THE INTERPRETATION OF
THE NEW TESTAMENT
1861–1961

THE INTERPRETATION
OF
THE NEW TESTAMENT
1861–1961

The Firth Lectures, 1962

by

STEPHEN NEILL

LONDON
OXFORD UNIVERSITY PRESS
NEW YORK TORONTO

Oxford University Press

LONDON OXFORD NEW YORK
GLASGOW TORONTO MELBOURNE WELLINGTON
CAPE TOWN IBADAN NAIROBI DAR ES SALAAM LUSAKA ADDIS ABABA
DELHI BOMBAY CALCUTTA MADRAS KARACHI LAHORE DACCA
KUALA LUMPUR SINGAPORE HONG KONG TOKYO

ISBN 0 19 283005 8

© *Oxford University Press 1964*

First published (with corrections) in Oxford Paperbacks 1966
Third impression 1975

*Printed in Great Britain
by Fletcher & Son Ltd, Norwich*

PREFACE

THIS book has grown out of the Firth Lectures delivered in the University of Nottingham in November 1962. My appointment to this lectureship both gave me great pleasure, and compelled me to put into shape material which I had been rather unsystematically assembling over a number of years.

I knew 'Budge' Firth fairly well. It is typical of his modesty and simplicity that I never had any idea that he was a wealthy man, and I was surprised to learn that it was he who had founded the Firth Lectureship. Having known him, I thought that I understood exactly what he had intended by this foundation—a Christian witness in the University on the highest possible intellectual level, yet presented in such a manner as not to repel those who have no technical acquaintance with theology. When I announced as my subject 'The Interpretation of the New Testament', I was warned not to be surprised if my hearers were rather few. I was greatly encouraged both by the number of those who came to the lectures, and by the close attention with which tightly packed and rather lengthy discourses were followed. This has confirmed my impression that many outside the charmed circle of theologians are anxious to know what the theologians are at, if only the material can be presented in a form that does not make demands for previous knowledge that they are unable to meet.

This is a not a book for the expert. As far as possible the necessary apparatus of scholarship has been relegated to the footnotes. I have tried to provide a narrative that can be read without too much trouble by the non-theologian who is anxious to know and is prepared to devote some time and thought to the subject. The difficulty throughout has been that of selection. I have tried to feel the movement of thought over a century, to concentrate on a small number of writers rather than to expatiate over many, and at the risk of over-simplification to draw attention to what seems to me to be of permanent significance.

At a great many points I am indebted to Professor C. F. D. Moule of Cambridge, who has encouraged me by his enthusiasm for the book, has saved me from a number of errors, and has drawn my attention to points that I would otherwise have overlooked. I am grateful to the authorities of the Oxford University Press, who have accepted without demur responsibility for the publication of a book that has grown considerably beyond the limits at first assigned to it. Once again Miss G. I. Mather has accomplished prodigies of skill and intelligence in deciphering and reproducing almost flawlessly a complicated manuscript.

Looking through the list of writers referred to in the book, I am moved to find how many of these scholars I have been privileged to know personally during the forty years since I first devoted myself to the intensive study of the New Testament. During most of this period I have had to be an onlooker rather than a participant in the game; but, if any of these learned men should chance to read my book, I hope that they may feel that I have not wholly failed to profit by the laborious researches in which it has not been possible for me to share.

S. N.

Hamburg
April 1963

The production of a paper-back edition of this book has made it possible to correct a number of errors and misprints, surprisingly few considering the range of country covered. I am grateful to reviewers and others who have helped to make these corrections possible, and to many friends who have been good enough to say that they have found my book useful.

January 1966   S. N.

CONTENTS

Chapter I

CHALLENGE TO ORTHODOXY

I

BRITAIN has never been able to make up its mind whether it is part of Europe or not. At times, as under William the Conqueror and throughout the Plantagenet period, the connexion was close, and the English Channel merely a troublesome accident of geography without religious or political significance. In the seventeenth and eighteenth centuries Englishmen seemed to spend most of their time fighting everyone else in every conceivable part of the world; and it is not surprising that by the end of the Napoleonic era Britain, and the English Churches, were as much isolated from the continent of Europe as they had ever been in their history. There were exceptions; but it is probably true to say that, at the turn of the eighteenth century, hardly anyone in England was aware of the great things that had been happening in the intellectual world of Germany.

Germany, in fact, came late on the scene of European intellectual development. In the early eighteenth century England had been the teacher of Europe. The influence of Locke and Newton, Berkeley and Hume was omnipresent and persuasive.[1] About the middle of the century a change took place, and the siren voices of Voltaire and Rousseau tended to drown those of the older and more technical philosophers. Frederick II of Prussia was not alone in finding Voltaire very much to his taste; in the Germany of his day to be able to speak French well was the mark of an educated gentleman. The young English lord still made the grand tour, when war was not positively keeping the roads closed; he came back with a good knowledge of French, a collection of Italian pictures, some first-hand ideas about the Palladian style of architecture, and at least a smattering of the

---

[1] This has been brilliantly shown by Paul Hazard in his great book *La Crise de la conscience européenne*, 3 vols. (Paris, 1935: English trans., *The European Mind, 1680–1715*, 1953).

Italian tongue. In most cases it did not occur to him to learn German.

The recovery of Germany from the dreadful devastation of the Thirty Years War was necessarily slow and painful. Whole areas had been depopulated. The country was divided up into endless petty principalities, without political or economic unity. Some of the most famous universities of the country had not yet been founded.[1] In those that existed, scholarship was pedantic and lethargic rather than adventurous. There were learned men, but there seemed to be little originality in their contribution to the world of letters.

Then, about the middle of the century, everything was changed within a few years by the emergence of an astonishing constellation of men of eminence in almost every department of learning, thought, and literature. In small and remote Königsberg, Master Immanuel Kant (1724–1804) sat and brooded on all the mysteries of thought and existence; having destroyed metaphysics with one hand he proceeded to restore it with the other, and has perhaps a stronger claim than Descartes to be the founder and creator of modern philosophy. Just across the road from him, Johann Georg Hamann (1730–88) saw more clearly than any of his contemporaries, or indeed than anyone else for long after his day, the significance of history as the medium of revelation.[2] The friend and pupil of both, Johann Gottfried Herder (1744–1807), spoke in tones which heralded the coming of the German Romantic movement; and by his book—*Vom Geist der Hebräischen Poesie* ('On the Spirit of Hebrew Poetry') (1782–3)—prepared the way for a new and more living understanding of the Old Testament and its message. Philosophy, history, and poetry are not the same as religion; yet each is a proper concern of men to whom the Christian understanding of the world is of paramount importance.

Outside the Königsberg circle, Gotthold Ephraim Lessing (1729–81) gave new form to the German language as a means of literary expression; in *Laokoon* (1766) laid new foundations for literary criticism; in *Nathan der Weise* (1778–9) put forward a notable plea for freedom and tolerance in matters of religion; and through his publication of the so-called *Wolfenbüttel Fragmente* of Hermann Samuel Reimarus (1774–8) set a-going that quest of the historical Jesus of which Albert Schweitzer was to write the story more than a century

---

[1] Göttingen dates from 1734; Berlin only from 1810.

[2] This in part accounts for the revival of the study of Hamann over the last thirty years; the meaning of history is one of the major theological preoccupations of the present day.

later. Johann Wolfgang von Goethe (1749–1832), with his almost universal interests in all directions, developed a strain of German lyric poetry which was without precedent except in the greatest of the Lutheran Christian hymns. Two later figures, whose achievements begin to be notable before the end of the century, are Georg Wilhelm Friedrich Hegel (1770–1831), who in 1818 moved from Heidelberg to Berlin; and Friedrich Daniel Ernst Schleiermacher (1768–1834), whose famous *Speeches (Reden) on Religion to its Cultured Despisers* were delivered in 1799.[1]

It is a memorable record. And, of all this, at the turn of the century, England was almost wholly unaware. Few had troubled to learn German; there were not many translations, and those that there were had been produced by hacks rather than by scholars.

One of the first to recognize the importance of Germany and of the new German thought was the poet Samuel Taylor Coleridge. Coleridge spent the greater part of the year 1798 in Germany, attended lectures in Göttingen, and applied himself to the study of the language with such zeal that he was able in a few weeks to produce a translation of Schiller's *Wallenstein*. Coleridge was one of the first to realize the importance of Kant; and no doubt some of the oracular wisdom of the Sage of Königsberg was heard to echo through the oracular utterances of the Sage of Hampstead. The influence of Coleridge on British philosophical and theological thinking can be traced throughout the whole of the nineteenth century; though not himself a theologian, he was one of the first to attempt to deliver the British mind from what he was perhaps the first to call bibliolatry,[2] that literal and pedantic understanding of the Bible which is too narrow to allow it to speak in the freshness of its own original and glowing inspiration.

The most notable of all the interpreters of the new Germany to Britain was Thomas Carlyle. It is hard to imagine by what strange process of hidden affinity Carlyle arrived at his boundless admiration for Goethe; it would be almost impossible to imagine two men more different in every respect. But somehow the affinity was there, and the devotion it engendered lasted over many years. The first outward manifestation of it was the· translation of *Wilhelm Meister* which appeared in 1824. Hardly anyone today reads Carlyle's endless book on

[1] English trans. by John Oman (1893), now available in paperback form (New York, 1958).

[2] The *Oxford English Dictionary* has an earlier reference: 'If to adore an image be idolatry To deify a book is bibliolatry', 1763; but this does not seem to be used specifically of the Bible.

Frederick the Great; it bears witness both to Carlyle's erudition, and to his indomitable determination to make all things German an intelligible reality to the British public.

II

Of the theological ferment which accompanied the German Enlightenment rather more than an echo had reached England by the end of the eighteenth century. What was happening in Germany was an awakening of the critical spirit in a new form, and particularly in relation to the use and handling of historical evidence. In the past much had been taken for granted; now nothing was to be taken for granted. In earlier days authority in Church and State had had the last word, almost as much in Protestant Europe as in the lands still controlled by the Roman Catholic Church; for within fifty years of Luther's death Lutheran Orthodoxy had hardened down into a scholasticism as rigid and unimaginative as anything that the Middle Ages had produced. The doctrine of the verbal inspiration and inerrancy of every part of Scripture, treated as one single whole without any recognition of the differing value of different parts, made an intelligent and imaginative approach to the Bible almost impossible, and tended to brand as infidelity any attempt to apply the principles of historical criticism to the sacred text. But, once the critical spirit had been aroused, no boundaries could be set to the areas to which it would be applied; the Scriptures have played so important a part in the life of Europe that it was quite certain that sooner or later, and whatever the cries and horrified protests of orthodoxy, criticism would lay hands on the sacred books, and would ask with inexorable persistence every kind of question as to their origin, nature, and authority.

English no less than German orthodoxy had accepted the doctrine of the verbal inerrancy of Holy Scripture. The man who first made the English-speaking world aware that it was possible to doubt this doctrine and still to remain a Christian was Herbert Marsh (1757–1839), Professor of Divinity at Cambridge in 1807, Bishop of Llandaff in 1816, and Bishop of Peterborough in 1819. Marsh has a little niche of his own in English church history. He had an intense dislike of Evangelicals, and was determined to have none in his diocese, if he could possibly prevent it. Long before the better-remembered Bishop Henry Phillpotts of Exeter (1778–1869) he hit upon the device of framing a series of eighty-seven questions, a 'trap to catch Calvinists', to which no Evangelical could possibly give a satisfactory answer (from the bishop's point of view); and so none were licensed to serve in the diocese of Peterborough. But Marsh has better claims to fame than this. In the first place, he was the first in the theological school at Cambridge to abandon the age-old tradition according to which all lectures in divinity had been given in Latin, and to give his own lectures in English. Secondly, wishing to introduce to English readers an idea of the New Testament different from that to which they had traditionally been accustomed, between 1793 and 1801 he translated into English and published the *Introduction to the New Testament* of the Göttingen professor Johann David Michaelis. This was the fruit of earlier adventure on the part of Marsh. He was one of the few English theological students who in the eighteenth century penetrated the world of Germany and mastered its secrets for themselves. In 1785 and following years he was in Göttingen, and sat at the feet of Michaelis; it was the work of his own master that he had decided to make available in English.[1]

J. D. Michaelis (1717–91) was one of the most remarkable figures of the eighteenth century. At the age of thirty-three he became professor of oriental languages at the University of Göttingen, and made that the centre of his activity for the remaining forty-one years of his life. He worked with enormous diligence and wrote on a great many subjects connected with the Old Testament, the New Testament, and dogmatic theology. He was one of the first to see the importance of Arabic for the understanding of classical Hebrew, and to insist that the Old Testament must be read historically, and interpreted in the light of the times and of the situation of those to whom it was addressed. When he turned to the New Testament, his aim was to read it and to interpret it without dogmatic presuppositions. An illustration will make clear what he meant by this. The orthodoxy of the time took it for granted that, because the New Testament is divinely inspired in every part, it is *a priori* impossible that there should be any contradictions between the Gospels; any apparent contradiction must be due only to the imperfection of our understanding, and must be susceptible of resolution into harmony. Michaelis was prepared to face the

[1] Both the lectures and the books of Marsh were highly popular. Though Michaelis's work fills four considerable volumes, edition after edition came from the press, each enriched by additional studies from the pen of Marsh himself. The edition which I have used myself is the fourth—of 1824. Apparently no life of Marsh has ever been written; I am sure that the subject would well repay detailed study.

possibility that there really might be contradictions. His own views were generally conservative; but, as we shall see again and again in this study, what matters is not so much the particular views that any scholar holds as the validity of the methods which he uses, and the integrity of his devotion to them. Michaelis accepted the ancient view that what guarantees the inspiration of a New Testament book is its apostolic authorship. No claim to apostolic authorship has ever been made on behalf of Mark, Luke, or Acts; therefore, they do not stand on the same level of inspiration as Matthew and John. Michaelis could regard Hebrews, James, and Jude as being, in the strict sense of the term, non-canonical works. If, however, we are prepared to go as far as that, the unity and integrity of the Canon as one single inspired whole falls completely to the ground. But, Michaelis goes on to say, this does not really very much matter; Mark, Luke, and Acts are historical works; even though they be not supernaturally guaranteed as free from error, we can still learn just as much from them as we can from any other historical work regarding the general historical reliability of which we have become convinced on purely rational grounds.

Up to about 1770 the reputation of Michaelis was prodigious; honours were heaped upon him both by government and in the learned world. But his later years were darkened by discredit which came upon him by reason of his own lack of scruple in certain transactions. At the same time, it was felt by the learned that he had not kept himself up to date with the movement of thought and scholarship in that era of rapid progress. By the time at which Marsh translated his great work, he had become a legendary figure, but was no longer a living influence.

English opinion was in general so conservative at the time that it can occasion no surprise that Marsh's publications aroused no small contention. John Randolph, Bishop of Oxford, condemned Marsh's researches as 'derogating from the character of the sacred books, and injurious to Christianity as fostering a spirit of scepticism'—an objection to which Marsh replied in what Randolph complained of as 'a coarse strain of low abuse'.[1] But beyond the learned world of the universities this side of Marsh's activities seems to have aroused no more than passing attention.

It was by a very different route that the modern methods of critical study as developed in Germany came to exercise a deep and lasting influence on English thinking. In 1810–12 a Prussian diplomat

[1] See *Dictionary of National Biography*, vol. xxxvi, p. 212.

named Georg Bartold Niebuhr published two volumes of a history of Rome. This book marked an epoch, since it was the first clear manifestation of a new form of learning—critical history; that is, the writing of history in the light of the new critical method that had been developed in the first half of the eighteenth century in relation to the physical sciences, and was now being progressively extended to other spheres. Niebuhr's influence on all the later historians of the nineteenth century was immense; they went to him to learn the delicate art of handling historical material and of weighing historical evidence.[1] G. P. Gooch, no mean authority, has referred to him as 'the first commanding figure in modern historiography, the scholar who raised history from a subordinate place to the dignity of an independent science, the noble personality in whom the greatest historians of the succeeding generations found their model or inspiration'.[2] Niebuhr's aim, like that of Michaelis, was to approach his subject without presuppositions; two questions only are to be asked: What is the evidence? What is the value of this evidence? No tradition must be allowed to stand merely because it is venerable or is supported by endless later authorities. Niebuhr's 'scepticism' produced devastating results in his chosen field, the early history of Rome. Fifty generations had devoutly accepted the stories of the seven kings of Rome as literal history; Niebuhr had little difficulty in showing that the traditions preserved by Livy and the other ancient historians had little, if any, foundation in fact; to account for their origin, he made use of the fruitful, but dangerous, concept of 'myth'.[3]

Niebuhr was fortunate in finding as disciples in England two of the most notable men of the age. Thomas Arnold (1795–1842), who was to become famous as headmaster of Rugby School (1828), was himself planning to write a history of Rome when his attention was drawn to the work of Niebuhr; he became an immediate enthusiast for the new methods and their results, and, though critical of Niebuhr at certain points, made up his mind never to differ from him, unless he was quite certain that the difference rested upon necessary considerations. Connop Thirlwall (1797–1875) was perhaps an even more remarkable

[1] I am inclined to think that Niebuhr's influence was greater in Britain than elsewhere. On the continent of Europe it seems to have been to some extent neutralized by the very different influences stemming from the school of Hegel.

[2] *History and Historians in the Nineteenth Century* (1913), p. 47, quoted in J. C. Thirlwall, *Connop Thirlwall* (1936), p. 41.

[3] Dangerous, as we shall see later, because the word has so constantly been used in theology without the precaution of adequately careful definition.

figure than Arnold. He was certainly one of the greatest Christians of the nineteenth century, and no man in that troubled age made a greater contribution to sanity in religion and to true freedom of thought. Justice has hardly been done him by later generations, perhaps because his best writing is hidden away in the eleven comprehensive charges which he delivered to the clergy of the diocese of St. David's. Thirlwall's attention had been directed to German thought and literature by his friend Julius Hare (1795–1855), himself a man of considerable learning though little originality.[1] As a young fellow of Trinity College, Cambridge, Thirlwall had not very much to do, so threw himself with avidity into the task of assisting his friend in the translation of Niebuhr's *Roman History* (1828–32).

Now, if critical methods can be applied to the early history of Rome, they can be applied to the early history of Israel. Niebuhr himself was well aware of this possibility, and, though it was not his special subject, had made some passing comments on Genesis which could not be reconciled with the doctrine of verbal inspiration. This was enough to alarm the cohorts of orthodoxy, and even the fanatically loyal Arnold passed through some anxious moments. His doubts were allayed when he was able to visit Niebuhr at Bonn in August 1830. 'I . . . talked with him for three hours', he wrote to a friend, 'and I am satisfied from my own ears, if I had had any doubts before, of the grossness of the slander which called him an unbeliever.'[2] A review of the translation in the *Quarterly Review*, which referred to 'works . . . pregnant with crude and dangerous speculation', called forth the wrath of Thirlwall, who replied to it in defence of Niebuhr. In a letter to the Chevalier Bunsen written in 1831 he remarked:

In Germany I hear most persons were at a loss to conceive on what grounds Niebuhr could have been assailed in England as irreligious. That persons of this description would be scandalised by Niebuhr's divergency from the book of Genesis I knew to be an unavoidable misfortune, and I only hoped that his speculations might not fall into their hands. But I had scarcely imagined that the *Quarterly* would have degraded itself by such a stupid and bestial attack as that with which it evaded the more difficult task of reviewing the book.[3]

[1] Hare was the only Anglican in more than a century to write anything on Luther that is worth reading. His *Vindication of Luther* (1855) is scientifically objective, and for its date a remarkably percipient piece of work. Hare at the age of ten had first 'learnt to throw inkstands at the devil' at the Wartburg in 1805.

[2] Letter to the Rev. George Cornish, in Stanley's *Life and Correspondence of Thomas Arnold, D.D.* (4th ed., 1891), pp. 152–3.

[3] Quoted in J. C. Thirlwall, op. cit., p. 47.

But translation of books on Roman history was not the only means employed by Thirlwall to fall foul of the paragons of Biblical orthodoxy. In 1825 he had had the temerity to translate Schleiermacher's *Critical Essay on the Gospel of St. Luke* (1821). This is far from being Schleiermacher's best work. He was not primarily a historical or literary critic; his book on St. Luke had no lasting influence on the progress of the study of the Synoptic problem in Germany or elsewhere. It is interesting to note, however, that, abandoning the idea of an 'original Gospel' which was supposed to underlie our present Gospels, he maintained the view, not unlike that which much later was to be associated with the school of 'Form-criticism', that the Gospel material had earlier circulated in the form of brief 'memorabilia', on which the evangelists had later worked, each with a particular understanding of the life of the Lord in his mind. What was clear was that Schleiermacher's view, and any view remotely resembling it, was incompatible with a belief in verbal inspiration; Thirlwall translated the book because he wanted to make a wider circle of English readers acquainted with a view which he believed to be important. Schleiermacher had couched his views in language of considerable obscurity, as 'the best method of keeping off improper readers'; Thirlwall laboured to be lucid; but it cannot be said that either the translation, or the able account of the various competing theories with which he prefaced it, makes easy reading.

The result is well known. In the furore that followed, the name of Schleiermacher became a kind of bogey word, as standing for infidelity in its most virulent form. And some of the odium naturally attached itself to the translator. A good many years later, in 1837, Lord Melbourne, himself no mean scholar, was anxious to recommend Thirlwall, whom he recognized to be one of the ablest scholars in the English Church, for the bishopric of Norwich. The feeling against Thirlwall was too strong, and this came to nothing. Three years later Melbourne returned to the charge in connexion with the vacancy in the remote and impoverished see of St. David's. He was, however, particularly anxious to appoint no bishop suspected of heterodoxy. It took a considerable time, and consultation with the Archbishop of Canterbury, before the Prime Minister's anxieties could be set at rest. The story of what happened when the offer had been made and accepted has passed into history. The Prime Minister received Dr. Thirlwall in his bedroom; after an interview of some length, Melbourne turned to his departing guest and said: 'I have done you a favour by presenting you with a bishopric; now I want you to do me a favour in return.' Thirlwall having agreed in advance, Melbourne continued: 'Then what the devil made you translate Schleiermacher?' History has, alas, concealed the answer to the question.[1]

The next stage in the enlightenment of the British public brings us into touch with two unexpected actors.

In May 1825, two months after the publication of Thirlwall's offending translation of Schleiermacher, Hugh James Rose (1795–1838), one of the forerunners of the Anglo-Catholic movement in its Cambridge form, preached a series of four sermons from the university pulpit on *The State of the Protestant Religion in Germany*. He had recently spent nearly a year in that country for the sake of his health, and had been horrified by what he had discovered; he was deeply concerned that such poisonous views should not penetrate England. The Church in Germany, according to Rose, was 'the mere shadow of a name', the scene of 'an abdication of Christianity', in which rationalism reigned supreme, reason was made the judge of every doctrine, and ministers held themselves free to preach from the pulpit whatever views happened to appeal to them, without any regard for the historical confessions of faith to which they might at one time or another have pledged their loyalty. Rose's book was translated into German, and not unnaturally was very badly received; what the Germans criticized was not simply the views of Rose, which might be regarded as due to ignorance and spleen, but also the whole state of academic and ecclesiastical life in England, judged by them to have become completely identified with obscurantism and the suppression of free inquiry.

It happened that in 1826 Edward Bouverie Pusey (1800–82) was in Germany, spending fourteen hours a day perfecting his knowledge of the Hebrew and Arabic languages, and sitting at the feet of some of the greatest scholars of the day. His attention was drawn to Rose's book, and, living in the midst of German friends, he could not but be aware of the universally unfavourable reaction to it. He decided to write and present a different point of view. His study, entitled *An Historical Enquiry into the Probable Causes of the Rationalist Character of the Theology of Germany*, is a most remarkable production to have

[1] The authority for this appears to be Professor A. H. Sayce, the Assyriologist, who records it in his *Reminiscences* (London, 1923), p. 91. But it seems to be one of those tales supported only by an oral tradition; Sayce cites no authority other than his own memory, which is likely to be reliable, as he was born in 1845 and had many opportunities of meeting Thirlwall, who died in 1875.

come from the pen of a young man of twenty-seven, already heavily engaged in his own professional obligations. Pusey, although not robust in health, must have been possessed of amazing powers of concentration to have attained in so short a time to such a mastery of the history of German theology since the Reformation. And no less remarkable than his knowledge is the width of his sympathies, in directions which are unexpected in the light of his later developments. He sees in the Pietists, and in particular in his hero Philipp Jakob Spener,[1] a stream of pure spiritual life in Churches that had been smothered under the weight of a dead conformity to which he gave the name of 'Orthodoxism'. But he took a much less hopeless view of the situation than Rose; while there was much that could, from the Christian point of view, be regarded only as deplorable, there were signs of life in many quarters; and the development of the scientific spirit and freedom from prejudice could never be harmful to the true spirit of the faith.

Pusey was not sanguine as to the reception which would be accorded to his book:

I do not expect very merciful handling from reviews. The sentiments scattered up and down [the book] will fare still worse than the style; and I expect to be thought one-third mystic, one-third sceptic, and one-third (which will be thought the worst imputation of all) a Methodist, though I am none of the three.[2]

As far as Germany was concerned Pusey need have had no anxiety; as soon as a translation was published, his book was commended for its accuracy, its fairness, and the breadth of its observations.[3] In England things were worse even than Pusey could have anticipated. Rose read, misunderstood, and fulminated. Pusey had written that historical passages of the Bible in which no religious truth was contained should not be regarded as equally inspired with other passages of Scripture. Rose quoted this, substituting 'parts' for 'passages', and accused Pusey of undermining faith in the historical sections of the Bible, in which of course the Gospels can be included. Pusey, to defend himself, published in 1830 a second part of his work. He

[1] It is interesting to note that F. W. Farrar, in his Bampton Lectures on the *History of the Interpretation of the Bible* (1887) also speaks very warmly of Spener.
[2] Quoted in H. P. Liddon, *Life of Edward Bouverie Pusey*, vol. i (1893), pp. 152–3. Liddon gives a full and temperate account of the whole episode.
[3] It is interesting to observe that a translation was needed. Then, as at all times, German scholars seem to have been doubtful whether anything existed in English which could compensate them for the labour of learning the language.

continued to expand, to explain, and to justify. But it was long before the reputation he had earned for unorthodoxy in the matter of Biblical inspiration was allowed to die a natural death.

The consequences for Pusey were grave. He came to regret the publication of the two books as a mistake. In his will, dated 19 November 1875, he expressed a wish that these books should not be republished. He retreated into a rigid conservatism, which refused even to see that certain questions might need to be reopened, certain old doctrines re-expressed. Fifty years after the period of his studies in Germany, he was still writing on the Old Testament in a manner which implied that nothing had happened in theology since the days of those ancient fathers of the Church, of whom he had so monumental a knowledge, and whom he was able to cite with such perfect appositeness in illustration of the doctrine of the Minor Prophets.[1]

III

If Englishmen, having dealt with the mild unorthodoxies of Mr. Pusey, imagined that they could settle down untroubled to the enjoyment of their traditional beliefs, they were destined to undergo before long a rude awakening. In 1835 David Friedrich Strauss (1808–74) published the two volumes of his *Life of Jesus*. This year and this book marked, as few others have done, a turning-point in the history of the Christian faith.

In order to understand Strauss one must love him. He was not the greatest, and not the deepest of theologians, but he was the most absolutely sincere. His insight and his errors were alike the insight and the errors of a prophet. And he had a prophet's fate. Disappointment and suffering gave his life its consecration. It unrolls itself before us like a tragedy, in which, in the end, the gloom is lightened by the mild radiance which shines forth from the nobility of the sufferer.

So Albert Schweitzer in his famous *Quest*.[2] The terms are rather rhetorical; they do justice, however, to the fact that the godly of

[1] 'Pusey on the Minor Prophets' is a spiritual classic. But no one, reading it, would guess what had been happening in the world of Old Testament studies in the nineteenth century.

[2] *The Quest of the Historical Jesus* (Macmillan Paperback Ed., 1961), p. 68. It is to be noted that Karl Barth, in his far from unsympathetic study of Strauss, takes the view that he was a very *untragic* figure. See *Die Protestantische Theologie im 19. Jahrhundert* (1947: English trans., *From Rousseau to Ritschl*, 1961), pp. 490–516. Here and for the rest of this chapter I am much indebted to what, in my opinion, is the best book that Karl Barth has ever written, and the one that is likely to have a longer life than any other.

Strauss's day recognized, however muddily and unfairly, that, if Strauss's interpretation of the Gospels came to be accepted, Christianity as it has been understood through the centuries would come to an end in a generation.

Emanuel Hirsch, in his account of Strauss, remarks, rightly in my judgement, that 'out of the power of truth a question-mark has been set up over against our religion, with which up to the present day theology and the Church have not dealt adequately and in the manner appropriate to the question'.

What, then, was this revolutionary doctrine? Strauss had realized that, in the interpretation of the Gospels, the supernaturalists who accepted everything more or less as it was written, and the rationalists who were prepared to explain almost everything if not to explain it away, had run themselves to a standstill, and that there was an urgent need that some new principle of interpretation should be found. This principle Strauss believed himself to have discovered in 'the mythical'. Wherever our sources indicate the presence of the supernatural or abnormal, the mythopoeic faculty has been at work; only by recognizing this can we do justice to the sources that we have.

Strauss never defined too clearly what he meant by the mythical, and many woes have descended on theology through this lack of precision. The word 'myth' is commonly used in one of three connexions. A myth may relate to the doings of gods and other more-than-human beings; in many cases we can see that the myth is a rude and poetic attempt to understand the world, in fact, a kind of 'philosophy before philosophy'. Secondly, the word is used of those majestic tales, such as the early stories in Genesis, in which a profoundly religious understanding of the human situation, such as can hardly be better conveyed than through such a tale, is made known to us. In the third place, as in the case of the Oedipus sequence, the myth may be a projection outwards of the human sense of man's inner problems as he wrestles with a dark and perplexing destiny. In none of these cases has the myth any direct connexion with history; and it makes no difference to the significance of the myth whether there is any basis in history for the tale or not. For a different kind of exercise of the creative imagination, other words—for instance, saga and legend—are used. Here the action takes place definitely within the field of history; imagination has been at work on the historical material to interpret it in accordance with certain categories of understanding which do not necessarily arise out of the material itself. Most readers of the great saga of Gideon will recognize the purely human and historical features in it; this is a story of courage and adventure, of a self-taught military genius and his achievements. The imagination of Israel, however, saw this tale as part of the dealings of God with his chosen people; he is, of a truth, the only deliverer; it must be made plain that Gideon is only an instrument in the hand of the LORD most high. But history and interpretation cannot be completely separated; the deliverance could not have taken place in this way, unless Gideon had been the kind of person depicted in the narrative of the book of Judges. Not many modern readers, probably, take as literal history the story of the wolf of Gubbio, who was converted by St. Francis and died at a great age in the odour of sanctity. Yet who that has read the exquisite tale in the *Fioretti* doubts that it is 'true'? Unless Francis of Assisi had been the kind of man that we know him to have been, this kind of tale would not have been made up about him. The legend is not history; but in its own way the legend bears witness to the truth of history.

Nothing could be more dangerous than to use the term 'myth' without the clearest possible delimitation of the sense in which it is being used. At the very outset, we encounter one of the imperfections of the method of Strauss. The 'mythical' is used as the key to unlock all the mysteries of the Gospels; but in point of fact the Gospels are a phenomenon far too complex to be unlocked by any single key, especially when that key is itself so simplified and lacking in subtlety.

Let it be agreed, however, that the admiration of the early Christians for Jesus found expression in the fashioning of myths, in Strauss's sense of the word. But this process does not take place *in vacuo*; what were the raw materials on which the minds of the disciples worked in order to produce this particular kind of myth and no other? Here Strauss is at once ready with his answer. The two main factors are the supernatural elements in the Old Testament, and the conviction of the disciples that Jesus was the Messiah of Jewish expectation. The handling of the story of the Transfiguration provides a typical example of the application of the method:

We may suppose, then, that we have here a myth, in which two diverse tendencies are apparent. The first is the desire to repeat the transfiguration of Moses in yet higher measure in the experience of Jesus; the second to bring Jesus as Messiah into contact with his two forerunners; and through this appearance of the Lawgiver and the Prophet, the founder and the reformer of the Jewish theocracy, to present Jesus as the perfecter of the kingdom of God, as the fulfilment of the law and the prophets; and furthermore to represent his messianic dignity as confirmed by a voice from heaven.[1]

By the time that Strauss has finished this work, there is very little in the Gospel records that has not yielded to the mythical disintegration. The book is called *The Life of Jesus*; but in what sense is the title appropriate? Strauss has his answer ready for this, as for all other questions. The life of Jesus cannot be written.[2] To write the life of Jesus means to fit him into our ordinary human categories, to make that life a part of the existence of the human race. But that is exactly what the Gospels refuse to do. Throughout and in every part they present Jesus as the one who breaks through all these categories, who refuses at any point to be fitted into them.[3] If we come to the Gospels with questions which were never asked by the writers, and which they never intended to answer, we may produce a pious work of our own imagination, but this will bear little or no relation to the reality of Jesus as this is presented in the Gospels. This does not, of course, mean that there is no historical substratum to the Gospel story. Strauss expressly safeguards himself against this idea: 'The author of this work wishes especially to guard himself in those places where he declares that he knows not what happened, from the imputation of asserting that he knows that nothing happened.'[4]

In another sense also Strauss affirmed that it was impossible to write the life of Christ. When we consider the differences in order between the several Gospels, the way in which sayings of Jesus are reported in different contexts, the inner contradictions, we become aware that what we have are no more than isolated fragments, on which some kind of order has been imposed by the evangelists. The facts and sayings are like a necklace of pearls, of which the string has broken. 'The hard grit of these sayings of Jesus has not indeed been dissolved by the flood of oral tradition, but they have been worked away from their original position and like rolling pebbles have been deposited in

[1] D. F. Strauss, *The Life of Jesus Critically Examined* (reprint of 1906), p. 545. The parallel which Strauss later draws between the transfiguration of Jesus and the 'transfiguration' of Socrates in Plato's *Symposium*, highly characteristic of his method, is perhaps not likely to carry conviction to many readers.

[2] Later in life Strauss was to make certain concessions to more traditional opinions; but there is no reason to doubt that his basic conviction to the end of his life was that which has just been stated.

[3] We shall see later that at this point the voice of Strauss was genuinely prophetic, and that the greater part of modern scholarship would go with him in this general principle, though not in every detail of its application.

[4] Strauss, op. cit., p. 92.

places to which they do not properly belong.' If we try to write the
life of Christ, we shall merely be imposing another order, purely
subjective, on materials the true order and connexion of which must
for ever escape us.

Strauss himself is not unduly concerned at this volatilization of the
story of Christ, since he is convinced that all that has been taken away
by historical criticism is given back by philosophy. The all-important
thing is the idea. The central idea in the Christian faith is the over-
coming of the natural by the spiritual. Traditionally, faith has seen
this process concentrated and perfectly achieved in one individual,
Jesus Christ. What we now have to realize is that the subject in this
great drama is not one individual but mankind as a whole. And this is
reasonable; for it is the nature of an idea not to pour out its fulness in
one single example, but to make known its fulness in a number of
examples which mutually complement one another.[1]

Mankind is the union of the two natures, the incarnate God . . . Mankind
is the child of the visible mother and the invisible father, of spirit and of
nature. It is the miracle worker, in so far as in the course of human history
spirit ever more completely asserts its mastery over nature. It is the sinless
one, in so far as the course of its development is blameless . . . Mankind is
the one who dies, who rises again and ascends to heaven, since from the
negation of the element of nature ever higher spiritual life arises. Through
belief in this Christ, that is, in his death and resurrection, man is justified
before God.[2]

At a later stage in his development Strauss was to put the question:
'Are we still Christians?', and was to answer it in the negative, at
least in so far as any traditional content can be read into the word.
But there is no reason to doubt that, from his own point of view,
he was a sincere believer, and was convinced that only through an
interpretation of the Gospels such as he had given was it possible to
save the Christian faith for the nineteenth century.

England did not immediately become aware of Strauss—the
language barrier was still strong. But certain intellectual circles were

---

[1] His actual words, in the concluding section of his second volume, are: 'This is by no
means the way in which the idea realizes itself, pouring out its whole abundance upon
one example and begrudging itself to all others. Rather it likes to unfold its wealth in a
diversity of examples which complement each other, in the interchange of individualities,
one in decline, the other rising.'

[2] Strauss, op. cit., p. 780.

deeply interested in the new movement of thought in Germany, and from them awareness of the ideas of Strauss began to spread. It was felt desirable that the *Life* should be translated; and this work was entrusted to no less a person than George Eliot the novelist. The task was not completed until 1846.[1] In Germany, however, as may be supposed, the *Life* attracted immediate attention, and the furore was tremendous. Various attempts were made to have the book suppressed;[2] answers poured from the press, most of them characterized by a failure to grasp what the issues really were, and none of them successful in striking at the foundations of the great edifice that Strauss had erected.

In what sense is it ever possible to *answer* a great work of the intellect? It is possible to go through it point by point, indicating inaccuracies or errors in detail. Such demonstration is usually highly tedious; and for the most part it is ineffective, because it leaves the main structure unshaken. A principle may still be valid, even though the working out in detail of its applications may leave much to be desired. In dealing with such a work as that of Strauss, there are only two possibilities. Either it must be shown that the method adopted is inappropriate to the material to be considered, or, granted that the method is not illegitimate, it must be shown that the application of the method has been vitiated from the start by concealed presuppositions and prejudices, by the neglect of relevant evidence, or by the failure to see what kind of conclusions really follow from the evidence adduced, and what kind of evidence must be produced if certain conclusions are to be maintained as tenable.

In point of fact, Strauss's method and his conclusions were vulnerable at a number of crucial points.

In the first place, he had not subjected his sources, the Gospels, to any careful literary and historical criticism before beginning to work upon them. He had, for instance, played off John against the Synoptic Gospels, and the Synoptic Gospels against John, without taking serious account of the historical, literary, and theological characteristics which separate John from the other Gospels, and account of which must be taken if the use of it as a historical source is not to lead

[1] 'She found much of it repulsive, especially his "dissecting the beautiful story of the Resurrection". She could only endure to continue her task by gazing at a cast of Thorwaldsen's figure of the risen Christ' (*Life*, i, p. 112). See L. E. Elliott-Binns, *Religion in the Victorian Era* (1936), p. 183.

[2] The conservative theologian J. A. W. Neander (1789–1850), very greatly to his credit, was one of those most strongly opposed to the suppression of a book of which he most heartily disapproved.

to confusion. Strauss himself admitted that textual and literary criticism of this kind did not really interest him; yet the drudgery of this kind of approach has to be gone through, if historical reconstruction is to have any chance of proving itself permanently valid.

Secondly, Strauss overlooked the most obvious fact of all—the existence of the Christian Church. Here is a tremendous movement in history, which started in Palestine in the first century A.D., which spread rapidly through the ancient world, and the spiritual impulses of which have not died away after so many centuries. How is all this to be accounted for? What was the power that launched the movement? What kind of a stone could it be that, once thrown into the pool of human existence, could set in motion ripples that would go on spreading until the utmost rim of the life of the world had been reached? When Strauss has finished his critical work, and given us Jesus as he understands him to have been, has sufficient account been given of what lies at the origins of a great world movement?[1] To this there can be only one answer. As Strauss understands it, Jesus lived on in the faith of his disciples, and this faith was strong enough to create the belief in his resurrection. But the kind of Jesus who is indicated in Strauss's pages was not the kind of person to create that kind of faith. The causes, as suggested by Strauss, do not measure up to the consequences; something in the evidence that is of the greatest significance must somehow have been overlooked.

We have learned a good deal in recent years of the relationship between personalities and movements. Historians have tended of late to think and speak in terms of movements almost as though they came into being automatically and of themselves; Carlyle's view of history in terms of 'Heroes' has been out of fashion. But it is impossible completely to discount the role of personalities in the fashioning of history. If every word written and spoken by Adolf Hitler had completely disappeared, it would still be possible to reconstruct a fairly complete picture of Hitler from the movement of which he was the directing mind and spirit. Napoleon became a legend in France; much of the legend is unhistorical,[2] but it would never have come into existence at all if Napoleon had not had the gift of imposing himself

---

[1] It is to be noted that in his first *Life of Jesus* Strauss made no attempt to bring together in a single picture the dismembered fragments into which he had reduced the Gospel.

[2] F. A. Simpson, in *The Rise of Louis Napoleon* (1909), p. 15, has written of the Frenchmen of 1848, who 'turned from the realities of a not very glorious present to the glories of a not very real past'.

on the imagination of men and calling out their utmost devotion. Jean Pierre de Béranger, in his touching poem *Les Souvenirs du Peuple*, has caught exactly the accent:

> On parlera de sa gloire
> Sous le chaume bien longtemps.
> L'humble toit, dans cinquante ans,
> Ne connaîtra plus d'autre histoire.

It is certain that a great deal in Jesus Christ will always remain mysterious to us; it is equally certain that the figure which stands behind the Christian movement is greater than either Hitler or Napoleon. That is the way in which history happens; and it can happen in no other way.

IV

One of the men who recognized the first great weakness in the work of Strauss and set himself, not to put the clock back, but to work over the material in a far more critical fashion, and to reconsider Strauss's work in the light of the results of this documentary criticism, was Ferdinand Christian Baur (1792–1860).

Baur, who had earlier been one of Strauss's teachers, was called in 1826 to be professor at Tübingen, and there remained till the end of his life.[1] The type of interpretation which he called into being is commonly called that of the Tübingen school. Baur was a heroic figure, a representative of German scholarship at its best, in its tireless industry, in the range of its operations, and in its fearless eagerness to advance to the knowledge of the truth without regard for what the consequences may be in relation to convictions and traditions dearly held and cherished. He was at his desk by four o'clock every morning. The works published during his life-time amount to ten thousand pages; those published after his death from his notes or those of his students to another six thousand—the equivalent of a book of four hundred pages every year for forty years.

Baur's strength was in his capacity for seeing things as wholes. There is always a tendency in theology, as elsewhere, towards specialization. We think of the New Testament as a separate world, neatly

---

[1] Professor W. G. Kümmel refers to the influence of Niebuhr's *History of Rome* on the development of the thought and outlook of Baur, in the period before his election to the professorship at Tübingen during which Strauss had been his pupil. *Das neue Testament* (1958), p. 156.

framed off by the Canon, and observing laws of its own which are not applicable in other fields. It was one great contribution of Baur that he recognized that the New Testament itself is part of church history. There is indeed a difference—the apostolic age has a character all its own; but there is no break in continuity. Similarly, the history of doctrine does not begin where the New Testament ends; the New Testament itself is concerned with the work of interpretation; it shows men of very different backgrounds and points of view wrestling with the phenomenon of Jesus Christ, and reaching widely differing conclusions in their understanding of that phenomenon. Church history and the history of doctrine are only further stages in the working out of a process which already has its roots deep in the New Testament itself. With these convictions, Baur set himself nothing less than the gigantic task of working out a complete picture of Christian antiquity. The tasks of the exegete, the church historian, and the systematic theologian are very different, and require different training and gifts. The exegete is akin to the philologist and the literary critic; his concern is with language, with words and their meanings, separately and in sentences, phrases, and whole books. The church historian works on exactly the same methods, and requires exactly the same training, as the secular historian in the weighing of historical evidence and the assessment of historical probability. The systematic theologian is more akin to the philosopher; his task is to relate theological understanding to a total understanding of the universe and of human life within it. To reach eminence in so many varying disciplines is almost beyond the limits of human possibilities. But the task that Baur had set himself could not be accomplished without eminence in all three fields.

For all his greatness, Baur's work was marred by two weaknesses, which are to be found also in the work of a number of other German theologians—provincialism,[1] and special pleading.

Baur lived in a small German university town. Of all that was going on in Germany he had an acute awareness; to the rest of the world he seems to have paid less attention. This comes out interest-

---

[1] On this, see a fascinating essay by Paul Tillich on 'The Conquest of Intellectual Provincialism' in *Theology of Culture* (1959), pp. 159–76. Tillich writes: 'If one studied theology in the first decade of this century at famous theological faculties within Germany, such as those of Tübingen, Halle, or Berlin, one identified the history of theology in the last four centuries with the history of German theology . . . It was our feeling that only in Germany was the problem of how to unite Christianity and the modern mind taken absolutely seriously.'

ingly in what is perhaps the best book that he ever wrote, and the only one that today can be read for other than historical reasons—his *Die Epochen der kirchlichen Geschichtsschreibung* ('Epochs in the writing of Church History') (1852).[1] Starting from Eusebius, the father of church history, Baur delineates the various methods of writing history that have been followed by ecclesiastical historians up to his own time. Until he has dealt with the Magdeburg Centuriators and Cardinal Baronius in the sixteenth century, he is excellent; but then the book becomes a study of church history writing in Germany. There is no mention of either Gibbon or Bossuet. The omission of Gibbon is perhaps excusable; he was not strictly a church historian, though with only a slight stretch of language he might be called the greatest of all ecclesiastical historians. But Bossuet was the last great figure of the Middle Ages; and his *Discours sur l'histoire universelle* (1681) is the last attempt on a major scale to depict the history of the world in those categories of providence and divine purpose that are the guiding principles of Eusebius.

It was a great misfortune that in 1833 Baur became acquainted with the philosophy of Hegel and, like many of his contemporaries, fell deeply under its sway. Hegel had worked out the dialectic of thesis, antithesis, and synthesis. Progress takes place in human affairs when one movement is carried to such a point that it necessarily produces by reaction its contrary. Then in process of time the opposites coalesce into a higher unity, from which in time the same process can commence again. This is the dialectic which Karl Marx claimed to have caused to stand on its head. It may be disputed whether there is any sphere of human affairs to which the Hegelian dialectic is really applicable; certainly theology is not one of them; and in all the realms of theology there is none in which the principle is more wholly inapplicable than the study of Christian origins. But it was just here that Baur believed that Hegel had given him the needed illumination. Judaic Christianity, Pauline Christianity, the reconciliation of both in the Catholic Church—these things run like King Charles's head through the whole of Baur's researches; and this means that from 1833 onwards his work was gravely vitiated by an irrelevant and unproved presupposition.

[1] Of this book Emanuel Hirsch remarks that 'it has not yet been replaced by a comparable or better work' *(Geschichte der neuern evangelischen Theologie,* vol. v, p. 524), a judgement with which I heartily concur. It is strange that, in all the current debates on the meaning of history, so little reference seems to be made to this classic work.

Rarely can a theologian have received a more comprehensive
certificate of merit than that paid to Baur by Mark Pattison, Rector of
Lincoln College, Oxford. In his essay on 'Theology in Germany',
Pattison writes:

The characteristic of Baur's method has been already indicated. The
animation and force of his reasoning is derived from the directness and dis-
tinctness of his purpose. The vigour and inspiration, which many theorists
have drawn from theological passion, is supplied to him from his confidence
in his scientific method. Every fact with him tells and is referred to its place.
He is no historical painter, to bring forward events because they make a
good picture. He values nothing but what is significant. With the same fine
tact with which Niebuhr follows the trail of a national migration, Baur
tracks a dogma. Not an inflexion, however minute, escapes him; not a
complication, however perplexed, that he does not unravel. The traverses and
passes of dialectic, the flights and vagaries of mysticism, the solid and the
frivolous, the heights and depths through which the doctrine in its passage
down the stream of time has ranged, are all marshalled in their due relation
to the general development of the thought.[1]

Yet the question will not be stilled, whether Baur might not equally
well be the object of another brilliant piece of delineation, in which
Pattison indulged at the expense of a scholar whose diligence and
erudition were equal to those of Baur:

To take his side is at the beginning, and not at the end of his intellectual
process... He must start at once with a proposition, and then ransack
libraries for material out of which to forge the proof of it...The more
copious his citations, the more dexterous his ingenuity, the more irrefragable
his logic, the more vehement his determination to make us think so, the more
the reason revolts from the determination. The intellectual character
exemplified by Warburton is common enough in life. But it only attracts
wonder when it is coupled with powers and industry like Warburton's,
and dedicated to some literary theme of widely-extended interest... A
comprehensive general reading, an heroic industry in marshalling the parti-
culars of the proof, a dialectical force of aim, which would twist a bar of iron
to its purposes; and all brought to bear to prove a perverse and preposterous
proposition. The mischief done by such powerful efforts of human reason is
not in the diffusion of erroneous opinion on the subjects of which they
treat, but in setting brilliant examples of a false method.[2]

[1] *Essays* (collected and arranged by Henry Nettleship, 1889), vol. ii, pp. 231–2.
[2] *Essays*, vol. ii, pp. 165–6.

There is Baur to the life, in so far as incautious assumptions at the start lead him into error on every principal point of New Testament criticism. Baur's industry and erudition, and the brilliance of his critical insight at certain points, cannot compensate for the fatal weakness of the foundation on which the whole structure has been erected.

Baur saw, and here his intuition was perfectly correct, that the starting-point of all critical study of the New Testament must be the Epistles of St. Paul. These are the earliest Christian documents which we possess; here we come directly into contact with the life of the earliest Christian communities, and it is only through them and their faith that we can penetrate into the mysterious world of Jesus Christ, and of those events which lie at the origins of Christian faith. Baur started out from a conservative and orthodox position; gradually he was led to the conclusion that only the four great epistles, Romans, 1 and 2 Corinthians, and Galatians, are indubitably authentic; and it was on the study of these four that he based his reconstruction of Christian origins.

The study of the First Epistle to the Corinthians reveals to us the presence of parties and party strife among the earliest Christians. There seems to have been in Corinth a party which attached itself to the name of Cephas (Peter), the leader of the original apostles, questioned the apostolic authority of Paul, opposed itself to his teaching and set itself to destroy his work. A similar phenomenon presents itself in the Epistle to the Galatians. On this indubitable fact of tensions in the early Church arising out of different attitudes to the Law and to the faith of Israel, Baur bases his reconstruction of the history of the Church, a reconstruction which differs at almost every point from the traditional understanding. He sees the whole history in terms of bitter hostility between the Jewish and Gentile, the Petrine and the Pauline, wings of the new community. Members of the original Christian group in Jerusalem regarded themselves still as Jews; the Old Covenant retained its validity, and the one point of difference which marked them off from other Jews was the acceptance of Jesus as Messiah. Paul had set himself free from Judaism and the Law. He alone had understood the true significance of the work of Jesus; while not denying the Messiahship he does not emphasize it; for him Jesus has become the great deliverer, through faith in whose death man is reconciled to God and quickened through the presence of the Spirit. Gradually the sharp difference between these views led to a total separation between the communities, and one of the main aims of the Judaizing party was the hindering, and if possible the destruction, of the work of Paul. Pauline Christianity is far more authentic, since based on a deeper apprehension of the meaning of the work of Christ; it alone had within it the promise of universality, since it alone had broken free from the swaddling-bands of the old Jewish faith. But this was actually the weaker side, since the Jewish party could glory in the great names of Peter and the other apostles.

Here we have the thesis and the antithesis. The synthesis is to follow. It was impossible that two groups, both bearing the name of Christ, should for ever remain in separation. Gradually feelers, with a view to reconciliation, were put forward, the first from the side of the weaker or Pauline party. About the middle of the second century, final reconciliation took place, and, under the grave threats of the Gnostic movement, both parties found a home in the developing Catholic Church, in which something of each was retained but each underwent considerable modifications through its fusion with the other.

Having arrived at this general picture, Baur goes on to classify the documents of the New Testament, and of early Christian literature as a whole, according to the relationship which he traces in them to this history of strife and reconciliation. As we have seen, on the Pauline side the four 'authentic' epistles are our true and reliable guides. On the Judaizing side, the classic document is the Apocalypse, and later the pseudo-Clementine writings. The other books of the New Testament represent stages in the movement towards compromise. The Acts of the Apostles, which is throughout an eirenic book, minimizes the conflicts, and tries to present a harmonious, or at least a harmonized, picture of Christian origins.[1] The Epistle to the Hebrews represents a much earlier stage in this development:

The Epistle to the Hebrews is, perhaps, to be regarded as the first member of this group of eirenical writings, which form a separate class and belong to a specific period . . . With its own peculiar character . . . it can perhaps be regarded as a first and still somewhat ambiguous attempt to undertake the assimilation of the two parties, and the establishment of peace by means of the written word, through letters which were circulated in the name of the Apostles.[2]

[1] As Baur himself puts it, by making Paul look as Petrine as possible, and Peter as Pauline as possible.

[2] This is from an essay on the origins of the episcopate, published in 1838 in the Tübingen *Zeitschrift für Theologie*, and quoted in W. G. Kümmel, *Das neue Testament* (1958), p. 163.

It is hardly necessary to insist that this attempt to classify the varied literature of the New Testament according to one single principle leads Baur not infrequently to the use of methods which are neither critical, scientific, nor historical. An example is to be found in the essay from which we have just quoted. Next to the Pastoral Epistles in this field of reconciliation, says Baur,

> stands, as has become increasingly evident to me, the Epistle to the Philippians, in which, in addition to the reference to 'bishops' and 'deacons' in the opening sentences of the Epistle, and much else, into which this is not the place to enter, Clement the pupil of Peter is brought in as the first of the fellow-workers of the apostle Paul (4. 3).

This is the kind of aberration which in Baur so disconcertingly runs parallel with those brilliant historical insights, based on genuine scholarship, which make parts of his work permanently valuable. It is true that at a much later date anti-Pauline literature was circulating under the name of Clement. But in the first century there were as many people called Clement as there were people called Judas; and this identification of the Clement of the Epistle to the Philippians with the critic of Paul is a flight of fancy which rests on no evidence whatever, and has no shade of probability to recommend it.

Bishop Lightfoot complains somewhat tartly of this absurdity, and of others which had been piled on top of it by followers in the school of Baur. After quoting a passage from Matthew Arnold's *Essays in Criticism* (p. 57), where it is stated that 'an extravagance of this kind could never have come from Germany where there is a great force of critical opinion controlling a learned man's vagaries and keeping him straight', Lightfoot goes on to say that his own experiences of the critical literature of Germany have not been so fortunate. He adduces:

> Baur's suggesting that the pivot of the Epistle, which has a conciliatory tendency, is the mention of Clement, a mythical or almost mythical person, who represents the union of the Petrine and Pauline parties in the Church; then Schwegler, carrying the theory a step further, and declaring that the two names Euodia and Syntyche [Phil. 4. 2], actually represent these two parties, while the true yokefellow is St. Peter himself; then Volkmar improving the occasion, and showing that this fact is indicated in their very names, Euodia or 'Right way', and Syntyche or 'Consort', denoting the orthodoxy of the one party, and the incorporation of the other; lastly Hitzig lamenting that interpreters of the New Testament are not thoroughly

imbued with the language and spirit of the Old, and maintaining that these two names are reproductions of the patriarchs Asher and Gad, their sex having been changed in the transition from one language to another, and representing the Greek and Roman elements in the Church, while the Epistle to the Philippians is itself a plagiarism from the Agricola of Tacitus.[1]

At one crucial point at least Baur did make a permanent contribution to New Testament criticism. He recognized and asserted the difference in character between the Fourth Gospel and the other three. Until his time, almost all those who had dealt with the historical issues of the life of Jesus had taken the Fourth Gospel as their starting-point; the traditional ascription of its authorship to the beloved disciple had hardly been questioned; and who could be a better authority for the life and teaching of Jesus than the one who had lived in closest intimacy with him? This being taken as the basis, the other Gospels were then fitted in as well as possible into the picture. Baur saw, and argued persuasively, that the true relationship is exactly the other way round. If we wish to study the life of Jesus historically, the Synoptic Gospels bring us nearer to what we seek. Much of what Baur wrote about the Fourth Gospel is critically indefensible. Working still from his fatal principle of the division between Jew and Gentile as the central clue to Christian history, he affirms that the aim of the Fourth Gospel is not the writing of history but the presentation of an idea; and that the Johannine ideal (John 10. 16) 'of a Christian community made up equally of Gentiles and of Jews' belongs to a time 'in which Christianity has grown beyond the oppositions of its early days'. He is accordingly convinced that the Gospel cannot have been written earlier than the second half of the second century.

When he comes to the Synoptic Gospels, Baur continues to be misled by his presuppositions. Luke is the Gospel of the Gentiles, and is thus markedly Pauline in character. Now the Pauline understanding of the Gospel is authentic in that it has drawn out that which is essential in the Gospel message and which gives it its universal character. But chronologically this understanding comes later and can only to a limited degree bring us into contact with the original historical material. Wherever Luke and Matthew disagree, Matthew is to be unconditionally preferred. In Mark, Baur could find no trace of the opposition between Jew and Gentile. Therefore, on his principle, this must be a late

---

[1] J. B. Lightfoot, *Essays on 'Supernatural Religion'* (1889). The essay from which the quotation is taken was first published in the *Contemporary Review* in 1875.

document, belonging to the period not earlier than the middle of the second century, when reconciliation has finally taken place. So he takes Mark to be a compilation dependent on both Matthew and Luke, and written with the express purpose of reconciling the differences between them. Having disposed of the other Gospels, Baur now turns to Matthew. Here, too, from this point of view, much must be rejected as mythical in character and as later additions to the original narrative. But here, in this primarily Jewish Gospel and especially in the speeches, Baur believes that we can find at least some authentic evidence of what Jesus believed and taught.

V

Ferdinand Christian Baur has enjoyed an immense reputation in Germany, both during his lifetime and since his death. The Tübingen school, of which he was the central figure, dominated the scene for a whole generation. As we have seen, up to a point the reputation of Baur was well deserved by his immense industry, by his steadfast refusal to take anything for granted—this is the starting-point of any serious critical study—by his insistence that every book of the New Testament must be considered in relation to the historical circumstances of its origin in so far as that can be ascertained, and by certain brilliant insights of permanent validity. But there is a great deal to be set on the other side. At very few points indeed has subsequent investigation confirmed the rightness of Baur's solutions, even when it has approved his formulations of the questions. This suggests that either the method employed was basically wrong or that there were grave imperfections in the application of it. It is in the field of its presuppositions, which in themselves have nothing to do with critical or historical method, that the whole great structure of the work of Baur comes to grief. Again and again, when the presuppositions are exercising their unfortunate influence, critical method is for the time being abandoned.

It is impossible for any of us to work without presuppositions. What is important is that we should ourselves be aware of what our presuppositions are, and that we should make allowance for the distorting influence that they are likely to have on work which professes to be critical and unprejudiced. Baur was well aware of this. In the introduction to his history of the Church he tells us that the task of the historian is 'to place before ourselves the materials given in the history as they are objectively, and not otherwise, as far as that is possible'.[1] Yet a little later he can quote Schelling to the effect that 'history proves satisfying to the intellect when the empirical causes have been used as the means to the manifestation of a higher unity'.[2] It is from the dominance of the idea that the danger comes. Critical and historical study must be purely empirical; assumptions must be reduced to the minimum possible or the work cannot be carried out with any hope of success. If history is no more than the self-realization of the idea according to the laws of an immanent necessity, history really ceases to be history, and the Christian faith, as a faith rooted in history and conditioned by it, ceases to have anything more than relative significance.

This point has been correctly grasped by two twentieth-century scholars, neither of whom could be accused of any prejudice against Baur.

Horst Stephan writes:

The use of the Hegelian ideas proved to be a Procrustes' bed. Baur could not grasp the richness of concrete historical life, the importance of *personal* life and of the outstanding personality, the supra-historical factor, which cannot simply be absorbed into the idea. This use of the idea makes it possible to present Church history as a necessary, dialectical, advancing process, and takes from it the living character which it derives from the Christian belief in God.[3]

Karl Barth's comments and questions are alike penetrating:

From this point of view, then, we may ask Baur without a sneering sense of superiority, but also without levity, how the concept of the idea of history, according to the characteristics determined by him, may be related to the concept of God. What is history? Baur's answer is that history 'is the eternal clear mirror, in which Spirit beholds itself, contemplates its own visage in order to be for itself and in its own consciousness that which in itself it is, and to recognize itself as the moving power of that which historically has come to be' (*Dogmengeschichte*, p. 59). 'Really?' we may be inclined to ask. But, if it were the case that the history of the Church is that kind of history in which *God* speaks to us in our neighbour, and in which God speaks to us *in our neighbour*, would it be right that the history of the Church also should be understood and presented as that kind of self-contemplation?[4]

---

[1] *Vorrede* to *Kirchengeschichte*, vol. i (3rd ed., 1863), p. vii, English trans. (1878), p. x.
[2] Ibid., vol. ii (2nd ed., 1863), p. vi.,
[3] H. Stephan, *Geschichte der evangelischen Theologie* (ed. of 1960), p. 148.
[4] K. Barth, *Die protestantische Theologie im 19. Jahrhundert* (1947), p. 458.

VI

While Baur and his colleagues had been endlessly studying the New Testament in Tübingen, English theology had been in the main concerned with other things.[1] In the year (1845) in which Baur gathered together his thoughts on the Pauline problem in his great book *Paulus der Apostel*, John Henry Newman reached the end of the long pilgrimage which finally brought him to haven in the Church of Rome. England was rocked by this controversy, which may well have seemed more important than obscure dissertations on points of New Testament grammar and exegesis. Just in the same period, Frederic Denison Maurice with his friends was developing those views on Christian Socialism which have served as an active leaven in the Christian thought of England up to the present day. The frenzies of the Baptismal Controversy and the Gorham case (1847–50) kept bishops and journalists alike busy. And then came the Great Exhibition of 1851, the war in the Crimea, the Indian Mutiny—public opinion had a great deal on which to exercise itself.

But isolation cannot last for ever, and sooner or later the clear awareness of what was happening in Germany was bound to break in on the English-speaking world. The explosion came in 1860, with the publication of a book called *Essays and Reviews*, in which seven scholars, mostly of the University of Oxford, put forth their views on the contemporary situation in relation to Christian thought and faith. It was stated that there was no common planning between the writers; the book was an attempt 'to illustrate the advantages derivable to the cause of moral and religious truth from a free handling, in a becoming spirit, of subjects peculiarly liable to suffer by the repetition of conventional language and from traditional methods of treatment'. *Essays and Reviews* is a dull book, and, like so many other manifestos of the kind, would have passed unnoticed, except for a chance circumstance—the *Westminster Review* congratulated the authors on their courage, but urged them to go further and to cut themselves off more completely from those trammels of orthodoxy by which they were still fettered through their position in the established Church. The *Quarterly Review* came to the defence of orthodoxy, and then the book began to sell.

[1] Two of Baur's works have been translated into English—*Paul, the Apostle of Jesus Christ* (1873–5) and *The Church History of the First Three Centuries* (1878–9); as so often happens, the books were translated into English after they had begun to lose influence in the country of their origin.

From their own point of view, the orthodox had every reason to be alarmed. The Rhine and the Main were flowing into the Thames; German theology had overflowed its banks and flooded into England with a vengeance. One of the writers in *Essays and Reviews* was the Reverend Benjamin Jowett of Balliol College, who a good many years before had studied in Germany (1845–6), and was in part responsible for that Hegelian influence by which much Oxford theology was coloured for a considerable period.[1] In 1855 Jowett had published a commentary on the Epistles to the Romans, Galatians, and Thessalonians in which he had maintained what were held to be unorthodox views on the Atonement. The book had, however, been reviewed in somewhat favourable terms by a young fellow of Trinity College, Cambridge, in the *Journal of Classical and Sacred Philology*. J. B. Lightfoot, while criticizing rather sharply the weaknesses of the book in matters of accuracy and precise knowledge of the language of the New Testament, drew attention to its importance as the first serious attempt in England to apply to the New Testament the critical methods which were being developed on the continent of Europe. Mark Pattison, whose views on Baur we have already quoted, chose for his contribution a safe subject—certain aspects of religious thought in England in the seventeenth and eighteenth centuries. But he was known to have an immense admiration for the German university system, and spent his whole life in the vain pursuit of a total erudition, like that of the great renaissance scholars, Casaubon and the Scaligers, of whom he wrote so admirably.[2]

Put in the simplest words, the question that orthodox Christians had to face was this: 'Is the Bible to be treated like any other book or not?' Of course, the question is too simple; we do not treat Shakespeare as we treat Edgar Wallace. Yet it does go to the heart of the problem. Traditional Christian reverence held a view of Biblical inspiration which separated it off from every other book; these were the authentic words of God himself; and though up to a point grammatical, textual,

[1] The most notable Oxford Hegelian was T. H. Green (1836–82), whose rather unorthodox Christian faith made possible for many young men faith in spiritual realities as against the closed mechanical view of the world which was prevalent at the time. There is a sympathetic study of Green in W. Sanday, *Christologies Ancient and Modern* (1910), pp. 65 ff. The succession was carried on by F. H. Bradley (1846–1924) and Bernard Bosanquet (1848–1923). The only Cambridge Hegelian of eminence was J. McT. E. McTaggart (1866–1925).

[2] Pattison is best known from his own admirable *Memoirs* (1885); but V. H. H. Green, *Oxford Common Room* (1957), throws much light on the story of an unhappy and frustrated man.

and linguistic criticism might have their place, all awkward questions were supposed to be stilled by the protection of inspiration. It must be remembered that at that time almost all good Christians in England were what would now be called 'fundamentalists'. Whether it was Mr. Newman or Dr. Pusey, Lord Shaftesbury or Dean Close, Mr. Gladstone or Dr. Dale, there was very little between them; all accorded the Bible an unqualified reverence, and all believed that, if its inerrancy were successfully impugned, the whole Christian faith would collapse. Not many were prepared to take the temerarious position that, if the Bible is inspired, its inspiration is likely to shine all the brighter as a result of patient, impartial, and ruthlessly honest critical work upon it.

The handling of *Essays and Reviews* by the Church is a warning to all times that may be faced by a similar crisis. Everything was done exactly in the way in which it ought not to have been done. The Upper House of the Convocation of Canterbury condemned the book. The Lower House by a large majority commended the action of the bishops. Ten thousand Anglican clergymen signed a memorial to the bishops condemning the Essayists. Legal proceedings were started against them in the Court of Arches. The airing of ecclesiastical controversy in the law courts is one of the more deplorable aspects of the history of the Church of England in the nineteenth century.

No proceeding could possibly be more useless than the official condemnation of a book such as *Essays and Reviews*. It could reasonably be held that the writers, as clergymen of the Church of England, had gone against obligations which they had taken upon themselves when they were ordained. It could be maintained that the *Essays* were a bad piece of work, and that the evidence produced by the Essayists did not as a matter of fact support the conclusions which they put forward. But the tide could not be turned back. It was quite certain in 1860 that criticism had come to stay, and that henceforward the Bible would be treated like any other book. No holds would be barred. The Scriptures would be subjected to ruthless investigation. Unless they were able on their own merits to stand up to the challenge, the cause might be held to be lost in advance.

For it must be recognized that the threat presented to the Christian cause by the school of Tübingen was very grave. It is, of course, a fact that no one is saved merely by believing that certain events happened a long time ago. But it is a long way from this naïve belief to the bland assertion that the idea is all that matters, that the historical self-clothing of the idea is in a certain measure fortuitous, and that the validity of the idea would remain even if it could be proved that none of the historical events, which have been regarded as the foundation of the Christian faith, had ever occurred at all. If the incarnation of Jesus Christ is the great act of God in history, then much does depend on the extent and reliability of our historical evidence for what happened. If the Gospels were written well on in the second century, what faces us is a set of tendencies, faint memories, reconstructions, tales invented to give historical form to what in reality are theological and not historical convictions. This is not, of course, to say that because certain critical conclusions are inconvenient from the point of view of our faith, faith or inspiration should be called in to impede the work of historical criticism. It does mean that we should be careful not to pretend that one thing is another, and to imagine that the Christian faith as presented by Strauss or Baur is the same as the Christian faith of the Church in the earlier centuries.

In the years that followed 1860, Christians in England were almost in a state of panic. The *status quo* could never be restored. A way out of the panic could be found only if men would come forward who would carry out the work of critical investigation in a spirit of complete fearlessness, with willingness to face every fact and every issue, to meet them less hampered by presuppositions than the representatives of the German schools, and to show on the basis of minutely critical work that the answers given to the critical questions in Germany between 1830 and 1860 were not the only answers that were compatible with the known facts. The hour brought forth the man; in 1861 Joseph Barber Lightfoot was appointed to the Hulsean Professorship of Divinity at Cambridge, being then thirty-three years of age.

Chapter II

THE NEW TESTAMENT
AND HISTORY

FOR forty years, from 1860 to 1900, Lightfoot, Westcott, and Hort were names profoundly venerated throughout the whole world of scholarship, and especially in the English-speaking world. Hardly ever in the history of the Church have three men of such distinction worked together over so long a period on the accomplishment of what was essentially one great purpose.

At certain points the three men very closely resembled one another. There was little difference in age, Brooke Foss Westcott being a little older than the other two.[1] All three were Scholars, and later Fellows, of Trinity College, Cambridge. All had made an intensive study of the Latin and Greek classics, and were masters of both languages in their classical form. All were members and ministers of the Church of England. All were profoundly committed to the faith of the incarnation, holding that in Jesus Christ God himself had entered into human life for the redemption of that life from all evil. The differences, however, were also many and interesting; it was because of these differences that each of the trio was able to make his own special contribution, and at certain special points to compensate for the weaknesses of the others. Lightfoot was the only one of the three who was able to live a continuously academic life. In their day Fellows of colleges who married had to resign their fellowships. Thus it came about that for eighteen years Westcott was a master at Harrow School, and Hort was incumbent of the parish of St. Ippolyts cum Great Wymondley, some twenty miles from Cambridge, from 1857 till 1872. What these men produced is all the more remarkable in view of the heavy demands made on their time and strength by these other responsibilities. Hort was not altogether suited to parish life; his son has described how he would sit for hours with an uncompleted sermon in front of him, unable because of a curious kind of literary aphasia to add a single word to what he had written.

[1] Brooke Foss Westcott (1825–1901); Joseph Barber Lightfoot (1828–89); Fenton John Anthony Hort (1828–92).

Though all shared many gifts in common, Lightfoot was primarily the historian, Hort the philosopher, and Westcott the exegete.
When Lightfoot's first great commentary, that on the Epistle to the
Galatians, appeared (1865), Hort was inclined to criticize it on the
ground that some of the doctrinal problems involved had been
inadequately treated.[1] But Lightfoot knew his own limitations. What
he could handle as an historian he would handle superbly; what was not
within his field must be left to others whose gifts were different from
his own. Hort, who among other things had taken high honours in the
School of Botany and Physiology at Cambridge, had a far wider
knowledge of philosophy and of natural science than the others, and
was more aware of the changing climate of thought resulting from the
writings of Darwin and other discoveries in the field of science.
Westcott had an extraordinary sensitiveness to shades of spiritual
meaning, and this made him an almost ideal commentator. Of the three,
Hort had the strongest feeling for the institutional side of the Christian
religion, and Lightfoot, though he became a highly successful bishop,
the least interest in that aspect of it.

The three scholars were well aware of the rising tide of criticism in
Germany. Baur, who died in 1860, had attempted single-handed the
vast enterprise of a complete survey of the whole of Christian antiquity, and had reached conclusions which appeared to the Cambridge
three to be vulnerable at a great many points. *Essays and Reviews* had
brought the critical problems to the notice of every thinking Christian
in England.[2] The only way adequately to deal with this situation was
to carry out an equally comprehensive survey, on basically the same
critical principles, but far more soberly, far more realistically, with far
greater attention to accuracy, and with far fewer presuppositions than
those which Baur had brought with him into the field. The three
friends planned nothing less than a complete commentary on the
New Testament, to be based on a critically edited Greek text, to be
philological, historical, exegetical, and doctrinal, and so to present

---

[1] A. F. Hort, *Life and Letters of Fenton J. A. Hort*, vol. ii (1896), pp. 79–80: 'Certainly
his doctrinal statements are far from satisfying me. One misses the real attempt to fathom
St. Paul's own mind, and to compare it with the facts of life which one finds in Jowett.
On the other hand, he is surely always admirable on historical ground . . . as also in all
matters of grammar and language and such like essential externalities.'

[2] Lightfoot, Westcott, and Hort, while disagreeing with the writers of *Essays and
Reviews* at many points, felt that they had been scurvily treated by the church authorities,
and that far too little recognition had been given to their genuine honesty of purpose.
They even for a short time contemplated writing a reply, but fortunately this plan was
given up—a very different approach to the whole problem was needed.

the whole panorama of Christian truth against the setting of its historical origins. Lightfoot was to deal with the Pauline Epistles and Hebrews, Westcott with the Johannine writings, to which Hebrews was later added, and Hort with the other books of the New Testament. The plan was never carried out in its entirety; what we have from the three originators of it is a magnificent fragment, and much of their achievement is of permanent and unchangeable value.

From the moment of his appointment to the professorship at Cambridge in 1861 Lightfoot was an immense success as a lecturer and teacher. Nothing like his lectures had been heard before in Cambridge. The New Testament had been treated as a repository of grammatical peculiarities, or of proof-texts, to be quoted and co-ordinated in support of the traditional doctrines, with little regard to the origin or background of any particular text. Lightfoot's method was from the start strictly historical. As he expounded the Epistle to the Galatians, the old words came to life, and the hearers became aware of the Apostle standing at one of the great crises of his life, as the whole stability and continuity of his work was menaced by 'the other gospel' brought in by the Judaizers. So great was the number of those desiring to hear Lightfoot's lectures that they had to be moved to the Hall of Trinity College. A great many people felt that something was astir in the theological world.

Lightfoot was a tremendous worker. It was said in Cambridge that, however late you went to bed, you would still see the light on in his rooms in the Great Court of Trinity College. His mind was systematic, clear, and vigorous, his memory capacious and exact. Bishop Westcott has given a convincing picture of his method of handling his materials:

His method of working was characteristic. When a subject was chosen, he mastered, stored, arranged in his mind, all the materials which were available for its complete treatment, but he drew up no systematic notes, and sketched no plan. As soon as the scope of the Essay was distinctly conceived, he wrote continuously and rapidly, trusting to his memory for the authorities which he used, and adding them as he went forward, but so that every reference was again carefully verified in proof.[1]

In the hands of anyone else this method could well have been dangerous; but undoubtedly it was for Lightfoot the right method. He was fortunately gifted with a style of singular lucidity; and the

[1] Prefatory Note to *The Apostolic Fathers: Part I. S. Clement of Rome* (1890), p. vii. This note was written about a year after Lightfoot's death.

vigour of the thought is reflected in the forthright, manly, and unaffected presentation of it.[1] And the integrity of Lightfoot's mind and the scrupulous accuracy of his scholarship make it impossible to imagine that his work ever suffered from haste or carelessness. He had earned to the letter the praise accorded to him by Westcott, who at the end of the tribute from which we have already quoted comments: 'the last mature fruit of labours pursued with unwearied devotion at Cambridge, at St. Paul's, and at Durham, by one whose "sole desire" it was, in his own words written a few months before his death, in "great things and in small, to be found συνεργὸς τῇ ἀληθείᾳ"—.'[2]

Like Baur, Lightfoot had recognized that the Epistles of Paul must always be the starting-point for the historical study of the New Testament. During the twenty years which followed his appointment to the professorship at Cambridge, a great deal of his time was given to the preparation of his stately series of commentaries on the Pauline Epistles. In 1865 his first series of lectures was brought together in the commentary on the Epistle to the Galatians, a work so valuable that by the date of Lightfoot's death in 1889 it had already passed through ten editions. This was followed by commentaries on the Epistle to the Philippians (1868), and on Colossians and Philemon (1875), which have proved no less indispensable to the serious student of the New Testament, and have been reprinted again in America in quite recent times.

During this period Lightfoot was drawn almost accidentally into an exciting controversy directly related to those radical views of the New Testament and of Christian origins which had been put forward by the Tübingen school. A writer of very small distinction named J. A. Cassels in 1874 published anonymously a book under the title *Supernatural Religion*. Cassels was convinced that the supposedly supernatural element in religion, as opposed to its ethical content, was harmful and ought to be eliminated: 'We gain far more than we lose in abandoning belief in the reality of Divine Revelation. Whilst we retain pure and unimpaired the light of Christian Morality, we relinquish nothing but the debasing elements added to it by human superstition.'[3]

[1] The same, alas, cannot be said of Bishop Westcott. In 1919 I heard Henry Jackson say in a lecture that Westcott had once told him that he had never rewritten a single sentence; 'and that', said Jackson, 'is perhaps why I find some of his sentences so extraordinarily difficult to understand'.

[2] Op. cit., p. viii.

[3] *Supernatural Religion* (1874), vol. ii, p. 489.

Having acquired a superficial knowledge of the Tübingen theology and its reconstruction of early Christian history, Cassels set to work with the help of its methods to show that the Gospels in particular are so far removed in time from the events they purport to record that they are in fact historically worthless, and can afford no solid foundation for that structure of revelation which has been built up upon them.

In those gusty and combative days of the Victorian era there were many who were doubtful whether the Christian faith was true, and perhaps as many more who were very eagerly desirous that it should not be true. *Supernatural Religion* seemed to provide the answer to these anxieties and hopes. In no time the book became the vogue; edition after edition was called for, and the publishers could hardly keep up with the demand. And then suddenly the wind changed.

At one point Cassels had gravely over-reached himself. He had criticized the scholarship of Canon B. F. Westcott in terms which seemed to impugn that great man's intellectual integrity. The matter was brought to the notice of Lightfoot, who was incensed, and was readily persuaded to deal faithfully with *Supernatural Religion* in a series of articles in the *Contemporary Review*. With his perfect mastery of all the evidence, Lightfoot was able to write rapidly and easily, and with a zest which immediately communicates itself to the reader. He has no difficulty in tearing to shreds the borrowed robes of Cassels' supposed scholarship, in vindicating the integrity and accuracy of his friend, in showing how grossly the argument from silence has been mishandled and misapplied, and in presenting the case for a much more favourable estimate of the historical value of the Gospels. The effect was immediate and deadly. Stone dead hath no fellow. 'In no time *Supernatural Religion* was a glut in the second-hand market.'[1] A book which is so permanently and justly dead is hardly even of historical interest today; but Lightfoot's *Essays on 'Supernatural Religion'* (1889) are still a joy to read, as the best controversial writing in English since Bentley wrote on the Letters of Phalaris (1699) and delivered 'the most crushing blow that was ever dealt to insolent and aggressive sciolism'.[2]

This parenthetical controversy has drawn our attention to the immense importance of the dating of the New Testament documents. The Tübingen school had questioned the dates ascribed by tradition to most of the New Testament books, and had brought them down to a period at which, though they might be of the greatest

[1] G. R. Eden and F. C. Macdonald, *Lightfoot of Durham* (1932), pp. 9 ff.
[2] R. C. Jebb, in *Dictionary of National Biography*, vol. iv, p. 310.

value as evidence for the thought of the Church in the second century, they must be almost without value in relation to Jesus Christ himself and to the earliest stages of the Christian story. Almost at the beginning of his studies Lighfoot had become convinced that many New Testament problems can be solved only when the New Testament is considered not only in itself, but in relation to the whole corpus of Christian literature of the first two centuries. Where there is so much doubt as to dating and chronology, is it possible to find outside the New Testament itself a fixed point, chronologically exact and determined, an Archimedean point on which it is possible to take one's stand, and from there to shake the world?

In the modern world we are so accustomed to history books, in which each event is assigned to a precise date, and to the modern printed book, the date of the publication of which is clearly indicated on the title-page, that it is difficult for us to realize the patient and tedious labour by which the chronology of the world's history has gradually been established on a scientific basis. Many nations have had little interest in chronology, indeed in history itself. The dates given in the Bible are notoriously inadequate from the standpoint of modern historical research; it is astonishing but true that we cannot fix with absolute certainty the date of those crucial events in the history of the world, the birth and death of Jesus Christ. At a number of points we are reduced to mere conjecture, or to reasonably probable inference from wholly insufficient data.

The extreme case is the early history of India. We possess an immense and classic literature in the ancient Vedic and Sanskrit tongues; yet in all this vast field there is hardly so much as a single indication, through which the dates of the documents, and of the events to which they refer, can be established. We are dependent on an external and almost fortuitous occurrence; the invasion of the Punjab by Alexander the Great in 330 B.C. provides the Archimedean point from which it is possible to survey Indian history backwards and forwards and to bring order out of chaos. Starting from this one fixed point, it has been possible to determine, with reasonable accuracy, the course of the development of Indian thought and literature, and to fix in time such crucial turning-points as the life and teaching of Gautama the Buddha.[1]

---

[1] It is interesting to note that the learned Abbé Dubois, writing in 1817 (English trans., 1897) of the manners and customs of the Hindus, tentatively assigned the Buddha to the twelfth century B.C. Modern scholarship has fixed the date of his birth, with fair precision, in 563 B.C., and of his death in 483 B.C.

Some ancient documents contain precise information as to their authorship and date, but a great many do not. To the former class belong such works as the *Commentaries* of Julius Caesar and the *Letters* of Cicero. Hardly anyone has ever doubted the authenticity of these works. If they are authentic, they give us clear and lucid information, such as we have for hardly any other period of ancient history, concerning life and thought in the Roman world in the middle of the first century B.C. To the second class belong the Gospels. No one of them gives, in its text, the name of the author; the titles which we find in the ancient Greek manuscripts form no part of the original text. No one of them gives any indication as to the date and place of writing. If an ancient writing is of this anonymous and homeless character, by what means, if any, is it possible to fix it in time, and to establish with some probability the name of the writer?

Use can be made of a number of delicate criteria—of literary style, of attitude and atmosphere, of reference or absence of reference to known historical events. Any reader who is interested in trying out this method can satisfy himself of its validity by a chronological study of that charming series of tales *The Irish R.M. and his Experiences*. The stories evidently form a sequence, and there are subtle clues as to the period of time that they cover. But at only two points are they related directly to any period in the history of the world outside the charmed sphere in which they move. The first is the point at which the Major purchases a motor-car. The second, far more precise, is the departure of Mr. Flurry Knox for the South African war; this can have taken place only in one of two years, 1900 or 1901; and much more probably the former. This fixes for us, beyond all doubt, the period to which the stories refer. Many little points of detail make it certain that the stories can only have been written by authors who had themselves lived in the period that they record; all the internal evidence goes to show that the stories were written down within that period or very shortly after.

But how long after? Is there any criterion by which we can fix with absolute certainty the latest date by which a document can have been written? There is. If a document is quoted in another document, of which the date is previously known, it is unshakeably certain that the first antedates the second. Now we find that Sir Arthur Quiller-Couch, King Edward VII Professor of English Literature in the University of Cambridge, devoted one of his professorial lectures to the writings of E. Œ. Somerville and Martin Ross, and referred in particular to the glorious *peripeteia* in the story 'Lisheen Races Secondhand'. The lecture was published, in the book entitled *The Poet as Citizen*, in 1934, but internal evidence suggests that it was actually delivered in 1917 or 1918. It is, then, absolutely certain that the story was written before that date. It is a reasonable, though not an absolutely certain, supposition that we must allow a period of not less than ten and more probably of twenty years for the story to become sufficiently well known to become a suitable subject for a professorial discourse.[1]

Precisely such are the methods that are applied by scholars to the New Testament books, as to all other ancient documents. Using such methods, can we determine the very latest date at which the New Testament books can have been written?

A century ago early Christian literature was in confusion. Little had been done to sort out the genuine works from the spurious compositions that clothed themselves with such great names as those of Athanasius, Ambrose, and Augustine. A great many problems of chronology remained unsolved; for instance, the dates of so famous an early Christian writer as Justin Martyr were still a matter of controversy. On our immediate problem, however, the dates of the New Testament books, it was possible to make one certain and incontrovertible statement; every book of the New Testament, except the Epistle to Philemon, is quoted by Irenaeus, who became bishop of Lyons in the South of France somewhere about A.D. 178 and died probably not later than 200. It is, therefore, impossible that the New Testament books should have come into being later than this date. This is not irreconcilable with the view of the Tübingen school, which as we have seen was inclined to judge that considerable sections of the New Testament were written about the middle of the second century, though this leaves rather little time for the books to acquire the unquestioned authority in the Church which Irenaeus seems to ascribe to them. The question arises whether it is possible to move the absolute *terminus ad quem* back to an earlier period than that of Irenaeus. This was the question that Lightfoot set himself to answer.

There were in existence two considerable bodies of Christian literature, for parts of which at least the claim had been made that they arose in the very early years of the second century, or, in the case of

[1] Of course, the date of the writing of 'Lisheen Races' is perfectly well known. *Some Experiences of an Irish R.M.* was published by E. Œ. Somerville and Martin Ross in 1899. I am asking the reader to use his imagination, and to suppose himself to have encountered in the heart of Africa an undated copy of the *Irish R.M.* and a dated copy of Quiller-Couch's lectures, and to have employed his leisure in scientific chronological study.

one of them, even in the closing years of the first. It was clear that, if this claim could be made out, the effect on the critical study of the New Testament would be immense.

The Clementine writings are a highly miscellaneous collection. Apart from a first Epistle, purporting to have been written by a certain Clement on behalf of the Church of Rome to the Church of Corinth in a time of crisis, and a second 'Epistle', which is in reality a sermon, this literature consists of a whole variety of more or less romantic documents, of which the most important are the *Clementine Homilies* and the *Clementine Recognitions*.[1] The *Homilies* describe the travels of Clement in the East, and the conflict between Peter and Simon Magus, which Clement claims to have witnessed. This work, ascribed by Baur and his colleagues to an early date, became almost the cornerstone of the Tübingen theory, since these scholars believed that the name Simon Magus really concealed no less a person than the Apostle Paul, and found here striking confirmation for their view that the clue to the whole of early Christian history is the passionate opposition between the Pauline and Petrine parties in the Church. But Baur denied any connexion between any part of this literature and that Clement of Rome who was believed to have been the successor of Peter as bishop of the Roman Church.

The name of Ignatius, who was bishop in Syria, and died as a martyr in Rome not later than A.D. 115, had become attached to a number of letters or collections of letters, some addressed to churches and some to individuals. A number of these were obviously very late documents, the character of which made it clear that they could have had no connexion with any historical Ignatius. The authenticity, or spuriousness, of the thirteen older letters had long been a subject of learned and acrimonious debate. Baur would not admit the authenticity, or early date, of any of the letters; since, if the authenticity of any of them could be established, the whole Tübingen structure would be undermined at its most sensitive and precarious point; none of the Ignatian letters shows any awareness of the kind of tension between the Petrine and the Pauline factions, which was the cornerstone of the Tübingen theory.

Lightfoot was convinced that somewhere in this mass of literature, and principally in the Ignatian letters, his Archimedean point was to be

---

[1] For a complete list of the documents, and an admirably concise statement of the problems arising from them, see *The Oxford Dictionary of the Christian Church* (1958), p. 301.

found. With unwearied diligence and perspicacity he set himself to the elucidation of the truth.

The Ignatian problem with which Lightfoot proposed to deal was one of extraordinary complexity; only the essential elements in it can be briefly sketched in this chapter.

Nothing is known in detail of the life and work of Ignatius as bishop of the Church in Syria at the beginning of the second century. But various records of his martyrdom, not at Antioch but at Rome, have been preserved. Eusebius in his *Ecclesiastical History* gives an account of it, in which he informs us that Ignatius was the second successor of Peter in the episcopate at Antioch.[1] He quotes at length from the Epistle of Ignatius to the Romans, in which Ignatius expresses his eagerness for martyrdom, and picturesquely speaks of himself as 'bound to ten leopards'—the soldiers of the maniples who were entrusted with the duty of guarding him—'who the better they are treated, the worse they become'. Furthermore, Eusebius gives a list of seven letters written by Ignatius, six to churches and one to Polycarp the bishop of Smyrna.[2] The *History* of Eusebius was one of the most widely read books in the ancient world; and this passage alone was sufficient to keep alive the memory of Ignatius. But, in addition, letters bearing his name were in circulation, and were specially popular with the Monophysites because of certain passages which seemed to favour the Monophysite position. If these seven letters are genuine, and date from about 110, they will shed a flood of light on that dark sub-apostolic period about which we know so little. If they can be shown to be spurious, they are of course of no value whatever as evidence for that period and that stage of Christian development.

The letters of Ignatius were among the earliest of the monuments of Christian antiquity to be printed. A Latin translation was published at Paris by J. Faber (Stapulensis) as early as 1498, to be followed by another edition, produced at Cologne, in 1536; and by the Greek text, once more at Paris, in 1557. But the trouble was that in these editions there were too many letters of Ignatius. Eusebius had given the names of seven—but the first Latin edition included eleven, the second twelve, and the Greek again eleven. Altogether thirteen were known. What was to be thought of the six of which no mention had been made by Eusebius,

---

[1] Origen states that Ignatius was the direct successor of Peter.
[2] Eusebius, *Ecclesiastical History*, III, 36, 1–15. Translation by H. J. Lawlor and J. E. L. Oulton, vol. i (1927), pp. 95–97; see also the notes in vol. ii (1928), pp. 106–9.

which are never cited by any of the ancient authors before the sixth century, and which seem to show clear signs of having been written at a date considerably later than the second century? To make matters worse, in the seven letters recognized by Eusebius, along with much that seemed to be primitive there were passages which appeared to bear the stamp of later times; and, when the printed text was compared with the quotations in Eusebius and Theodoret of Cyrrhus (d. 458), many divergencies were noted. Bad money always tends to drive out good. The presence of these doubtful letters and doubtful passages brought discredit on the collection as a whole; Ignatius seemed to be a very shaky witness for the period to which he was alleged to belong.

The sixteenth century was a learned rather than a critical age, and anxiety as to the authenticity of the letters did not immediately develop. In fact, views on the questions tended to develop as a function of views about episcopacy rather than on the basis of a careful and critical handling of the material. The New Testament says hardly anything about episcopacy. Ignatius says a great deal. Writing at a time at which the Church was gravely threatened by heresy, he regards the bishop as the very centre of the unity of the Church and as the guardian of its life. He presents no doctrine of succession as that was later to develop in, for instance, the writings of Irenaeus. But, even without that, the letters provided plenty of material for violent controversy in the sixteenth century, in which some churches, having abandoned the only form of church order known in more than a thousand years, were looking about for justification for their actions, and others which more conservatively had retained the episcopate were looking for historical as well as theological support for their position. If you approved of episcopacy, Ignatius was just your man; if you disapproved of episcopacy, Ignatius just would not do.

One of those who disapproved of bishops, and therefore of Ignatius, was John Milton, who expressed himself on the subject in a typical tirade:

Had God intended that we should have sought any part of useful instruction from Ignatius, doubtless he would not have so ill-provided for our knowledge as to send him to our hands in this broken and disjointed plight; and, if he intended no such thing, we do injuriously in thinking to taste better the pure evangelic manna by seasoning our mouths with the tainted scraps and fragments of an unknown table, and searching among the verminous and polluted rags dropt overworn from the toiling shoulders of Time, with these deformedly to quilt and interlace the entire, the spotless, and un-decaying robe of truth.[1]

Anglican divines, on the contrary, taking a gentler view of bishops, on the whole read Ignatius with pleasure and without suspicion. Richard Hooker and Lancelot Andrewes seem alike to have accepted the thirteen letters as genuine. But the dating of documents and questions of their genuineness cannot be settled on the ground of prejudice or *parti pris*; only a rigid and impartial scrutiny of the internal and external evidence can provide the materials for an answer. It was time that Ignatius should be tried by these methods and no others.

Within a year or two of Milton's diatribe, remarkable new light was thrown on the whole question as the result of one of the most remark-able pieces of detective work in the whole history of Christian scholar-ship. Archbishop James Ussher is known to most people today only as the man who worked out those curious dates (4004 B.C. the creation of the world, etc.) which till very recently adorned the pages of most Bibles printed in England; or as the prelate who tried to soften the rage of the sectaries by proposals for a mild form of episcopacy diluted by presbytery. But Ussher was much more than this. He was a man of immense learning—Mark Pattison, who knew a great deal about the seventeenth century, once referred to him as the most learned man of his age—and of impeccable critical acumen. He had noticed that quotations from Ignatius in the Latin works of three English writers of the thirteenth and fourteenth centuries agreed exactly with the quotations in Eusebius and Theodoret as against the printed versions. He rightly concluded that at that period a Latin translation of the Epistles in this earlier form must have existed in England, and hoped that some manuscripts of this version might survive.[2] Now about this there could be no certainty; many factors of chance enter into the survival or destruction of manuscripts, and Ussher's researches might well have been in vain. But good fortune was with him. He was able to find two Latin manuscripts, one in the

---

[1] J. Milton, *Of Prelatical Episcopacy* (*Works*, vol. iii, p. 72). This was written in 1641. Ignatius can be troublesome in the twentieth century as well as in the seventeenth. During the discussions on church union in South India, the Swiss A. Streckeisen of the Basel Mission on 21 March 1938 wrote to the American Congregationalist J. J. Banninga: 'I therefore do not think to trouble more about it, but to leave my Ignatius during holidays in the bookshelf, enjoying the same rest he had had practically all these years.' B. G. M. Sundkler, *The Church of South India* (1954), p. 410.

[2] Reasons have been given for thinking that this version was actually made by the great Robert Grosseteste, Bishop of Lincoln, about 1250.

library of Caius College, Cambridge, and one in the library of Bishop Richard Montague of Norwich. These gave a Latin translation, which is so literal that the original Greek can be almost exactly reconstructed from it; and the text so reconstructed agrees exactly with the quotations in the ancient fathers at every point where comparison can be made.[1] All that was lacking to Ussher was the uninterpolated Greek text; two years after the publication of his book in 1644, the lack was supplied by the Dutch scholar Isaac Voss, who was able to track down a manuscript in Florence, of which Ussher had heard but which he had been unable to acquire or consult, and from it to print the Greek text of six epistles in their original and uninterpolated form.[2] The reader who was familiar with Greek now had in his hands the original text, freed from the interpolations of later times, of this very early witness to the Christian faith outside the New Testament.

Ussher's book ought to have settled the main question for good and all; but Ignatius was destined to have a further long and controversial history. In 1666 the Swiss Protestant pastor Jean Daillé (Dallaeus, 1594–1670) entered the lists with a large controversial work on the writings which pass under the names of Dionysius the Areopagite and of Ignatius. With regard to the former Daillé had an easy task; no one now believes the writings of the so-called Areopagite to be other than the work of a monk of the sixth century, who had become deeply imbued with the neo-Platonic philosophy in its later form. With Ignatius he is less successful. Few are likely to believe that the Ignatian letters were unknown till about the end of the third century, at which time they were forged. It is hard to resist the impression that Daillé is more concerned to defend his own views as to the late origin of episcopacy, which he places as late as the beginning of the third century, than to take seriously the literary and historical evidence for the authenticity of the seven letters of Ignatius which was available in his time. Daillé's challenge was met by the great John Pearson (1613–86), Bishop of Chester, who in 1672 brought forward once again all the arguments in favour of the genuineness of the Epistles, in his *Vindiciae Epistolarum S. Ignatii*. In most parts of the world his work seemed to have been accepted as closing the controversy.

[1] Ussher made the mistake of rejecting as spurious the letter to Polycarp, which subsequent scholarship has accepted as genuine.

[2] The Medicean manuscript did not contain the letter of Ignatius to the Romans; this was later discovered, and printed for the first time in Paris in 1689. Translations in Armenian and Syriac, and in part in Coptic, have since been added to the textual evidence for Ignatius.

From one point of view the work of Daillé was wholly justified. The shelves of the libraries are weighed down by spurious and apocryphal works from the early Christian centuries. It is essential that the genuine works should be enabled to emerge from the chrysalis of the spurious in which they have become enveloped. The recovery of the genuine Ignatius by Ussher and Pearson made it possible to see in its full extent the work of the interpolator, who composed the whole of six letters, and inserted passages of considerable length into the seven which are now held to be genuine. Who was the interpolator, and where did he work? Once again, the detective genius of Ussher gave the right answer. The interpolator lived in Syria, probably in Antioch, in the last third of the fourth century A.D. His work so closely resembles that of the author of the so-called *Apostolic Constitutions* that Ussher came to the conclusion that we here have to do with one man and not with two—the author is the interpolator, a view which in modern times can claim in its support the more than respectable authority of Harnack.

The work known as the *Apostolic Constitutions* deserves a brief paragraph, in illustration of the theme that the accurate dating of early Christian documents is of the utmost importance. This work, which is now recognized by all to have been composed not earlier than the middle of the fourth century, was first printed at Venice in 1563. Most critical readers with any capacity for weighing historical evidence recognized that the book had only the most tenuous of connexions with the Apostles. But the eighth book contains a document of really great significance—the so-called Clementine Liturgy, the oldest complete Eucharistic liturgy that we possess. A whole succession of devout Anglican scholars, who were deeply interested in liturgy and in liturgical reform, believed that this was the original apostolic liturgy, to which all others ought to be made to conform.[1] This is one of the

---

[1] One of the most passionate and extravagant defenders of this point of view was William Whiston (1667–1752), the successor of Newton in the Lucasian Chair of Mathematics at Cambridge: 'These Constitutions . . . will well deserve to be considered by every Christian with that caution and awful regard to their contents which the Authority of the Apostles of Christ, nay of Christ himself, and of God his Father, so visibly appearing therein does demand from us. And indeed I must own, as to myself, that I cannot read them without the same regard that I pay to any book of the Bible, since I have fully satisfy'd myself that they are Genuine, Sacred, and Apostolical; and the Original Repository of those Sacred Laws of Christ, by which he will govern his Church' (*Primitive Christianity Reviv'd* (1711–12), vol. iii, pp. 11–12, quoted in W. J. Grisbrooke, *Anglican Liturgies of the Seventeenth and Eighteenth Centuries* (1958), p. 57). But Whiston was not alone in his opinion. There was a danger, though only a passing danger, that the liturgy of the Church of England might come to be influenced by the views of an unknown

points at which critical scholarship has said a decisive No; the thoughts of the late fourth century cannot be read back into the apostolic age, or into that Ignatian age which followed so closely upon it. The work of Ignatius himself and that of his interpolator have been finally and permanently separated from one another.

We come now to the nineteenth century, in which two new factors brought the Ignatian letters back to the centre of attention in the world of learning. The discovery of a short Syriac version of only three letters raised once again the whole question of the authenticity of the Vossian seven.

Ussher and many others had believed with some confidence that a Syriac version of the Ignatian Epistles was in existence; but all their efforts to trace it and to discover a manuscript ended in failure. This was the state of affairs when, in 1845, Dr. Cureton, a Canon of Westminster, at last published the Syriac Ignatius. But the publication contained a great surprise; only three letters were to be found in the Syriac text—the Epistles to Polycarp, to the Ephesians, and to the Romans, and these in a form considerably shorter than the Greek text. At once the question arose whether the Syriac was a shortening of the Vossian form of the seven letters, which in that case could still be taken to be original; or whether the short Syriac represented the original, which at some later date had been expanded into the longer and Vossian form. The discussion was vigorous and lively, and opinion was sharply divided. Cureton, with natural pride in his own discovery, maintained against all comers that the Syriac represented the original. He found a number of supporters, among them the outstanding German scholar Albrecht Ritschl (1822–89). Lightfoot himself for a considerable period held this view, and changed it only when extensive study of the whole field of the Ignatian problem convinced him that it was untenable. Others, notably Baur, continued to deny the authenticity of any of the Ignatian Epistles in any form. A few defended the seven Vossian letters as authentic and truly Ignatian.

This matter was brought closer to settlement by the great conservative scholar Theodor Zahn (1838–1933), who had been working on the Ignatian problem for many years. In 1875 he came out with his big book, the most important work on the subject which had appeared in any language since the *Vindiciae* of Bishop Pearson just two centuries before. Zahn was by temperament so conservative that he was

author of the fourth century, on the mistaken understanding that he was directly the mouthpiece of the Apostles.

inclined to maintain positions which had been given up even by other conservative scholars; but here he was on solid ground. He showed clearly that the Curetonian letters *could* have been produced by shortening from the Vossian, and that it was almost impossible that the shorter version should have been expanded into the longer. Lightfoot worked independently, and in greater detail, on the same lines; since the publication of his work hardly a single scholar had been found to maintain the priority of the Curetonian form.

Here, then, at last is an answer. We can be done with the thirteen letters and the three; only the seven remain to instruct or to trouble us. Eusebius, so to say, has been vindicated; the seven letters known to the ancient Church are the only ones which have any claim to authenticity. But to say that they have a claim to authenticity is not to say that they can be accepted without question as authentic. Eusebius could have been mistaken in attributing the seven letters to Ignatius, the martyr of two centuries earlier. We have to go further back in time. The external evidence of quotations and allusions has to be looked at. Further testing on the grounds of internal consistency and probability, further checking of alleged anachronisms, have to be carried out. Here Lightfoot expends many pages in going into every single difficulty that had been raised, and showing that some of these rested on misunderstandings of the text, others on unfamiliarity with the thought and practices of the times; but that in the end the probability of their genuineness immensely outweighs anything that can be said on the other side.

Two instances may be given as an illustration of the range of Lightfoot's knowledge, the practical intelligence which he brought to every question, and the vigour and trenchancy of his style.

One point refers to those 'leopards' who had been set to guard the martyr on his way to Rome. A scholar named Bochart had maintained that the word 'leopard' was not known in Greek before the age of Constantine, two centuries later, and therefore could not have been used by Ignatius writing in A.D. 110. Lightfoot was able to point out that the word does occur in Greek in a writing of the physician Galen only about fifty years after the time of Ignatius, that it occurs also in a rescript of the emperors Marcus and Commodus (177–80); and that the elder Pliny, writing in Latin fifty years before Ignatius, refers to *leones quos pardi generavere* ('lions brought forth by pards'). With characteristic modesty he writes: 'As a very imperfect knowledge and casual research have enabled me to supply these important passages, which have hitherto escaped notice, it is not unreasonable to surmise that in the extant literature of the intervening period other examples may occur, which have not yet been brought to light.'[1]

Critics had raised the question: How could a prisoner carefully guarded by ten leopards find means to write letters and to communicate freely with his friends? The question betrays a modern attitude to prisons which is quite different from that of the ancient world. In all the records of the early persecutions of Christians nothing surprises the modern reader more than the freedom enjoyed by the prisoners to receive their friends, to communicate with them, and to write. The best-known example of all is that of the *Acts of Perpetua and Felicitas*, to which Lightfoot refers; but there are many others. He then proceeds:

Unhappily for criticism, but happily for humanity, history is not logically consistent. Men are not automata, which move on certain rigid mechanical principles, but complex living souls with various motives, impulses, passions, reluctances. The keepers of John Hus at Constance were far more deeply and personally interested in preventing his disseminating the opinions which had locked the prison doors on him and for which he ultimately suffered, than the keepers of Ignatius at Smyrna and Troas. Indeed it is not probable that the human 'leopards', who maltreated this early martyr, cared a straw whether Ignatius made an additional convert or not. The Bohemian prisoner too was guarded far more rigidly and treated far more cruelly than the Antiochene. Yet John Hus found means to communicate with his friends, enunciating his tenets with absolute freedom and denouncing his judges without any reserve of language. Here is a passage from one of his letters:

'Oh, if the Lord Jesus had said to the Council "Let him that is without the sin of simony among you condemn Pope John", me seemeth they would have gone out one after another ... The great abomination is pride, covetousness and simony ... Written on the festival of S. John the Baptist, in a dungeon and in fetters, in the recollection that John was likewise beheaded in a dungeon and in fetters for the sake of God's truth' (Wratislaw's *John Hus*, p. 370 sq.).

... with much more to the same effect. Is John Hus then a myth, or the Council of Constance a fiction?[2]

There is much more of the same kind, and this must all be read in detail, if the full excitement of the chase is to be realized, and the

---

[1] *The Apostolic Fathers*, Part II, vol. i, p. 412. Lightfoot was probably right; but the latest edition of Liddell and Scott's *Greek Lexicon* (1940) does not in fact cite any earlier instance.

[2] *Ibid.*, pp. 359–60.

patient methodical precision with which each detailed point is handled is to be appreciated. But at last the chase comes to an end; Ignatius is finally vindicated, and we can be assured beyond all reasonable doubt that we have here a considerable body of literature outside the canonical New Testament, but dating from exactly that period to which some of the later books of the New Testament almost certainly belong.

Research into the nature and history of another very ancient document, the so-called first Epistle of Clement, was going on at the same time. Here the problems were much less difficult, the main complication being, as we have seen, the existence of a whole collection of other works bearing the name of Clement, in which a strictly Judaistic form of Christianity is defended and Paul is the arch-enemy. But, when these have been correctly dated in the first half of the third century, the first Epistle of Clement, which in certain churches was for a long time regarded as canonical or almost canonical, emerges as an authentic production of the Church of Rome in about A.D. 96. The circumstances are well known. There had been divisions in the Church of Corinth, in the course of which some of the presbyters had been repudiated by one section of the congregation. The Church in Rome has for a time been greatly disturbed by persecution (this can hardly be other than the persecution under the Emperor Domitian in or about A.D. 95 and 96); but now that peace has been restored the Church of Rome can write to the sister Church in Corinth in terms of quiet but affectionate authority, endeavouring to bring the dissenting brethren to a better mind. The letter is attributed to Clement, who can hardly be any other than that Clement who is referred to by other authorities as the second or third bishop of the Church in Rome. The author does not refer to himself as bishop—in fact there is no reference in the Epistle to a bishop in Rome; the letter is written on behalf of the Church as a whole, and it is the authority of the Church that is throughout invoked. If this dating and identification are accepted, as they are by almost all scholars today,[1] we are brought even nearer to the world of the New Testament.

Now comes the crucial question. The reader may have wondered why it has seemed worth while, in a book on the New Testament, to

---

[1] Einar Molland, in his article on the Clementine Epistles in *Die Religion in Geschichte und Gegenwart*, ed. 3, mentions two exceptions in modern times—Merrill (1924) and Eggenberg (1951). We shall note a little later the attitude of the Tübingen school to this earliest of the Clementine writings.

devote so much space to matters which lie outside the Biblical material. The chase may have been exciting, but is it really of more than archaeological interest? Is it relevant to the interpretation of the New Testament? The answer of the historian must be that it is of cardinal importance; these texts give us a picture of the life of the Church at the end of the first century and the beginning of the second, invaluable as a point of departure, from which we can turn back to look at the New Testament documents themselves. By great good fortune these letters do not come to us from obscure corners of the Church. Antioch, Ephesus, Rome, the three greatest centres of early Christianity outside Jerusalem, are represented in them. Ignatius has been bishop in Syria. He is passing through Asia Minor, and there he writes his letters to the various churches. He is on his way to martyrdom in Rome. And in the letter of Clement the great Church of Rome, which is to play such an immense part in the life of the Church, for the first time becomes vocal. What kind of picture of the life and thought of these churches is to be derived from the Clementine and Ignatian letters?

It has to be admitted that Ignatius is a peculiar and not altogether attractive person, unlike any other of whom we have record in the early Church.

He writes a very odd kind of Greek—short staccato sentences, difficult and sometimes almost unintelligible. An English scholar, Wilfred Knox, refers to 'the extraordinary medley of New Testament phrases and heathen religious and astrological language, which forms the Greek of Ignatius'.

The eagerness for martyrdom and the passionate desire *not* to be delivered from it, which Ignatius expresses, suggest a pathological or neurotic strain which is less than attractive to the modern reader. But this trait has been very much exaggerated. In six of the seven Epistles Ignatius makes no reference at all to martyrdom, though he speaks often of his captivity and its hardships. It is only in the letter to the Romans that he refers to his approaching death. In the later records of the persecutions there is undoubtedly a pathological strain; we read of those who deliberately provoked the anger of the crowds and of the authorities in order to compass martyrdom—the Church had to rule that those who thus voluntarily brought about their own death would not be included in the official roll of martyrs. But this is not the case with Ignatius; there is no suggestion that he had sought arrest or tried to secure his own condemnation. Once condemned, he glories in the fact; he had perhaps heard that influential friends in

Rome might try to bring about his release, and this he did not desire, since he was convinced that the cause of Christ would be promoted by his death and could be hindered by his survival. This is not, perhaps, the way in which we would write today; but that is not to say that it would be felt to be inappropriate by the recipients of the Roman letter. The fact that this letter exercised so profound an influence on the understanding and delineation of martyrdom in the later years of the Church suggests that, on the contrary, what Ignatius wrote was felt to be proper and suitable. And, even if it were otherwise, why should we suppose that even fathers of the Church must always be wise and temperate? As Lightfoot most appositely remarks:

A like answer holds with regard to any extravagances in sentiment or opinion or character. Why should Ignatius not have exceeded the bounds of sober reason or correct taste? Other men in his own and immediately succeeding ages did both. As an apostolic father he was not exempt from the failings, if failings they were, of his age and position.[1]

The weighty emphasis on episcopacy is surprising, when we compare Ignatius with the New Testament and its lack of emphasis on the formal organization of the Church. But here we see part of the defensive reaction of the Church against the threat of false doctrine by which its unity was imperilled. There is no trace in Ignatius of Gnosticism in its later and developed form, as we find it about the middle of the second century; he is concerned with docetism—the denial that Jesus had really come in the flesh—and with the idea that the humanity of the Redeemer was only an appearance. Now this is exactly the problem that meets us in the first Epistle of John: 'Every spirit which confesses that Jesus Christ has come in the flesh is of God, and every spirit which does not confess Jesus is not of God.'[2] This Epistle almost certainly had its origin in Asia Minor; and all the evidence suggests that this was the area in which episcopacy, as it gradually came to be universally accepted in the Church, first appeared in a developed form. Under the threat of dissolution, the Church found it necessary to have in every place a recognized centre of unity, of authority, of teaching, and of ministry.

We must turn once again to look at the reconstruction of Christian history provided by Baur and his colleagues of the Tübingen school.

---

[1] *The Apostolic Fathers*, Part II, vol. i, p. 423.
[2] 1 John 4. 2-3.

THE NEW TESTAMENT AND HISTORY

If Clement and Ignatius are accepted as authentic, what effect will this have on their theories?

It will be recalled that the main plank in the Tübingen platform is the theory of an intense opposition between Jewish and Gentile Christianity, between Peter as the representative of the one party and Paul as the leader of the other. It was only, we are told, towards the middle of the second century that the reconciliation between the two factions became an accomplished fact. If this is a correct account of the history, it would be expected that clear traces of the conflict would be found in Clement and Ignatius: either the reconciliation has not taken place, or it is so recent that memories of the great controversy will still be living and vibrant. In point of fact in neither Clement nor Ignatius do we find any trace that there had ever been such a conflict. It is specially to be noted that each refers to Peter and Paul together, Ignatius writing to the Romans, 'I do not commend you, like Peter and Paul' (§4), and Clement referring to the two Apostles as the two chief among the Christians of their time (§5). In neither case is there any hint that either of the writers has ever heard of any lasting controversy between the two Apostles. The churches represented by Clement and Ignatius are churches of the Gentiles, but they show no trace of any hostility towards churches of the Jewish tradition. They show singularly little understanding of the real significance of the teaching of Paul, but equally no sign of any idea that this teaching stands in radical opposition to the teaching of any other Apostle. It is clear that the bitter hostility to Paul displayed by certain sections in the Church is not a primitive feature, overlaid as time went on by the spirit of compromise; but that it is a later, second-century development, as Judaic Christianity took on that highly negative form which ultimately led to its disappearance.

If Baur was right, large parts of the New Testament were written subsequently to A.D. 130. The letters we are studying give no support whatever to this view, and at certain points emphatically contradict it. It is true that neither writer gives the impression of being aware of the existence of anything like a Canon of New Testament Scripture, a collection of sacred books venerated by all the churches, such as we find already in Irenaeus (c. A.D. 180).[1] Moreover, there are few actual quotations from New Testament books. The tendency, especially in Ignatius, is far more to refer to Christian writings of an earlier date, to

[1] In Ignatius, γέγραπται, 'it is written', is used to introduce quotations from the Old Testament only.

summarize their teaching, or to represent it in language less exact than that of quotation. Similarly, Clement refers to the Gospels, to Epistles of Paul, to the teaching of the Epistle of James, and again and again to the teaching of the Epistle to the Hebrews. There is nothing specifically Johannine; but, if Clement is rightly dated in A.D. 96, this is exactly what is to be expected; even if the Gospel of John had been written as early as this, its diffusion seems to have been limited for a considerable period to Asia Minor and perhaps to Egypt. It is important, however, that though Ignatius never quotes the Fourth Gospel, and indeed does not refer at any point to John the Apostle, his letters are full of Johannine material; it is unlikely that he knew the Gospel in written form, but he seems to have lived in the same theological world which is the background of the Fourth Gospel, and out of which the written Gospel eventually assumed shape and form.[1] In so far as these early writers have a theology of their own, it is a theology compounded of almost all the strains of Christian thinking which are to be found in the New Testament; the New Testament as a single volume is only very gradually taking shape, but it is in essentials already the common possession of the Church.

Baur himself had been aware from an early date that all his theories stood or fell with the spuriousness of the Clementine and Ignatian Epistles. In his study of the origin of the episcopate,[2] he had put forward as early as 1838 the view that the Ignatian letters were forged in Rome some time in the second half of the second century, at a time at which the place of the episcopate in the Church was a matter of living controversy.[3] This was a singularly unfortunate suggestion. As we have seen, Ignatius refers constantly to the episcopate in his letters; there is one single exception—in his letter to the Romans there is no reference to the episcopate or to the bishop. This attitude exactly corresponds to the period 105–115. There is reason to think that in Rome the episcopate, as a separate and central office, developed more slowly than in centres of Christianity further to the east. But it is almost incredible that a forger, writing in Rome at a time at which the

[1] This is exactly what we should expect, if Dr. W. Sanday was right in thinking that there was 'an anticipatory stage of Johannine teaching, localised somewhere in Syria, before the apostle reached his final home in Ephesus' (*The Criticism of the Fourth Gospel* (1905), p. 199), an idea recently taken up and defended by T. W. Manson, *Studies in the Gospels and Epistles* (1962), pp. 105–22.

[2] 'Über den Ursprung des Episcopats in der Christlichen Kirche' (*Tübingen Zeitschr. für Theologie*, 1838).

[3] It is to be remembered that Baur, who died in 1860, never had the advantage of acquaintance with the careful researches of Zahn and Lightfoot.

bishops of Rome were already coming to play a considerable part in the life of the Church as a whole, should have made no reference at all to the bishop, or to that idea of succession in apostolic authority which we know to have developed not long after the middle of the second century.

For the Clementine letter Baur had a different solution. We know of two people named Clement in the first century at Rome. One was Flavius Clemens the consul, a relation of the Emperor Domitian, who was put to death during the persecution in A.D. 95 or 96. The other was the 'bishop' and reputed author of our letter. Until the nineteenth century it was always taken for granted that these were two distinct people. But Baur and other theologians of his school put forward the idea that there was only the one Clement in Rome, the consul, who is also the Clement referred to in Philippians 4. 3. Out of a variety of confusions later Christian thought invented the legend of the bishop who never really had any existence at all. The Clementine writer is an entirely different Clement, who lived not at Rome but in the eastern part of the Roman Empire. This remarkable theory became so popular in Germany that Lightfoot is able to quote the nineteenth-century scholar Hasenclever as saying that 'later Protestant theology almost without exception has declared itself for the identification'. But the identification of the two Clements rests, in point of fact, on no evidence whatsoever and belongs purely to the realm of fantasy; it is never heard of today, and the student is unlikely to find any reference to it unless he delves into books written the best part of a century ago.

Zahn and Lightfoot had done their work. They had identified the precise point at which the Tübingen theories were most open to attack; if the attack was successful here, the champions of the Tübingen theories would have no power to defend themselves elsewhere. The theories had been killed stone dead.

It is not often that a theory can be so completely overthrown. Most theories, even though heavily attacked, can find something to say for themselves, at least as an alternative theory if not as the only possible theory. But occasionally the contrary evidence is of such a kind that the theory has no possibility of survival at all. It may be interesting to give one example, which will make clear exactly what is meant. Two generations ago Dr. D. S. Margoliouth, Laudian Professor of Arabic in the University of Oxford, was not merely one of the most erudite of orientalists, but also one of the most notable spinners of theories in the learned world. He was convinced that the Book of Ecclesiasticus (Sirach) had originally existed in Hebrew. In an essay published in a book called *Lines of Defence of the Biblical Revelation* (1900) he had maintained that, if the Greek text were translated simply back into Hebrew, it would be found that the words would fall into a simple rhythmical, even metrical, form.[1] Until the very end of the nineteenth century, no Hebrew text of any part of Ecclesiasticus was known. But between 1896 and 1898 considerable fragments of the Hebrew Ecclesiasticus were found in a Geniza[2] in Cairo; at no point did the Hebrew text thus discovered correspond to the Hebrew text as provided by Margoliouth through retranslation from the Greek, and it presented no signs of the rhythmical structure which Margoliouth believed himself to have discovered. No more was heard of this particular theory.[3]

Hardly less crushing was the blow delivered to the Tübingen theories by the genuine Clement and Ignatius. If the theories were correct, certain phenomena should have been observable in these letters. In point of fact, not merely is none of these phenomena to be observed, but what is to be found is so contradictory of what was to be expected as to raise the question whether any of these phenomena were ever at any time anywhere to be found in the Christian world. To Baur and his colleagues we shall always be indebted for the sharp raising of many questions, and for a number of brilliant insights. But the whole mythology of the enmity between Peter and Paul, of the later reconciliation in the Church, and of the dating of New Testament books in the middle of the second century, had collapsed like a house of cards.

This significance of the work of Lightfoot was at once and generally recognized in England. Bishop A. C. Headlam, no mean authority, affirms that Lightfoot had accomplished exactly what he set out to do; he had brought the study of Christian antiquity back from the realms of theory and fantasy to the sober realities of genuinely critical

[1] Op. cit., pp. 32 ff.: 'Ben-Sira's verses can ordinarily be restored by simple retranslation from the Greek' ... 'That rhythm is, as we should expect, analogous to the rhythm employed in the contemporary Canaanitish document, the Punic of Plautus: both are imitations of Greek metres.'

[2] The chamber attached to a synagogue into which manuscripts which were no longer in use, but which were too sacred to be destroyed, were thrown.

[3] In fairness it should be added that Professor Margoliouth was not convinced even by this evidence; he stoutly maintained (*The Origin of the 'Original' Hebrew of Ecclesiasticus*) that the Hebrew fragments from Cairo were not original but represented a late retranslation from the Greek. He has had very few followers in this view.

THE NEW TESTAMENT AND HISTORY

investigation.[1] The general sense of British scholarship approved and applauded what he had done.

In a sense he had done it too well. Every elementary text-book of church history today takes for granted the authenticity of the letters of Clement and of the seven letters of Ignatius, and uses them as primary source material for the history of the sub-apostolic age. As a result the majority of theological students do not even know that their authenticity was ever seriously questioned, and that one of the greatest critical battles of the century was fought about them. Who now reads Newton's *Principia Mathematica*? We all know the conclusions; who troubles himself today with those proofs which it took the great mind of Newton fifteen years to work out? This is a pity. It is good sometimes to go back over the tracks of the great discoverers, to rethink their thoughts and to learn from the sobriety and discipline with which they developed and followed up their methods. If I had my way, at least five hundred pages of Lightfoot's *Apostolic Fathers* would be required reading for every theological student in his first year. I cannot imagine any better introduction to critical method, or a better preparation for facing some of the difficult problems of New Testament interpretation that yet remain unsolved.

Opinion in Germany was less unanimous. But notable among those who recognized at once the significance of the work of Lightfoot was Adolf Harnack (1851–1930), at the time of the appearance of *Ignatius* Professor in the University of Giessen. Harnack was just coming to the fore as one of the most distinguished Biblical scholars in Germany. A few years later his *History of Dogma* (1886–9) was to make him famous; and until his death he was one of the most influential thinkers in the whole world of Christian theology. He had no hesitation in hailing Lightfoot's work as the greatest treatise of the century in patristic theology. When Lightfoot died, Harnack wrote of him that his work was 'of imperishable value . . . There was never an apologist who was less of an advocate than Lightfoot.' By these words Harnack meant to indicate Lightfoot's complete freedom from *parti pris*, and from that spirit of special pleading which we noted as one of those vices of scholars under which New Testament interpretation has suffered. He is never pleading a cause; he is never trying to make

[1] G. R. Eden and F. C. Macdonald, *Lightfoot of Durham* (1932). Chapter by A. C. Headlam, 'Bishop Lightfoot as a Historian', pp. 136–41. Note especially p. 136: 'For myself as for Church history, the publication of Lightfoot's *Ignatius* represented a quite definite epoch. It was the definite assertion of the scientific method of study over the speculative for early Church history.'

C

out a case. His one concern is to present the whole of the evidence clearly and without prejudice, to let facts speak for themselves, and to support no position unless it seems to be based, with probability approaching to certainty, on an absolutely impartial consideration of the evidence.

It was in this connexion that Harnack let fall his famous remark about 'the return to tradition'. By this he did not mean a return to traditional methods of study, or to the acceptance of the New Testament merely on the authority of earlier ages in the Church. The clock can never be put back in that way. Nothing may be accepted on authority. Every tradition, however venerable, must be questioned, and no more respect may be accorded to it than is justified by the evidence on which it rests. What Harnack meant by the return to tradition was something quite different. In the two generations before his rise, critical scholars had rejected almost all the traditions that were current in the ancient Church with regard to the origin and growth of the books of the New Testament, and of the Christian Church which produced those books. It had now become clear that that rejection had been hasty and intemperate, and that the resulting picture of the early Church had been not historical but imaginary. Working on just the same critical principles as his predecessors, but with a wider outlook and a keener historical sense, Harnack arrived at much more conservative conclusions than they.[1] In his book *Luke the Physician*, published in 1906 (English trans., 1907), he maintained the view that the Gospel of Luke and the Acts of the Apostles are by the same author, and that author Luke the Physician, the travel-companion of Paul; this was a startling reversal of views which had been confidently held by a great many scholars for sixty years.

One of the curious features in German theology is that no ghost is ever laid. A century after his death Baur still walks abroad, and echoes of his ideas are found in all kinds of places.[2] It is still not uncommon to hear references to the 'four undoubted Epistles of Paul' (Galatians, 1 and 2 Corinthians, and Romans), a view which was first put forward by Baur. It is odd that the phrase should have had such a long life.

---

[1] Much confusion is caused by the use of the word 'conservative' in two radically different senses. A conservative may be one who refuses to face the challenge of evidence that may disturb his comfortably accepted conclusions. He may be one who faces all challenges, considers all evidence, and comes to the conclusion that there is no need radically to change the views which have been generally held on a particular subject. It is, of course, only in the latter sense that Harnack was conservative.

[2] At the time of writing, plans are in hand for the republication of the more famous of Baur's many works.

In the first place, these four are not undoubted. For instance, the Dutch scholar Van Manen, in his article on Romans in the *Encyclopaedia Biblica* (1903), refused to admit the Epistle to the Romans as genuine; those who are interested in the gentle art of special pleading should read the article in order to see what a surprisingly strong case Van Manen is able to make out for what is generally regarded as an eccentric view. On the other side, very few critics have doubted 1 Thessalonians or Philemon; there is an increasingly strong consensus in favour of Philippians; and British scholarship is almost unanimous in accepting the authenticity of Colossians.

The continuing influence of Baur goes deeper than this. A Danish scholar, Professor Johannes Munck, has pointed out that, although the literary results of the Tübingen school have been universally abandoned, the historical results attained on the basis of those abandoned views continue to meet with wide acceptance:

> But though the literary hypotheses were dropped, the historical points of view of the Tübingen School were still regarded as valid. While the Scriptures were [now] assigned to the first and early second centuries, the contrast between Paul and the primitive church, between Gentile and Jewish Christianity, remained. The contrast that was originally thought to have lasted through two centuries was transferred to approximately the three decades between Paul's conversion and his death ... The picture of Paul therefore becomes the picture of a lonely apostle, giving all his strength in the unparalleled effort of calling into life church after church of newly converted Gentiles, but losing those churches at once to the Judaizing emissaries from Jerusalem who follow hard on his heels ... Instead of a richly-faceted historical reality, there has been found a colourless homogeneity, caused by making inferences everywhere from a one-sided interpretation of early Christianity.[1]

The whole of Professor Munck's elaborate study of 350 pages is devoted to the careful consideration of this theme. He has his own point of view, and it is not likely that all his conclusions will in the long run prove acceptable. But his main point is well taken: historical study of the New Testament has been long and widely distorted by the acceptance of assumptions which rest on no evidence whatever. The truly historical reconstruction of the story of the primitive Church is still in its very early stages.

Again and again in this chapter stress has been laid on the importance of the accurate dating of documents, wherever this is possible. Harnack

[1] J. Munck, *Paulus und die Heilsgeschichte* (1954), English trans., *Paul and the Salvation of Mankind* (1959), pp. 69 ff.

took up this matter, and one of his great books is entitled *Chronologie der alt-christlichen Literatur*, 'The Chronology of Early Christian Literature' (1896). Much has been done, and many problems have been definitively solved. But at one crucial point we still await our Zahn or our Lightfoot. The complete Greek text of the first and second Epistles of Clement was published from a manuscript discovered in Constantinople in 1875. Another of the treasures contained in this manuscript, and published for the first time by the Metropolitan Bryennios in 1883, was the little book known as the *Didache*, or the *Teaching of the Twelve Apostles*. The *Didache*, which consists of two parts, a simple moral catechism and the outlines of a 'church order', contains many features that seem to be extremely ancient. When and where in the world did it come to be written?

To this simple question nothing approaching a definite answer can be given. Since fragments of the book have been found in Latin, Coptic, Syriac, and Arabic translations, it is clear that it was widely known and used. Lightfoot was inclined to place it as early as the closing years of the first century. Quite a number of scholars, believing that the *Didache* is deliberately archaizing and not genuinely archaic, place it as late as the end of the second century or even later. Others, and this seems on the whole to be the most probable view, think that the book came into existence in Syria some time in the first third of the second century. But we have to admit that we simply do not know; and perhaps, without the discovery of new evidence of manuscripts or other early works, we may never know. Our ignorance here is a warning against hasty conclusions in other spheres, where the evidence is almost as fragmentary and conclusions are equally uncertain.[1]

Christianity as seen in the *Didache* is curiously thin and arid, if we come to it from the Fourth Gospel or even from the Apocalypse. Yet it does contain one of the great prayers of Christian history: 'Let grace come, and let this world pass away.'

[1] The most recent study of the *Didache* is by Jean-Paul Audet, *La Didaché: Instruction des Apôtres* (Paris, 1958). On the basis of an immensely learned survey of all the materials, Fr. Audet comes to the conclusion that the *Didache* was written in Syria between A.D. 50 and 70. It is hardly likely that this conclusion will meet with general acceptance; but it is exciting to consider the possibility that we have here a work outside the New Testament which may have been written earlier than most of the New Testament books. See review by J. N. D. Kelly in *Journal of Theological Studies*, New Series, vol. ii, October 1961, pp. 329–33.

Chapter III

WHAT THE NEW TESTAMENT
SAYS, AND WHAT IT MEANS

A. WHAT IT SAYS—THE TEXT

I

THE need for critical study of the Scriptures had come to be generally admitted. Essential questions had been asked. Mistaken methods of inquiry, leading to demonstrably wrong conclusions, had been put on one side. The field was at last wide open for the positive and scientific interpretation of the New Testament documents.

But before we can set to work on the interpretation of an ancient writer, quite a lot of preliminary jungle-clearing and bridge-building has to be accomplished. In the first place, it is not a bad idea to ascertain as far as possible what the ancient document actually says.

Nothing in the history of New Testament study is more astonishing than the willingness of scholars through generation after generation to put up with what they knew to be an inferior text of the New Testament.[1]

At this point it may be useful to make clear what is meant by a good and an inferior text of an ancient author, or of the New Testament. We are so used to printed books that it requires a great effort of imagination to put ourselves back into the world of only five centuries ago, when everything had to be written by hand, and the multi-plication of books was a slow and laborious process. Yet anyone who has written a book or even read the proofs of one knows well that even the printed book has passed through exactly the same hazards and the same possibilities of error as an ancient manuscript, and that,

[1] English readers are fortunate in having available in most attractive form, reliable material on the New Testament manuscript tradition in Sir F. G. Kenyon's *Our Bible and the Ancient Manuscripts* (1st ed., 1895), a book which has been translated into German and very warmly received in Germany. The fifth edition, revised by A. W. Adams and published in 1958, records all discoveries and progress up to that date, but has been subjected to some unfavourable criticism by the experts.

though these possibilities have been greatly reduced by modern methods, the human brain and eye and hand remain imperfect instruments, just as they were two thousand years ago.

It is practically impossible to copy a manuscript without making a mistake. This is true today even when a writer is copying a quotation from print; the likelihood of mistake is immensely increased if the text to be copied is itself a manuscript, and naturally increases still further, if the manuscript is old, worn, and imperfectly legible. Some types of mistake are so common, in ancient as in modern times, as to be easily classifiable. Among the commonest of all is the inversion of two letters, or the omission of one letter to make a familiar but wholly inappropriate word; 'scared' for 'sacred', and 'fiend' for 'friend', have long since ceased to surprise any proof-reader. The repetition or omission of a word or a line is a frequent occurrence — and the omission of a single word can have somewhat grave consequences, as when the printers of the so-called Wicked Bible accidentally omitted the word 'not' in the Seventh Commandment.

In most cases such errors can be easily corrected. But much more serious causes of corruption lie near at hand. A sentence which has been accidentally omitted is written in at the bottom of the page; the next scribe to copy the manuscript carelessly introduces it in the wrong place. What was really a reader's comment in the margin gets incorporated into the text. There is an inveterate tendency for a scribe to substitute a familiar form for an unfamiliar, especially when copying proper names; the pool with five porches in John 5 appears in the Authorized Version as Bethesda, but quite a number of Greek manuscripts read Bethsaida, others Bezatha or other forms; and no really ancient manuscript gives the verse about the angel coming down and troubling the water. Quite often a scribe writes down what he remembers and not what he sees. On what is now page 591 of the *History of the Ecumenical Movement 1517–1948*, there occurred what struck me as a curious reference to the duty of the Church 'to teach both young and old to observe the *ten* commandments'. Eventually, after several readings of the proof, I checked it against the report of the Oxford Conference (1937) on Church, Community and State, *The Churches Survey their Task*, and found that the eminent Church leaders at the conference had spoken of the '*divine* commandments'. The only possible explanation for the error was that the secretary who typed the chapter had been misled by memory into putting in a very familiar phrase instead of the less familiar one which actually stood in the text before her. An error of this kind, which makes tolerably good sense, is far more difficult to detect than one which makes nonsense.

There are three still graver causes of corruption, which are not uncommonly at work. The first operates when a scribe cannot make out what is in front of him and in faithful fulfilment of his task writes down a meaningless jumble of letters. The second, and worse, occurs when the scribe sees, or thinks, that what is in front of him is nonsense, and tries to correct it by the light of his own unaided intelligence; there is only a slender chance that he will accidentally get things right. The last, and worst case of all, is when the scribe disagrees with what he sees in the text, and deliberately alters the text to suit his own understanding of orthodoxy. So, where the Seer of the Apocalypse wrote in Rev. 21. 24 that 'the nations shall walk in the light of' the heavenly city, some less generous-hearted scribe turned it into 'the nations of them which are saved'—and you will find this error in your Authorized Version.

We have to face the fact that every ancient manuscript, even the best, is full of errors. It is obvious that the more often a manuscript is copied, the more numerous the errors which become incorporated in its descendants, and that, in general, we may say that the older the manuscript the better and truer it is likely to be. This is not always the case. A scribe of the fourteenth century who had the luck to copy a manuscript of the fourth century might give us a very valuable text indeed; and, conversely, the careless copyist of a good text may produce such a botched and depraved copy that his work is little better than useless.

The New Testament is a very old book. The latest part of it can hardly have been written later than the year 116. This means that for fourteen hundred years, until 1516, it was exposed to all the hazards of manuscript tradition. Whatever view we may hold of the inspiration of the New Testament, we are bound to admit that it has been immune from none of the chances, the perils, and the corruptions which have assailed all other manuscript traditions of similar length. When those who have no expert knowledge of the subject hear of all these errors and corruptions, they tend to be afflicted with grave anxiety as to the reliability of the New Testament. Have we any means at all of knowing what Jesus and the Apostles really said or wrote? Here it may be said at once that only in very bad manuscripts indeed is the substance of the text gravely affected by the errors. Indeed, I think it is no exaggeration to say that the very worst Greek manuscript now in existence (I have no idea which it is) contains enough of the Gospel in unadulterated form to lead the reader into the way of salvation. But, when this has been said, it is still clear that the careful study of the manuscripts is important. Even in the case of Shakespeare, we want to know, if we can, amid the confusions of the Folios and Quartos, what he really wrote. Far more worth while is it to spend any amount of labour in order to come a little nearer, if we can, to the authentic words of Jesus Christ and the Apostles.

The printed New Testament in Greek had got off to a bad start. Erasmus (1516) had worked from only four late manuscripts, one of them imperfect.[1] A few other manuscripts later became available, and some improvements were made in the text, though without any real understanding of the critical problems involved. By the middle of the seventeenth century the world settled down with some equanimity to the use of what came to be called the *Textus Receptus*, the received text,[2] on which Dr. Hort tartly remarks: 'This arbitrary and uncritical variation gave way to a comparative fixity equally fortuitous, having no more trustworthy basis than the external beauty of two editions brought out by famous printers.'[3] And so things remained for nearly two centuries. It is easy to understand why this was so. The *Textus Receptus* had become so familiar to the scholars of the time that they knew it almost by heart; and it was also very near to the text which underlay the various European versions—German, French, English— which churchmen north of the Alps used in church, and often at their family devotions. We all love the familiar, and prefer not to be disturbed. In any case, the science of the critical study of ancient texts was still in its infancy.

The first serious questions about the New Testament text seem to have been raised in consequence of the study of Codex Alexandrinus (A), the splendid manuscript presented to James I of England by the unfortunate Patriarch of Constantinople, Cyril Lucar.[4] The text of 'A',

[1] The other early sixteenth-century text, the Complutensian (1522), was rather better, and was widely used by Roman Catholics.

[2] This term has no authority other than that of a note in the second Elzevir edition of 1633, informing the reader that he has in his hands 'the text now received by all'. Much unfortunate superstition later became attached to the term, as though the 'Received Text' was infallible and beyond criticism.

[3] *The New Testament in the Original Greek* (1881), p. 12. Richard Bentley caustically remarked that this text, produced originally by the Swiss publisher Stephanus, was venerated 'as though his compositor had been an angel'.

[4] The manuscript arrived in London in 1628; in consequence the arms it bears on its present cover are those of Charles I.

as it is generally called, differed at a great many points from the *Receptus*. As other manuscripts were discovered and studied, it became clear that, though the great majority of them agreed at most points with the *Receptus*, this was very far from being the only possible type of New Testament text. Scholars in England, such as Bishop Fell (1625–86) and Brian Walton (*c.* 1600–61), and Richard Simon (1638–1712) in France, were well aware of the unsatisfactory state of the text, but little was done to take account of the new evidence, or to work directly towards a new and improved text.

The first enunciation of the principles on which a critical text ought to be constructed was made, in 1716 and 1720, by the greatest of all English classical scholars, Richard Bentley, Master of Trinity College, Cambridge (1662–1742). Bentley had had wide experience in the editing of classical texts, and astonishing skill, amounting almost to genius, in emending them where they were faulty.

Bentley saw the cardinal importance of agreement between evidence of Greek and of Latin provenance; he maintained, correctly, that where we find New Testament quotations in the Greek father Origen (A.D. 170–240) in agreement with the text of the Latin Vulgate, we shall have before us the text of the New Testament as it was at the time of the Council of Nicaea in A.D. 325. He believed that we can go further; he claimed more than once that it should be possible to 'make the text so undoubtedly true *ut a manibus apostolorum vix purior et sincerior evaserit*' (that it hardly came from the hands of the Apostles themselves in a purer or more faultless state). Bentley did not go so far as to produce a text of the Greek New Testament; perhaps it is as well that he did not do so. Authoritarian and haughty in his personal habits, he was authoritarian and haughty also in his attitude towards classical manuscripts; in the remarkable expression of Professor A. E. Housman, he was rather inclined to treat them as though they were refractory fellows of Trinity, and, if they did not say what he felt that they ought to have said, to take steps to ensure that they should. His emendations of the text of Milton's *Paradise Lost* are plain evidence of the occasional perversity of genius. A New Testament text edited by Bentley would almost certainly have been brilliant, illuminating, and perverse. Yet, in the two specimen pages which he did produce, in spite of the limited materials at his disposal he set forth a text which is almost as correct as anything in the most modern editions.

The greatest service to the improvement of the New Testament text, prior to 1831, was rendered by John Mill (1642–1707), who a few days before his death brought out the Greek text with a valuable introduction, and an elaborate *Apparatus Criticus* showing the variations from the Received Text in a large number of Greek manuscripts, in the ancient translations, and in quotations in the fathers of the Church.[1] Mill's work was laborious, patient, and accurate; it showed something of the wealth of the evidence, and of the complexity of the problems that had to be dealt with if order was ever to be brought out of the chaos of these apparently conflicting materials. What Mill failed to supply was any theoretical principle to serve as a guide in sorting out the immense mass of evidence that he had collected. It was left for later generations to work out sound principles for the classification of the manuscripts which were being recovered in ever increasing numbers, and a scientific exposition of the methods that must be followed by the textual critic, if he is to arrive at conclusions which are genuinely determined by the evidence and not dependent merely on his personal preferences.

The period between Mill and the middle of the nineteenth century is filled by a number of famous scholars, who worked on the critical problems of the New Testament text. The greatest contribution of this period was made by J. J. Griesbach (1745–1812),[2] whose work appeared in the years 1774–1800. He had clearly grasped the principle that no final results can be obtained until a complete classification has been made of all the materials according to the *families* of manuscripts to which they belong. It may be well at this point to explain just what is meant by the principle of 'genealogy', of families of manuscripts.

At first sight, it might appear that the important thing is the number of manuscripts which contain a particular reading, let us say, 'Who has loosed us from our sins' as against 'Who has washed us from our sins' in Rev. 1. 5.[3] But a little thought will show that mere number is of no value whatever as a criterion. If ten copies have been made from one

1 There is a quite admirable study of the work of Mill in Canon Adam Fox's *John Mill and Richard Bentley: A Study of the Textual Criticism of the New Testament 1675–1729* (1954), a book which deserves to be better known than it appears to be. Not long ago I had in my hands Dr. Hort's own copy of Mill's *Greek Testament*; it is now in the possession of Archdeacon Naylor of Montreal, having been given to him by Dr. Philip Carrington, at that time Archbishop of Quebec.

2 Griesbach was building on the very important work of J. A. Bengel (1687–1752), who first introduced the idea of seeing the manuscripts as 'families, tribes, and nations'; and of J. S. Semler (1725–91).

3 In Greek there is a difference of only one letter, *lusanti*, against *lousanti*.

manuscript, and we have both the original and the ten copies, we can disregard all the copies, since they tell us nothing that is not already to be learned from the original; that is to say, *they have no independent weight*. They may be shown as belonging to a family; but all together they can carry no more weight than that of the single older manuscript from which they were copied.

If all manuscripts were perfectly copied, none would be of any greater value than any other, and the latest would give us as true and reliable a text as the earliest. But, in point of fact, as we have already stated, hardly any copy is perfectly free from error. Even in our modern world, with all the superior accuracy of typescript and printing, with all the labour of proof-reading and correction, it is hardly ever the case that a book reaches the point of publication entirely free from error; and nothing is more extraordinary than the errors which escape the notice of author, readers, and correctors, and remain until they are spotted by some careful reviewer.[1] All ancient manuscripts are full of errors in copying. Naturally, a mistake once made will appear in all subsequent copies of the text in which the mistake appears, unless it is corrected either by an intelligent scribe, or by comparison with some copy which has retained a better text. It is by comparing the errors and the deviations that it is possible to arrive at a classification of manuscripts according to their origins, and in many cases to determine what the original text must have been.

It may be interesting to give an illustration of the practical use to which this method can occasionally be put. Many years ago, when I was teaching in a high school in India, I had given my class some work to do in their own time, and had told them that they were not to get help from one another. When the papers came in, it was quite clear that collaboration had taken place. I decided to see whether, by close application of the methods of textual criticism, and particularly by noting the errors in the various texts, I could work out the process of this collaboration. It quickly became evident that the source of all the incriminated papers was the work of one clever boy. He had lent his paper to two boys, each of whom had lent his to others; and so it went on. As far as I remember, eleven boys were involved. I was able to write up on the blackboard a chart in the form of a family tree,

---

[1] I may give a personal illustration. It was only in correcting the proofs of my book *Anglicanism* that I noticed that the text stated that Cardinal Wolsey had become Bishop of Touraine in 1513; the name should have been Tournai. I have not been able to check at what point in the production of the book the error crept into the text. The hardest cases to deal with are those in which the error itself seems to make perfectly good sense.

showing exactly what had happened, and who had copied from whom. The boys were fain to admit that my chart was exact in every particular. To them this seemed little short of witchcraft, but then they had not had the advantage of studying the first principles of textual criticism.[1]

It quickly became clear to Griesbach that the vast majority of the then-known manuscripts, including those with which Erasmus had worked, and all those on which the *Textus Receptus* was based, belonged to one single family, which he called the Constantinopolitan. This goes back to a carefully prepared edition of the text, which by the eighth century had acquired almost official status in the Greek-speaking churches, which because of this official status came to be far more often copied than any other, and which gradually came to reign almost alone. To discover the general character of this edition, no more is needed than to read through a chapter of the Gospels in the Authorized Version, comparing it verse by verse with either the English Revised Version or the Revised Standard Version; a chapter I particularly commend for this purpose is Luke 9. Through the study of the older manuscripts available to him, Griesbach became aware of the existence of two other and older families, to which he gave the names 'Western' and 'Alexandrian'; in neither case was the name particularly well chosen, and this analysis was a simplification of a highly complex situation. But Griesbach was on the right lines; chaos was beginning to yield to the principles of order.

Unfortunately Griesbach was not entirely successful in carrying out in practice the excellent critical principles he had worked out, and his editions of the New Testament, published from 1774 onwards, were less valuable than might have been expected. He retained as the basis of his text the *Textus Receptus*, instead of going back to what he himself recognized as the older and better authorities; and he was not always successful in handling the rich and varied materials that he had collected.

In 1831 the classical scholar Karl Lachmann (1793–1851) brought out the first text which abandoned the *Textus Receptus*, and was based on the most ancient authorities. Lachmann was followed by Tregelles (1813–75), and Tregelles by Tischendorf (1815–74). Much of the work of textual criticism consists of patient poring over partly illegible manuscripts, trying to make out exactly what they say, and of

---

[1] One of the most notable examples of the identification of a group of manuscripts related to one another is that of the so-called Ferrar group, all of which have the common characteristic that they give the story of the woman taken in adultery not after John 7. 52 but after Luke 21. 38. Twelve manuscripts of this type are known to exist.

endless minute comparison of one manuscript and its readings with the traditions to be found in others. But Tischendorf was successful in bringing something of an element of romance into this so often tedious study. He travelled far and wide in the search for manuscripts. Every book on the New Testament text tells the story of his visits in 1844 and 1859 to the convent on Mount Sinai, where he discovered, lying amid the waste paper of the monks and likely shortly to be burned, what proved to be one of the most ancient and valuable of all New Testament manuscripts—the Codex Sinaiticus, which was for many years in St. Petersburg (Leningrad) and is now in the British Museum in London.[1] Tischendorf was a great collector of materials; the eighth edition of his text, published in 1894 some years after his death, is still the most complete presentation of the evidence, though, of course, it is now badly in need of revision.[2] One of the advantages enjoyed by Tischendorf was that the authorities of the Vatican had at last allowed the readings of its famous manuscript, the Codex Vaticanus, B, to become known; earlier scholars, who had had to work without accurate knowledge of this manuscript, were condemned to operate to some extent in the dark, being deprived of one of the most important of all our sources of information.

II

Such, roughly, was the situation when the two great Cambridge scholars, Westcott and Hort, decided that a more critically reliable text of the New Testament was an indispensable preliminary to that great work of reinterpretation which they had taken in hand. The idea was by no means new to them. We can identify the moment at which Hort became aware of the problem of the New Testament text from a letter written on 29 and 30 December 1851, when he was twenty-three years old:

[1] Codex Sinaiticus (ℵ), which contains, in addition to the Canonical books, the Epistle of Barnabas, and part of the 'Shepherd' of Hermas, was written almost certainly in the latter part of the fourth century A.D. At the time of its discovery it ranked with Codex Vaticanus (B) as the oldest of all known manuscripts of the New Testament in Greek.

[2] Many plans for 'a new Tischendorf' have been made; but we still await the accomplishment of the task. Two volumes, containing the Gospels according to Mark and Matthew with a very complete statement of the evidence, were published in 1935 and 1940 respectively by Mr. S. C. E. Legg. But the work is far too heavy to be undertaken by one man alone, and these volumes have not escaped criticism. Vigorous work is being carried on in Germany under the direction of Professor K. Aland, and we may hope that not many years will pass before the results become available.

I had no idea till the last few weeks of the importance of texts, having read so little Greek Testament, and dragged on with the villainous *Textus Receptus* . . . Tischendorf I find a great acquisition, above all, because he gives the various readings at the bottom of his page, and his Prolegomena are invaluable. Think of that vile *Textus Receptus* leaning entirely on late MSS; it is a blessing that there are such early ones.

It is a blessing to learn that Hort, whose later style was so excessively restrained and unemotional, could on occasion express himself so pungently. He did not know, in those cold nights of December, that he had been drawn into a consuming interest which would never leave him.

The two friends set to work in 1863. The results of their labours appeared from the press in 1881. But, once again, there was an essential preliminary; before tackling the question of the text itself, the scholar must settle the question of the method which he is going to follow. The time had come when textual criticism must finally be rescued from the slap-dash methods of hit and miss, and put on the basis of a reasoned and scientific technique.[1]

Since the invention of the printing press and the rediscovery of the Greek language in western Europe, a great deal had been done by scholars towards providing clear and accurate texts of the ancient writers. But the New Testament posed what was in effect a new problem. In discussing 1 Clement Lightfoot had remarked that, for the determination of the text of this letter, we are much better placed than in the case of the majority of Latin and Greek writers. At that time we had as authorities for the text of Clement one incomplete and imperfect Greek text in a manuscript of the fourth or fifth century; one complete but very badly written Greek text of the eleventh century; and a Syriac translation, so literal as usually to enable us to see what Greek text must underlie it. With this we are *better* off than for most Greek or Latin writers. Lightfoot is not exaggerating. For parts of the Greek dramatist Aeschylus we depend on a single late manuscript. For the Roman poet Catullus we depend on one late manuscript, which

---

[1] Dr. G. Zuntz in *The Text of the Epistles* (1953), pp. 10–11, rightly points out the *limits* of science and reason in this connexion: 'This tradition . . . is essentially a historical phenomenon, and history is not rational. There are ways of dealing scientifically with irrational phenomena, but these cannot be subjected to the same categories as rational objects. We must strive to combine the indications which the extant evidence so amply supplies with a coherent picture of the tradition in its constant flux and change.' This is a necessary warning; but it in no way reduces the obligation resting on scholars to push the use of scientific methods to the utmost limits of the service that they are able to render.

was known in the fifteenth century and was fortunately copied, but has since disappeared. No other ancient writing can compare with the New Testament in the wealth of the evidence by which it is supported; only in the case of Virgil is anything like comparison even remotely possible.

Where manuscripts are few, late, and corrupt, the greater part of textual criticism can be concerned only with conjectural emendation. At many points the scribes have misunderstood their text and reduced it to nonsense; the editor must do his best to guess what the original may have been, and to put back sense in place of nonsense. A few scholars have had especial gifts for this cross-word puzzle kind of work. The two greatest of whom we have record anywhere were Richard Bentley, already referred to, and Richard Porson (1759–1808), Professor of Greek in the University of Cambridge,[1] both of whom could look at a hopeless jumble of Greek or Latin letters, and by some mysterious sixth sense divine what the hidden original must have been; but Porson was more reliable than Bentley, since Bentley had a tendency to emend where no emendation was really necessary, and to delight a little too much in the ingenuity of his own speculations.[2]

If more than one manuscript existed, the scholar had a number of possibilities before him. He might decide that one manuscript was the best and follow it through thick and thin, through sense and nonsense —a procedure mercilessly castigated by that notable textual critic A. E. Housman. Or he could make a selective text, relying on inner intuition to guide him as between the various readings offered by the manuscripts where they differed. Or he could try to classify manuscripts according to date, origin, and mutual dependence, and to assess their value accordingly. But, though a good deal of progress had been made, no one had ever set out in plain terms just what textual criticism is, how the textual critic should proceed, and what exactly he may hope to achieve. It was this gap that Hort set out to fill; and the study of the manuscripts of the New Testament gave him exactly the material on the basis of which it was possible to proceed to the formulation of a genuinely scientific method of textual criticism.

[1] Porson rendered one direct service to the problem of the text of the Greek New Testament. In his *Letters to Archdeacon Travis, on the Spurious Verse 1 John 5. 7* (1790) he shows beyond the possibility of doubt that the verse about the 'three heavenly witnesses', which appears in the English Authorized Version as 1 John 5. 7, cannot possibly have formed part of the original text of the Epistle.

[2] We all exercise this faculty in an elementary way, when we correct almost automatically and unconsciously the misprints which are not uncommon in our daily newspapers.

One of the troubles is that he did his work too well. In fifty-three pages of the Introduction to *The New Testament in Greek*, published in 1882, Hort set out the complete theory and science of textual criticism. Nothing like this had previously been written in any language. Nothing of comparable value was to be written, until A. E. Housman published in 1903 his celebrated Preface to *Manilius*, a work of a very different character, enlivened by the author's characteristic and mordant wit. And, in point of fact, the work never had to be done again in exactly the same way. Hort's statement is definitive; his principles have been so generally accepted that few students trouble to read the original work in which they were first set forth.[1] The canons of criticism established by Hort have passed into every manual on the subject, and into every Introduction to the New Testament, often without acknowledgment. No sane scholar would ever think today of tackling the work of textual criticism on any principles other than these; but he may be unaware of the direction in which his main indebtedness lies.[2]

These priceless fifty pages were written in a cool, judicious, perfectly lucid prose; so orderly, so closely connected, so unadorned, so concentrated, that it is almost impossible to abridge or summarize them, and almost any passage could be quoted in illustration of the tone and method of the whole.

Hort starts with a general statement of what textual criticism is all about:

Every method of textual criticism corresponds to some one class of textual facts: the best criticism is that which takes account of every class of textual facts, and assigns to each method its proper use and rank. The leading principles of textual criticism are identical for all writings whatever. Differences in application arise only from differences in the amount, variety and quality of evidence; no method is ever inapplicable except through defectiveness of evidence.

We are then led, through the internal evidence of readings with their problems of intrinsic and transcriptional probability, to the crucial

---

[1] This author, who has been interested in textual criticism for a good deal more than forty years, read it for the first time as part of the preparation for the writing of this book.

[2] Naturally there is progress in this field as in every other. Notable introductions to the study of textual criticism have been written in later times, among them the *Critique Textuelle* of the French Dominican scholar Père Lagrange. But every one of these is based ultimately on the principles which Hort so lucidly laid down.

section—The Internal Evidence of Documents; a characteristic passage makes clear the subject under discussion:

A moment's consideration of the process of transmission shews how precarious it is to attempt to judge which of two or more readings is more likely to be right, without considering which of the attesting documents or combinations of documents are the most likely to convey an unadulterated transcript of the original text; in other words, in dealing with matter purely traditional, to ignore the relative antecedent credibility of witnesses, and trust exclusively to our own inward power of singling out the true readings from among their conterfeits, wherever we see them ... The first step towards obtaining a sure foundation is a constant application of the principle that KNOWLEDGE OF DOCUMENTS SHOULD PRECEDE FINAL JUDGEMENT UPON READINGS.[1]

Next follows the long central section on the principle of genealogy, the nature of which we have already indicated—the affiliation of manuscripts with one another, and the possibilities and the limitations of this method. Textual criticism is no irrational procedure; like any other science, it moves forward as fast and as far as it is able in the direction of 'rationally framed or discovered rules'; and thus it serves to impose 'salutary restraints on the arbitrary and impulsive caprice which has marred the criticism of some of those whose scholarship and insight have deservedly been held in the highest honour'. But, however effective and extensive the rules, it is impossible to eliminate the element of personal choice and decision. There are situations in which the evidence is so complex that no solution can be worked out as by mathematical formulae:

Here different minds will be impressed by different parts of the evidence as clearer than the rest, and so virtually ruling the rest: here therefore personal discernment would seem the surest ground for confidence. Yet here too, once more, the true supremacy of method is vindicated; for it is from the past exercise of methods that personal discernment receives *the education which tends to extinguish its illusions and mature its power*. All instinctive processes of criticism which deserve confidence are rooted in experience, and that an experience which has undergone perpetual correction and re-correction.[2]

'To extinguish its illusions and mature its power.' Could the

---

[1] Hort, op. cit., pp. 30–31.   [2] Ibid., pp. 65–66. Italics ours.

Cambridge philosophy of education possibly find more precise and more pregnant expression? Certainly the words sum up the career of Hort himself—massive knowledge, intense concentration and minute accuracy, quiet humility, and an adoring reverence for truth. Germans have not always had the highest opinion of British scholarship; but it was a German who wrote of Hort that

he was a great man, and at every moment a complete man, whether he was caring for the children suffering from scarlet fever in his rural parish, or occupying himself with the translation of Plato, or discovering and describing some new plant, or recovering some forgotten utterance of a Father of the Church, or sitting in his study wrestling with some problem of the transmission of a text, or standing on the summit of the Matterhorn and concerned to identify the surrounding mountains ... He was a student of the things and the people whom God has created; and in this study he forgot one thing only—himself.[1]

Like Griesbach, Hort was not always so successful in the application of his principles as in the formulation of them. Carrying the work of Griesbach a step further, he identified a further family of textual tradition, to which he assigned the title 'Neutral', and which he found represented specially in the two great and ancient manuscripts Sinaiticus (ℵ) and Vaticanus (B), both of the fourth century. Each of the other three families, which he called Syrian, Western, and Alexandrian, he regarded as being due to deliberate and conscious revision; the Neutral he believed to represent a purer tradition than any other, as having escaped the hand of the reviser, and in the main representing unaltered the true apostolic tradition. We now know that the text represented in Sinaiticus and Vaticanus is also the result of a revision, a very scholarly and sober revision indeed, but still a revision, and we see that Hort's dream of an uncorrupted and unadulterated text is one of those illusions from which he himself had not yet been set free.

Yet Hort was, after all, not so far astray. B is by far the greatest and the best of all the manuscripts of the New Testament that have come down to us. Like every other ancient manuscript it is marred by countless errors; but most of these are trivial and easily corrected. If every

---

[1] Caspar René Gregory in *Realencyklopädie für protestantische Theologie und Kirche* (1900), vol. viii, p. 370. Gregory (1846–1917), an American by birth, who became a professor in Germany (Leipzig), was also a distinguished authority on the text of the New Testament, and was largely responsible for fixing the Sigla, the conventional signs by which the New Testament manuscripts are known among scholars.

other manuscript of the New Testament had perished, and the text was printed from B alone with only the correction of the obvious and superficial errors, we should still have in all essentials a true text of the words of Jesus and the Apostles.

When Westcott and Hort published their Greek text in 1881, the scientific study of the New Testament took a long step forward. For reasons that have just been given, this could not be the final and definitive text. But it was an immense advance on anything that had preceded it. In a vast number of places the errors and additions of the scribes had been cleared away and the true reading restored. The effect was comparable to that which is attained when an ancient Greek statue that has lain for hundreds of years at the bottom of the sea is raised and cleaned and seen again in its pristine beauty. Many scholars to this day use this text in preference to any other.

The Westcott and Hort text, which is in the main though not exactly the Greek text which underlies the English Revised Version (1881), was so revolutionary that, though its value was immediately recognized by almost everyone competent to judge, it was not to be expected that it would everywhere be accepted with enthusiasm. It was, in point of fact, subjected to fierce and virulent criticism by a number of conservative scholars, most notable among them Dean Burgon of Chichester (1813–88) who still clung with blind and touching devotion to the inerrancy of the *Textus Receptus*. Burgon is described in the *Oxford Dictionary of the Christian Church* as 'famous for his support of a long series of lost causes'.[1] He carried his conservatism to the point of defending (1871) even the authenticity of Mark 16. 9–20, though the massive evidence of the older manuscripts makes it plain that these twelve verses are an ancient addition to the Gospel, the authentic text of which as we have it ends abruptly at 16. 8.[2] For the Westcott and Hort text he had no single good word to say. These controversies have long since been forgotten in England; but Burgon's influence still lives on in out-of-the-way places to which his book has penetrated. The new Tamil translation of the Bible was subjected, twenty years ago, to bitter and vitriolic attacks on the part of some South Indian Christians, who had read their Burgon, and believed that the new translation was a subtle attempt to debase and deprave the pure word of God— a charge all too readily listened to by simple Christians, whose love

---

[1] p. 208, s.v. 'Burgon, John William'.
[2] We shall later have occasion to consider the significance of this remarkably abrupt ending.

for the Bible is greater than their understanding of the problems which it presents.

III

The achievement of Westcott and Hort was notable, and of permanent value. The work, however, did not stand still. Hitherto unknown Greek manuscripts have come to light, notably one of the ninth century from Koridethi in the Crimea, a coarsely written manuscript, which in spite of its late date has proved to be highly important, because it undoubtedly represents a very ancient tradition.[1] The ancient translations—Syriac, Latin, Armenian, Georgian, Coptic, and the rest—have been intensively studied, their texts published in careful and critical editions, and evidence gathered through them for a period earlier than that of any .Greek manuscript that has survived. Better texts of the early Fathers have given us their Biblical quotations in reliable form; some of those who quote the Bible most extensively, such as Clement of Alexandria and Origen, also lived at a period earlier than that of the oldest of our existing Greek manuscripts.

The most exciting discoveries, however, are those of the great papyri, most notable among them the Chester-Beatty and Bodmer Papyri, dug up in Egypt, which have carried our direct evidence backwards in time by at least a century and perhaps by a good deal more. Scholars are of the opinion that the Chester-Beatty papyri cannot have been written much later than A.D. 200. The Biblical papyri in this group are all imperfect, but we have in them large sections of the New Testament; and this new evidence, together with that of other and more fragmentary papyri, brings us face to face with a whole new set of problems, and has led to a considerable revision of our picture of the way in which the New Testament has come down to us.

We have referred to the general, and reasonable, assumption that the older the manuscript, the fewer errors it is likely to contain. But, in the case of the New Testament, fact does not seem to march with theory. The evidence suggests that the early Christians were voracious and avid readers; no sooner were 'the apostolic writings' recognized as having normative value for the Christian life than the faithful wished to have their own copies to possess and to read for themselves. These

---

[1] This manuscript, commonly known as Θ, is one of the chief representatives of a fourth type of tradition, identified by Dr. B. H. Streeter and others as 'Caesarean'.

Christians seem to have been at least in part responsible for a remarkable change in the theory and practice of book-making. The traditional form of the book had been the papyrus roll; the author knew roughly the limits dictated to him by the length of the ordinary roll—the Acts of the Apostles represents about the extreme limit of what can be written without overflowing on to a second roll. It is obvious that the papyrus roll is extremely inconvenient for purposes of reference— you have to go on turning the roll in one direction or another, until you reach the particular column that you happen to need. From a very early date Christians seem to have preferred the Codex—the form with which we are familiar in the modern book. This had obvious advantages—if you wished you could have all the four Gospels bound up together; and later, as technical skill increased, the whole New Testament could be brought together between the covers of one single volume.[1]

In the ancient world the copying of manuscripts was a highly developed profession. In the *scriptorium* a whole gang of thoroughly trained men, usually slaves, would be steadily employed, writing from dictation. When a popular author like Martial (first century A.D.) completed a book, a considerable number of copies would be made, and the book would be almost immediately on sale at an astonishingly moderate price. Copying was on the whole accurate, and considerable care was taken to check and to correct the copies. The early Christians were on the whole poor people, and had no such facilities; their copies were cheaply made by amateurs, and from a time not later than the beginning of the second century inaccuracy in copying, multiplied and repeated, began to play havoc with the correctness of the text. Moreover, people of that time and of that level of culture had a very different attitude towards the text of an author from that which is current among us today. We regard precise accuracy as all-important—

an attitude of mind almost the opposite of that which, at the time, prevailed among Christians of all classes and all denominations. The common respect for the sacredness of the Word, with them, was not an incentive to preserve the text in its original purity. On the contrary, the strange fact has long since been observed that devotion to the founder and His apostles did not prevent the Christians of that age from interfering with their transmitted utterances. The reliance of the believers upon the continuing action of the Spirit easily

[1] Note, however, that almost all the greater among the ancient manuscripts are written on parchment, which is a much more durable material than papyrus.

led them to regard the letter less highly; where the two appeared to be at variance, the urge to interpolate what was felt to be true was not always resisted.[1]

This is well and truly said. The result was that the second century, so far from being a period in which the books of the New Testament circulated in a small number of carefully controlled copies, was in fact what Dr. Zuntz has picturesquely called 'the wild period'—many copies in existence, uncontrolled, copied at random, corrected from one another; so that there was a real danger that the purity of the original text might be irreparably lost, and the words of Christ and the Apostles submerged under the traditions of men. But fortunately there were those, even at that early period, who realized the danger and set themselves, by the collection of better manuscripts and the control of aberrations, to see that the text was not allowed to depart too far from what had been originally written. There was a tradition of careful textual scholarship among the Greeks, as we can see from the tradition of the texts of such writers as Homer and Plato. The centre of this tradition was Alexandria, which had become the home of a great Christian tradition probably no later than the closing years of the first century. It is almost certainly to Alexandria that we should look— though this is based on inference, and not on direct evidence—for this second tradition of the New Testament, based on careful scholarship and the weighing of evidence. If this view can be accepted as correct, the great manuscripts ℵ and B represent a rather late form of this process of revision. The Alexandrian scholars were not always right; but we owe them an immense debt for their careful work, and for the preservation of a textual tradition that without their help might easily have been lost.

The papyri have opened up to us a phase of the New Testament tradition earlier than any of which we previously had knowledge, and scholars are engaged today in the work of interpreting this new evidence, and of working back ever nearer to what was originally written by the Apostles. Yet strangely enough the possession of this new evidence makes us less certain than we were, and than Bentley was, of being able to get back to the wording of the original texts.

This need not seriously trouble us. We have a far better and more reliable text of the New Testament than of any other ancient work whatever, and the measure of uncertainty is really rather small. But the

---

[1] G. Zuntz, op. cit., p. 268.

question will not be stilled, whether with all the varied evidence that we have there may not be certain passages in which the corruption goes so far back that no manuscript at all gives us what was originally written. In regard to the text of almost all ancient authors this is certainly true; manuscripts are few, and in passage after passage it is certain that none of them presents what the author himself can possibly have written. In that case there is nothing for it but to emend conjecturally. This is not mere guess-work; it takes account of all the evidence that there is of the author's style and vocabulary, and of what he is likely to have written. In some cases, the conjecture is almost certainly right; in others many guesses have been made, and all we can say is that some are more likely than others. We cannot rule out the possibility that the same may be true of the New Testament, and that in certain passages, which are likely to be very few, nothing but inspired guess-work will take us back to the original.

The great conservative scholar C. H. Turner (1860–1930) believed that in one famous passage the correct reading is not to be found in any Greek manuscript that we possess, but that the right clue is given by one manuscript of the Old Latin, a version which dates from the second century. In Mark 15. 35–36, the Greek manuscripts give 'Behold, he is calling Elijah ... Wait, let us see whether Elijah will come to take him down.' Now there seems no particular reason why these pagan soldiers should know anything about the Old Testament prophet Elijah; the change of a single letter would give us *Helion*, the sun. At once perfect sense is restored. The sun was widely regarded in the ancient world as the supreme God, or as the manifestation of the supreme God. At the time of the crucifixion the sun's light had failed; what more natural than that the victim should call upon the sun, by whom he has been deserted? I think that Turner is right.[1] In the same Gospel, 10. 32, we read: 'Jesus was walking ahead of them; and they were amazed, and those who followed were afraid.' Turner believed that, in the face of all the manuscript evidence, we should read '*he* was amazed'. As Jesus goes up to face his cross, he enters into the very human cloud of dismay and anguish, of which Gethsemane is a second manifestation. Once again I think that Turner is right.[2]

In regard to two passages, I am convinced that what is needed is a change not of words or of letters, but of order. In our texts of Romans 7. 25, Paul, after his joyful outburst 'Thanks be to God through

[1] *A New Commentary on the Holy Scriptures* (1928), p. 118.
[2] C. H. Turner, *The Study of the New Testament, 1883 and 1920* (1920), p. 62.

Jesus Christ our Lord', goes back to the melancholy note of 'So then, I of myself serve the law of God with my mind, but with my flesh I serve the law of sin', thus making nonsense of his whole argument. If this clause is transferred a little higher, say after verse 23, it fits in there perfectly with the sense; and 'Thanks be to God' is followed immediately by the joyful continuation of the argument, 'There is therefore now no condemnation . . .' in 8. 1.

In the Sermon on the Mount, commentators have found very puzzling the sequence:

> You have heard that it was said to the men of old,
>   'You shall not kill:
>   and whoever kills shall be liable to judgement'.
> But I say to you
>   that everyone who is angry with his brother
>   shall be liable to judgement;
>   whoever insults his brother
>   shall be liable to the Council,
>   and whoever says 'You fool'
>   shall be liable to the hell of fire.

This is not at all the kind of thing that we should expect Jesus to say; this legal logic-chopping is not in the least in the style either of his utterance or of his thought. Peace is restored, if we see that the last four lines should be moved up ahead of 'But I say to you'. This kind of argument is exactly in the style of the Pharisees; it is they who would be likely to speak of the Council and of the fires of hell. The answer of Jesus then stands in its brief and lapidary splendour—'everyone who is angry with his brother shall be liable to the judgement of God'.

At certain points it seems impossible with the evidence that we have to decide which of two readings is correct. In Mark 1. 41 'Jesus, being moved with pity', stretched forth his hand and touched the leper and made him clean. But a number of old and very important witnesses read 'being moved with anger', and this has been adopted by the New English Bible. Now one of the canons on which we constantly rely is that the harder reading is to be preferred to the easier; a scribe is hardly likely to invent the harder reading; he is very liable to change a hard reading into something easier. 'Moved with anger' is certainly the harder reading here; I suppose that as a critic I ought to accept it, and yet I feel that it is certainly wrong, though I cannot explain the origin of this reading,[1] nor can I logically defend my prejudice against it.

There are such passages. Probably there always will be. The astonishing thing is that they are so few. Anyone who reads the New Testament in any one of half a dozen recent Greek editions, or in any modern translation, can feel confident that, though there may be uncertainties in detail, in almost everything of importance he is very close indeed to the text of the New Testament books as these were originally written.

B. WHAT IT MEANS: WORDS, SENTENCES, AND BOOKS

I

It is a great thing to know what the New Testament says. The next point to be considered is what the New Testament means. A book is made up of words; words have histories; they are flexible, living things; only rarely, if ever, is it possible to tie a word down to one unchangeable meaning that it will retain through all the changes and chances of language. This is true of even apparently simple words like 'table' and 'chair'. In Greek 'table' frequently has the secondary sense 'a banker's table'; in Matthew 25. 27 'the exchangers' are literally 'the men who sit at tables'.

Yet another of the achievements of that extraordinarily prolific nineteenth century was the invention and development of Comparative Philology. The starting-point was the discovery, announced in 1798 by Sir William Jones in Bengal, of the affinity between Latin, Greek, and the ancient classical language of India, Sanskrit. Grammar and vocabulary became the subject of extensive and excited study; Latin and Greek were seen in an entirely new perspective; and it was impossible that the study of the New Testament should be unaffected by these new ideas and these new methods. One of the most effective popularizers of the new science was another Trinity man, Richard Chenevix Trench (1807–86), who became successively Dean of Westminster and Archbishop of Dublin. In 1851 Trench had published a little book, *The Study of Words*, and followed this up in 1855 with *Synonyms of the New Testament*. Both books were reprinted many times, and exercised great influence. Trench was not himself a great

[1] Professor C. F. D. Moule has communicated to me in a letter the suggestion made by Dr. W. F. Howard that 'moved with anger' may have been originally a marginal comment in explanation of the difficult word translated 'sternly charged him'.

scholar,[1] but his words inspired others to great enterprises; his criticism of existing English dictionaries had no small share in setting in motion that tremendous work of scholarship, *A New English Dictionary on Historical Principles*, commonly known as *The Oxford English Dictionary*.

A century ago the student of the New Testament who wished to make a scientific study of its vocabulary had much less to help him than his successor today. The greatest weakness was on the side of the Old Testament and the Semitic languages: scholars had realized how much light could be shed on ancient Hebrew by the study of classical Arabic, but most of the philological work still remained to be done, and the results of the new discoveries which had made the Assyrian and Babylonian languages available to the scholar were only gradually finding their way into the dictionaries. For Latin and Greek things were rather better. Liddell and Scott had published in 1843 the first edition of their famous *Greek Lexicon*, which in its ninth revision (1950) is still the classic lexicon in English. For the New Testament, Hermann Cremer (1834–1903) was at work on a book which was to appear in 1866–7, a Biblical and theological dictionary of New Testament Greek, to be followed in 1867 by Grimm's *Greek-Latin Dictionary of the Books of the New Testament*. Cremer's work was of special importance; he had recognized that, though the words of the Greek New Testament might be the same as the words of classical Greek, something had happened which had put new content into them; the experience of Christian faith had brought about a revolution, as a result of which the starting-point and the goal of human thought had been emotionally changed. It was the purpose of his work to bring to light the new content in this living language, the new energy which it derived from the Christian experience. Yet when all the helps had been amassed, it remained true that a great deal had still to be done. In consequence much of the time of the great scholars of a century ago was spent on lexical work.

Lightfoot, Westcott, and Hort were agreed as to the lexical method to be followed. The Old Testament lies at the root of the New. So, when any word is to be handled, we must first question it as to its Jewish origins. At least as important as the Hebrew for this inquiry is the ancient Greek translation, the Septuagint. But here once again we see the difficulties. The first scientific text of the Septuagint still lay far

---

[1] The biography recently published under the title *The Man of Ten Talents* does him more than justice.

in the future (H. B. Swete's short Cambridge edition of 1887–94); and Hatch and Redpath had not yet begun that monumental *Concordance* (1897), which is today one of the indispensable companions of the advanced student of the New Testament. For the later Jewish thought of the scribes and Rabbis there were certain helps, and good work had been done in the seventeenth and eighteenth centuries.[1] But here, too, there was a large field which had hardly been surveyed.

Greek words, however, are Greek words; and their history in the Greek-speaking world is of primary importance for their meaning in the New Testament. There are some specifically Christian words, and others which have come in through the Septuagint;[2] but the greater part of the vocabulary of the New Testament is made up of perfectly familiar Greek words. Sometimes the history of the word cannot be traced, since so much of Greek literature is lost to us; but in many cases there is a sense of continuity, even when the exact steps of the succession cannot be shown. Lightfoot showed extraordinary perception, when in a lecture delivered in 1863, commenting on a New Testament word which at that time was otherwise known only from the historian Herodotus more than 400 years before, he remarked:

You are not to suppose that this word ... had fallen out of use in the interval, only that it had not been used in the books that remain to us; probably it had been part of the common speech all along. I will go further, and say that if we could only recover letters that ordinary people wrote to each other without the thought of being literary, we should have the greatest possible help for the understanding of the language of the New Testament generally.[3]

Sometimes the continuity is delightfully clear and illuminating. In Acts 12. 13 we read in the English Authorized Version that a damsel named Rhoda came *to hearken*. The word used here is ordinarily translated 'obey'; and it had considerably puzzled the revisers of the Tamil translation of the Bible. It happened that I remembered my Aristophanes, one of my favourite Greek classical writers; in his days in Athens, if you went to visit a friend, you beat upon the door and shouted 'Pai, Pai', just as in India you shouted 'Boy'; and then the

---

[1] In a subsequent chapter we shall encounter the work of the first Lightfoot (1602–75).

[2] Dr. P. Katz has made the very interesting observation that the Septuagint practically coins a number of new Greek words by using them in entirely new senses because of a resemblance in sound to certain words in the Hebrew text. (Quoted by N. Turner, 'The Language of the New Testament' in Peake's *Commentary on the Bible* (new ed., 1962), p. 662.)

[3] Quoted in L. E. Elliott-Binns, *Religion in the Victorian Era* (1936), p. 305. For the experimental confirmation of Lightfoot's view see the next chapter.

slave came—here is exactly Rhoda's word—to 'answer the door'—
only in Tamil you have to translate 'came to ask Who is it?' So there,
in the narrative of Acts five hundred years later, is exactly the word and
the idiom that is familiar to us from the golden age of Attic literature.[1]

But Greek is a language that had undergone many changes in the
course of centuries. It was important not to forget later writers, and
especially those, such as Philo of Alexandria and Josephus, who were
Jews writing in Greek. And, since the New Testament is in a real
sense popular writing, the contemporary popular writing in Greek is
of the greatest possible importance. Here, as we shall see in the next
chapter, we have riches such as were not available to the scholars of a
century ago.

Of course, the literature of the New Testament itself had to be
carefully surveyed. And here the need for an alert and flexible mind
becomes immediately apparent. Take a familiar word such as 'faith'.
With the help of a concordance trace it through the New Testament.
Is it not the case that we find almost startlingly different uses of the
word in Paul, in James, and in the Epistle to the Hebrews? And what
are we to make of the fact that the Fourth Gospel, in which the word
'believe' is so common, never once uses the substantive 'faith'? It is
clear that our study of words is going to land us in a great variety of
problems. We are accustomed to keep the New Testament books
separate from all others. For this kind of study, it is important not to
separate them from those other writings of the early Church which are
almost contemporary with the New Testament itself, and in which the
vocabulary is still to a considerable extent fluid and original. Occasionally we can use these later writings for the interpretation of the
New Testament; but this has to be done with care, since the New
Testament itself is so creative that in most cases it is necessary to
work forwards from it, and not backwards towards it from later uses
of the language.

As we have said, the scholars of a century ago had a keen sense for
words and for study of words. Without this preliminary knowledge
they felt that it was not possible to go on to the study of the larger
complexes of sentences, paragraphs, and books. Some of their studies
have become classical; and with all the new light that has come through
a century of further study, only a few modifications have to be made in

---

[1] Kittel, *Theologisches Wörterbuch zum neuen Testament*, s.v., refers to Plato and
Xenophon. The idiom is not uncommon, but it could easily be overlooked by someone
who had not studied classical Greek.

their conclusions.[1] But scientific work on the New Testament does not stand still; and the work of the dictionary-makers has gone forward, mainly in Germany, in two directions.

The first is that of the dictionary as such, in which the aim is to find, in each connexion, the nearest German (or English) word which will convey the meaning of the Greek.[2] Here the latest and most admirable tool that we have in our hands is the lineal successor of the work of Grimm nearly a century ago. Carefully revised a number of times by Walter Bauer (1877–1960), who devoted the greater part of a lifetime to this lexical work, this dictionary has now been translated into English by an American Lutheran, Dr. Arndt,[3] and printed in beautiful format by the Cambridge University Press. Here is every word in the New Testament, and in the other very early Christian writings, with the views of various scholars as to what every word may mean, and copious references to books and articles with the help of which the student can find his way through the learned research of the last sixty years.

The other great work is far more ambitious and on a truly monumental scale—Kittel's *Theologisches Wörterbuch zum neuen Testament* ('Theological Wordbook of the New Testament', T.W.N.T.) In writing the Preface to this work in 1932, the editor Gerhard Kittel (1888–1948) stated plainly that he and his colleagues understood their work as the continuation of the work of Cremer. Every word in the New Testament which has any theological significance (including Old Testament names, such as Adam, Abraham, and so forth, which are used in the New Testament with theological significance) is to be considered in the light of those new factors, that new vigour, which have come in with the revelation of God in Jesus Christ. The word *Theologisches* in the title is the operative word. This gigantic work has been appearing in parts over thirty years, and is not yet at an end; it looks as

[1] I find that Professor C. K. Barrett, in his characteristically careful and thorough study of *Westcott as Commentator* (1958), pp. 17–18, has drawn up a list of twenty-four Greek words or groups of words on which Westcott has left notable studies, in some of which he 'strikingly anticipates recent conclusions' and the method followed in Kittel's great *Wörterbuch*. What he has written of Westcott is no less true of Hort.

[2] See an illuminating passage on 'elucidation by translation' as the primary function of a dictionary in the new *Cambridge Italian Dictionary* (1962), p. x. 'An example of an unnecessary paraphrase in Hoare [2nd ed., 1925] is *maglia*: "closely knitted body-covering worn by dancers to simulate nudity". The word required is "tights".'

[3] Whose death shortly after the completion of this noble work of scholarship was a sad loss. In the later stages much help had been given by Dr. Gingrich, whose contribution was also notable, and whose name rightly appears on the title page together with that of Dr. Arndt.

though it might rival Herod's temple which was forty-six years a-building. It is the end-product of an incomparably complete assemblage of materials from every kind of source, Greek, Jewish, and Biblical. It may be questioned whether it may not defeat its own purpose through sheer weight and mass; as it nears the end the articles seem to get longer and longer, until one wonders whether the final page will ever actually be reached.[1]

As we shall see later, this great work has been subjected to certain fundamental criticisms; at times it seems as though the principles adopted by the contributors stood in the way of the successful fulfilment of their own purpose. Yet, whatever its defects·may be, Kittel presents, on the largest scale, information as to the history and background of Greek words; and starts from the correct presupposition that we cannot know what is new and dynamic in the New Testament usage unless we know what words meant, and how they were used, before the New Testament writers took hold of them and poured into them the new content derived from the new act of God in Jesus Christ. What the great men of the nineteenth century had indicated in outline has been raised to a higher power in the twentieth by the co-operative labours of a multitude of scholars.

II

As we have seen, one of the aims of Lightfoot, Westcott, and Hort was to produce a complete commentary on the books of the New Testament.

Almost from the beginning of the Christian era, Christians have been writing commentaries of every sort. One of the earliest and most famous in history is the commentary of Origen on the Gospel according to St. John. Many of the commentaries of the ancient Church take the form of homilies; thus the great John Chrysostom preached steadily through whole books of the New Testament, taking a few verses at a time, and trying to make plain the significance of these verses for his hearers at their own particular conjuncture of history.

With the rise of the critical method, an entirely new type of commentary was found to be necessary. Germany stepped into the breach with the famous series edited by Heinrich August Wilhelm Meyer (1800–73) in sixteen volumes between 1832 and 1852. Meyer himself

---

[1] The firm of A. & C. Black is to be congratulated on its enterprise in making a number of translations of the articles on the key-words available in English. Each of the longer articles makes a small book in itself. The reader must be warned that in certain cases shortenings have been carried out, and these are not always clearly indicated in the text.

contributed the volumes on the Gospels and on some other books as well; an English translation was issued between 1873 and 1895. The series has been edited and re-edited; in some cases the same scholar has produced two or three editions of his own commentary, revising all the time; in others, as one volume has become antiquated, some other scholar has been asked to take over the work and carry it out entirely afresh. The copy of Rudolf Bultmann's commentary on the Gospel according to St. John which stands on my shelves belongs to the eleventh edition. As far as I know, this enterprise is unique in the world, and many of the commentaries have been and are classics of their kind.

The strength of the early Meyer commentaries was on the philological side. Let us pay the most minute attention to the Greek words and to the formation of Greek sentences, and the meaning will emerge. The better this work is done, the more certain we shall be of the meaning of the original text—and then the work of the commentator is done, until fresh evidence compels him to reconsider his conclusions. It may at once be conceded that work of this kind is indispensable. But is this really all that a commentary is required to do? Does not the real work begin when the philological work has ended? The New Testament is made up of religious documents; must not the commentator move forward, dangerous as the task may be, into the field of theological interpretation?

Lightfoot, Westcott, and Hort wrestled with this problem, and from the beginning they were agreed on certain principles which diverged rather radically from those generally accepted by the Germans. A New Testament commentary, they held, must be *critical*; it must be based on the most accurate Greek text that could be produced. It must be *linguistic*, and must accept the necessity of minute philological study of the meaning of words and sentences. It must be *historical*, relating each book to the situation in which it appears to have been written, but at the same time seeing it as part of an immensely broad revelation of which history is the scene and the medium. It must be *exegetical*; it must endeavour to make plain to the reader what the words meant, as far as we can grasp this, to the one who wrote them and to his first readers. It must not aim directly at edification. There is a place for the devotional commentary; but in strictly scientific work edification must come only as a result of the manifestation of the truth. The Christian is naturally convinced that out of any careful study of the New Testament edification will emerge; but in this connexion it must emerge spontaneously from the value of the text considered, and not as something deliberately aimed at and fostered by the commentator. On all this there would be wide agreement among Biblical scholars of every school.

To these general principles, however, the Cambridge Three added one further principle of the greatest significance. Their work was to be done 'from faith to faith' (Rom. 1. 17 A.V.). This demands some explanation. The exposition of a religious document by one who does not share the religion set forth in the document presents enormous difficulties. We owe a great debt to the Christian scholars who have made available to us the treasures of the Islamic faith through critical and sympathetic study; yet an exposition of the Qur'an by a Muslim must always have in it a certain element of understanding from which the Christian scholar, by his own religious profession, is debarred. We owe much to the Jewish scholars—C. G. Montefiore, Martin Buber and others—who have written on the New Testament; but at all times the Christian feels himself to be in possession of certain keys which are not in their hands. The Cambridge Three were convinced and practising Christians; accepting Jesus Christ as Revealer, Redeemer, and Ruler, they believed themselves to share the faith of the early Christians among whom and for whom the New Testament was written. The use of the key of faith they regarded as wholly compatible with a strictly scientific use of evidence, and in no way as a substitute for it.

Clearly, this attitude points the way to the solution of certain problems, but it at once brings to light a number of others. To what extent does faith mean that certain dogmatic affirmations are accepted as true and in no circumstances to be questioned? For the Roman Catholic the answer is clear; any conclusions he may reach as a result of his scientific studies must be found to be compatible with a number of dogmatic declarations as to the faith, and a number of authoritative decisions with regard to the inspiration and authorship of a number of Biblical books.[1] But this is a position which cannot be taken up by the

[1] The resultant difficulties can be seen by comparing the text and the notes in Mgr. R. A. Knox's translation of the New Testament. The translation is made from the Latin Vulgate, which is still the official Bible of the Roman Catholic Church, a noble and powerful translation, which yet at many points does not correctly represent the meaning of the Greek. Truth has often to be looked for not in the text, but in the footnotes, in which the delicate linguistic scholarship of Mgr. Knox is to be seen. It should be mentioned that the attitude of the Vatican has become steadily more liberal in recent times: 'In September 1943 the publication of the "liberating" encyclical *Divino afflante Spiritu* brought official sanction to serious Biblical study and definite encouragement to scholars to advance prudently on a path of progress.' R. Aubert in *Twentieth Century Christianity* (ed. S. C. Neill, 1961), p. 55.

completely independent student. His position is 'dialectical'. He starts, perhaps, as a convinced Christian; but he must maintain a completely open mind, with the conviction that absolutely anything may be true provided that it does not offend against the logical law of contradiction, and also the readiness to modify even his deepest convictions, if the evidence makes it clear that they can no longer be held.

This is a difficult position to maintain; and the problem is illustrated by a most interesting controversy between the two intimate friends West-cott and Hort. Westcott, great man as he was, seems to me to have been a timid man, and to have been afraid to ask questions to which the answers might prove to be deeply disturbing.[1] At a certain point he became anxious lest certain lines of investigation which were being followed might lead to a weakening of what to him were essential convictions, and wrote to Hort asking for a guarantee in advance that the results of the investigations would be satisfactory from the point of view of orthodox convictions with regard to the nature of divine revelation. The asperity of Hort's answer is interesting and revealing. He was prepared to go on in collaboration with his friend only if he could be assured of absolute freedom in the carrying on of the investiga-tion. Nothing must be injected on the ground of faith which could not be found in the evidence. If this guarantee of complete academic freedom could not be given, he was prepared to withdraw from the work.[2] Hort was himself a man of profound Christian faith; he was convinced that the kind of investigations that he was carrying on could tend only to the strengthening and amplification of the faith; that the discovery of new truth might involve the modification of positions previously held, but that no new truth was likely to shake the foundation of the Christian faith as the Church had understood it for centuries. But this confidence in the general direction in which the evidence was moving was something quite different from the claim that the evidence must be made to conform to certain conclusions which had been reached independently of it. Misunderstandings were removed by the corres-pondence; the difficulty was overcome, and the friends continued to

---

[1] The late John Baillie once remarked to me of another great scholar, a friend of his and mine: 'The man was afraid to ask ultimate questions.'

[2] See the letters of 1 May, 2 May, and 4 May 1860 in A. F. Hort, *Life and Letters of Fenton J. A. Hort* (1896), vol. i, pp. 418–22; and especially the phrases: 'If you make a decided conviction of the absolute infallibility of the N.T. practically a *sine qua non* for co-operation, I fear I could not join you . . . I shall be glad to know whether, after this express explanation, you still are perfectly content to take me as a coadjutor in the commentary.'

work together in harmony; but the episode is revealing, and the problem is no less difficult in 1962 than it was when the two friends so nearly fell out over it a century ago.[1]

The Cambridge commentaries of the nineteenth century are only a fragment of the whole which had been planned; but they are a stately and impressive fragment. They are unique, both in the general agreement that underlies them, and in the fascinating divergence of individual talent and idiosyncrasy by which the work of the three contributors is marked.

Lightfoot's great commentaries are evidence of a capacious and forthright mind. Everything he writes is marked by vigour, lucidity, and an extraordinary command of the whole subject with which he is dealing. Perhaps he missed some of the deeper issues, but, as we have earlier suggested, he knew his own limitations and was prepared to work within them. Again and again he astonishes by the extent of his erudition. A few years ago, in a book called *The Apostolic Ministry* (1947), the late Dom Gregory Dix dwelt at length on the Jewish concept of the *shaliach*, the delegate or representative, 'a man's *shaliach* is as himself'—and for some years *shaliach* was one of the terms most constantly heard in academic debate about the origins of the Christian ministry. Professor C. F. D. Moule pointed out to me that everything that needs to be said on the subject of the *shaliach* is already there in half a page of Lightfoot's *Commentary on the Epistle to the Galatians*[2]—and the Jewish background to Christian beginnings was one of the fields in which he never claimed to be a master. To his *Commentary on the Epistle to the Philippians* Lightfoot appended a dissertation on the origins of the Christian ministry. This was later published separately with some answers to criticisms. Some evidence has come to light since Lightfoot wrote; but his dissertation is still after eighty years the best introduction to the subject.[3] A few sentences will make clear the range of Lightfoot's understanding, and the kind of approach which he made to every subject of theological significance:

The Kingdom of Christ, not being a kingdom of this world, is not limited by the restrictions which fetter other societies political or religious. It is in

---

[1] C. K. Barrett (op. cit., pp. 7–13) deals interestingly with this episode, and contrasts the views and methods of Westcott with those of Jowett.

[2] Ninth edition (1887), pp. 93–94.

[3] A very different but equally thorough discussion of the evidence has recently been made available in W. Telfer's *The Office of a Bishop* (1962).

the fullest sense free, comprehensive, universal. It displays this character, not only in the acceptance of all comers who seek admission, irrespective of race or caste or sex, but also in the instruction and treatment of those who are already its members. It has no sacred days or seasons, no special sanctuaries, because every time and every place alike are holy. Above all it has no sacerdotal system. It interposes no sacrificial tribe or class between God and men, by whose intervention alone God is reconciled and men forgiven. Each individual member holds personal communion with the Divine Head. To him immediately he is responsible, and from him directly he obtains pardon and draws strength.[1]

Hort's production was lamentably limited. As C. R. Gregory remarks in the article already cited, much of the best of Hort went into the work of other, and often lesser, men, to whom he was endlessly generous in the way of help, stimulus, and encouragement. In early life he had injured his health by the excessive ardour of his studies, and later was debarred for weeks and months at a time from any concentration on serious theological work. And he was influenced in extreme degree by the typical Cambridge hesitation to publish anything, lest one might be caught out in one single mistake, or be shown to have overlooked one minute fragment of the evidence. As a result, he wrote little, and we lack any major commentary from his hand.[2] In the fragments that we have, we note the steady determination to approach the subject from every possible angle, the patient fitting together of all the pieces of evidence into a pattern, the combination of an acute sense of the value of words with an understanding of the relation of words to thought. But, as a result of this concentration on detail, it is sometimes difficult for the reader to win through to any grasp of the whole. In a whole terms's lecturing he would cover perhaps ten verses of an Epistle. The more intelligent of his students retained the deep impression of his methods to the end of their lives; the average man sat bewildered by a multitude of evidences which he found it impossible to draw together into a unity.

As a commentator Westcott was the most famous, though not necessarily the most distinguished, of the three.

At one point he possessed unquestioned supremacy; he had a wide knowledge of patristic literature, especially of the Greek

[1] J. B. Lightfoot, The Christian Ministry (ed. of 1901), p. 1.
[2] The First Epistle of St. Peter i. 1-ii. 17 was published after his death, in 1898, as were his Hulsean Lectures, The Way, the Truth, and the Life (1893), Judaistic Christianity (1894), and The Christian Ecclesia (1897).

commentators on the New Testament; indeed, one of his great contributions was the introduction of British scholars to the world of Greek patristic thought. Much in the patristic commentaries is quaint, unscientific, even absurd. But Westcott's attention to this source of information was not just a waste of time. As he often pointed out, Origen, Athanasius, and Chrysostom used Greek as their own language, a thing that none of us can ever do, and therefore had an instinctive knowledge of the language such as no foreigner can ever possess. As a freshman I once heard Sir John Sheppard remark in a lecture: 'None of us knows enough Greek to say what that means.' Supposing that one who could lecture so divinely on Greek literature must know absolutely everything about it, I was deeply disconcerted by this remark; what had I then come to Cambridge for? Many years later Professor C. H. Dodd remarked to me in conversation: 'It is surprising how little of the New Testament there is of which we can say that we know exactly what it means.'[1] Now it is not the case that the early commentators always understood the New Testament correctly; they spoke and wrote Greek in a different way, and they had their own prejudices and shortcomings. But they stood far nearer than we to the time and the world of the originals; the quotations that Westcott brings in from these ancient writers both Greek and Latin are almost always apt, and sometimes brilliantly illuminating.

It is strange that Westcott's *Commentary on St. John's Gospel* in English, which appeared originally in 1880, should have been republished in 1958. In between, if we take account only of English works of major stature, there have been three stately commentaries, those by Archbishop Bernard (1928), by Sir Clement Hoskyns (1940), and by Professor C. K. Barrett (1955), not to mention Archbishop Temple's invaluable *Readings in St. John's Gospel* (1939–40), Professor C. H. Dodd's monumental introductory study, *The Interpretation of the Fourth Gospel* (1953), and a moving and sensitive commentary by Professor R. H. Lightfoot (1956), the last work from his patient and careful pen, beautifully edited and produced after Lightfoot's death by his friend Professor C. F. Evans. And yet, as Canon Adam Fox remarks in his Introduction to the new edition: 'Westcott remains in its own way the classic exposition.' 'This is due', he says, 'to the author having had a great fund of learning, a profoundly analytical and penetrating mind,

---

[1] The word 'exactly' is of course the operative word. The *general* sense of the New Testament is, happily, open to anyone who reads it with patience and humility.

and a deep reverence for every word of the Gospel, as well as a great familiarity with it.'[1]

Of the reverence there could be no doubt. One of his pupils records that, when he and a fellow-student had rashly expressed their opinions on a certain passage and then turned to the master for guidance, Westcott stated in hushed tones that this was a passage on which he had never as yet ventured to express an opinion. This humble respect for the text meant that for Westcott no labour was too great, if it would help him to determine the exact meaning of a single particle. But he had the defects of his qualities. He could be tiresomely detailed in elucidating shades of meaning which did not really exist;[2] he often seemed so absorbed in the detail as to have lost the sense of the whole. The text is sometimes treated as though it had fallen down directly from heaven—'Did he ever ask himself what the Epistle can have meant to those who first read it?' was the comment of a not unintelligent student of his *Commentary on the Epistle to the Hebrews*. Perhaps for that reason his best work was done on the Johannine writings, in which the theological content can be treated without direct reference to time and circumstance, in a way that is not possible in handling the Epistles of St. Paul.

The strength of Westcott is that his is a profoundly theological mind. Behind the particularities of text and particles and grammar lies a revelation of the living God; until the message is received as revelation, it cannot be understood; and since, with all the changes in the climate of human thought, the revelation itself is unchanging, there are elements of permanent value in any exposition that penetrates to the heart of what is there to be understood. This is far from being true of all commentators. It is true of Augustine, from whose sermons on the Gospels Westcott quotes so often and so appositely; of Calvin; and of some other great expositors. It is this penetration that accounts for the value which readers still attach to Westcott's exposition.

The nature of his theological approach is admirably and succinctly set out in what he has to say of the plan of the Fourth Gospel:

This is, to express it as briefly as possible, the parallel developments of faith and unbelief through the historical Presence of Christ . . . He makes no promise to compose a life of Christ, or to give a general view of his teaching, or to preserve a lively picture of the general effect which he produced on

---

[1] Westcott's *St. John* (1958), p. ii *a*.
[2] On the defects in his understanding of New Testament Greek, see the next chapter.

average observers, or to compose a chapter on the general history of his own times, or to add his personal recollections to memoirs of the Lord already current; nor have we any right to judge his narrative by the standards which would be applicable to any one of such writings.[1]

Two brief quotations from the commentary may indicate the kind of method by which Westcott makes his impression on our minds.

On 7. 17, 'If any man will do his will, he shall know of the doctrine, whether it be of God', he writes:

Religion is a matter of life and not of thought only. The principle is universal in its application. The *will of God* is not to be limited to the Old Testament revelation, or to the claims of Christ, but includes every manifestation of the purpose of God. A fine saying is attributed to Rabban-Gamaliel, the son of R. Jehudah ha-Nasi: 'Do his will as if it were thy will, that he may do thy will as if it were his will' (Aboth, II. 4).[2]

On 16. 16, 'Ye behold me no more ... ye shall see me':

As contrasted with the world the disciples never lost the vision of Christ. Their life was unbroken even as his life, and so also their direct relation to him. But on the other hand, the form of their vision was altered. The vision of wondering contemplation, in which they observed little by little the outward manifestation of the Lord (θεωρία), was changed and transfigured into sight (ὄψις) in which they seized intuitively all that Christ was. As long as his earthly presence was the object on which their eyes were fixed, their view was necessarily imperfect. His glorified presence shewed him in his true nature.[3]

The only other commentaries of that period which could be reprinted with any hope of being read today are the very different works of the learned and devout Swiss, Frédéric Godet (1812–1900) of Neuchâtel (*Luke, John, Romans, 1 Corinthians*). Fifty years ago these were to be found in translations in the library of almost every pious clergyman in England. Godet is diffuse and long-winded. He is not a match for his English contemporaries in learning. But of every text he asks implacably the question, 'What does this really mean?'; he goes on patiently until he thinks that he has discovered the answer, sets out the results with all the lucidity of the French mind, and leaves no doubt at all as to what he believes to be the message of the text for the reader.

[1] Westcott's *St. John*, p. xlii.   [2] Ibid., p. 118.   [3] Ibid., p. 231.

III

The Cambridge Three left behind them a vast mass of work done, methods and principles thoroughly tried and tested by experience, and a great many tasks still to be accomplished. The Cambridge tradition of exegesis is still a living thing, which has found expression in a notable series of commentaries; the original impulse given by Lightfoot a century ago has not yet finally died away. In the generation immediately following the pioneers, H. B. Swete (1835–1917) dealt with St. Mark (1895) and the Apocalypse (1906), and Armitage Robinson (1858–1933) with Ephesians (1903), a most elegant piece of work. A little later A. E. Brooke (1863–1939) produced a solid, cautious, and as yet unsurpassed commentary on the Johannine Epistles in the International Critical Commentary (1912). A. H. McNeile dealt with St. Matthew in what is still the best large-scale English commentary on the Gospel (1915), though some would hesitate to put it in the same class with the other works mentioned. J. B. Mayor expounded James (1892) and 2 Peter and Jude (1907) heavily and with enormous erudition. Alexander Nairne accomplished delicate and memorable work on the Epistle to the Hebrews (1913, 1917). Later still, E. G. Selwyn brought out a commentary on 1 Peter (1946), classic in scale and quality, though maintaining views that have not proved acceptable to all scholars. And so, at the end of the century, we come back to Colossians and Philemon in the small, expert, and admirable volume of Professor C. F. D. Moule (1957). Lightfoot might have been gratified by the testimonial to the excellence of his work rendered by a patient and independent scholar nearly a century after the appearance of the original Cambridge *Colossians and Philemon*.

No human work is perfect, and the achievement of even the greatest theologians is open to criticism at certain points. A variety of criticisms has been directed at the Cambridge school of New Testament exegesis.

In the first place, it is maintained, and rightly, that these great scholars were men of their own time and suffered under its limitations. They were born just at the wrong time for those studies in which they most greatly excelled. They had been brought up in the rigid English tradition of classical studies, and all had won distinction in this field before turning to theology. They came just too early to profit by the enormous enrichment of our knowledge of the world of the New Testament, which will be the subject of another chapter, and by the consequent changes in our understanding of the Greek of the New Testament. Some of their exegesis is antiquated; and some things that they said truly we would wish to express otherwise today.

It has often been maintained that they were unwilling to face fundamental problems. At one point we have seen reason to think that this was true of Westcott. But perhaps the formulation is not really correct. The task of New Testament interpretation was so gigantic that it almost wholly absorbed the energies of these men. But, behind this task, other questions necessarily emerge. What do we mean by revelation? What do we mean by inspiration? What is the nature of faith? What is the process by which the knowledge of God can be received by men? These are not questions of Biblical exegesis; they belong to the realm of systematic theology, of the philosophy of religion, or of the border line between the two. Anyone who has looked at Lightfoot's sermons in St. Paul's Cathedral, still more at Hort's Hulsean Lectures, *The Way, the Truth and the Life*, is immediately aware that these men were not ignorant of the problems of their times, and of the new perplexities that had come into being with the rise of natural science and the widespread adoption of a mechanistic view of the world. But, with the exception of Hort, they were not specially well qualified to deal with these questions; they concentrated on those things which they could do excellently, and believed that other men would be raised up to fulfil the tasks which were beyond their reach.

The gravest failure of the Cambridge school seems to me to have been its neglect of the problems of the Synoptic Gospels and of the life of Christ. The three great scholars were led by the circumstances of their time to the study of St. Paul, of the Johannine writings, and of other Epistles. As we said, in dealing with Baur, this must always be the starting-point of scientific study of the New Testament. But behind these writings lies the question of Jesus Christ himself. It was not enough to say that Strauss and Baur had not provided the right answer. The questions raised by them were still clamant, and were being asked in a great variety of forms by others. The central question, which cannot be evaded, and which faith attempts to evade only at great peril to itself, is always this: 'What think ye of Christ? Whose Son is he?' But, before we come to theology, the historical question demands an answer; the next stage in New Testament interpretation, left almost untouched by the men of Cambridge, could not but concern itself with what are commonly called the Synoptic Gospels, and with the historical problems of the life and death of Jesus Christ.

EXCURSUS: ON THE TEXTUAL CRITICISM OF A MODERN AUTHOR

Those who are unfamiliar with the processes of textual criticism sometimes receive the impression, as they hear all this talk of variations and corruptions in the manuscripts of the New Testament, that we are very far from having any certainty as to what the original text really was; and Muslims, who have become aware of what is in the wind, not infrequently use the uncertainties of the New Testament text, as contrasted with the complete uniformity and reliability of the text of the Qur'an,[1] as an argument against the truth and trustworthiness of the New Testament. There is no need for any alarm. Textual criticism is only one aspect of a problem and a process which goes to the making of every single book that has ever been produced. As long as the human eyes and fingers are imperfect servants, errors will creep in, and it is by no means certain that they will all be eliminated.[2]

It is sometimes thought that, now that we have the printed book, with all the paraphernalia of compositors, proof correction, printers' readers and all the rest of it, the possibility of error has been eliminated, and that textual criticism is a hobby of aged professors poring over crabbed and half-illegible manuscripts. It may be interesting and helpful to submit one example, drawn from one of the best-known modern classics, to show that this is very far from being the case. Some years ago, the chance reading of a review in the *Tribune de Genève* put me on to a modern detective story calculated to be quite fascinating to anyone who like myself has a liking for ancient texts, and so closely parallel in remarkable ways to some features of the history of the transmission of the New Testament text as to be by no means irrelevant in a book on the interpretation of the New Testament.

[1] The text of the Qur'an is of course, in fact, neither as uniform nor as reliable as the Muslims suppose!

[2] Let me note one which has always given me a good deal of pleasure. When Trinity College, Cambridge, celebrated the sixth century of Michaelhouse in 1924, an attractive history of the early foundation was written. When the proofs were being read, one of the authorities of the college wrote to the author and mentioned that, though he himself would have no objection to the phrase 'the antics of the medieval monks', there were those to whom it might give offence. The writer replied that what he had actually written was 'the *duties* of the medieval monks'; from which it is possible to infer rather accurately what the handwriting of this particular author must have been like!

The problem related to the letters of Madame de Sévigné, a favourite French classic of the second half of the seventeenth century. This work has been printed and reprinted dozens of times. Yet it is the strange fact that it was not until 1953 that anything like a reliable text saw the light. This is the remarkable phenomenon which is the subject of this excursus.

Marie de Rabutin-Chantal, Marquise de Sévigné, was born in 1626 and died in 1696. For the greater part of her life she lived in Paris, and was an acute and often irreverent observer of all that happened in that great city in that great century of great men and great events. She was attached by links of passionate, and indeed of almost pathological, affection to her daughter the Comtesse de Grignan; and, whenever the two were separated, two or three times a week she set pen to paper to communicate to her daughter, in lengthy, anecdotic, and often highly indiscreet letters, all the events which were passing around her in their gay, significant, and not rarely scandalous forms.[1] After the death of Madame de Sévigné and Madame de Grignan, the collection of more than 500 letters passed into the possession of the daughter of the latter, Madame Pauline de Simiane. Some letters of Madame de Sévigné had appeared in the memoirs of those to whom she had written, and the interest aroused was such that it seemed likely that there would be a demand for a more extensive selection of her letters. Accordingly Madame de Simiane engaged a copyist, and set him to work to reproduce in fair copy the collection of the letters Six large quarto volumes, covering about half the letters, were the result of this excellent arrangement. In the meantime, however, Madame de Simiane had lent a collection of 137 letters, to which a further fifty were later added, to the Abbé Celse de Bussy in Paris. De Bussy, who had become Bishop of Luçon, lent the letters to two friends, one of whom lent them to Voltaire. Voltaire, in whom scrupulousness was not one of the most highly developed characteristics, at once realized the value of the material that had come into his hands, and handed the text of thirty-seven letters to the printer Lefèvre at Troyes, with the result that a printed text of these letters was soon ready and awaiting publication. Word of this came to the ears of Thiériot, one of the friends of de Bussy, who succeeded in getting the piratical edition of Voltaire suppressed before it had even been published, so successfully that only three copies of it are known to survive. But, perhaps in order to fore-

---

[1] I take it that the Marquise is the original of the lady in Thornton Wilder's *Bridge of San Luis Rey*, who is linked to her daughter by a similar passion of epistolary devotion.

stall further tricks, of the same kind, the two friends proceeded to
publish all that they had in their hands, and in 1726 they produced at
Rouen an edition of 138 letters in two volumes comprising 705 pages.

Madame de Simiane was furious, and desired to have the entire
edition withdrawn. But for this there were no legal grounds; the
only result of her protest was the publication of a further edition of
642 pages which appeared at The Hague. The only way to suppress bad
material is to replace it by better. Pauline decided to place the entire
correspondence in the hands of a trusted friend, Denis Marius Perrier,
in Paris, with orders that he should produce a complete edition,
including a great deal of material that had not been printed in any of
the three earlier editions. But strict orders were issued to Monsieur
Perrier as to the manner in which he was to carry out his work.
He was to suppress everything that could cause embarrassment to
persons still living or to the descendants of those recently dead;
everything that related rather too closely to great affairs of state; everything that suggested quarrels or disagreements between the devoted
mother and her daughter; phrases and expressions that the temper of
the eighteenth century found rather too bold; references to sordid
details of household management and economy, and anything that
might cast doubt on the strict Christian orthodoxy of Madame de
Sévigné. A formidable list, and one involving considerable expurga-
tions. Madame de Sévigné was to be presented to the world not as she
was, erratic, spontaneous, intense in her affections · and sometimes
violent in her expressions, but tamed, domesticated, nicely made up
in order to secure the respect and approbation of future generations.

In 1734 Monsieur Perrier published four volumes of the correspondence between Madame de Sévigné and her daughter in the form
prescribed, with many passages omitted, and many modifications of
the actual phrases used in the original letters. The result was an
immediate explosion; Perrier had been far from successful in excluding
all the offending passages: Madame de Simiane complained that she
had been inundated with millions (*sic*) of letters. Her first act was to
burn all the letters addressed by her mother Madame de Grignan to
Madame de Sévigné, a sad loss to the world. Then she told Perrier to
send back to her all the originals, especially those which had not yet
been printed, with the intention of destroying them. Perrier hedged
and excused himself; in 1737 he brought out two further volumes,
containing 212 letters to add to the 402 already published. Madame de
Sévigné, revised and civilized, was now, for good or ill, in the hands of

the world. This was the completion of version number two.

But Perrier had not yet finished his devoted labours. He set to work and produced a third version of Madame de Sévigné. During the seventeen years in which this work was going on, Perrier to a considerable extent restored the matter of the letters, but took even greater liberties with the form. Many of the passages formerly suppressed as indiscreet were now reintroduced; but Madame de Sévigné was coerced into a strict observance of the rules of French grammar and epistolary etiquette of a kind that she had never felt to be necessary during her lifetime. Thus, she had almost always addressed her beloved daughter as 'ma bonne', an affectionate but not very elegant form of address; this will not do at all for Monsieur Perrier, who nine times out of ten changes it to 'ma fille', 'ma chère enfant', 'ma chérie'. Monsieur Perrier would have been entirely at home with the Alexandrian editors of ancient texts!

So in 1751 the third Madame de Sévigné appeared from the press, with a good deal of her irrepressible verve restored, but talking an impeccable French that was not her own. And for two centuries this was in fact Madame as the world knew her. In the seventy years between 1751 and 1821 a certain number of her letters had turned up from a variety of sources, and even a small number of original letters written with her own hand. And so matters remained, until in 1818–19 Monsieur Monmergué produced the first modern and scientific edition of the letters. But what could he do? In 1784 the originals had finally been destroyed, in accordance with the orders left fifty years before by Madame Simiane at her death. The work of Monmergué was careful and critical; but in effect he produced nothing but a Perrier revised and restored, and the image of Madame de Sévigné remained much as Perrier had devised and embellished it.

Then occurred one of those chance events for which the literary editor waits eagerly, and almost always in vain. A certain Marquis de Grosbois had in his castle in Burgundy a thick manuscript volume of 1,055 pages, well bound, and bearing on the cover the title *Lettres de Madame de Sévigné*. He had never bothered to read it; but, having acquired the admirable edition of Monsieur Monmergué, he entered into contact with the editor and lent him the manuscript. No sooner had Monmergué begun to read than he felt like Keats's watcher of the skies; he knew that a treasure had been discovered. The manuscript was in many ways an abomination; it had accumulated every kind of fault that a manuscript can have—misreading, misspelling, blanks,

omissions, confusions. Since I read of it, I have always thought of it as
Θ, that late Koridethi manuscript of the Gospels, so ugly and so ill-
written, and yet so important since clearly it was copied from an old
and excellent manuscript. Monmergué discovered in this folio fragments which were not to be found in any of the current texts of
Madame de Sévigné; at point after point it evidently went behind all
existing printed texts to something much nearer the original—this was
plain, when the style of the letters in this manuscript was compared
with that of the few autograph letters of Madame de Sévigné which
had come to light. Monmergué was naturally enchanted; he had in his
hands something far nearer to the originals than anyone had ever seen
since these were destroyed in 1784. He worked patiently for forty years,
and in 1862 produced his new edition, fourteen volumes of the Letters
of Madame de Sévigné, her family, and her friends.

Unfortunately Monmergué had fallen a victim to that vice, so
severely castigated by Housman, of always relying on 'the best
manuscript'. He had fallen in love with his own discovery, and printed
the readings of the Grosbois folio, whether they made sense or not.
Thus, in a letter of 19 April 1694, Madame is made to say of God
'Cet hôte divin, avec qui on ne saurait rien faire du bien'—a scarcely
reverent remark; we now know, from a source which will appear
immediately, that what Madame really wrote was: 'Cet hôte divin
avec qui *on ne compte jamais assez, et sans qui* on ne saurait rien faire
du bien.' The sentiment is perfectly orthodox, indeed pious; the
wretched copyist had simply omitted a line, his eye having been caught
and misled by the repeated *on ne*, and this, as every palaeographer
knows, is one of the commonest causes of errors in manuscripts.

We are not yet at the end of this strange history. The scene now
passes to the charming little fortified town of Semur-en-Auxois.
In 1872 the possessions of a once prosperous family named Massol
were being sold by auction; the owner of a second-hand shop in
Dijon, Madame Caquelin, found herself almost unwillingly the posses-
sor of six large manuscript volumes entitled *Lettres de Madame la
Marquise de Sévigné*. These volumes lay for thirteen months exposed on
a stall to all passers-by; but no one is interested in manuscript copies
of a work which has long been printed, and the books remained
unsold. Then a professor of law at the University of Dijon, Charles
Capmas, moved by some impulse, acquired the lot. He started to
compare the text with that of the Hachette edition of 1862; in
the inspired phrase of the most recent editor, Monsieur Gérard-

Gailly, he found that he had just discovered Herculaneum and Pompeii.

Careful research has made it certain that we have in our hands the actual copies of half the letters made from the originals by orders of Madame de Simiane from 1720 onwards, and then discontinued. We shall never know the originals, since these, as we have seen, were destroyed in 1784; but we have a copy taken directly from the originals, and a very good, neat, and careful copy at that, marred only by such errors as are invariably to be found in any manuscript.

The excitement aroused by the discovery was tremendous. But, before use could be made of it, the relationship between the Capmas copy and the Grosbois copy had to be established. Were they independent authorities, or was one dependent on the other? Methodical study of the kind that we have indicated elsewhere in this book has shown conclusively that the Grosbois text is simply a copy of the Capmas text. Someone, we do not know when or where, must have borrowed the six Capmas volumes for a limited time, and, because of their intrinsic interest, arranged to have a copy made of them. As time began to press, the copyist wrote more and more rapidly, omissions and errors begin to multiply, and the value of the text decreases steadily towards the end. With all its faults, Monsieur Monmergué was right in regarding it as an exceedingly valuable piece of evidence. But now, since the Grosbois is a copy of the Capmas and we have recovered the earlier manuscript from which it was made, it loses all independent value and becomes simply a curiosity.

Because of the magnitude of the labour involved, the Hachette text was not re-edited; the new discoveries made by Monsieur Capmas were put together in two supplementary volumes. But now at last a critical text based on all the existing evidence has been produced in the Pléiade edition by the Paris publishers Gallimard. In 1953, more than two centuries after the appearance of Monsieur Perrier's first efforts, for the first time something like a critical and reliable text of one of the best-known and best-loved of French classics has appeared. But, even now, it is important to notice the limitations of what the editor has been able to achieve. For nearly half the letters we have no better text than that provided by Monsieur Perrier—the originals have even been destroyed without having been copied, and there is hardly a possibility that any other evidence for their text will ever be forthcoming. So Madame de Sévigné stands before us, even in this magisterial edition, in four different degrees of verity:

1. There are the few letters of which the original autographs have been found. Here we know exactly what Madame de Sévigné wrote, because we have it from her own hand without change or alteration.

2. We have the excellent copy of nearly half the letters provided by the Capmas volumes.

3. We have certain letters in the early editions of Troyes and Rouen, a text hurriedly prepared but unedited and uncorrupted.

4. We have the revised and manipulated text of Perrier, which for a considerable part of the collection is all that we have and all that we are ever likely to have.

It has been thought that this history of the adventures of a modern classic might prove not uninteresting to those who are unfamiliar with the processes of textual criticism. So many of the problems that have to be faced in dealing with the New Testament reproduce themselves with singular exactitude here. And, if all this can happen in the age of printing to the work of a woman who died less than three hundred years ago, we may well be amazed that we have anything like reliable texts for many of the ancient classics. But, miraculously, it is just the fact that for the most part we have a better and more reliable text of the letters of the Apostle Paul than we have of the letters of Madame de Sévigné.

The principal lesson to be derived from this history is that you never know what may turn up. How did the Capmas text ever get to Semur-en-Auxois, and how did it come about that it had never been destroyed? We do not know. In our own country and in our own time we have had the astonishing discovery of the Boswell manuscripts that everyone had supposed to be irretrievably lost. All the known libraries of the world have been so carefully searched for Biblical manuscripts that it is not likely that any great new discoveries will be made in that direction. But what do the sands of Egypt and the caves of the Dead Sea still hold? There may still be treasures of darkness awaiting us or our children, to bring us ever nearer to that perfect text of the New Testament to which we aspire.

Note. Lest any reader should give me credit for having carried out research to which I lay no claim, I must make it clear that I have done no more than to summarize pp. 62–93 of the Pléiade edition of the Letters of Madame de Sévigné (Paris, Gallimard, 1953). My knowledge is limited to the admirable presentation of the facts by the editor, Monsieur Gérard-Gailly.

Chapter IV

JESUS AND THE GOSPEL

I

WE have seen that one of the greatest weaknesses in the work of Lightfoot, Westcott, and Hort was that none of the three had done any intensive work on the Synoptic Gospels and their problems. This was at the time natural and inevitable. All scientific New Testament study must start with the letters of Paul. If we place the Epistle to the Galatians between the first and second 'missionary journeys' of St. Paul, as many do, and accept the authenticity of 1 Thessalonians, then in these two letters we stand at a distance of not much more than twenty years from the events of the Cross and Resurrection; and in history an interval of twenty years is a very short period indeed. So Lightfoot and his colleagues were right to start where they did. But sooner or later we must come back to the Synoptic Gospels; there all the most acute and burning problems are to be found, and our judgement as to the value of these three Gospels as historical evidence will to a large extent determine our understanding of the Christian faith as a whole.

The general agreement of the first three Gospels as against the fourth is so obvious that no reader of the New Testament, however unskilled theologically, could fail to notice it. As long as the theory of verbal inspiration held the field, it was generally supposed that the Fourth Gospel, being the work of the beloved disciple, was the most authoritative of the four; a great many ingenious harmonizations of the Gospels were carried out, but almost always with the Fourth Gospel as the starting-point, and the material from the other three inserted into the framework provided by it. In this way it was possible to minimize the differences between the Gospels, and to give the impression that they all really say the same thing.

One of the first to realize that this method would not do was Griesbach, whom we have already met in connexion with the text of the New Testament. Griesbach saw clearly that all four Gospels cannot be treated together, and so separated off the fourth from the other three. Then he committed himself to 'the heresy', as he himself called it, that not very much can be gained by the attempt to create a harmony even of the first three Gospels, since it is not likely that any one of the evangelists strictly followed chronological sequence, and our evidence is insufficient to make plain what the chronological order of events actually was. What can be done is to arrange the first three Gospels in a *Synopsis*, printing them in three parallel columns; and this is what Griesbach actually did, thus for the first time making possible accurate assessment of the resemblances and differences between the three Gospels. It is for this reason and for no other that these three are now universally known as the Synoptic Gospels; the word has no mysterious inner significance, as though the writers had all written from the same, or from a similar, point of view, or had all followed a common impulse. All it means is that these three Gospels can be, have been, and still frequently are, arranged in this way in three columns in the form of a Synopsis, in which the whole text of each of the three is printed, and no attempt is made to combine them.

When these Gospels are thus set side by side, it is clear that they present a literary problem which is as fascinating as it is formidable. How are we to explain the obvious similarities in general outlook and construction between the three, and at the same time account for the startling differences in order, in emphasis, and in expression?

Our first business is to ascertain the facts and to locate the problems. For this purpose there is one, and only one, satisfactory method—the student must acquire a Synopsis, and work at it on his own, not trusting to anyone else's results, until he begins himself to see the extraordinary complexity of the lines of similarity and change.[1] We tend today to like quick returns, and all too easily to suppose that, because someone else has worked at a problem, there is no need for us to apply our own brains and energies to it. There is also, perhaps, a tendency to think that such minute attention to the text of the Bible is pedantic and enslaving. For this reason I was delighted to find, in one of the books on the Gospels which I have most recently read, that the learned author, Dr. Frederick C. Grant, makes exactly the suggestion that I would have made myself. As a first guide in method he suggests the following:

Go through Matthew and Luke and mark the exact equivalents to Mark by underlining the words in *unbroken* black lines (breaking the lines only to indicate inversions in order) and underlining in *dotted* black lines words

---

[1] The most practically useful Synopsis is that of Albert Huck, *A Synopsis of the First Three Gospels* (9th ed., revised by H. Lietzmann, of the Greek text: English edition by F. L. Cross, 1951). See also *Gospel Parallels* (R.S.V.) (2nd ed., 1957).

and groups of words which are similar and represent only slight grammatical changes (person, case, tense, mood, voice, or number). This is
laborious and minute work; but it is worth all the trouble—one gains a
grasp of the problem and of the proposed solution which nothing else can
supply . . . Nothing can take the place of that first-hand acquaintance with
the text which will result from the minute and exacting work, carefully
and accurately done, which this task involves.[1]

It is likely that only professed theological students will have time to
carry out such work for the whole Gospel; but to do it carefully even
for a single chapter would be an experience of the utmost value for the
ordinary student of the Bible, who is prepared to bring to his studies
the expenditure of some time and trouble. Once this has been done,
the student will be in a position to judge how much of the material in
Matthew and Luke is also to be found in Mark, and how much is
independent of him; he will begin to observe, as he studies the differences, certain habits and mannerisms which seem to be characteristic of
Matthew and Luke.

This is only a first step; for a thorough study, various other processes
have to be gone through, and the expert will probably be using all
the colours of the rainbow before he is finished.

And now, having some of the materials before us, we come to the
heart of the problem. What is the relationship between these Gospels?
Have they all borrowed from some common source? Or have they borrowed from one another? Or, although entirely independent of one another, have they come by some mysterious process to be singularly alike?

Every conceivable hypothesis has been put forward at one time or
another, each being supported rather by intelligent guess-work than
by careful and scientific reasoning. One theory which had a long run was
that of an original Aramaic Gospel, now lost, on which all the three
evangelists depended. Another hardy plant was the theory of oral
transmission; it is quite clear that there must have been a period, before
anything was written down, in which the deeds and words of Jesus
were passed on from one witness to another only by word of mouth;
it is probable that this oral tradition contained a great deal more than
has ever found its way into any written Gospel.[2] This oral material,

[1] F. C. Grant, *The Gospels: their Origin and their Growth* (1959), pp. 41–42.
[2] As evidence for this, we may take the interesting example of the verse about a man
working on the Sabbath day which is found in the Codex Bezae (D), and in no other
manuscript, in place of Luke 6. 5: 'the same day, seeing someone working on the Sabbath
day, he said to him: "My man, if you know what you are doing, you are blest; but if you
do not know, you are accurst and a law-breaker." '

it is supposed, was available to each of the evangelists, though no doubt with local variations; each took as much as he needed to carry out his own particular purpose, leaving aside much which has found its way into the pages of one or more of the other evangelists. One of the earliest books of Bishop Westcott was an *Introduction to the Study of the Gospels*,[1] in which he committed himself to the theory of oral transmission. Unfortunately he allowed the book to be reprinted time and time again without ever subjecting it to a thorough revision; as a result it is the least satisfactory of all his works, taking no account of the progress in the understanding of the problems of the Gospels which was one leading feature in New Testament studies in the second half of the nineteenth century.

Each of these theories contains a measure of truth. The Gospel was originally preached in Aramaic, and to some extent traces of this Aramaic origin can be identified even in the Greek Gospels as we have them today.[2] Similarly, no theory of the relationships between the Gospels can do justice to the complexity of the facts, unless it takes into account the period of purely oral transmission. But each theory falls down on the same point. The resemblances between the Gospels *in Greek* are at points so close as to be inexplicable, unless there was some kind of literary dependence between them after some part at least of the Gospel material had been written down, and written down in Greek.

If this is true, who was dependent on whom, and how?

Among the evangelists, Mark has always had a rather poor press. Augustine spoke somewhat contemptuously of him as a follower and abbreviator of Matthew.[3] Augustine's authority was so great throughout the Middle Ages that this view was generally accepted. It is reflected in the fact that of the more than seventy Gospel lections for Sundays and Saints' Days in the Prayer Book of the Church of England only three are drawn from Mark.[4] It is easy to see how this judgement was reached; Mark has very few of the words of

---

[1] First edition, 1851; many times reprinted.

[2] See M. Black, *An Aramaic Approach to the Gospels and Acts* (2nd ed., 1954), a cautious and reliable survey of the evidence.

[3] *Marcus eum [Matthaeum] subsecutus tanquam pedisequus et breviator eius videtur*— 'Mark seems to have followed Matthew as a kind of camp-follower and abridger.' Augustine, *De Consensu Evang*. ii.

[4] An interesting parallel is to be found in the sermons of John Donne. Of the 160 sermons which have survived, thirty-seven were preached on texts from the Gospels: Matthew is represented by sixteen texts, John by ten, Luke by nine, and Mark by only two. See E. M. Simpson and G. R. Potter, *The Sermons of John Donne*, vol. x (1962).

Christ; it is to Matthew and Luke that we are indebted for most of the parables, and in particular for the Sermon on the Mount. Mark seems inferior in grandeur and beauty to the other two. Baur, also, took a rather low view of Mark. He found in him few signs of 'tendency', and so relegated him to the position of the latest and therefore historically least valuable of the Gospels.

But, before Baur had reached this conclusion, a change in thought was quietly and gradually taking place, which was exactly to reverse Baur's judgement, to recognize that Mark is the earliest of all the Gospels, and to ascribe to this little book unique historical value.

II

When did the priority of Mark come to be generally accepted? It is exceedingly difficult to say. In 1850 the idea was little known even as a hypothesis. Twenty years later it was coming to be seriously reckoned with as a possibility. From then on it was very much in the air. By the end of the century it had come to be looked on as one of the assured results of the critical study of the New Testament.

The first scholar to approach the correct solution of the problem on the basis of careful observation of the facts seems to have been Karl Lachmann, whom we have already met as the editor of the first Greek text of the New Testament to be genuinely based on the evidence of the manuscripts. In 1835 Lachmann produced an article on 'The Order of the Narration of Events in the Synoptic Gospels'.[1] In his studies of the New Testament text Lachmann had found it impossible to accept the generally received theory that Mark had made use of the Gospels of Matthew and Luke. He now pursued his intuition further, using for his study the simple, but extraordinarily valuable and fruitful, criterion of the order in which events are narrated in the Gospels: 'I intend here to consider only the order of events. Since this is the simplest of all points of departure, and, as far as I am aware, has has previously been taken by no one—we are to consider at what definite results we may arrive by taking this as our starting-point.'[2]

When comparison is made on the basis of this principle, it is at once clear that, where Matthew and Luke are using the material which

---

[1] 'De Ordine Narrationum in Evangeliis Synopticis', *Theologische Studien und Kritiken*, 8 (1835), pp. 570 ff. Lachmann wrote, like many of his contemporaries, in Latin and not in German.

[2] Ibid. Quoted in W. G. Kümmel, *Das neue Testament*, p. 181.

is also found in Mark, the order of events in the two very nearly corresponds; but when they are using material which is not found in Mark, there is no such correspondence in the order of events as they relate them. From this fact Lachmann drew the conclusion that all three Synoptic Gospels used an older written or oral source, but that Mark had followed more exactly the order of events as presented in the older source, and that therefore he represents to us more accurately than either of the other two the tradition of the Gospels at an earlier stage of its development than is available to us in any written source. This was a deduction based on correct scientific observation of the facts. Lachmann, starting with the assumption that Matthew and Luke could not have had a copy of Mark before them, does not go on to make the further inference as to the priority of Mark as a *source* of the other two.[1] He does point in the right direction, and indicates, what later scholars were more fully to realize, the supreme historical value of the Second Gospel. His article seems not to have attracted much attention at the time; years were to pass before the second step in the inference was clearly taken.

Shortly after the appearance of Lachmann's article, the question of the priority of Mark was taken up by another scholar, Christian Hermann Weisse (1801–66), who was primarily a philosopher, not a theologian. In his critical study of the Gospels, which appeared in 1838, Weisse made two acutely penetrating remarks. It had long been noticed that the account of various events in Mark is fuller than that in Matthew and Luke, and that Mark adds a number of vivid touches, such as the '*green* grass' in Mark 5. 39 on which the multitudes are told to sit down.[2] Those who held the view that Mark had copied from Matthew and Luke supposed that he had added the details, if not to give 'verisimilitude to an otherwise bald and unconvincing narrative', at least to lend a certain liveliness to the scene. But Weisse saw, and his

[1] It is constantly stated in later authorities that he did take this step. The Abbot of Downside, Dr. B. C. Butler, makes it plain, with the relevant quotations, that he did not do so: *The Originality of St. Matthew; A Critique of the Two-Document Hypothesis* (1951), chap. v, 'The Lachmann Fallacy', pp. 62 ff. It is characteristic that in Schweitzer's great survey, *The Quest of the Historical Jesus*, Lachmann's epoch-making contribution is dismissed in a single sentence, or rather part of a sentence, in which he is linked with the wholly undistinguished Credner. Schweitzer has, however, noted at some length that Herder, with the literary intuition of genius, had recognized and defended the priority of Mark (*Quest*, pp. 34–37). But Herder was not a technical scholar; he could not advance the scientific reasons for what he knew and felt to be true.

[2] Incidentally this word 'green' is much more than a merely picturesque touch. Since in Palestine the grass is green for such a short time in the year, this is an important chronological indication.

observation is confirmed by what we see of the expansion of Gospel narratives in the apocryphal Gospels,[1] that this is not the kind of detail that is added by an author who wants to touch up an original picture. There is a strong probability in the opposite direction—that Matthew and Luke omitted many of the details in Mark, because they needed their space for other purposes and regarded these details as trivial. If this is true, it seems natural to conclude that Mark is independent of, and perhaps older than, Matthew and Luke. Weisse, like Lachmann, did not suppose Matthew and Luke actually to have used the Gospel of Mark. His view was that Mark had reproduced more simply and fully than the other two an older document, which was one common source of all the three. He then followed up this observation by another—that Matthew and Luke must have had another common source, a written collection of the sayings of Jesus, from which much of the material that is common to both of them is derived. Here we find in embryo the 'Two-Source' theory of the composition of the Gospels, which at the end of the century was to hold the field. It is striking to find it put forward as early as 1838, though without the support of the necessary weight of scientific argument.

Lachmann and Weisse had worked to a large extent by intuition. The patient, careful work by which alone a hypothesis can be verified was provided by Heinrich Julius Holtzmann (1832–1910), who at the age of thirty-one produced a notable work on the Synoptic Gospels.[2] Holtzmann was a typical German professor of the late nineteenth century. Slow, ponderous in style, without a trace of humour and with no concessions to the possible human weaknesses of his readers, he moves rather laboriously from point to point. But, when he has done his work in his own way, something of real value has been established. Holtzmann survived by forty-seven years the publication of his first great work, and had to his credit a long list of other compositions; but it is doubtful whether he ever produced anything of importance comparable to that of his first work on the Synoptic Gospels.

Holtzmann has, of course, his own eccentricity, such as must be allowed to learned men. He invents a wholly unnecessary document A, supposed to be prior to our Mark, and to have been shortened by Mark through the omission of the speeches which it contained. But, when allowance has been made for one such aberrant hypothesis, with Holtzmann we are in the main on solid ground. Mark is the original apostolic

---

[1] Notably in the story of the resurrection in the apocryphal Gospel of Peter.
[2] *Die synoptischen Evangelien: Ihr Ursprung und geschichtlicher Charakter* (1863).

document, and can be treated as being for the most part historically reliable. Here, as Holtzmann himself remarks, we part company with the Tübingen school; they would have allowed us no more than the echoes of conflicts and tendencies in the primitive Church, from which we could pick up faint gleams and shadows of a real Jesus of Nazareth. If Holtzmann is right, we are almost a hundred years nearer to the actual events than Tübingen had admitted; a real encounter with Jesus of Nazareth as he actually was becomes possible. Holtzmann goes further than this; accepting the view that behind Matthew and Luke, where they agree, lies a written document consisting mainly of speeches or utterances of Jesus, he proceeds with considerable perspicacity to work out the kind of document that this must have been.[1] Both documents, according to him, are historically reliable, and evidence for this is their agreement in the kind of picture of Jesus that they give. If we are to make a choice, it must be in favour of Mark. Holtzmann gives evidence of his acuteness as a critic by his remarks on the Passion narrative; here at point after point we see how the later writers have softened down a little the roughness and almost violence of the Marcan narrative; we have the impression that our picture of Jesus has, through these later contributions, 'gained in completeness, rather than in the intensity of its living contents'.

The materials were now present for the beginnings of scientific study of the life of Jesus. Unhappily neither Weisse nor Holtzmann was able to free himself from the distorting influence of that German idealistic philosophy which had wrought havoc in so many directions. Each allowed himself to be influenced by considerations which had nothing to do with historical method or with the evidence of the Gospels themselves; and the result was, inevitably, failure to wrestle scientifically with the evidence. The Gospels show that the kingdom of God, as Jesus understood it, is a power that breaks in upon men from without through the direct and personal action of God himself. We may disagree as to the interpretation of the Jewish 'eschatological' vocabulary in which this fact finds expression. As to the fact itself there can be no doubt. But, in the circles in which Weisse and Holtzmann had grown up, the kingdom of God had been understood as an inner and spiritual change within the hearts of men; this is to be a kingdom of reason, intelligence, and good will. And so the Gospels, instead of

[1] This is the later-to-be-famous and ever memorable 'Q'; but this term had not been invented in the days of Holtzmann; we shall have later to consider the doubts as to its actual parentage.

serving as the critic and the judge of all human imaginings, have to be
reduced to the level of what scholars in the middle of the nineteenth
century regarded as possible and suitable. Jesus is spiritualized; the
kingdom of God is reduced to a psychological phenomenon. For another
forty years men will go on writing liberal lives of Jesus, each more
subjective, more 'situation-conditioned', than the last. The time for
the beginning of fully scientific work on the life of Jesus had not yet
come.

III

For another reason, scientific work on the Gospels was hardly
possible in 1863. If we are to work in detail on the Gospels, we must
know with some accuracy what the Gospels really say; and at that
date, as we have seen, no fully reliable text of the Gospels in Greek
was yet available.

The text of the Gospels has suffered more than that of any other
part of the New Testament from what is called assimilation, the
inveterate tendency of the scribes to put into one Gospel what really
belongs to another. The scribe may have written without due attention,
with the result that what he wrote down was what he had often
heard in church, and not what was actually before him in the text
that he was copying; or, if the text was shorter than that with which
he was familiar, he might insert what seemed to him to be the missing
words, in the honest desire that nothing of the Gospel should be lost.
It is easy for the reader to check this for himself. Nothing is more
difficult than to remember exactly what is in each Gospel. If the reader
will write down what he remembers of one familiar passage, such as the
story of the paralytic who was first given the forgiveness of his sins
and then healed of his infirmity, or the parable of the sower, and will
then compare it carefully with the three Gospels, in all of which these
passages are to be found, he will almost certainly find that what he has
written down is a *conflation*—bits and pieces of all the Gospels have been
brought together into something which does not exactly correspond
to any of them. It is in this form that Christians, for the most part, carry
the Gospels in their heads.

Instances of scribal assimilation are numbered by the hundred. A
particularly interesting example is to be found in John 6. 69; the later
and assimilated texts read 'thou art the Christ, the Son of the living
God', and this appears in the Authorized Version of the Bible in

English. But it is quite certain that the original reading was 'thou art the holy one of God'. This is not found in so many manuscripts; but it is found in those which by their age and reliability, when they agree with one another, enable us to say with absolute certainty that this or that was the original reading. What has happened is that a scribe, or a number of scribes, at a rather early date, correctly spotted that this passage is the Johannine parallel to the story of Peter's confession in Matthew 16, and either unconsciously or deliberately put into the mouth of Peter here the words which are to be found in all the best manuscripts of Matthew 16. The most interesting thing of all is that the scribal conscience seems to have been not wholly unperturbed by this interference with the original reading, and that we have in consequence at this point an extraordinary variety of readings in the manuscripts:

Thou art
(1) the holy one of God
(2) the Christ, the Son of the living God
(3) the Christ, the holy one of God
(4) the Christ, the Son of God
(5) the Son of God
(6) the Son of the living God
(7) the Christ.

This variety does not at all affect what I have called our certainty as to the original reading; it does illustrate the kind of variation that we shall find in the manuscripts in hundreds of passages of the Gospels.

The result of this process of assimilation, as must be plain to the reader, is that in the later manuscripts, and in the printed texts derived from them, we have a dimmed and obscured picture of the various evangelists. A family likeness has been imposed upon them, and something of the characteristic features of each has been suppressed. Now, if we are to work out the literary history of the Gospels, and so to work critically on the evidence for the life of Christ, a great deal will depend on details, on even minute differences in style and expression. We shall not be able to get very far until we have in our hands a scientifically established Greek text of the Gospels. It is for this reason that the publication of the Greek New Testament by Westcott and Hort in 1881 produced a revolution in this, as in so many other fields. Scientific work on the literary history of the Gospels was at last able to begin.

In the period up to 1881 Britain had produced nothing of any very great value on the Gospels.[1] There was nothing to compare, in thoroughness and precision, with the work of H. J. Holtzmann. But now at last Britain took a hand. In the forty years that followed on 1881, the greater part of the genuinely scientific work on the Gospels was done in Britain, and particularly in the University of Oxford.

It was by now generally agreed that Mark was the earliest Gospel. But this meant that scholars had to take a new look at the Gospel, as though they had never seen it before. The effect of this adventure was in many cases astonishing. Supposing Mark to have been a tame abbreviator of the work of others, as Augustine had held, scholars had paid far less attention to him than to any of the other three evangelists. Now, when they read him for himself and without presuppositions, they discovered to their amazement that this tame copyist, though endowed with only moderate literary capacity, was in fact a writer of immense originality and power. From being the despised poor relation, Mark's Gospel came to be accepted as the primary historical source for all our knowledge of the life of Jesus Christ; indeed, the reaction went almost too far, and there was a tendency to establish a kind of verbal inerrancy of St. Mark.

When scholars looked with new eyes and without prejudice at the figure of Jesus of Nazareth as he is presented to us in this Gospel, they rubbed their eyes and wondered how they could have been so blind before. One of those who caught from the Gospel the new vision of Jesus was Francis Crawford Burkitt of Cambridge. Burkitt was an extraordinary man, an artist to his fingertips, whose whole personality was expressed in his magnificent and perfectly legible handwriting; an enthusiast for J. S. Bach—perhaps his translation of the old German chorale *Wachet auf* will live longer than anything else that he wrote. *Nihil quod tetigit non ornavit.* When he died in 1935, the *Journal of Theological Studies* set apart a whole number as a memorial to him, and listed his work under thirteen headings: Syriac Studies, Textual Criticism, Hebrew and Old Testament Studies, Early Christian Literature and Life, On Gnosticism, On Mandaeism, On Manichaeism, Liturgical Studies, Franciscan Studies, Archaeological Studies, Philological, The Past and the Present, Biographical. In addition to his technical competence, Burkitt had the rare gift of making complex theological problems

---

[1] The popular life of Jesus Christ by Dean F. W. Farrar (1874), which went through twelve editions in a single year, is edifying but scientifically worthless, though it is a great deal better than many of the lives of Jesus for which Dr. Schweitzer has found a place in his great survey. It has just been republished (1963) by the firm of Cassell.

completely intelligible to his readers. In a little book with the title *The Earliest Sources for the Life of Jesus* he caught the attention of my generation with the striking phrase 'the stormy and mysterious Personage portrayed by the second Gospel'.[1] This is exactly right. What has this Jesus to do with the mild Galilean peasant of Renan's fancy? Here is a man of more than Napoleonic stature, who spreads around him astonishment and dismay; whose words are perplexing in the extreme; who goes on puzzling his disciples to the very end; who flouts the conventional piety of his day; and yet who all through remains human, without a single trait characteristic of the Greek hero, the θεῖος ἀνήρ. Here are problems galore, if at any time we should venture to take it in hand to write a life of Jesus; and we may be certain that what we write will be wholly unacceptable to those who like their Jesus tamed and conventionalized, and are not willing to be led away to the bleak uplands on which he moves in the Gospel according to St. Mark.

By the end of the nineteenth century, then, scholars were almost unanimously agreed that St. Mark was the earliest of the Gospels. But it would be unfair to the reader to allow him to suppose that this is a kind of mathematical axiom which it is impossible to challenge. In historical research there are few axioms; and it is good that periodically every alleged conclusion should be challenged and tested in the light of fresh evidence, or of a change in the premises on the basis of which the evidence is weighed. This, in point of fact, is what has happened to the theory of the priority of Mark. The first to raise the question afresh in Britain was a fine Roman Catholic scholar, Dom John Chapman (1865–1933), Abbot of Downside. He began work on the question in 1926, and at his death in 1933 left a mass of material, which was reduced to order by Mgr. J. M. T. Barton and published in 1937 under the title *Matthew, Mark, and Luke*. This big and complicated book attracted limited attention. Much more stir was caused when another Roman Catholic scholar, Dom B. C. Butler, also Abbot of Downside, produced a book with the challenging title *The Originality of St. Matthew* (1951).

[1] F. C. Burkitt, *The Earliest Sources for the Life of Jesus* (2nd ed., 1921), p. 49: 'Till our eyes become accustomed to the atmosphere it is difficult to recognise the conventional Saviour, with the gentle unindividualised face, in the stormy and mysterious Personage portrayed by the second Gospel.' A little later on Professor Burkitt quotes the remark of Professor B. W. Bacon (*Beginnings of the Gospel Story*, p. 108) on 'the sane and well-poised mind of the plain mechanic of Nazareth', and a remark of the great Wilhelm Herrmann about Jesus giving utterance to 'ethical ideas that are the essential element in the spiritual experience of the modern world' (*Sources*, pp. 56 and 73), as examples of the unwillingness of modern scholars to see what is so plainly there in the Second Gospel.

Butler scored a strong point in showing that those who supported the priority of Mark had been guilty of a *logical* fallacy. They had shown that Matthew and Luke were both related to Mark, and not related directly to each other; Mark was the *link* between Matthew and Luke. They then assumed that the only possible explanation of this was that Mark came first, and that Matthew and Luke both made use of his Gospel. But *logically* it is equally possible that Mark made use of, and abridged, Matthew, and that Luke then in turn made use of Mark. This thesis is then patiently worked out in great detail and with considerable skill. Although Butler's argument runs contrary to a whole century of work on the New Testament, scholars have had to take it seriously, and to reconsider all the positions that they have traditionally held.

But the arguments of the Roman Catholic scholars have not proved convincing. They have shown the *possibility* that Matthew is the oldest Gospel; they have not established this as a probability. Mark contains only about half the material to be found in the Gospel of St. Matthew. It is hard to see why, if he had all this material before him, he omitted so much of it. It is easy to see how Matthew, if he had Mark before him, could have taken Mark as the framework into which to introduce the vast mass of fresh material which he had at his disposal. 'The point may be put like this: Given Mk, it is easy to see why Matt. was written; given Matt., it is hard to see why Mk was needed.'[1]

In the last years of the nineteenth century, however, the learned world was untroubled by such doubts. The great new revelation of the priority of Mark filled the sky, and was accepted by all except some stubborn adherents of the old theory of oral tradition. But the acceptance of the principle raised far more questions than it answered. The Marcan theory gave some solid ground on which to stand; it made possible a general picture of the relationships between the first three Gospels. But, once scholars moved forward from principles to details, the problem of the origin, the history, and the relationships of the Gospels still presented itself as immensely complicated. And it is usually by patient attention to detail, and by nothing else, that positions in historical or literary research can be firmly established.

In 1898 Professor (later Dean) Armitage Robinson, in a speech at the Church Congress held in that year, laid great stress on the amount of

[1] G. M. Styler, 'Excursus IV: The Priority of Mark' in C. F. D. Moule, *The Birth of the New Testament* (1962), pp. 223–32. This is the best brief study of the 'Matthaean thesis' known to me. Mr. Styler continues: 'In spite of the postulates of the Form critics, it is likely that Mk's sprawling and circumstantial stories are more original than Matt.'s shorter and more formal ones' (loc. cit., p. 231).

preliminary work that needed to be done before even an approach
could be made to the solution of the Synoptic problem: 'In England,'
he said, 'so far as published work is concerned, we are at the very
beginning—the foundations of the study have not yet been laid.'[1]
Just at that time, a patient toiler, who is remembered for nothing
except his work in this field, was preparing to publish some of his
results. Sir John Hawkins was a canon of St. Albans; over a number of
years he had employed his leisure in minute and careful studies of the
first three Gospels, and in drawing up what were in the main statistical
tables to illustrate the characteristics of each, and the resemblances
and differences between them. With characteristic modesty he called
his book *Horae Synopticae*, to indicate that he was concerned only with
the preparatory approaches to the problem and not as yet with any
attempt at solution:

I have only been trying to help in that preliminary process of collecting
and sifting materials which must be carried much further than it has yet
been before we can be ready for the solution of the Problem—or, as I would
rather express it, of such parts of it as are not now insoluble. For while it
seems to me on the one hand that there are some aspects of it as to which
we are not likely to advance beyond statements of conflicting probabilities,
unless there are some fresh discoveries of documents in Egypt or elsewhere,
on the other hand I believe that not a few conclusions—and those of the
most important kinds—are likely to be made so clear and so practically
certain by the patient and careful investigations of the language of the
Gospels which are now being carried on, that before long they will meet with
general acceptance.[2]

The work of Hawkins was so careful and thorough as to earn a paean of
commendation from one of the leading New Testament scholars of the
time:

The character of Sir John Hawkins' work is well known: . . . as Mark
Pattison said of Bishop Butler, 'every brick in the building has been rung
before it has been laid'; its extreme sobriety and caution, never overstepping
the limits of proof, and always scrupulously discriminating degrees of proof;
the clear distinction that is observed between assured results and speculative
probabilities or possibilities.[3]

[1] Quoted in J. C. Hawkins, *Horae Synopticae* (1899), p. v.
[2] *Horae Synopticae*, pp. v, vi.
[3] W. Sanday in *Oxford Studies in the Synoptic Problem* (1911), p. xii. Harnack shared
this opinion: 'it is impossible', he wrote, 'to overrate Hawkins'. Quoted by A. C. Headlam
in *The Life and Teaching of Jesus Christ* (1923), p. 6.

Hawkins's work is for specialists rather than for amateurs. The headings of some of the sections will indicate the kind of immensely detailed and patient work that has gone into his results: 'Rude, harsh, obscure, or unusual words or expressions [in Mark], which may therefore have been omitted or replaced by others'; 'Traces of numerical arrangements in Matthew'; 'The alterations and small additions in which Matthew and Luke agree against Mark'. And most important of all: 'The source largely used by Matthew and Luke, apart from Mark'. Here all the materials for study are set out with minute accuracy. What shall we make of them, if we try to approach nearer to the solution of the problem of Gospel origins?

Four great principles suggest themselves on even a superficial study of the material:

1. Neither Matthew nor Luke treats Mark as we would treat 'inspired Scripture'. Each takes the utmost liberty to edit, to rewrite, and to alter the material that is before him. But the method of writing of the two is very different. A careful study of their differing editorial methods is an essential part of work on the Synoptic problem.

2. In building up the structure of their Gospels, Matthew and Luke make very different use of Mark. Matthew follows in the main the order of Mark, and inserts at suitable points great blocks of his own independent material. Luke largely departs from the Marcan order; the structure of his Gospel is his own, and he makes use of Mark as and when it suits him.

3. In the sections in which both Matthew and Luke are independent of Mark, they sometimes show such close agreement as to suggest that each had before him another common source which already existed in writing, and in Greek.

4. But Matthew and Luke both contain a considerable amount of material in which each is independent both of the other and of Mark.

Is it possible to go further than this in building up a theory of the materials which have gone into our Gospels, and of the way in which they have been used?

Scholars devoted an immense amount of time to discussing the question whether the 'Mark' which Matthew and Luke had before them was our Gospel of Mark, or an earlier and shorter version of the Gospel, an *Ur-Markus*, to use the German term ('original' or 'primitive' Mark). After long debate opinion has generally settled down to the view that there never was more than one Mark, and that the Gospel as used by the other evangelists was exactly or almost exactly the Gospel as we have it today.[1]

Then comes the notable question of that other source, used by Matthew and Luke, which scholars have agreed to call Q.[2] Had Matthew and Luke another written source in Greek, apart from Mark? If so, is it possible to determine with any degree of certainty what it contained, and when and where it came into existence?

The reader is likely to understand this question better if he is prepared to take a little trouble to make soundings in it for himself. This can easily be done by comparing, in Matthew and Luke, some of the most familiar sections of the Gospels. The two narratives of the temptation are strikingly similar in many ways; but the order is different, the second and third temptations in Matthew's account being reversed in Luke's. There are many and great similarities between the Sermon on the Mount in Matthew 5–7 and the Sermon on the Plain in Luke 6. In both we find the Beatitudes, the command to love our enemies, the command not to judge, the parable of the two houses. Yet the differences in detail are as striking as the resemblances; and much that is found in Matthew in the Sermon on the Mount (e.g. the Lord's Prayer), is found in Luke in other contexts. Can we find one satisfactory explanation for all these phenomena?

---

[1] The best discussion of the problem known to me in English is that by F. C. Burkitt in his *Gospel History and its Transmission* (1906), pp. 42–58. Burkitt quotes J. Wellhausen as saying in his *Einleitung in die drei ersten Evangelien* (1905), p. 57: 'Mark was known to the other two synoptic writers, when it was already in the same condition as we now have it, both in text and contents.'

[2] Why Q? Hereby hangs a delightful critical tale. As students we were always told that Q stood for the German word *Quelle*, source. But in a fascinating footnote to his *History and Interpretation in the Gospels* (1935), pp. 27–28, Professor R. H. Lightfoot tells us a different story. Dr. Armitage Robinson had told him that, when lecturing on Gospel origins at Cambridge in the 1890s, he had been accustomed to refer to St. Mark's Gospel as P ('reminiscences of St. Peter') and to the presumed 'sayings-document' as Q, simply because that was the next letter in the alphabet. He believed that this use had been carried to the Continent, where the Germans had 'soon found an explanation that no doubt seemed to them both more satisfactory and more rational'. But apparently Dr. Armitage Robinson was wrong. It seems that Johannes Weiss (1863–1914) was using the expression not later than 1892, and that he gives a hint of having learned it from his father Bernhard Weiss (1827–1918), another great scholar, whose work was of lasting value in several directions. (See C. F. D. Moule, *The Birth of the New Testament*, p. 84, n. 1, where reference is made to an article by W. F. Howard in the *Expository Times*, 1938–9, pp. 379 ff.). This little tale is an awful warning to scholars. If it is so hard to arrive at certainty concerning a matter so near our own time, how careful must we be not to assume certainty about much more distant matters, on which our information is so much more limited!

At the turn of the century there was widespread agreement that there really had been a Q, a very early collection of the sayings and teachings of Jesus, perhaps with some narratives attached, which probably existed first in Aramaic, but was soon translated into Greek, perhaps in a variety of unofficial versions. Various attempts at reconstruction of Q were made. The boldest was that of Harnack, who believed that it was possible to arrive, by critical comparison of Matthew and Luke, at the original order of the sections in Q (with the exception of some doubtful passages), and to a large extent at its actual wording. In 1907 he published his version of Q under the title *Sprüche und Reden Jesu* ('Sayings and Speeches of Jesus'). This was an exciting piece of detective work; but, in spite of the eminence of the author, most scholars felt that this was going a good deal too fast, and that much more careful and detailed work would be needed before any confident statement could be made.[1]

As we have already indicated, much of the indispensable preliminary work was carried out in the University of Oxford, where for a considerable number of years the seminar that gathered around William Sanday, the Lady Margaret Professor of Divinity, devoted its attention to the problem of the Gospels. In Germany, the seminar is a gathering in which the professor collects under his wings a number of fledgling students, whom he will later send out to propagate his views or to develop their own. In Britain, in so far as the method exists, it tends rather to take the form of a fellowship of scholars, of whom one is president or director, for the leisurely discussion of current problems, in the course of which a common point of view may gradually emerge. Sanday had gathered around him a notable group of men; there was J. C. Hawkins, whom we have already met, W. C. Allen who produced the commentary on Matthew for the *International Critical Commentary*, J. V. Bartlet, the eminent nonconformist, who later had much to do with the plans that led to the formation of the Church of South India, B. H. Streeter, of whom we shall hear again, and the

---

[1] A much more cautious reconstruction is to be found in V. H. Stanton's *The Gospels as Historical Documents*, Part II (1909), pp. 76–106, a monument of patient and careful industry, which in my opinion has been undeservedly forgotten. Stanton was Regius Professor of Divinity at Cambridge from 1916 to 1922. Reviewing Harnack's work in the *Journal of Theological Studies* for April 1907 (pp. 454 ff.), F. C. Burkitt aptly remarked: 'We see clearly enough that we could not have reconstructed the Gospel according to St. Mark out of the other two Synoptic Gospels, although between them nearly all Mark has been incorporated by Matthew and Luke. How futile, therefore, it is to attempt to reconstruct those other literary sources which seem to have been used by Matthew and Luke, but have not been independently preserved.'

young and brilliant N. P. Williams, whose later work was to be in other fields.[1]

Sanday has left an interesting picture of the method of work:

> It has been our custom to take the Synoptic Gospels section by section, with Tischendorf's handy *Synopsis Evangelica* as our basis, but of course calling in the many excellent *Synopses* that are in use, especially Rushbrooke and Wright and among the Germans, Huck. We have taken the section, and have had reports upon it from one or two leading commentaries, usually beginning with the very close and careful treatment of Dr. Bernhard Weiss; we have then discussed it freely among ourselves over the table. In this process opinion has gradually ripened—individual opinion, that is, rather than collective; for we have never sought to fix a corporate opinion, beyond the natural convergence of individual minds.[2]

It is hard to imagine a more pleasant setting for such work, or a better atmosphere than that which Sanday managed to create about him. For these scholars were not dry academics; they were men of profound Christian conviction; what upheld them in the long and often tedious processes of critical study was the hope that at the end of the search they might find that they had come a little nearer to the Son of Man.

After a good many years of study in common, the group resolved to publish a joint volume of essays, and in 1911 *Oxford Studies in the Synoptic Problem* appeared from the press.[3] Here we find ourselves still in the realm of minute detail. Had Mark any acquaintance with Q? What was the original extent of Q? A fresh reconstruction of Q by Dr. Allen. Had Luke one special source, from which he derived all the material which he shares with neither Mark nor Matthew?

All these are important questions, and to none of them is the answer simple. But study cannot go on for ever in this phase of minute research. Sooner or later someone must attempt to create a synthesis; to bring together in one common picture all the scattered fragments with which the preliminary research has had to do. In the years after

[1] A broad-minded seminar! 'We have twice, I think, had lady members for a few meetings'! I like the scholarly 'I think'; Dr. Sanday could not commit himself to certainty about the frequency of so scandalous an invasion.

[2] *Oxford Studies in the Synoptic Problem* (1911), p. viii.

[3] The student will find it fascinating to compare with this volume the *Studies in the Gospels: Essays in Memory of R. H. Lightfoot*, published by another group of Oxford men (slightly diluted by Cambridge!) under the editorship of Professor D. E. Nineham in 1955. In no other way will he be able so quickly to grasp the difference between New Testament study fifty years ago and New Testament study today.

E

the First World War two Oxford scholars attempted to produce the kind of synthesis that would make the results of learned research available to a wider circle.

IV

Of Burnett Hillman Streeter (1874–1937), as of so many others among the scholars who have come before us in this survey, it is impossible to write without affection, tinged in his case with a little amusement. This extraordinarily shy and retiring man succeeded in winning the confidence and affection of generation after generation of undergraduates, the respect of colleagues, and the animosity of some who feared the liberal tendencies of his thought. His interests were large. One of his best-known books, *Reality* (1926), dealt with the problem of science and religion in the modern world. *The Buddha and the Christ* (1932) faced the challenge presented to the Gospel by more ancient and non-Christian philosophies. But perhaps he will be longest remembered for his work on the New Testament. Here, as everywhere, his work was marked by his inveterate habit of asking questions, his refusal to be satisfied by anyone else's answers, his determination to get to the original sources, and a quality of imagination which made his writing always interesting and suggestive even where it did not carry conviction.[1]

In 1924 Streeter published a large book of over 600 pages, called *The Four Gospels: A Study of Origins*, a comprehensive gathering together of the results of the scientific study of the Gospels up till that time. That this is a great book will not, I think, be doubted by anyone who has ever used it. Part of the trouble is that Streeter tried to bring in more than any single book can hold—the manuscript tradition, the Synoptic problem, the Fourth Gospel. Inevitably some parts of the book are much better than others; some sections have aged rapidly and can no longer be regarded as authoritative. But it was a work that needed doing, and much of it was done surpassingly well.

As an illustration of the range and freshness of Streeter's knowledge I may quote a short passage which deeply interested me, when I first read the book nearly forty years ago. Discussing the apparent belief

[1] His own attitude is beautifully summed up in the quotation from Bacon, which appears on p. vi of the book which we are just about to consider. 'The enquiry of truth, which is the love-making or wooing of it; the knowledge of truth, which is the presence of it; and the belief in truth, which is the enjoying of it—is the sovereign good of human nature.'

of the early Christians (John 21) that the Parousia would take place before the death of the last of the original believers, Streeter cites a fascinating modern parallel:

There are those alive who can remember the feeling of trepidation with which members of the Irvingite Church watched the declining years of the last survivor of those twelve 'Apostles' within the life-time of whom Edward Irving, the founder of the community, had prophesied the visible return of Christ. And when the last of these did die, and the Lord did not return, that community received a grievous shock.[1]

The most original contribution of Streeter was in the development of a 'Four-document' theory of the origins of the Gospel. The nineteenth century had known of two—Mark and Q. Streeter was convinced that this investigation could be pushed further, and that it is possible to find in our Gospels traces of other written documents (allowing of course for the almost certain influence of oral tradition at many points). In the outline of the chapter which deals with this theme (pp. 223–70), he summarizes concisely what he believes to lie behind his hypothesis:

It is assumed that a hypothesis which reduces the number of sources to a minimum is more scientific . . . But a plurality of sources is historically more probable. In particular, if Mark is the old Roman Gospel, it is antecedently to be expected that the other Gospels conserve the specific traditions of Jerusalem, Caesarea and Antioch.[2]

Streeter had come to the conclusion that Luke's Gospel appeared, or had at least been prepared, in two different forms. First, a writer had combined the material of Q and the material which is peculiar to Luke (including such notable features as the parables of the Good Samaritan and of the Prodigal Son) in one single document, which Streeter wished to call Proto-Luke. At a later date, the same writer or another writer combined this already existing Gospel with certain

[1] *The Four Gospels*, p. 477. The last Apostle died on 3 February 1901. It is immensely to the credit of the Catholic Apostolic (Irvingite) Church that it had the grace and courage simply to admit that it had made a mistake.

[2] Ibid., p. 223. This idea of *local* church traditions plays a very important part in the development of Streeter's view. It is interesting to read a vigorous defence of this view in the posthumous work of Dr. T. W. Manson, *Studies in the Gospels and Epistles* (1962), pp. 105–22.

selections from Mark, a work with which at an earlier date he had probably been unacquainted. As to the identity of the person who carried out this twofold process of conflation, here are Streeter's views in his own words:

I suggest that the author of Proto-Luke—the person, I mean, who combined together in one document Q and the bulk of the material peculiar to the Third Gospel—was no other than Luke the companion of Paul. And I suggest that this same Luke some years afterwards expanded his own early work by prefixing the stories of the Infancy,[1] and by inserting extracts from Mark—no doubt at the same time making certain minor alterations and additions. For reasons summarised in the last chapter of this volume, I hold that the author of the Third Gospel and the Acts was Luke the companion of Paul.[2]

Proto-Luke has not on the whole found many friends in the world of scholarship. Dr. Vincent Taylor, the Methodist scholar who was later to produce a lengthy and valuable commentary on Mark's Gospel (1952), came out strongly in support of it. But Professor J. M. Creed, who was at that time working on his *Commentary on St. Luke's Gospel* (published in 1930), felt that there was little to be said for the theory, and dismissed it almost contemptuously in a footnote. Creed's authority in such matters was great;[3] British scholarship has tended to accept his judgement, German scholarship was by this time engaged in other lines of research, and seems never to have devoted much attention to Proto-Luke. Yet perhaps this judgement was premature; Streeter's suggestion was an attempt to take seriously the structure of Luke's Gospel, as it is now in our hands, and to account for the peculiarities of that structure as compared with the structure of Matthew. In handling such a complex question it is rarely possible to reach more than reasonable probability; scholarship may yet come

---

[1] It is worth while noting that Dr. Sanday held that, in view of its very strongly Jewish character, the Infancy Narrative in Luke may well have been the *first* part of the Gospel to exist in written form—a view from which I have never seen any reason to dissent.

[2] Op. cit., p. 218.

[3] Creed was an excellent classical scholar, a slow, patient, meticulous worker, unwilling, in the good Cambridge tradition, to print anything until he was sure that he had considered the whole of the available evidence. He had come deeply under the influence of the 'religio-historical' school in Germany, with which we shall be concerned in chapter v, as is evident from his *Commentary on Luke's Gospel*. His death in 1940 at the early age of fifty was a grave loss to English New Testament schorlaship.

round to the view that reasonable probability is exactly what Streeter has been successful in establishing.[1]

Turning now to Matthew, Streeter thinks that here we can see traces of another written document, this time with markedly Judaistic tendencies. Matthew takes Mark as his framework, and then very skilfully combines into five great discourses material which he has taken from Q and other material which he has taken from his own source M. Thus, Luke in its present form is made up of an independent Proto-Luke (L + Q) into which sections of Mark have been introduced; Matthew is an enlarged form of Mark, into which Q and M have been inserted at appropriate points. In each case, of course, the writer finally responsible for the Gospel is an author and not a mere compiler; he has his own interests and his own theology, and exercises wide liberty in the handling of his material, from whatever source it may originally have come.

This is, perhaps, as far as any documentary theory can go. It accounts for almost the whole of our existing Gospels on the basis of four pre-existing documents, all of early date, only one of which, our Mark, has survived. It is ingenious and plausible, based on the consideration of innumerable details, and serious in its attempt to do justice to all the phenomena. The 'four-document theory' was widely welcomed, as giving a fuller and more satisfactory account of Gospel origins than anything else that had preceded it; and, in view of Streeter's reputation for liberal theology, many of his readers were surprised that on the whole his conclusions were so conservative—the Gospels are accepted as generally reliable historical documents, and as based on elements which date from a period removed by less than the span of a single human life from the events which they record. No book has quite taken the place of Streeter's; any serious student of the Gospels is bound to read it, though at many points he may feel free to dissent from its conclusions.[2]

It has to be recognized, however, that Streeter stood at the end of an age, summing up the results of sixty years of intensive research

---

[1] I note that Professor T. W. Manson was prepared to take Proto-Luke seriously: 'It seems to me that Streeter was right in his main contention that the document Proto-Luke was a definite stage in the composition of our Luke and that the next step was the incorporation of extracts from Mark with Proto-Luke rather than the expansion of Mark by the insertion of Proto-Luke material.' *Studies in the Gospels and Epistles* (1962), p. 54. The essay from which this quotation is taken was written in 1944.

[2] For instance, Streeter gives the best short account known to me of the reasons for supposing Mark to be the earliest Gospel (op. cit., pp. 157–81).

since the days of H. J. Holtzmann. When his book appeared, the reaction was already setting in.

The first reaction was against the attempt to define precisely documents which no longer existed, and the existence of which is only inferential. At one time it almost seemed that we could lay our hands on Q—just a little further in the pursuit, and we would have him. Now a great many scholars would prefer to talk of Q-material rather than Q. There is no reason to doubt that collection of the sayings of Jesus began at a very early date, and quite probably in areas of the Christian Church in which Aramaic was still spoken.[1] But the contradictions in which we land ourselves as soon as we try to draw up more exactly the contents of this hypothetical document warn us that it is better to leave the matter a little vague rather than to seek for certainty where certainty is not to be had.[2] The gap between 1924 and 1962 is, however, greater than can be expressed merely in terms of the modification of one hypothesis. Dr. A. M. Farrer has set it out for us cogently and well:

It would be impertinence to suggest that the scholars who established the Q hypothesis reasoned falsely or misunderstood their own business; no less an impertinence than to talk of the great Scholastics so. St. Thomas understood the business of being an Aristotelizing Augustinian, and if I am not his disciple it is not because I find him to have reasoned falsely. It is because I do not concede the premisses from which he reasoned. And if we are not to be Streeterians, it will not be because Dr. Streeter reasoned falsely, but because the premisses from which he reasoned are no longer ours.[3]

It is the business of any history of opinion to take account of the subtle and at the time hardly observed changes, not so much in what

---

[1] Few today hold that Matthew's Gospel as we have it today can be the work of the Apostle Matthew; more favourable consideration can be given to the idea, supported by a rather enigmatic saying of Papias, about A.D. 130, which connects Matthew with 'Oracles of the Lord written in the Hebrew tongue', that Matthew the Apostle did have a hand in the collection, and possibly the writing down, of material of this character.

[2] Dr. A. M. Farrer has contributed to the volume of *Studies in the Gospels* (1955), pp. 55–88, a paper under the engaging title 'On Dispensing with Q', in which, with characteristic verve and ingenuity, he tries to show that Q is one of those entities which, according to late medieval philosophy, are not to be multiplied beyond what is necessary. Consider the possibility that Luke had read Matthew, and John all the other three, and all will be simple. I do not find myself in agreement; I think that Q has come to stay, in the sense explained in the preceding paragraph. I find myself supported by Professor R. H. Fuller, *The New Testament in Current Study* (1962), p. 74, n. 1: 'It is hard to think that the patient work over many years . . . can be blithely dismissed in a few pages.'

[3] *Studies in the Gospels* (1955), pp. 55–56.

men think as in the way in which they think. Dr. Farrer is right in holding that between 1920 and 1950 there was a shift not so much in views and opinions as in the kind of question that scholars asked and in their assessment of the weight to be attached to different kinds of evidence. It will be our business in a later chapter to consider the causes and the nature of that shift. For the moment we are still concerned with the first quarter of the twentieth century, and must consider two others among the outstanding products of the thought and researches of that period.

V

We may remind ourselves that there will always, and necessarily, be three aspects of New Testament study—criticism and analysis of the documents, reconstruction of the history, and theological interpretation. To put it in less technical language, we are entitled to ask three separate and distinct questions: (1) What evidence have we, and what kind of evidence does it prove to be? (2) To what extent, if any, can we answer the simplest question, What happened? (3) Was the event which happened significant, and in what way, if any, is it significant for us today? In the study of Christian origins, it is impossible to keep these questions rigidly separate—they tend to overlap at every point. But it is essential to recognize that they are three separate and distinct questions, that different techniques are needed to deal with them, and that, because the questions are different questions, the kind of answers we may hope to find to them will not be the same kind of answers.

Streeter was primarily concerned with the first of these questions. While he was writing his book on the four Gospels, another notable Oxford scholar was wrestling with the second question—given such evidence as we have, how far is it possible to establish the story of Jesus of Nazareth as a part of human history?

Arthur Cayley Headlam (1862–1947) seemed to be a man born to success. All Streeter's brilliance had brought him little in the way of public honour and recognition. Headlam moved, with a certain inevitability, from one post of distinction to another. In the last twenty-five years of his life he was one of the best-known figures not only in the Church of England but in the whole Church of Christ. To those who did not know him well he seemed cold and aloof. He certainly did not suffer fools gladly, and at times his caustic tongue got him into trouble. Intimate friends, however, have left a very different picture of him; one of the secrets of his power was an ideally happy marriage which lasted for twenty-seven years. Headlam had an almost unlimited capacity for work, and his learning extended into many realms.[1] His mind was capacious, but a little inflexible; once he had made up his mind on a subject, he found it very hard to change, and was inclined to give less than due weight to criticisms of his position which others had found to be valid.[2] This made for clarity of thought and lucidity of expression; it did mean that Headlam, for all his learning, could be out of touch with the movements of thought around him.

Most important of all for our purpose, Headlam had studied ancient history in preparation for 'Greats' at Oxford. While not sharing to the full the belief of Lord Acton in the possibility of a pure and passionless historical study, the results of which would be as unassailable as those of physical science, he was convinced that there is a real objectivity of history. Given certain historical documents, we may hope to attain to reasonably certain historical results, if we handle them in accordance with the rigid rules of historical method.

It was in this spirit that Headlam approached the Gospel records. The results of many years of study were set forth in *The Life and Teaching of Jesus Christ*, a work which appeared in January 1923, just at the time at which Headlam was consecrated to be Bishop of Gloucester.[3] It is an extraordinarily able book; it is not surprising that within four months of publication it had to be twice reprinted. In the Preface Headlam tells us what he hopes to do:

I have aimed, in the first place, at showing that, accepting the results of modern criticism, there is every reason to think that the subject-matter of the first three Gospels represents the traditions about the life and work of Jesus of Nazareth as they were current in the earliest years of the Christian

---

[1] During the discussions on Prayer Book revision in the years following 1920, Headlam formed the impression that Walter Frere (1863–1938), Bishop of Truro, the only competent liturgiologist on the bench, was getting his way too much. Knowing nothing of the subject, Headlam spent £20 on liturgical books, for six months got up an hour earlier every morning; and then, as he remarked to a friend: 'Frere didn't get his way quite as much as he had before.'

[2] This was notably the case with his book *The Doctrine of the Church and Reunion*, which when first published in 1920 aroused a considerable furore of criticism. The fifteen-page Preface to the second edition does little more than reassert Headlam's position: 'In the present edition I have confined myself to making some few corrections, almost entirely verbal. *I have seen no reason for making larger changes*' (op. cit., 2nd ed., p. xxi; our italics); this is Headlam all over!

[3] I think that the book appeared on 25 January, the very day of the consecration; but of this I cannot be sure.

Church. Then, secondly, that it harmonizes with all that we know of the times when Jesus lived and the environment in which he taught. Thirdly, that the teaching of Jesus is harmonious throughout, natural in its language and form to the circumstances and representing a unity of thought transcending anything that had existed before. And then, fourthly, that the life as narrated forms a consistent whole.

If we transpose these four statements into the form of questions, they give us an impeccably precise formulation for the historical approach to the problem of Jesus of Nazareth. And Headlam is right in insisting throughout that what we have to explain is the Christian Church. In history consequences cannot be greater than causes. Here is a great spiritual movement, which has withstood the changes and chances of nineteen centuries. How are we to account for it? The Roman Empire would be inexplicable without Julius Caesar and Augustus; what was the corresponding factor in that other movement in the first century A.D., which led to the birth and growth of the Christian Church?

So Headlam leads us with great erudition through the history of the times, the Jewish background, the Gospel sources, the evidence for the ministry and teaching of Jesus, the growth of opposition to him, his own understanding of his work. Much of this is excellently done; whole sections can still stand, with only minor modification in the light of later research. Unfortunately, Headlam breaks off at the Transfiguration; he had intended to complete the task, but the burdens of the episcopate led him away to other things, and the second volume was never written. But, by the end of this volume, Headlam was satisfied that by the application of purely historical methods it had been possible to arrive at a reasonably reliable outline of the life and teaching of Jesus:

Our purpose was to construct a life on the basis of the material before us, without presuppositions either positive or negative; not to assume what Christian tradition has taught about Jesus, but not to deny it. The one presupposition that we have allowed ourselves is that we must be able to account for the fact of Christianity. A religion of such universal spiritual significance could not be the result of astral fancies or any such thing. Our method has been to construct our story out of our material, primary and secondary, as we might do in secular history, and then consider whether we have succeeded in producing a coherent and consistent narrative. . . .

Jesus was the Messiah. As such he fulfilled all that the Old Testament had to teach, but he always transcended it. As the Son of God he lived in intimate union with the Father. As the Servant of God he fulfilled God's will on earth. As the Son of man he was the Judge of mankind. . . .

I would suggest to you that there is a homogeneity and consistency about the life and the teaching, which we cannot but look upon as a strong proof of authenticity, and the teaching bears the impress of a single mind . . . The teaching of Jesus, as contained in the Gospels, is not a collection of different opinions held by various individuals during a period of fifty to seventy years, but a homogeneous whole coming from one teacher of intense spiritual power.[1]

A sound historical method; but applied to what? In what sense are the Gospels historical documents? Like his contemporary, F. C. Burkitt, Headlam never wavered in the conviction that what we meet in Mark's Gospel is history. There can never be *history*—though there can be annals—without interpretation. But, in the opinion of these scholars, Mark is basically faithful to the facts; following his outline, and supplementing it critically from our sources in the other Gospels, we shall not be far from the original events as they actually took place. This was precisely the conviction that had already been challenged when Headlam's book left the press. He had taken it for granted that Mark's Gospel, allowing for the differences in theme, is history in much the same sense as the *Histories* of the Roman historian Tacitus. A new school was arising which was to maintain that, if we wish to regard the Gospels as being in any sense history, we cannot use the word as we use it of any other document in the whole literature of mankind. Reading Headlam today, we have to project ourselves back into another world which is different from our contemporary world of theological scholarship.

VI

We come now to our third question—that of theological interpretation. What do the Gospels mean to us today? For the classic answer to this question, as given in the period which we are now considering, we have to go back another twenty years to another country and to a scholar of more massive eminence than either Streeter or Headlam. It is hardly possible for the English reader to picture to himself the position occupied by Adolf von Harnack in the world of theological scholarship at the beginning of this century. For nearly

---

[1] Op. cit., pp. 313, 315–16. This is in effect the conclusion of the book.

forty years he bestrode that world like a colossus, as Schleiermacher and Ritschl had done before him, and as, in a rather different way, Karl Barth has done in the years between 1930 and 1950. His productivity was enormous; he touched on every aspect of the study of the New Testament, of early church history, and of the development of doctrine. But he was by no means the typical dry-as-dust professor living immured in his study. He took a prominent part in public life, and one of his main concerns was the relationship between the Gospel and the culture of the times.

When it became known that this great man had delivered in Berlin, in the winter semester of 1899–1900, a series of non-technical lectures under the title *Das Wesen des Christentums*, 'The Essence of Christianity', there was intense excitement. Professor Paul Tillich has described how, immediately on their publication, the railway station at Leipzig was crowded with immense consignments of the books about to be dispatched to every corner of the civilized world. 'By 1927 the volume had already been through fourteen printings, and had been translated into as many languages.'[1] It was received with both enthusiastic acclamation and bitter criticism.

In the Preface to the first English edition Harnack indicated something of his purpose: 'This I know: the theologians of every country only half discharge their duties if they think it enough to treat of the Gospel in the recondite language of learning and bury it in scholarly folios.' It is impossible not to be reminded of Schleiermacher and his *Speeches on Religion to its Cultured Despisers*, which had been delivered, also in Berlin, just a century earlier in 1799, and at last translated into English by John Oman in 1893. Harnack, like Schleiermacher, is conscious of the alienation of the great mass of the educated public in the Germany of his day from the Church and the Gospel. He stands as a prophet, saying, 'Hear ye the word of the Lord'; and trying to proclaim that word in a form which will be relevant and intelligible to a generation the mind of which has been conditioned by many other forces and many other doctrines. His understanding of his task is set forth with great simplicity in the opening sentences of the lectures:

The great English philosopher, John Stuart Mill, has somewhere observed that mankind cannot be too often reminded that there was once a man of the name of Socrates. That is true; but still more important is it to remind

[1] R. Bultmann, Introduction to the reprint issued in Stuttgart in 1950, available in English in the paper-back reprint of 1957.

mankind again and again that a man of the name of Jesus Christ once stood in their midst. The fact, of course, has been brought home to us from our youth up; but unhappily it cannot be said that public instruction in our time is calculated to keep the image of Jesus Christ before us in any impressive way, and make it an inalienable possession after our school-days are over and for our whole life. And although no one who has once absorbed a ray of Christ's light can ever again become as though he had never heard of him; although at the bottom of every soul that has once been touched an impression remains, a confused recollection of this kind, which is often only a 'super-stition', is not enough to give strength and life. But where the demand for further and more trustworthy knowledge about him arises, and a man wants positive information as to who Jesus Christ was, and as to the real purport of his message, he no sooner asks for it than he finds himself, if he consults the literature of the day, surrounded by a clatter of contradictory voices.[1]

What, then, can we do to help this modern man to find himself again in relation to Jesus Christ?

What is Christianity? It is solely in its historical sense that we shall try to answer this question here; that is to say, we shall employ the methods of historical science, and the experience of life gained by studying the actual course of history. This excludes the view of the question taken by the apologist and the religious philosopher.[2]

How far has Harnack been successful in carrying out his own intention?

It goes without saying that *Das Wesen des Christentums* is a great and powerful book. In 1950 it received a notable and rather unexpected tribute from Rudolf Bultmann, whose own ideas are very different from those of Harnack:

Harnack's book is a theological-historical document of the greatest importance. Every theologian who would be clear about the present situation in theology and its origins should be familiar with it. It should, moreover, be a part of required theological training and education ... It should be stressed that this understanding of Christianity, though one may label it 'liberal', is in no wise a lifeless residue of a vanished era which no longer needs to be taken seriously. On the contrary, the liberal understanding, at the very least, contains active impulses which though now obscured never-theless preserve their legitimacy and will recover their validity.[3]

[1] Op. cit. (reprint of 1957), pp. 1–2.   [2] Ibid., p. 6.   [3] Ibid., p. viii.

Bultmann quotes with extraordinary aptness some sentences of Karl Barth:

The theology of every age must be sufficiently strong and free to hear, calmly, attentively, and openly, not only the voices of its favourites, not only the voices of classical antiquity, but all the voices of the past in its entirety. We cannot prescribe who among the collaborators of the past will be welcomed to participate in our own work, and who will not be. For there is always the possibility that in one sense or another we may be in particular need of wholly unexpected voices, and that among them there may be voices which are at first entirely unwelcome.[1]

In Bultmann's opinion Harnack is one of those voices, today perhaps unwelcome, to which we cannot but pay attention.

In reading *Das Wesen des Christentums* it is convenient, as with so many great books, to read the last chapter first, and so to see what the book is really all about. If we start here, we shall find that Harnack is deeply concerned about the threat to Protestantism as he understands it. The threat is threefold—from the State, from the indifference of the masses, and from the timidity of those who desire to rest upon the support of some outward authority for their faith. All these tend in the direction of the Catholicizing of Christian faith. To Harnack the Catholic Church in both its Eastern and its Western forms is the betrayal of the Gospel, since it identifies faith with a doctrine and the community of brethren with a hierarchically controlled organization. Luther's Reformation had been a great blow struck in the cause of spiritual liberty; but Luther himself had been too enmeshed in the medieval tradition to see the full significance of his own rediscovery of the Gospel. Now the danger is acute:

In the face of these three so different forces, what we have to do is to maintain Christian earnestness and liberty as prescribed in the Gospel. Theology alone is unavailing; what is wanted is firmness of Christian character. The evangelical Churches will be pushed into the background if they do not make a stand. It is out of such free creations as the Pauline communities that the Catholic Church arose. Who can guarantee that those Churches, too, will not become 'Catholic', which had their origin in 'the liberty of a Christian man'?[2]

We now know where we are. To Harnack the Gospel is the great

[1] *Die protestantische Theologie im 19. Jahrhundert* (1947, English trans., 1960), pp. 2 ff.
[2] Op. cit., pp. 297–8.

declaration of the spiritual liberty of mankind; this is the clue which will guide him in all the intricacies of his researches; this is what he will primarily look for in the message and mission of Jesus Christ. It is in this sense that Harnack can be spoken of as a representative of the liberal tradition in the interpretation of the life of Jesus.[1]

This sense of liberation runs through the whole of Harnack's exposition of the Gospel. What was the difference between Jesus and the Jews to whom he first proclaimed the message?

They thought of God as a despot guarding the ceremonial observances in his household; he breathed in the presence of God. They saw him only in his law, which they had converted into a labyrinth of dark defiles, blind alleys and secret passages; he saw and felt him everywhere. They were in possession of a thousand of his commandments, and thought therefore that they knew him; he had one only, and knew him by it. They had made this religion into an earthly trade, and there was nothing more detestable; he proclaimed the living God and the soul's nobility.[2]

This is a fine programme of spiritual liberation. As Harnack sees it, the proclamation of it by Jesus can be summed up under three headings:

The kingdom of God and its coming.
God the Father and the infinite value of the human soul.
The higher righteousness and the commandment of love.

But in point of fact these all coalesce: 'for ultimately the kingdom is nothing but the treasure which the soul possesses in the eternal and merciful God. It needs only a few touches to develop this thought into everything that, taking Jesus' sayings as its groundwork, Christendom has known and striven to maintain as hope, faith and love.'[3]

We cannot evade the question of the relation of Jesus himself to the Gospel which he preached; but 'there are phenomena which cannot, without the aid of symbols, be brought within the range of the understanding'. Jesus was convinced that he is the Son of God in a sense in which no other man is Son of God. He was convinced that he is the way to the Father, and as he is the anointed of the Father, so he is the judge as well.

---

[1] But his possession of a sound historical method marks him off radically from the writers of the 'liberal' lives of Jesus in the nineteenth century.

[2] Op. cit., pp. 50–1.

[3] Ibid., p. 77.

Was he mistaken? Neither his immediate posterity nor the course of subsequent history has decided against him. It is not as a mere factor that he is connected with the Gospel; *he was its personal realization and its strength, and this he is felt to be still.* Fire is kindled only by fire; personal life only by personal forces . . . History shows that he is the one who brings the weary and heavy laden to God; and, again, that he it was who raised mankind to the new level; and his teaching is still the touchstone, in that it brings men to bliss and brings them to judgement.[1]

These brief selections will give the reader some impression of the intense sincerity of Harnack, and of the rhetorical skill with which he presents his arguments. They may indicate, also, some of the questions which are suggested, and left unanswered, by this profoundly impressive book.

The kingdom of God is here made a matter of ethical, spiritual, and interior renewal. But is this what the kingdom of God really is, as proclaimed by Jesus in the Gospels?

It is true that Jesus is all this in the experience of men. But how does it come about that he is able to do all this for us? Who, in fact, is he? It is true that, when we speak of the relationship of God to men, of eternity to time, we can speak only in the language of symbols. But, is it not the case that, in his use of the New Testament symbols, Harnack has deftly evacuated them of their meaning? We cannot permanently evade the question as to the relationship of Jesus to God. Our ultimate question is not about Jesus, but about the Father; and for the answer to our question the Christian doctrine of the Trinity is the developed symbol.

Furthermore, if this was all that Jesus ever said and did, why should anyone ever have wished to crucify him? No doubt his message, even as set forth by Harnack, is challenging and disturbing, but perhaps rather to the individual than to a whole order of society. But it is clear from the Gospels that Jesus was felt by the Jewish leaders to be disturbing in a far more radical way than this. The question he asked was literally a question of life and death. From their own point of view they were absolutely right in giving the answer that they did.

It cannot be said that Harnack's presentation is at any point false. The weaknesses in it are much more a matter of selection and of emphasis. For all his sound historical method, Harnack has fallen into the error of trying too much to make Jesus into a man of our age instead

[1] Op. cit., p. 145.

of letting him remain firmly planted in his own. Although he disclaims the role of an apologist, perhaps he is trying a little too hard to make Jesus Christ acceptable to the men of his own day. But one thing is quite certain—that, though Jesus Christ can always be made intelligible to the men of every generation, his Gospel will always be a scandal, an offence, except to those who through faith are prepared to accept that destruction of the old order and that renewal of themselves for which the Crucifixion and the Resurrection of Jesus Christ stand as the changeless symbols—an eternal reality firmly planted in the midst of time.

You may expel theology with a pitchfork, but she will always return. All the ultimate questions about man and his life are theological. The moment I begin to think about my own existence, I am faced by unfathomable mysteries. I may deny the existence of these mysteries. What I cannot do is to domesticate them, to find pretended solutions in the non-mysterious categories of the visible world and of day-to-day experience. The danger for the liberal lies always in his tendency to domesticate Jesus Christ, to make him out to be less dangerous than he really is, to rob him of his mystery, and to offer solutions of the Gospel problems which are no real solutions. When that happens, the mystery will painfully and violently reassert itself; theology driven out by the back door will re-enter at the front. When Harnack gave his famous lectures, the men were already born who would create the theological revolution of our day. Since they have taught and written, Harnack is irrecoverably dated; his work is of permanent value, but it belongs to a period, and expresses an outlook, which are no longer ours.

Chapter V

GREEKS AND CHRISTIANS

I

THE doctrine of Biblical inspiration led men to separate the Bible from all other books, and so made it impossible for them to read it impartially and with open eyes. In exactly the same way belief in the truth of Christianity led scholars to view the Christian faith in isolation—as a separate whole revealed by God in its perfection, and therefore only slightly if at all related to other ideas and other traditions. The continuity of the Christian faith with Judaism was apprehended. The study of the Old Testament was essential for the elucidation of the New Testament texts; it was recognized that an understanding of the Jewish faith as it was in the time of Jesus and in the two succeeding centuries could contribute to our understanding of the Gospel and of the early Church. With the non-Jewish and Hellenistic environment it was otherwise. The faith was regarded as standing in opposition to this environment, threatened by its hostility, endangered by the penetrating influences which could produce heresy, but guarding its purity by loyalty to the faith once delivered to the saints.

If our attitude today is very different, this is due to one man more than to any other—Edwin Hatch, who was born in 1835 and died in 1889. Hatch was a great scholar, who somehow seemed never to receive the recognition that his merits demanded. It may be that his views were too liberal to meet with the approval of the authorities of his day; be that as it may, he was left in a position of comparative obscurity in Oxford, and never secured what is commonly called promotion in the Church. His most permanent legacy is the *Concordance to the Septuagint*, to which he devoted many years of work, and which was completed by Dr. Redpath—an indispensable aid to detailed work on both the Old and New Testaments. He also produced two notable sets of lectures. His Bampton Lectures on *The Organization of the Early Christian Churches* (1881) aroused immediate attention in Germany, and had the unusual honour of being translated by no less a person than Harnack—a notable example of one great scholar being translated by another. His Hibbert Lectures on *The Influence of Greek*

Ideas on Christianity (1889) were also translated into German, this time by E. Preuschen, and published with additions by Harnack in 1892. It is only rarely that English work receives such immediate recognition in Germany.

In introducing the new paper-back edition of *The Influence of Greek Ideas*,[1] the distinguished American scholar Dr. F. C. Grant remarks that 'this book ... is a part of the priceless legacy which nineteenth-century historical scholarship has bequeathed to the twentieth—and possibly to the twenty-first. With others of its kind, these are works which age cannot wither nor time decay, but are permanent contributions to knowledge—like those of Darwin, Kelvin, and the elder Huxley in the realm of physical science.'

Hatch opens his study by referring to the small amount of attention that had been devoted to the subject up to his time;[2] and then lays down two cardinal principles which are to guide the student in his handling of the materials:

1. It is impossible to separate the religious phenomena [of a given race] from the other phenomena, in the same way that you can separate a vein of silver from the rock in which it is embedded ... They are separable from the whole mass of phenomena, not in fact, but only in thought. We may concentrate our attention chiefly upon them, but they still remain part of the whole complex life of the time, and they cannot be understood except in relation to that life.

2. No permanent change takes place in the religious beliefs or usages of a race which is not rooted in the existing beliefs and usages of that race. The truth which Aristotle enunciated, that all intellectual teaching is based on what is previously known to the person taught, is applicable to a race as well as to an individual, and to beliefs even more than to knowledge. A religious change is, like a physiological change, of the nature of assimilation by, and absorption into, existing elements.[3]

---

[1] Harper and Brothers, New York, 1957.

[2] It is important to be clear as to exactly what is meant. Hatch is referring to the study of the *Hellenistic* world. A good deal had been done to illustrate the text of the New Testament from classical sources. Here one of the most notable pioneers was the polymath of Basel, Johann Jakob Wettstein (1693–1754), who in his great edition of the New Testament (1751–2) included in the commentary innumerable illustrative passages from classical and rabbinic sources. This inexhaustible granary has been used, with and without acknowledgement, by a great many later commentators. Various plans have been made for 'a new Wettstein'. The matter is now in the hands of the University of Utrecht. Just in time for mention here, I have received a copy of the lecture delivered by Professor W. C. van Unnik on 29 March 1963: *Corpus Hellenisticum Novi Testamenti* (in Dutch). For further details on Wettstein, see C. L. Hulbert-Powell, *J. J. Wettstein* (1938).

[3] Hatch, op. cit., pp. 3–4.

Hatch goes on to point out the difficulty that we have in transporting ourselves through imagination into the climate of thought of the ancient world—our unconscious presuppositions are so different from those of the Mediterranean world in the time of Paul that, unless we are careful to allow for them all the time, these presuppositions will distort the ancient material as we handle it. He gives an excellent illustration. We think of religion as an affair between the soul of man and God; but, in the ancient world,

it was a matter which lay, not between the soul and God, but between the individual and the State. Conscience had no place in it. Worship was an ancestral usage which the State sanctioned and enforced. It was one of the ordinary duties of life. The neglect of it, and still more the disavowal of it, was a crime. An emperor might pity the offender for his obstinacy, but he must necessarily either compel him to obey or punish him for his disobedience.[1]

Then, on the basis of a comprehensive knowledge of the literature, both Christian and non-Christian, Hatch draws a fascinating picture of Greek life in the early centuries of our era under various aspects— Greek education, Greek rhetoric, Greek theology, and so on—in every case with careful evaluation of the effect of the Greek on the Christian tradition. No summary or series of excerpts can do justice to the vividness of this living representation; its power depends upon the steady accumulation of detail, and it must be read as a whole. We have space only to take a glance at Hatch's conclusion:

The result is the introduction into Christianity of the three chief products of the Greek mind—Rhetoric, Logic, and Metaphysics. I venture to claim to have shown that a large part of what are sometimes called Christian doctrines, and many usages which have prevailed and continue to prevail in the Christian Church, are in reality Greek theories and Greek usages changed in form and colour by the influence of primitive Christianity, but in their essence Greek still ... The question which forces itself upon our attention as the phenomena pass before us in review, is the question of the relation of these Greek elements in Christianity to the nature of Christianity itself. The question is vital. Its importance can hardly be over-estimated.[2]

These words of Edwin Hatch, spoken in 1888, are of the most burning relevance today, when the question of the Semitic and the

[1] Op. cit., pp. 21–22. [2] Ibid., pp. 350–1.

Hellenistic elements in the Christian faith is once again the subject of one of the liveliest theological debates of our time. This will come before us in our last chapter. Before we come to that, we must take up certain other considerations that are suggested by the reading of Hatch's book. He deals mainly with the period of developed Christianity from the middle of the second century on; and his picture is drawn almost exclusively from literary sources, from the works of essayists, satirists, and philosophers. Clearly, two questions must be asked. The churches of the New Testament lived in a Hellenistic environment; is it possible to trace the Greek influence back into the time of the New Testament itself? Secondly, is it possible to go behind the literary records, which of their nature are bound to be a little artificial, and to have recourse to other sources of a different kind, which will bring us more closely into touch with the life of ordinary people in those distant times? The answer is that today we have in overflowing abundance non-literary material, out of which the patient labour of scholars has been able to reconstruct for us in quite astonishing detail the life, the hopes and fears, the religious thoughts of the folk of the days of Paul and James and John.

II

The first source of information is to be found in the thousands of inscriptions engraved on stone and scattered over the whole of the European and North African world. Almost any museum will offer specimens, and the observer of the twentieth century is often fain to admire the exquisite lettering in which the ancient stonemason displayed the excellence of his craft. Many of these inscriptions are on tomb-stones, brief, uninformative, giving only the name and age of the deceased; some are much longer, and include laudatory accounts of virtues and rough poems, not rarely remarkable by their disregard of the elementary rules of Greek and Roman prosody. But some are public inscriptions, set up by authority, and these give us a great deal of information concerning historical events of which we should otherwise be ignorant; by far the most famous of these is the *Monumentum Ancyranum*, the most complete of the surviving copies of the great record set up by order of the Emperor Augustus himself, in which he traces the events of his reign and his own interpretation of them.[1]

---

[1] The *Monumentum Ancyranum* was discovered in the neighbourhood of Ankara, in 1555; to the original Latin a Greek translation has been added. The classic edition, with commentary, is that of Theodor Mommsen (1865).

The nineteenth century was the period in which great collections of these inscriptions were made and published. It was obvious that they must contain a certain amount of material that would be useful to the Christian historian. Many have worked in this field; but one name stands out above all others as that of the scholar who has worked with greater patience and success than any other in the relating of the evidence of the inscriptions to New Testament interpretation. Sir William Ramsay (1851–1939) was Professor of Humanity at the University of Aberdeen. The long academic vacations gave him the opportunity to pursue his passion for research as a practical archaeologist. Not content with handling the published results of others, Ramsay went year after year to Asia Minor, saw for himself, and made his own discoveries. We have a charming description of him at work from the pen of another great and notable traveller, Gertrude Bell, who shared with Ramsay some of his journeys and researches, and was herself an archaeologist of considerable merit:

MADAN SHEHAR
Saturday, May 25, 1907

The Ramsays arrived yesterday. I was in the middle of digging up a Church, when suddenly 2 carts hove into sight and there they were. It was about 3 in the afternoon. They instantly got out, refused to think of going to the tents, Lady R. made tea (for they were starving) in the open and R. oblivious of all other considerations was at once lost in the problems the Church presented. It was too delightful to have someone as much excited about it as I was . . . .

DAILE
June 8, 1907

We are getting so much material that it will certainly make a book. Our plan is that Sir W. shall write the historic and epigraphic part and I the architectural. I think it will be worth doing, for this is the first time that an accurate study has been made of any one district in these parts, hitherto people have only travelled through and seen what they could see and gone on . . . I should have been helpless here without Sir W. and the more I work with him the more I like him and respect his knowledge. In fact it is being a magnificent success, quite everything I hoped it would be.[1]

---

[1] *The Letters of Gertrude Bell*, selected and edited by Lady Bell, D.B.E. (1927), vol. i, pp. 239, 242. My use of this quotation presents source critics with an interesting problem. Anyone who has read Dr. W. F. Howard's delightful *Romance of New Testament Scholarship* is likely to remember that he has quoted the same book and part of the same passage. How does it come about that we have both quoted a book that stands rather remote from our immediate theme? The obvious solution is that I have just cribbed from

The most notable of all Ramsay's discoveries (1883) was the funerary inscription of Abercius, Bishop of Hieropolis in the later years of the second century A.D. This unusual document tells us something of the bishop's life, but in such strangely allusive terms that some have thought that it springs not from Christian faith but from the mystery cult of Attis that was prevalent in those regions at the time. This idea has now been given up; this is an unmistakably Christian document, and is a most interesting illustration of the way in which in the early days, when persecution was still a possibility, Christians developed a kind of secret language in which every symbol would at once be intelligible to the Christian but might convey little or nothing to the uninitiated. Every Christian knew that the fish is a symbol of Jesus Christ;[1] how far is this likely to have been known to those who were not Christians at that time?[2]

Ramsay's investigations, however, carried him back also to New Testament times, and in particular to a minute checking of the accuracy and reliability of the Lucan writings. As he himself has told us, he had in his younger days been deeply influenced by the speculations of the Tübingen school, and approached Luke without any prejudice in his favour, indeed with rather strong scepticism as to his reliability as an historian. The story of his researches is also the story of his gradual conversion to the view that Luke is a most careful and trustworthy writer.

Luke is the one New Testament writer who can be called, in the strict sense of the term, an historian. Inevitably he refers often, and especially in the Acts of the Apostles, to contemporary events, situations, and forms of speech. If it can be shown that he is minutely accurate in

[1] Almost certainly from the initial letters in Greek—*Iesous Christos Theou 'Uios Soter* = *Ichthus* = Fish = Jesus Christ Son of God Saviour.

[2] The whole epitaph may be read as No. 64 in vol. i of B. J. Kidd's *Documents Illustrative of the History of the Church*. The Greek text, with translation, is conveniently to be found in Lightfoot's *Apostolic Fathers* (1889), vol. ii, I, pp. 492–501.

Howard. The real answer is much less likely, and one that no source critic could have guessed. When I decided to include a section on Sir William Ramsay, I recalled from my reading of thirty years earlier these passages from the *Letters of Gertrude Bell*, and decided, without even looking up or verifying the passage, to quote it. Some months later I read Dr. Howard's book, and found that we had quite independently agreed on the appropriateness of the quotation. Dr. Howard also quotes a very pleasant passage from D. G. Hogarth's *The Accidents of an Antiquary's Life* (1910), a book which was not familiar to me: 'Ramsay had made to himself a European reputation as an explorer of Asia Minor at a cost which another man would think scarcely sufficient for the tour of Germany; and it had become his principle, as for similar reasons it has become Petrie's, to suffer none but the barest means to his end' (pp. 5 ff.).

these points, that will raise at least a presumption that he is accurate in other matters, for which independent contemporary evidence is not available to us. One matter on which the inscriptions give us a great deal of information is the titles borne at various times by the officials of the great cities which Paul is stated to have visited in the course of his travels; and here we find that the writer of Acts knew the correct titles, and used them with unvarying precision. In the words of Ramsay: 'The officials with whom Paul and his companions were brought in contact are those who would be there. Every person is found just where he ought to be: proconsuls in senatorial provinces, asiarchs in Ephesus, strategoi in Philippi, politarchs in Thessalonica, magicians and soothsayers everywhere.'[1] The most remarkable of these titles is 'politarch', the ruler of the city. It is used in Acts 17. 6 of the chief men of the city of Thessalonica. Previously, this word had been completely unknown except for this passage of the Acts. It has now been found in nineteen inscriptions, dating from the second century B.C. to the third century A.D. Five of these inscriptions refer to Thessalonica, which had five politarchs in the reign of Augustus and six at later times. Exactly the right title is used at exactly the right time and place.

Experience shows that nothing is more difficult than to get titles exactly right. Our French neighbours seem to have given up the struggle in despair, and it seems almost a point of honour with them to get English titles hopelessly mixed, just as no French bibliography ever manages to cope adequately with the problems of English spelling and capitalization. But even the English writer is liable occasionally to slip, and to be a little uncertain as to the difference between Lady Brown, the Lady Agnes Brown, and Agnes Lady Brown. And anyone who is familiar with the universities both of Oxford and Cambridge knows the unimaginable pitfalls presented to the unwary by the difference in vocabulary between the two. At Oxford your tutor is a man who tries to teach you something; at Cambridge the last thing your tutor would ever think of doing would be to teach you anything—he sends you along to someone else for that purpose. It is precisely by errors in such minor matters that a writer gives himself away; and this is particularly true if there has been a change in style and title at a date which we can precisely identify.

Imagine an English city, which in 1962 has taken a step up in the

[1] The Bearing of Recent Discovery on the Trustworthiness of the New Testament (1915), pp. 96–97.

world, and has been provided with a Lord Mayor instead of a mere mayor. If a writer refers to a subsequent civic head of the city as 'the mayor', this does not necessarily mean that his information is defective; he may, through a slip of memory, have carried over to a later date a title which had an earlier and valid existence. But if, in writing of a period earlier than 1962, he refers to the Lord Mayor, he is certainly guilty of an anachronism—he is either unaware that a change of title has taken place, or reveals that he is unaware of the date at which the change was effected. Now this is exactly the kind of thing that was happening the whole time in the Roman Empire, as will be obvious to anyone who takes the trouble to find out which Herod was governing how much of Palestine at what time, and with what title. The man who manages to get everything right in relation to the time about which he is writing is certainly a careful, and almost certainly a contemporary, historian.

Ramsay was led by his study of the inscriptions to ask one specially interesting and important question: Who were the Galatians? When Paul cries out in his Epistle, 'O foolish Galatians', whom is he addressing? The old view was that the Galatians were the Gaulish inhabitants of the high central tableland of Asia Minor, whose territory Paul passed through on his second missionary journey. If this is correct, the letter to them cannot have been written earlier than A.D. 53, and we are faced with the difficult problem that it makes no mention of the 'Council of Jerusalem' recorded in Acts 15, nor of the decisions concerning the rights of Gentile Christians which were made at that Council. Now Baur, as we have seen, had laid down the correct principle that Paul's letters are our primary document, and that, in case of direct disagreement between the Acts and the Epistles, it is the Epistles that are to be preferred. It was, then, easy for the adherents of this school to explain why Paul never refers to the Council; he never refers to it because it never happened at all—it is a sheer invention of the writer of the Acts of the Apostles. This seems to attribute rather large powers of invention to the writer of Acts; but this view of his manner of writing history was widely held a century ago, and in consequence hardly any value was ascribed to his work as historical evidence for the events of the first century.

Ramsay, on the basis of his vast knowledge of the inscriptional material, came forward with a very different theory regarding the date and destination of the Epistle to the Galatians.[1] 'Galatians' in his

---

[1] *A Historical Commentary on the Epistle to the Galatians* (1899).

view referred to the inhabitants of the cities of Antioch in Pisidia, Iconium, Lystra, and so forth, whom Paul had encountered on his *first* missionary journey. These people were not Galatians by race, but they were inhabitants of the Roman province of Galatia; and so to address them as Galatians would have been correct, acceptable, and possibly even a little flattering to their vanity. But, if this identification is correct, there is no reason why the Epistle to the Galatians should not be brought forward to a considerably earlier date than that traditionally ascribed to it. It might well fall between the first and the second of Paul's missionary journeys. In that case, there would be a very good reason for Paul's failure to mention the apostolic Council—when the letter was written, it had not yet taken place. The visit to Jerusalem to which Paul refers in Galatians 2. 1–10 is not that described in Acts 15, but that referred to in Acts 11. The Galatian letter is written about the time at which Paul is thinking of or planning the visit to Jerusalem which will later be described in Acts 15. If this view, or anything like it, is correct, much of the alleged contradiction between the evidence of Acts and that of the Pauline Epistles proves to be no contradiction at all.

It cannot be said that unanimity has been reached by scholars on the subject of the Epistle to the Galatians. Until recently British scholarship was almost unanimous in accepting the 'South-Galatian' theory and the early date for the Epistle, though with many differences of interpretation in detail. German scholarship still favours the 'North-Galatian' view and the later date.[1] Very few German scholars have any personal acquaintance with the archaeological evidence, and it is possible that they tend to underestimate its significance.[2] This is one of the points at which further study may lead us to greater certainty than we possess at the present time. It is the merit of Ramsay to have opened up and supported with great erudition and originality a new and fruitful solution of one of the most complex and difficult problems in the whole field of New Testament interpretation.

The later work of Ramsay has tended to cast a shadow upon the value of his earlier contributions. In later years he came to be almost obsessed by the desire to prove the absolute accuracy of the New

[1] An exception on the British side is Professor A. D. Nock in his suggestive little book on St. Paul in the Home University Library Series (1938).

[2] It is characteristic of German scholarship that the name of W. M. Ramsay does not appear in either the text or the index of Professor W. G. Kümmel's admirable study *Das neue Testament* to which we have had occasion to refer from time to time. Professor F. F. Bruce, in the introduction to his commentary on the *Acts of the Apostles*, refers to the undue neglect to which the work of Ramsay has been relegated.

Testament in every detail, in the light of the kind of evidence that he could supply. This is neither necessary nor possible. What Ramsay had done conclusively and finally was to exclude certain possibilities. As seen in the light of the archaeological evidence, the New Testament reflects the conditions of the second half of the first century A.D., and does not reflect the conditions of any later date. Historically it is of the greatest importance that this should have been so effectively established. In all matters of external fact the author of the Acts is seen to have been minutely careful and accurate, as only a contemporary can be. But this does not prove, though it may suggest, that he is equally accurate in all other respects, and in his interpretation of the progress of the Gospel in the first generation after the Resurrection. Grateful as we are for every piece of help that archaeology may give, when it has done its utmost we shall still be left with a great many problems on our hands.

III

The second great revelation of the ancient world has come to us from the sands of Egypt. A certain number of papyri had been known as early as the eighteenth century, the first discoveries having been made in 1778; but their number was small and their importance was not generally recognized. It was only from 1877 onwards, with new discoveries in Egypt, that the trickle developed into a flood. Then in 1897 the rubbish-heaps of the ancient city of Oxyrhynchus began to be systematically searched. In the dry clear air of Egypt, where it hardly ever rains, decay of the kind that is universal in moister climates is unknown. Even delicate materials can survive for many centuries. Papyri in their thousands began to emerge from the sands, and a picture of the ancient world, such as no one had believed that it would ever be possible to recover, began to take shape before the eyes of men. The greater part of the work of decipherment and publication was carried out by two British scholars, B. P. Grenfell and A. S. Hunt (1898 onwards). We who have lived through the period of the Qumran discoveries, which will come before us in our last chapter, can well picture to ourselves the excitements of sixty years ago, as volume after volume of the Oxyrhynchus papyri appeared from the press. Quite literally no one knew what might turn up next.

The variety of the new material which we owe to the papyri is extraordinary. Some of them have given back to us classical texts, which were known to have existed, but which had almost completely disappeared—the lyric poet Bacchylides, the work of Aristotle on the constitution of Athens, the *Ichneutae* of Sophocles, several plays of the comic poet Menander.[1] A roll of the poetess Sappho turned up, and unfortunately disintegrated almost completely before it could be read.[2] A number of 'Sayings of Jesus', some of them previously entirely unknown, came to light. As we have seen, Biblical manuscripts of the utmost importance have come into our hands, and have carried our evidence for the text of the New Testament a hundred years nearer to the original than any manuscript which was previously in our possession. Even more precious than the great Chester Beatty papyri is a tiny fragment of St. John's Gospel, which the experts date not later than A.D. 130, and which, if the experts are right, brings us back within a very few years of the actual writing of the Gospel.[3]

By far the greater part of the papyri are, however, popular documents —bills, tax-receipts, fragments of letters—exactly the kind of thing which would be picked up out of the waste-paper baskets of any great city at the present time. A few of these are interesting, and have become famous—there is the letter from the naughty schoolboy to his father; the letter from the husband to the wife who is expecting a baby, telling her that if it is a son she is to bring it up, but if it is a daughter she is to expose it. There are letters from soldiers to their commanding officers asking for extension of leave.[4] Most of them, however, are extremely dull, and pabulum only for the scholar with some special antiquarian interest. Yet, dull or interesting, many of these papyri do give us exactly what the great Lightfoot had desiderated forty years before—specimens of the way in which people actually spoke and wrote in the days of the New Testament.

One of the first results of these new discoveries was a revolution in the estimate made by scholars of the Greek in which the New Testament was written. It had long been recognized that 'Biblical Greek' was not the same as classical Greek. But to a large extent the

[1] *The Times* of 22 June 1963 announced the discovery of considerable fragments of Menander's play *The Man from Sikyon*; it is believed by the experts that this papyrus was written not much more than seventy years after the death of Menander.

[2] One Greek comedy recovered from the rubbish heaps contained long passages in an unknown language, which was believed to be Indian; it has now been identified as old Canarese.

[3] Published in 1935 by C. H. Roberts, *An Unpublished Fragment of the Fourth Gospel*, with detailed arguments as to the dating of the fragment.

[4] All the more interesting examples known up to the date of publication have been assembled by G. Milligan in *Selections from the Greek Papyri* (1910). See especially pp. 32–33, 102–3, and the valuable summary on pp. xxxi–xxxii.

interpretation of it was vitiated by two assumptions which, consciously or unconsciously, were made by almost all scholars; the first was that the grammatical and syntactical standards of classical Greek could be applied to the New Testament—an erroneous idea which sent Westcott off on endless wild-goose chases after exact classical shades of meaning which had in fact long since disappeared from the language; the second that Biblical Greek was markedly distinct from the secular Greek of the time in which the New Testament was written. The papyri emerge from the grave; and, lo and behold, we find that New Testament Greek is simply the *Koinē*, the common form of Greek, simplified down from the classical standards, which had become widely used throughout the East as a result of the campaigns of Alexander the Great.

Where the New Testament differed from classical standards, it had been the habit of the pedagogues to treat it as 'bad Greek' or 'degenerate Greek'. Now it came to be seen that the *Koinē* really is a language with rights of its own.

A very elaborate and perfect form of human speech does not usually last very long—it makes too great demands on the patience and intelligence of ordinary human beings in a hurry. The elaborate perfection changes into something more simple and manageable. Classical Sanskrit is an instrument of extraordinary delicacy and flexibility; but almost before it had reached its perfection it had begun to break down into the *Prākrits*, the ancestors of the modern languages of northern India.[1] That very conservative people the Icelanders have kept their beautiful but difficult and highly inflected language almost in the form in which it existed when the Edda was composed seven hundred years ago; but in all the other Scandinavian languages disintegration and simplification have gone forward, the successive stages being marked in Swedish, Danish, and Norwegian. Attic Greek is unsurpassed as a vehicle for the expression of every possible shade of human thought and feeling; but it is found in its perfection in but few writers, among them the great writer of comedies, Aristophanes; in view of its extreme complexity, it is not surprising that very soon the tendency to simplification began to set in. The *Koinē* represents a rather late phase of disintegration and simplification.[2]

[1] The Buddhist Scriptures are written in Pālī, that Prākrit of which we have the largest literary remains.

[2] It must not be forgotten that though Attica produced a great proportion of Greek literature in its highest manifestations, many other forms of the Greek language besides the Attic were in existence, notably the Ionic, in which Herodotus wrote his history.

That this was the true nature of New Testament Greek was perhaps first grasped by the Greek scholar George Hatzidakis, who was naturally helped by his knowledge of modern Greek and its evolution.[1] But the incomparable popularizer of the new knowledge was the Berlin scholar Adolf Deissmann (1866–1937). His great book, *Licht vom Osten* (1908), translated into English under the title *Light from the Ancient East* (1st ed., 1910), went through edition after edition, and helped to change the mind of every reader. Many words which had previously been known only in 'Biblical' Greek were now shown to have been quite common in the language of New Testament times. Constructions or idioms which had previously seemed odd now found their ready explanation. We now know that 'the Prodigal Son did not vaguely "gather together" all his share of his father's substance: he "realized" it, converted it into ready money. St. Paul had not heard that some of the Thessalonians were "walking disorderly", but that they were "playing truant", not going to work, in expectation of the imminent end of the world. Judas carried the "money-box", not the bag.'[2]

All this is valuable and useful. One study of New Testament Greek after another has shown the deep influence of the papyrus discoveries. The pioneer in the application of scientific linguistic method to New Testament Greek in the light of the new information was the Methodist scholar J. H. Moulton (1863–1917), who succeeded, as even the Germans admitted, in making philology exciting; after his death his great *Grammar of New Testament Greek* (vol. i, 1906) was continued by another Methodist, equally admirable in scholarship, W. F. Howard, and is now at last completed by the publication, just as this chapter goes to press, of the third section, *Syntax*, the work of Dr. N. Turner. Parallel to this, in quite recent times has appeared the fine fruit of long years of endeavour, the ninth edition of the grammar of Friedrich Blass (1843–1907), prepared by Professor Debrunner, in both German (1954) and English (1961) editions, the English splendidly produced by the Cambridge University Press.[3]

---

[1] Hatzidakis published his grammar of modern Greek in 1892.

[2] E. C. Hoskyns and N. Davey, *The Riddle of the New Testament* (1931), p. 24.

[3] Albert Debrunner (d. 1958) was responsible for the fourth edition, a comprehensive revision of the work of Blass, which appeared in 1913, and made the perfection of the book his life-work. The English edition, by Robert W. Funk, is a good deal more than a mere translation; Professor Funk was able to use a number of notes prepared by Professor Debrunner before his death, and by rearrangement greatly to improve the order and the perspicuity of the material.

That which is new is always exciting, and there is an inevitable tendency for its importance to be overestimated. Some of our experts today speak as though the *Koinē* was a world to itself unrelated to all that had come before it, and as though a knowledge of classical Greek was almost a drawback to the student of the New Testament. This view of the *Koinē*, important as is the new knowledge which has led to our better understanding of it, simply cannot be maintained. Not long ago, I read through the New Testament in Greek in three months at the rate of three or four chapters a day. The thing that impressed me, as a student of classical Greek, was not that all this is strange and new, but that on the whole these writers handle the Greek language so extraordinarily well. They do not write exactly as Plato or Demosthenes wrote; but they knew what they wanted to say, and went straight to their object with that directness and economy of words which is the indispensable condition of great writing. There is an immense difference between the vigour and general correctness of the New Testament writers,[1] and the halting, broken jargon of so many writers of the papyri. This is literature. T. R. Glover, who had an exceptionally wide knowledge of the literature of the time, both Greek and Latin, once remarked to me that Paul is obviously the greatest writer of the first and second centuries after Christ, an opinion which was shared by the most notable classical scholar of this century, von Wilamowitz-Moellendorff.[2] Of course Paul does not always write correct and tidy Greek. His use of prepositions is the nightmare of his commentators, and his syntax very frequently breaks down under the weight of what he has to say. I have often pictured Paul dictating so fast that the wretched Tertius (Romans 16. 22) simply got down all he could and left the rest to chance![3] But these letters have survived because they are great literature, and not only because they are great religious truth.

[1] The Apocalypse is, of course, an exception, with its astonishing Semitic Greek, perhaps deliberately adopted by a writer who could write much more correctly when he wished.

[2] 'This Jew, this Christian, thinks and writes in Greek for all the world, though primarily for the brethren whom he directly addresses. His Greek is dependent on no tradition and no model; unaided it wells up in an irresistible stream directly from his heart. Yet it is Greek, and no translation from Aramaic, as are the words of Jesus. All this constitutes Paul one of the classic writers of Hellas. At last, at last we encounter a man who speaks in Greek out of a fresh and inner experience of life . . . This epistolary style is Paul's and Paul's alone.' *Die Kultur der Gegenwart* (3rd ed., 1912), p. 232.

[3] Professor Moule, in a personal communication, questions whether Paul can actually have dictated: 'in a good many passages I think he has imposed his distinctive and powerful mind, and in large part his vocabulary, but not always precisely his own sentences'.

There is another point at which a warning has to be uttered against placing more weight than they will bear on these new discoveries. What the writers of the New Testament wrote was in the main the Greek of their own time; but it was Greek with a difference. It had the background of a long Jewish tradition; and it was concerned with religious events which were without parallel in the history of the world. I can quote, with great satisfaction, the protests of two eminent Cambridge scholars against an exaggerated estimate of the importance of the *Koinē* in itself. First, E. C. Hoskyns, whom we have met already from time to time:

There is a strange and awkward element in the language which not only affects the meanings of words, not only disturbs the grammar and syntax, but lurks everywhere in a maze of literary allusions which no ordinary Greek man or woman could conceivably have understood or even detected. The truth is that behind these writings there lies an intractable Hebraic, Aramaic, Palestinian material ... No single New Testament author for one moment imagines that he can interpret his material apart from the knowledge of the Jewish sacred Scriptures. The tension between the Jewish heritage and the Greek world vitally affects the language of the New Testament.[1]

And then with characteristic caution from Professor C. F. D. Moule:

The pendulum has swung rather too far in the direction of equating Biblical with 'secular' Greek; and we must not allow these fascinating discoveries to blind us to the fact that Biblical Greek still does retain certain peculiarities, due in part to Semitic influence (which must be far stronger in the New Testament than in an equivalent bulk of colloquial or literary 'secular' Greek, even allowing for the permeation of society by Jewish settlements), and in part to the moulding influence of the Christian experience, which did in some measure create an idiom and a vocabulary of its own.[2]

IV

The new discoveries can help us a great deal with the text and the

[1] *The Riddle of the New Testament* (1931), pp. 19–20.
[2] *An Idiom-Book of New Testament Greek* (1953), pp. 3–4. Moule adds an admirable quotation from the Dominican Père Lagrange (1855–1938): 'Il n'en est pas moins vrai que lorsqu'un helléniste ouvre le NT, en particulier les évangiles, il se trouve transporté dans les tentes de Sem. L'exagération de quelques hellénistes a été, reconnaissant chaque objet, comme déjà vu dans le domaine de Japhet, de prétendre qu'il en venait toujours.' *Luc* (1920), p. xcvi.

language of the New Testament. Can they help us also to enter into the thought-world of those to whom the Gospel was originally preached? There can be no doubt whatever as to the answer. The papyri have cast a flood of light on the 'hopes and fears of the ordinary man'.[1] From our literary sources we know a good deal about the official beliefs and worship of the Graeco-Roman world, which, as we have seen, were more a part of civic stability and loyalty than of inner religious devotion. There was the worship of the Emperor, whose *Tychē*, good-luck, was the cement that held the whole empire together. There were the superb Olympian deities, whom Homer had made a picturesque though not always admirable reality for the whole Hellenic world; and also those strange rustic deities still venerated at Rome, whose priesthoods were held as a mark of honour by members of the noblest families in the city. The papyri have now revealed to us the underworld of religion, the popular ideas and forms of worship, of which we knew a certain amount, but never so much until these pathetic evidences reached us from the hands of very ordinary men.

The first thing that strikes us is the prevalence of magic in that ancient world.[2] This should be easily intelligible to us, since in our own troubled day there has been such a resurgence of astrology, with occasional evidences of darker realities such as Satanism and the celebration of the black mass. In times of grave uncertainty men feel that their whole life is a prey to unseen and unintelligible forces—to the stars which pitilessly determine the destiny of men, to fate which decrees the future, to luck, chance, which holds men in a grasp that is both capricious and irresistible. The natural reaction is to seek some way of escape; if only we can make a pact with these unseen powers, still better if we can in some measure get them under our control, we may be able to make a little world of liberty for ourselves in the midst of the prevailing determinism.

Ideas such as these are found in almost every part of the world. We now know that they go back very far in Greek history. Professor W. K. C. Guthrie quotes for us the earliest known example of a spell, intended to cast disease or injury on another: 'I put quartan fever on Aristion to the death'; this is certainly not later than the beginning of the fourth century B.C. Professor Guthrie further tells us that the

---

[1] The phrase is the title of chapter x of Professor W. K. C. Guthrie's *The Greeks and their Gods* (1950).
[2] An excellent account of this and other aspects of Hellenistic religion will be found in W. W. Tarn, *Hellenistic Civilization* (2nd ed., 1936), pp. 266–98.

terms *katadesmoi* and *katadeseis*, literally 'bindings', 'refer to curses which were scribbled on tablets, often, though not always, of lead, and left in tombs or buried in the ground where the spirits of the underworld, to whom they were commonly addressed, would be able to find and act on them'.[1] A slightly different form of sympathetic magic has left its mark on literature, in the splendid second Idyll of Theocritus, where we see Simaetha and her maid Thestylis carrying out all the gruesome ritual planned to draw home the absent and faithless lover:

Now will I burn the brew. And thou, Artemis, hast power to move Hell's adamant and aught else as stubborn. Thestylis, the dogs are howling in the town; the goddess is at the cross-roads. Quick, clash the bronze.
My magic wheel, draw to my house the man I love.[2]

Theocritus lived in the second century B.C. The material grows in volume, until we reach the collections of magical formulae which date from the third to the fifth centuries A.D., and include such formidable works as the 'great Paris papyrus' of the fourth century, which contains more than 3,000 lines of magical formulae and spells. All these works are an amalgam of Greek, Egyptian, Jewish, and Gnostic material— most surprising and significant, perhaps, is the extent of the Jewish contribution. Mr. Gow remarks pointedly that 'the most casual reader of such collections as Audollent's *Defixionum Tabellae* or Wünsch's *Antike Fluchtafeln* must be struck by the passion exhaling from these scrappy and frequently illiterate texts'.[3]

So we now know very well the kind of thing that those who practised magic arts in Ephesus were up to (Acts 19. 18–19). The magical papyri have filled in for us one very important part of the background of that world in which the early Christians lived. If this was the kind of thing that everyone around you believed in, it was not so easy to be delivered at once and completely from the fear of the unseen and almost certainly malevolent world.

Even more important for our purpose than the world of magic is a new understanding of the world of the mystery religions.

Here again the knowledge is not entirely new. As long ago as 1829

[1] *The Greeks and their Gods*, p. 271. The whole section 'Witchcraft and Curses', pp. 270–4, merits careful reading.
[2] Theocritus, Idyll 2, 'Magic and Charms', ll. 33–36. Trans. A. S. F. Gow.
[3] A. S. F. Gow, *Theocritus, Edited with a Translation and Commentary* (1950), vol. ii, p. 35.

Lobeck wrote his famous work *Aglaophamus*, in which he collected together all that was then known of this aspect of Greek religion.[1] The mysteries of Eleusis were famous; here the ancient myth of Demeter and Persephone, the earth-mother who gives the corn, and her daughter who must spend one-third of each year in the under-world in those months when the fields are bare and barren, was brought into contact with man's hope and desire for immortality. Whereas other men can expect nothing better than the drear and forlorn existence of Hades, the initiate may look for a far richer and happier life in Elysium. The secret was well kept; and we simply do not know what happened in the final experience of initiation, except that almost certainly it was an experience not of learning, of being told some secret, but of seeing, of vision. We do know a good deal about the preliminaries, baths and purifications and so on;[2] beyond that the initiates kept their secret. ' "A great awe of the gods holds back the voice" as the Homeric Hymn puts it, and a chorus of Sophocles says that a golden key is laid upon the tongue of mortals by the Eumolpid priests.'[3] These rites, too, have left their mark on great literature. We meet the Eleusinian initiates in the incomparable poetry of *The Frogs* of Aristophanes; and the concluding lines of their great introductory hymn indicate the combination of spiritual privilege and ethical responsibility, which was characteristic of the Athenian understanding of Eleusis in the great days: 'To us alone are given the sun and the pleasing light, to us who are the initiates, who observed a godly manner of life towards both foreigners and our fellow-citizens.'[4]

There were manifold mystery religions in the ancient world. Some, like those of Eleusis, seem to have been pure and austere; others, like those of Attis in Phrygia, were horrifying in their grossness. But all were alike in being related to the changing seasons of the year, to the death of winter and the rejuvenescence of spring, mythologically

[1] The philosopher, Friedrich Nietzsche, somewhat impolitely referred to Lobeck as 'a worm dried up in the midst of books'—his appreciation of the 'Dionysiac' element in human life was inadequate! Scientific scholars have almost universally acclaimed Lobeck's sober and balanced erudition.

[2] It is to be noted that in none of the mysteries was the lustral bath the central act of initiation, as baptism was in the Christian ceremony of initiation. Thus Clement of Alexandria says: 'It is not without reason that in the mysteries that obtain among the Greeks, lustrations hold the first place.' *Strom.*, 5, 11. He means first *in order of time*, not in order of importance, since, according to him, there follow the minor mysteries, and only after these the great mysteries.

[3] W. K. C. Guthrie, op. cit., p. 289. The latest research has confirmed the view that the secret of the Eleusinian mysteries was well kept.

[4] Aristophanes, *The Frogs*, ll. 455–9.

represented in the form of a dying and rising god. This annual death and rebirth was a natural subject for poetry and for dramatic representation. Of all the records of the mysteries the most famous is that given by the charming writer Apuleius at the end of his *Metamorphoses*. The unhappy Lucius has been transformed by malice into an ass; we have followed him through ten books of his lamentable adventures, in that harsh and cruel world of which Apuleius gives a more vivid picture than any other ancient writer known to me. It has been revealed to him that he can be restored to human form only through eating a garland of roses, and that this will be available to him in the hands of the high priest at the celebration of the great mysteries of the goddess Isis. And so it happens. In solemn cortège the high priest is advancing; Lucius sees with unutterable joy the promised garland.

But I did not let myself go in transports of joy. I did not hurl myself forward, reckoning that this sudden irruption of a quadruped would somewhat mar the order and peacefulness of the ceremony. No, with calm and steady pace, just as a man would have done, and taking care to draw no attention to myself, I slipped gradually through the crowd, which by some divine inspiration separated to let me pass. The priest at once stopped ... and of his own accord raised his right hand and brought the wreath within reach of my mouth. Then, trembling with emotion, my heart beating violently, I eagerly seized the wreath, so beautifully decked with roses, and devoured it, waiting instantly for the fulfilment of the promise. The heavenly promise was no lie. Immediately, the hideous face of an animal fell away from me. The shaggy mane fell off; the thick hide became tender again ... and finally the tail, the principle cause of so many miseries, just disappeared.[1]

This is all romantic and delightful. More significant for our purpose is the hymn of praise with which Lucius breaks out in the process of being initiated into the mysteries of the universal goddess:

Holy one, who watchest ceaselessly over the welfare of the human race, always generous in giving to mortals those good things by which they are preserved, to those who are in misfortune thou suppliest the tender care of a mother ... The gods of the heaven pay homage to thee; the gods of the lower world respect thee. Thou governest the movement of the universe; thou settest alight the sun; thou rulest the world; thou treadest the infernal regions underfoot ... Thou makest a gesture and the breezes blow, the clouds swell, the seeds germinate, the young plants grow. Thy majesty fills with awe the birds which fly in the heavens, the beasts which wander on the

<hr>

[1] Apuleius, *Metamorphoses*, xi, 13.

mountains, the serpents which couch beneath the earth, the monsters which swim in the ocean. My spirit is too poor to show forth all thy praise . . . but all that, in his poverty, a faithful believer can do, that will I be eager to do. Thy divine features, thy sacred person, I will keep for ever hidden in the secret place of my heart, and in spirit I will contemplate thee.[1]

It is improbable that Apuleius had come under Christian influence; it is important to remember that this was the kind of religious expression that the early Christians were likely to meet among their better-educated friends.

Isis was an ancient Egyptian goddess. Most of the mystery-gods had fairly respectable ancestry and a long history. The newcomer among them was Mithras, the god of the morning. Mithras came in from the eastern regions, and from that very ancient world of religion which we find in the classic scriptures of India and Iran.[2] He is depicted in friezes and monuments as the young warrior in conflict with the bull—his victory is the victory of the forces of light and order against the forces of chaos and darkness. His cult spread with astonishing rapidity, especially among and through the soldiers, to the extreme limits of the Roman Empire. As one descends into the depths of the earth in the church of San Clemente at Rome, below all the Christian remains one comes at last to what is almost certainly a Mithraeum. It was no great surprise to scholars when excavations in the City of London revealed what must certainly have been a temple of Mithras, probably of the third century, in a remarkably good state of preservation.

To most British readers Mithras will probably be familiar through Kipling's *Puck of Pook's Hill*. Kipling's Roman legionary on the threatened northern wall, with his very British and moral hymn to Mithras, is a highly romanticized figure. Yet perhaps Kipling, with the insight of genius, came nearer to understanding the attraction of the cult of Mithras for the soldier than many of the patient scholars, laboriously deciphering the ambiguous archaeological evidence. There was a moment at which it seemed that Mithras might be a rival to Christ in bidding for the faith and loyalty of the decaying Roman Empire.[3]

[1] Op. cit., xi, 25.

[2] For a very careful and important study of the original Iranian Mithras, see R. C. Zaehner, *Dawn and Twilight of Zoroastrianism* (1961), pp. 96–144.

[3] Our knowledge of the mystery religions and of their forms of worship has been enormously extended by archaeology, and by the material drawn from the inscriptions

V

It is evident that the Christian fathers, especially of the second century, were well acquainted with the mysteries. Clement of Alexandria tells us a great deal about them and claims to speak from special knowledge. Christians could not fail to note certain parallels between the sacred meals of the mystery cults and the sacraments of the Christians; the closer the parallels, the more convinced were the Christians that these pagan sacraments were a diabolical parody of the Christian rites, directly inspired by the evil spirits in order to lead the faithful astray. At no point have the fathers a good word to say for the mysteries; never once do they suggest that they were in some way a preparation for the Christian Gospel, or that they expressed in some dim way universal human aspirations to which the Gospel of Jesus Christ is the true answer.

Yet it was impossible for the Christians entirely to escape the mystery atmosphere. At point after point their vocabulary is seen to include elements which are common to Christian faith and mystery practice. Two instances will prove the point. From the time of Justin Martyr on, a term which is constantly used for baptism is φωτισμός, enlightenment. Now this is a word which is not absent from the New Testament;[1] by the time of Justin it seems to have acquired a technical significance, and this significance, if not derived from the mysteries, is at least very closely related to them, since there exactly the same terminology is to be found. Another Christian term, very common in later usage, is σφραγίς, the seal. Tertullian uses the corresponding Latin term of those who have passed the tests, and have been sealed.[2] Here again we have quite definitely a technical term of the mysteries, which has made its way into Christian usage; this very same word is to be found by no means infrequently in the Pauline writings.

The extent of this mystery-influence from the second century onwards had been generally recognized by Christian scholars. A new field for study was opened up, when the question was raised whether we must not trace this influence very much further back, and

[1] e.g. Hebrews 6. 4, 10. 32; Ephesians 1. 18.
[2] See E. Hatch, *The Influence of Greek Ideas*, pp. 295 ff.

and the papyri. The best survey of this whole field in English is still S. Angus, *The Mystery Religions and Christianity* (1925), though at a good many points this is now somewhat out of date. There is also an excellent brief account of the subject, and in particular of Mithras and Mithraism, in Sir Samuel Dill's *Roman Society: Nero to Marcus Aurelius* (1904), pp. 584–626.

recognize that the surrounding world exercised a profound influence on the language, the thought, and the theology of the New Testament itself. This was the field of the so-called religio-historical school, which affirmed that Christianity can be understood only if it is studied as one phenomenon among the many phenomena of religion in the decaying Roman Empire and the Levantine world. For forty years this was perhaps the strongest influence in the field of New Testament interpretation.

It seems that the first scholar to raise this question in quite specific form was Otto Pfleiderer (1836–1900), who has therefore earned the title of 'the father of religio-historical theology in Germany'. Pfleiderer was convinced that Paul's theology is a mixture of Jewish and Hellenistic ideas, so that it could be described as both 'Christianized Pharisaism' and 'Christianized Hellenism': 'We can confidently say that Paul's theology would not have been what it is, if he had not drawn deeply on Greek wisdom as this was made available to him through the Hellenized Judaism of Alexandria.'[1] Pfleiderer proceeds to ask whether Paul's views on baptism may not have been derived from the Eleusinian mysteries:

It may be appropriate to mention here that initiation into the Eleusinian mysteries was regarded as a kind of rebirth, and that, in particular the hierophant to the service of the temple had to take a sacramental bath, from which he emerged as 'a new man' with a new name, in which 'the first was forgotten', that is to say, the old man with his old name was put away. We may permit ourselves to ask whether Paul, when from Corinth he wrote Romans chapter 6, was not aware of this rite of the Eleusinian mystery, this 'bath of new birth', and described the sacramental significance of the Christian rite of baptism after this model. Just as in relation to the Lord's Supper he used the analogy of the pagan sacrificial meal, his mystical understanding of baptism may have stood in direct relation to the Greek mysteries.[2]

We may contrast the bold confidence of Pfleiderer in his interpretation of the Eleusinian mysteries with the discreet sobriety of Professor

---

[1] O. Pfleiderer, *Das Urchristentum* (1887), p. 170. Pfleiderer makes the astonishing claim that the Wisdom of Solomon must be recognized as one of the main sources of Paul's theology; in point of fact there are very few traces of an influence of the Book of Wisdom in Paul, and, where this exists, it is nearly always by way of violent *repudiation*; this kind of Hellenism is something that Paul knows and has rejected. Pfleiderer's chief book was translated into English and published under the title *Primitive Christianity* (1906–11).

[2] Ibid., pp. 303–6, quoted in W. G. Kümmel, *Das neue Testament*, p. 265.

Guthrie on the same subject. There is, in fact, much that is questionable in the paragraph that we have quoted. But it is clear that the question that Pfleiderer has raised is a legitimate one; the Church from its beginnings has never lived in a closed ghetto, it has acted and reacted with its surroundings; it is perfectly correct to inquire into the origin of its thoughts and words, and into the influence that the environment may have exercised on them.

This problem of the sacraments and their possible relationship to the world of the mysteries was taken up by two scholars in the fifteen years following Pfleiderer's first enunciation of the theme. Albert Eichhorn in his book on the Lord's Supper in the New Testament, *Das Abendmahl im neuen Testament* (1898), admits that he is unable to bridge the gap between what we may suppose to have happened at the Last Supper and the sacramental ideas that seem unmistakably to be present in Paul. He is convinced that advance must be along the lines of religio-historical investigation. No such hesitation assailed Wilhelm Heitmüller. In his book on baptism and the Lord's Supper in Paul, *Taufe und Abendmahl bei Paulus* (1903), he takes the line that it is quite clearly demonstrated that the origins of Paul's view of the sacrament are not to be found in the original Christian Gospel, that in fact they stand in sharp contrast to it. Paul's understanding of the Lord's Supper belongs to the 'mystical and enthusiastic' side of his teaching; in the Eucharist the Body and Blood of Christ are given; faith no longer plays any essential role. The very ancient idea of the eating of the god is to be noted; we are here on the ground not of the original Gospel, but of the general religious history of mankind:

The interpretation of baptism and the Lord's Supper stand, therefore, in unreconciled and irreconcilable incongruity with the central significance of faith in Pauline Christianity, that is to say with the purely spiritual and personal understanding of the religious relationship, which plays a leading role in Paul's own religion and in the world of his ideas . . . If Paul had not already found baptism and the Lord's Supper practised as sacraments, he would have been able from his own resources to turn them into sacraments. Not only so; from the standpoint of the philosophy of history, this is something which he was bound to do, if it was his purpose to conquer the world with his Gospel; for the world which he had to win was not yet capable of that purely spiritual apprehension of the Gospel which best corresponds to its true religious genius.[1]

[1] W. Heitmüller, op. cit., p. 35; quoted in W. G. Kümmel, *Das neue Testament*, pp. 323-4.

We note that in these statements of Heitmüller four principles are involved, which by constant repetition have become almost sacrosanct in many schools of contemporary theology:

1. There is a radical difference between the preaching of Jesus and the theology of Paul.

2. There is a radical contradiction at the heart of Paul's theology, of which he seems only in part to have been himself aware.

3. The cause of this contradiction was the intrusion into Paul's thought of elements from the Hellenistic world around him, which, however useful temporarily as accommodation to the world in which he lived, were nevertheless destructive of the true quality of faith as simple trust in God without the intervention of any intermediary, human or sacramental.

4. Here we see the beginning of 'catholicism', that reliance on the outward and visible, on ordinances, on the institution, which is always in deadly warfare against the true spiritual Gospel as understood by German Protestantism.[1]

The man who more than any other is remembered, and deservedly, in connexion with the dissemination of knowledge about this whole world of Hellenistic and eastern religion and its possible influences on the New Testament is Richard Reitzenstein (1861–1931). Reitzenstein had studied theology, but he was a professor of classical philology, and his independence in relation to technical theology was perhaps an advantage to him in his approach to this strange and unfamiliar world of religion. His best-known book, *Die hellenistischen Mysterien-religionen*, appeared in 1910. Here Reitzenstein maintains emphatically that Paul must have been acquainted with the religious literature of the Hellenistic world, and that this literature exercised a profound influence on his mind as he set himself to proclaim the Jewish faith in the alien world of the Hellenistic religions:

A fresh study of this religious literature became necessary from the moment at which the apostle prepared himself, with total self-dedication, for the work of preaching among the Greeks. ... He was bound to acquaint himself

---

[1] I am not sure who invented the term '*Frühkatholizismus*', 'early catholicism'; it may have been Heitmüller himself. We shall meet it again and again in German theology of this century, and always as a term of reproach—a curious example of the way in which we are all influenced by our prepossessions—'Catholic' in English is not ordinarily a term of reprobation.

with the forms of speech and the mental world of those groups which it was his aim to win, and to establish norms for the communities which he wished to bring into existence and could not organise after the pattern of the earliest Christian Church, and also for those forms of worship which he wished to establish among them. Is it really impossible to suppose that he adapted for this purpose, as perhaps his predecessors had done before him, forms which were already in existence?[1]

Reitzenstein goes on to note the standing contrast in Paul between his almost excessive self-confidence as a recipient of divine revelation, and his consciousness of a very human weakness and uncertainty. With this duality we are already familiar in the world of Hellenistic religion:

We find this sense of a duality of existence, in the strictest sense of the term, in the mystery-literature and in the mystery-religions; we find it again in the Gnosticism which grew out of them. Here the 'man of the Spirit' is essentially a divine being, and, in spite of his earthly body, has been caught up into another world, which alone has value and reality. We meet this basically Hellenistic religious experience as already present in Paul; and the religio-historical method of interpretation can find a place for him in this line of development not indeed as the first but as the greatest of all the Gnostics.[2]

At this point it is necessary to elucidate briefly the use of the terms Gnosis and Gnosticism in recent New Testament scholarship. Every student of church history is familiar with the Gnosis of the second century—that curious mixture of Christian, Greek, Jewish, and oriental elements, which in the work of Basilides and Valentinus grew into imposing systems, and attempted to supply the Christian faith with an elaborate philosophical undergirding such as seemed to be lacking in the simple presentation of the faith in the New Testament. The Church's struggle with Gnosticism is the fiercest that it has ever endured, and the whole of its subsequent history has largely been determined by the nature of that struggle, and by the manner in which the victory of the Church was secured. One of the leading features in all forms of Gnosticism is the idea that a certain number of fragments from a higher, spiritual world have become prisoners in this lower and physical world; these are 'the spiritual' who can be redeemed. It is the function of Christ to descend into this lower world, bringing the true Gnosis, the knowledge through which the spiritual, but they only, can

[1] R. Reitzenstein, op. cit., pp. 58, 60.   [2] Ibid., pp. 55-56.

be delivered from the bondage of corruption and return to their original home. In some of the later books of the New Testament we find a number of references to views which appear to be akin to those of the Gnostics, but in a much less developed form. It had, however, been taken as axiomatic by scholars that Gnosticism was a Christian heresy, a corruption of the original Christian message by the incorporation into it of a variety of alien elements.

We shall consider later under another aspect the question of the origin and development of Gnosticism. At this point it is to be noted that scholars of the religio-historical school became convinced, as a result of their researches, that Gnosticism was much older than had generally been supposed. Before the first appearance of Christianity in the world, there was in existence all through the ancient East a system of religious thought, dualistic and pessimistic in character, but with its own characteristic doctrine of redemption. The first preachers of the Gospel, we are told, entered into this Gnostic world, took over the framework of its thinking, introduced into it the story of Jesus of Nazareth, who in this Hellenistic atmosphere became identified with the heavenly man, the Gnostic supernatural redeemer, in whom the earliest Christians in the Hellenistic world had already believed before their conversion to the Christian faith.

But where, in point of fact, do we find evidence for a pre-Christian belief in this Gnostic divine redeemer? The sources from the Graeco-Roman world appeared to be silent on the matter, so Reitzenstein pushed his researches ever further eastwards. Beyond the Levantine world lies Persia, with its ancient traditions of the conflict between light and darkness, between Ahuramazda and Ahriman; here Reitzenstein believed that he had found the missing link in the chain of evidence, and from 1916 onwards Iran, and the supposed Iranian myth of redemption, formed the centre of his thinking.[1] Here, he believed, it was possible to find the origins of much that had previously passed as Christian.

Then light seemed to come from a region which had long lain in almost total obscurity. The Mandaeans are a small quasi-Christian sect living in Mesopotamia. Little was known of them with certainty until from 1905 onwards the Göttingen scholar M. Lidzbarski began

---

[1] The book in which this view was first put forth was *Das iranische Erlösungsmysterium* (1921). All that needs to be said about Reitzenstein's Iranian adventure has been expressed by our best living Iranologist Professor R. C. Zaehner in one rather unkind but truthful sentence: 'The Iranian *Erlösungsmysterium* is largely Reitzenstein's invention' (*Dawn and Twilight of Zoroastrianism* (1961), p. 347).

to produce reliable translations of their literature, and especially of their main literary possession, the *Ginza* (Treasure). For here, at last, we do find the heavenly redeemer, *Manda da Hayye*, the 'knowledge of life', also called *Enos Uthra*, who did of old descend to earth and overcame the powers of darkness, and so can guide lost souls, the imprisoned fragments of light, back to that world of light to which they belong. It is admitted that the Mandaean writings as we have them are late (seventh or eighth century); but they may contain very much earlier material. If it can be shown that their redemption myth goes back to a time earlier than the New Testament, then here at last we have the outlines of the Gnostic myth, which Paul and the Gentile Christians knew and took over, and into which they fitted their knowledge and understanding of Jesus Christ. The 'primeval man' of the Gnostic myth and Jesus the Christ are in a strange fashion joined to form the Christian Redeemer adored by the Hellenistic Christians.

The discovery and publication of the mystery-texts led to a perfect rash of books on the subject, many of them of little originality, but all developing the idea of the dependence of the Christian faith in one direction or another on the mystery-religions. In my judgement, one man stands far above all others as a contributor to the development of this religio-historical school of interpretation, which sees the New Testament as one part of a much wider historical phenomenon, the religion of the Levant in the period before and after Jesus Christ. Wilhelm Bousset (1865–1920) was an outstanding scholar, distinguished by width of outlook, accuracy of knowledge, and sobriety of judgement. His book on the religion of Judaism in New Testament times[1] was one of the first attempts scientifically to survey the whole field of Jewish religion before, during, and after the time of Christ. His book on the problems of Gnosticism[2] was a pioneer work, and after more than fifty years is still worth reading. His greatest book is *Kyrios Christos* (1913), in which he attempts to draw together all the threads of the religio-historical understanding of the Christian faith.[3]

---

[1] *Die Religion des Judentums im neutestamentlichem Zeitalter* (1903).

[2] *Die Hauptprobleme der Gnosis* (1907).

[3] I must confess to a special interest in Bousset. *Kyrios Christos* is the first German theological work that I ever read; exactly forty years ago I borrowed it from Clement Hoskyns to read during the long vacation of 1922. It is evidence of the haphazard way in which we do things that as far as I know this great book has never been translated into English. Dr. C. Colpe, in his book *Die religionsgeschichtliche Schule* (1962), points out that in 1913 Professor Bousset was no longer representative of the religio-historical school; his book is a summing up of results, but other members of the school had already gone beyond the point of view set forth by Bousset in his great book.

Kyrios Christos is a work on the grand scale. In it Bousset tries to give a sketch of the whole development of Christian thought till the time of Irenaeus towards the end of the second century. The method that he has chosen to follow is well grounded. Irenaeus marks a great division within church history; he may be called the first of the great 'Catholic' theologians. With little originality he sums up clearly and intelligently the teaching of the Church as it had taken shape through the tremendous struggle of the Church with second-century Gnosticism, and as in fact it was to remain for many centuries. Irenaeus, as we saw earlier, quotes from every book of the New Testament except the Epistle to Philemon, and thus shows at an early stage the way in which the New Testament came to be collected and recognized as 'canonical'. He is a bishop at a time at which the bishop has already become the recognized centre of authority and unity. Irenaeus gives us a fixed point of doctrine, from which, if we wish, we can work backwards through the various stages of development until we come to the New Testament origins themselves.

Bousset's great contribution is that he understood the early Christian groups primarily as worshipping communities. It was in worship that, more than at any other time, they realized their own being, the nature of their existence as a Christian fellowship. Bousset uses the term *Kyrios* as the clue to the significance of their worship.

The term *Kyrios*, Lord, is a perplexing one. It is used in the Septuagint Greek translation of the Old Testament as the equivalent of the mysterious unspoken name of the Jewish God, the Jehovah of our Authorized Version. But it seems clear that it was also a title frequently used of the mystery gods in the Hellenistic world, 'the Lord Sarapis', 'the Lord Attis', and so on; and that it was specially used in this way by the groups of worshippers who gathered around the mystery-god, to be renewed by partaking of his life in a sacramental meal, and ecstatically to feel his presence with them. It is this, according to Bousset, that accounts for the prevalent use of the term among the Gentile Christians of the early period: 'The Son of Man of the primitive Christian community is derived from Jewish eschatology, and continues to be an eschatological figure ... The *Kyrios* of the early Hellenistic Churches is a power which is *present* in the cult and in worship.' But this understanding of the significance of Christ, so Bousset goes on to tell us, resulted in a major shift in the Christian's outlook on his world, and of the purpose of God in it:

In this presence of the *Kyrios* in the act of worship, in the experiences of his apprehensible reality which came to Christians at worship, there was from the beginning a mighty alternative to the eschatological ideas of the earliest Christian communities—without observation, quite gradually, the centre of gravity of the faith began to shift from the future into the present. *Kyrios*-worship, liturgy and sacrament were the most dangerous and powerful foes of the earlier communities. For if this concept were ever to take its place in fully developed form, then the other must necessarily lose its élan, the vital power by which it swept everything along with itself. This, however, we may take to have been the development; to a very large extent the Son of Man has been forgotten, and remains in the Gospels as a hieroglyph, the true significance of which has been forgotten; the future belongs to the *Kyrios*, who is present in the act of worship.[1]

Bousset draws a number of other conclusions from his interpretation of the evidence. In many cases these Christian groups had been associations of mystery-worshippers before they became Christians. All that has happened is that their mystery-god has acquired a new name and a new character as Jesus of Nazareth. Naturally such worshippers have very little interest in the historic events of the life of Jesus. Everything for them is concentrated in the *drama* of the death and resurrection, a drama that is repeated among them Sunday by Sunday, into which they feel themselves ecstatically caught up. In the sacrament they receive the very Body and Blood of the God; they become partakers of his life, and so they have the assurance that they have passed from death to life. The eschatological tension of a future which has become already present has been changed into the sacramental tension of an outward which has become already inward, of a time-conditioned being which already enjoys timelessness.

As usual, there was a certain time-lag before these German ideas became widely familiar in England. The greatest contribution to their popularization was made by one of the most notable English New Testament scholars of the century. Kirsopp Lake (1872–1946), as a young man, had rather surprisingly gone to Leiden in Holland as New Testament Professor. In 1913, Trinity College, Cambridge, was about to appoint a theological lecturer. One of the favoured candidates was Lake. At the crucial moment word reached the great

[1] It has to be recorded with regret that Bousset remarks elsewhere that this 'curious duplication of the object of adoration in Christian worship would be unthinkable, except in surroundings where the monotheism of the Old Testament no longer rules as an assuredly and unconditionally accepted truth'. There is no evidence whatever that the Hellenistic Christian groups, deeply influenced as they were by the Old Testament, were less firm in their monotheism than any other part of the primitive Christian community.

Master of Trinity, Henry Montague Butler, that Lake was unorthodox in his views, and this, it must be confessed, was a mild way of putting it. The choice in consequence fell on the other candidate, Frederick Tennant, Lake's senior by seven years, and hardly a pillar of the kind of orthodoxy that Butler approved. No criticism can be made of the choice of a man whose *Philosophical Theology* is one of those classics that is likely to survive for centuries. Yet it cannot but be regretted that Lake was lost to America. There he did distinguished work, especially on the text of the New Testament—the little book on the subject that he prepared in collaboration with Silva New is still the best short introduction to New Testament textual criticism that exists in any language. Yet Lake never seemed quite to fulfil the promise of his earlier years.

In 1911 he had produced a book called *The Earlier Epistles of St. Paul,* which is a very notable book indeed. For the first time the conclusions of the religio-historical school were made known to the English-speaking world in most attractive and dramatic form. Some of Lake's positions could not be maintained today. And, as we came to read the German books which in fact he was summarizing and interpreting, we realized that Lake was not quite so original as we had supposed him to be. For all that, I think that those of us who read Lake when we were young will be inclined to think that this is one of the best books on the New Testament that has ever been written in the English language. This is the way it ought to be done. Under Lake's skilful guidance, we feel ourselves one with those new and struggling groups of Christians, in all the perplexities of trying to discover what it means to be a Christian in a non-Christian world. And there is the Apostle, so very much in working clothes and without a halo; we feel in our bones the passionate eagerness of Paul for better news from Corinth, the passionate relief when the good news arrives.

There were, of course, some very disturbing things in the book. Paul had always been regarded as the pillar of Protestant orthodoxy; what would Protestantism be without Paul's doctrine of justification by faith? Yet Paul, as Lake presents him, takes a very realistic view of the Lord's Supper in terms of the eating and drinking of the God. Anglo-Catholics were perhaps a little incautiously jubilant; their view of the Lord's Supper seemed to go back to much earlier times than had generally been supposed, and it appeared now to be possible to quote the Apostle of the Gentiles in favour of a view with which he was imagined by many to have been unfamiliar. Some Protestants were a little unduly alarmed. Wiser heads thought that, whatever view of the presence of the Lord in the Eucharist we may come to hold, the Hellenistic mystery-religions are not exactly the allies we would choose to have in the defence of our position. But, when we have made every allowance that can be made for later discovery and for the need for more prudent statement, nothing can alter the fact that Lake had made it necessary for every English student to take seriously the Hellenistic background of the New Testament. His interpretation might be wrong. There could be no evasion of the questions he had asked.

We waited long and eagerly for a complementary volume on the later Epistles of Paul; but somehow the book never came: *The Earlier Epistles* stands as a token, as the promise of a work that was never completed.

VI

In the previous section we have given a sketch of the development of a certain school and type of New Testament interpretation which draws heavily on the alleged influences of the Hellenistic environment on early Christian thought. The outcome of this process has been the erection of three structures of thought which are accepted by a great many scholars of this school as though they were self-evident realities. These three are the pre-Christian Gnostic myth, Gentile Christianity, and 'early Catholicism'. It is now time to turn on these three structures the light of scientific criticism and to consider how far they have really been established beyond the possibility of cavil or disproof.

1. The outlines of the Gnostic myth are summed up for us with admirable clarity by Professor Rudolf Bultmann in his article on the Fourth Gospel in the new edition of the great German theological encyclopaedia *Die Religion in Geschichte und Gegenwart*:[1]

The basic elements in the Gnostic myth of redemption, the concrete features of which can vary in detail, are as follows: A heavenly being is sent down from the world of light to the earth, which has fallen under the sway of the demonic powers, in order to liberate the sparks of light, which have their origin in the world of light, but owing to a fall in primeval times have been compelled to inhabit human bodies. This emissary takes a human form, and carries out the works entrusted to him by the Father; as a result

[1] Vol. iii (1959), col. 84.

he is not cut off from the Father. He reveals himself in his utterances ('I am the Shepherd', etc.) and so brings about the separation of the seeing from the blind to whom he appears as a stranger. His own hearken to him, and he awakes in them the memory of their home of light, teaches them to recognise their own true nature, and teaches them also the way of return to their home, to which he, as a redeemed Redeemer, rises again.[1]

2. Of Gentile Christianity the picture is rather less uniform, but there would probably be general agreement as to the following features. From a very early date, and even before the conversion of Paul, there existed in some of the great cities of the Roman Empire Christian communities of Gentile origin which grew up in almost complete independence of the traditions of the Jewish Church in Jerusalem. This had already been recognized by Baur and his followers of the Tübingen school; although developed to a point at which they could not be defended, these ideas were in the main sound. The Jewish concept of the Messiah had little meaning for these Gentile Christians, and the Jewish categories were very soon replaced by the familiar terms 'Son of God', 'divine man', and so forth, which these groups drew from the terminology of the other and non-Christian cult-groups around them. The rapid development of this type of Christology, which we find already so far advanced in Paul, is due to the taking over by the Christians of an already formulated scheme, into which they fitted their ideas of the Christ. There was little that they had to develop *de novo*; they had merely to adapt the material that was there ready to their hand. Such Gentile groups were, naturally, not very much interested in the earthly life of Jesus of Nazareth; they were concerned only about the living Christ, the dying god who had risen again, who was felt to be present among them in the ecstasy of worship, and the reality of their fellowship with whom was guaranteed to them by the Spirit in the automatically effective sacraments.

3. The development of *Frühkatholizismus* is depicted for us in summary form by Professor H. Conzelmann in his article on Gentile Christianity (*Heidenchristentum*) in the volume of *R.G.G.* referred to above.[2] His statement is as follows:

The relationship of the Church to the eschatological future loses in im-

---

[1] The curious and important phrase 'the redeemed Redeemer' refers to one element in the Mandaean form of the myth—the Redeemer himself falls victim to the powers of evil in the lower world, and has to be delivered by further action from the side of the powers of light.
[2] Vol. iii, col. 139.

portance in comparison with the present possession of 'means of grace' (*Heils-kräfte*, literally 'powers of salvation'), and their mediation to the individual; these are administered and experienced in the institutions of the cult. So the office of the priest acquires a new, that is to say constitutive, significance in relation to the salvation of the individual. Originally the office of the preacher had as its task the proclamation of the unconditional character and the immediacy of salvation for every individual; but now the priest acquires the new character of mediator intervening between God and man. In place of the proclamation of a salvation without presuppositions, which recognises no condition other than that of faith, and no means other than the Word, we encounter now the invitation to enter on a way of salvation under the guidance of the Church, and that means in fact under the guidance of ecclesiastical authority. The Church has become an institution for the transmission of salvation (*Heilsanstalt*), and that means that it stands in need of a new law. For the first time in the history of the Church it becomes evident that sacramentalism and moralism are brothers; to the sacramental administration of salvation is added of necessity the disciplinary administration, especially when the priesthood has reached its monarchical culmination in the office of bishop.[1]

In these three great structures we are presented with a comprehensive picture of Christian origins as these are related to the non-Jewish world. It is clear that, if this reconstruction of the history is solidly grounded, and as clearly proved as the scholars who have contributed to its formation believe it to be, the traditional understanding of the New Testament, and of the early years of Christianity, is no longer tenable.

We have already encountered a number of instances in which what were really no more than unverified suppositions have succeeded in passing themselves off as established truths. It will be convenient at this point to cite a judgement passed by Professor C. H. Dodd, whose judgements are always conspicuously fair and magnanimous, on one of the scholars whom we have had occasion to mention with considerable respect:

The whole process of reconstruction is a masterpiece of characteristic ingenuity, but it depends on too many arbitrary assumptions. It is not too much to say that in Reitzenstein's later work much of ancient literature became one vast jig-saw puzzle, to be dissected and reassembled by methods which often had too little regard for the maxim that a chain is as strong as its weakest link.[2]

[1] *R.G.G.*, iii, 139.   [2] *The Interpretation of the Fourth Gospel* (1953), p. 121 and n. 3.

It is in the light of this and similar warnings that we approach the critical consideration of the three main pillars of the 'religio-historical' interpretation of the New Testament.

1. The Gnostic myth and the mystery-religions

It is clear from the start that, for our consideration of the relationship between the Christian faith and its Hellenistic environment, the question of chronology is all-important. Who borrowed from whom? In which direction was the current of influence flowing? It is by no means always easy to determine; but this very fact lends increased importance to the dating of our evidence, in so far as this is possible, and demands of us great caution in the use of evidence to which no date can be ascribed with any degree of certainty. Otherwise we are liable to go seriously wrong. An illustration from modern times may help to make this clear.

It could well happen that an historian working in Ceylon in the twenty-fifth century, and stumbling on the fact that there existed in Ceylon in the twentieth century both a Young Men's Christian Association, and a Young Men's Buddhist Association, should conclude that the Buddhist Association was the earlier, and the Christian a pale imitation of it. After all, Buddhism is very much the older religion, and has been in Ceylon a great deal longer than Christianity. The inference could be regarded as highly plausible. But if the historian has at his disposal one-tenth of the evidence which is available to us, he will know with absolute certainty (and this is one of the cases, rather rare in historical research, in which we can speak in terms of *certainty*) that the plausible inference was in fact the incorrect one, that the Christian institution was prior, and that it was borrowed by the Buddhists at a date considerably later than that of its foundation because of its manifest success as an instrument of Christian propaganda.

Now, it is universally recognized that mystery-religions existed in the Mediterranean world from a very early date, and that many and various types of them were to be found in the first and second centuries A.D. There is therefore no *a priori* reason for excluding the possibility that the early Christian communities were influenced by the mystery atmosphere that surrounded them, and were inclined to borrow words, ideas, and possibly ceremonies from this ancient and well-established form of religion. It is when we try to put exact content into this general statement, and to determine the extent and nature of the borrowing, that we are liable to get into trouble, unless we pay careful attention to such chronological data as we have. Two illustrations will serve to make the matter plain.

Everyone who reads books on Christianity and the mystery-religions becomes familiar with a letter discovered among the papyri at Oxy-rhynchus which reads: 'Chaeremon invites you to dinner at the *trapeza* [the table, or festal meal] of our Lord Sarapis tomorrow.' By the time that one has met this quotation in a dozen books and articles, one is inclined to think that this is a common phrase, and the mind jumps at once to 1 Corinthians 10. 21: 'Ye cannot be partakers of the Lord's table and the table of devils.' Our Lord Jesus, our Lord Sarapis—what could be clearer? But in point of fact the phrase is by no means common. Not more than a dozen examples of it can be quoted from the ancient literature, the inscriptions, and the papyri. More important still is the question of the date. When was Chaeremon writing? The answer seems to be that the letter was written not earlier than the beginning of the third century. By that time Alex-andria, the great centre of the cult of Sarapis, was largely a Christian city; it had been the home of the great Christian teachers Clement and Origen. It is not impossible that, when Christians spoke of 'the table of our Lord' they were borrowing from mystery-usage; but we have to reckon also with the possibility that when Chaeremon writes of 'the table of our Lord Sarapis' the borrowing is really the other way.

Of course, ritual banquets of every kind had been held in heathen temples from the earliest times, and it is to this fact that Paul is alluding in 1 Corinthians 10. That excellent scholar Hans Lietzmann, in his commentary on the Epistle,[1] has a useful Excursus on the subject at this point. Of course, Chaeremon is quoted. But Lietzmann, careful scholar that he is, makes it clear that no evidence has as yet been found for a pre-Christian use of the phrase 'the table of our Lord X'. The phrase *may* have been used earlier. Here, as so often, we have to say simply that we do not know, and we are warned once more of the extreme uncertainty attaching to inferences based on what is in itself uncertain.

Another example of the significance of chronology in this con-nexion is yielded by one of the most striking of all the mystery phrases—*renatus in aeternum*, 'reborn for eternity', which has been interpreted by many Christian scholars, including Kirsopp Lake, as

[1] *Handbuch zum Neuen Testament*, vol. ix (1931).

throwing much light on the theology of baptism as that was understood in the early Church. Do we not find in this mystery phrase a
remarkably close parallel to the Christian concept of baptism as a
'rebirth to eternal life'? It has not infrequently been inferred that the
pagan phrase is the original, the Christian a borrowing from it. But
what are the facts?

The phrase *renatus in aeternum* occurs only in relation to the
Taurobolium, a sacrifice performed in connexion with the rites of
the Great Mother of Asia Minor or of Attis.[1] On the appointed day
the priest descended into a deep trench dug in the earth; this was covered
with a platform of wood on which a bull was then slain, the blood
descending through orifices cut in the wood on to the waiting priest
below. In this horrible ceremony we are clearly in touch with the
very ancient idea of blood as the most powerful magic—in many
societies the blood of a man is even more powerful than that of an ox—
and of the power of blood to renew and restore life, if life has been
weakened or impoverished. From the inscriptions it seems that on
occasion the priest who had undergone the ceremony, on emerging
bloodstained from the pit, was greeted by the watchers as *renatus in
aeternum*.

Here, once again, the question of the direction in which borrowing
took place, or may have taken place, can be determined only by careful
attention to chronology. The first recorded occurrence of the ceremony
which can be dated belongs to the year A.D. 143, the last to the very
end of the fourth century, when the triumph of Christianity in the
West was already assured. It is, of course, unlikely that the first
recorded instance is the first to have taken place; but all the evidence
that we have suggests that the ceremony became common only in the
third and fourth centuries. And what of the inscriptions and the
phrase *renatus in aeternum*? That immensely learned man Professor
Arthur Darby Nock once pointed his finger sternly at me, and said:
'Only three instances, and all of the fourth century.' Nock had an
amazingly wide knowledge of the whole world of Hellenistic religion,
and an accurate and careful mind. I have no doubt that he was right.
And, if so, there is an overwhelming probability that the phrase
renatus in aeternum is Christian in origin, and an overwhelming

[1] It is frequently stated that the *Taurobolium* formed part of the rites of Mithras. As
far as *inscriptions* are concerned there is as yet no evidence for this at all. Archaeological
remains *suggest* a connexion, as would be natural in view of the character of Mithras as
slayer of the bull; for the time being the question must be left open.

improbability that Christians could have borrowed it from any mystery source.[1]

We turn now from the mystery-religions as such to the problem of Gnosis or Gnosticism. As we have seen, Church historians recognized the existence, not later than the middle of the second century, of a vast movement in which the central concept was that of the imprisonment of particles of light or spirit in the gross and fleshly world and their deliverance through the descent of a heavenly being, who in one way or another had come to be identified with the Jesus of the Gospels. In recent years many scholars have come to believe that the roots of Gnosticism go back much further than is generally supposed, that there was a pre-Christian Gnosis, the influence of which was deeply felt throughout the Middle East, and that clear traces of this Gnosis are to be found in almost every part of the New Testament, and in particular in Paul and in the Johannine writings. Here, once again, it is clear that the question of chronology is of crucial importance; from what date onwards does it become possible to speak of Gnosticism in any recognizable form?

In this field we are embarrassed not because we know too little, but in a sense because we know too much; in hardly any other area has the progress of knowledge been so rapid in recent years—before a book that refers to the subject is in print, it is likely to have been put out of date by some later discovery.

Sixty years ago we had a good deal of knowledge of a rather late system of dualistic religion known from its founder Mani (216–266 or 267) as Manichaeism. Most of our information about this religion came from its Christian enemies; but at least the name of it was familiar to a very wide circle of readers, since the great Augustine himself was a Manichaean for a number of years before he became a Christian, and has written about Manichaeism at some length in his *Confessions*. Then in 1902 and 1903 explorations in Chinese Turkestan brought to light a number of original Manichaean documents in a whole variety of languages, including Chinese. In 1931 a smaller but very important group of Manichaean writings, including hymns in Coptic, turned up in Egypt. These discoveries have filled in a good many gaps in our

[1] Alas, that learned and kindly man died in January 1963, between the writing and the revision of this lecture. He was the man who could have given us a definitive and authoritative account of Hellenistic religion in the crucial period. His Gifford Lectures on the subject were delivered as long ago as 1939–40 and have never been published. Much is scattered in many articles of great value; but we shall never have from his pen the definitive book of which, in connexion with New Testament studies, we stand so sorely in need.

knowledge of a religious system which spread from China to the Atlantic coast, and presented itself for a time as a serious rival to Christianity.[1]

More startling than the Manichaean discoveries has been the recovery in 1945 or 1946 at Nag-Hammadi in Upper Egypt of a mass of Gnostic writings in Coptic. Thirteen volumes bound in leather have been found to contain no less than forty-nine treatises; some of these were known before, others are entirely new. For the first time we are able to meet the Gnostics not as they are represented to us by their enemies, but in their own words and utterances. Many of the treatises have not as yet been published, some have hardly been studied; but it is already clear that a wealth of new material for the reconstruction of the Gnostic system, as it had developed by the middle of the second century, is already in our hands. Jean Doresse, in his work *The Secret Books of the Egyptian Gnostics*, tells us that the treatises can be divided into four categories:

First that of the greatest, purely Gnostic revelations, with some commentaries expounding the myths that they contain; next some revelations that are no less important but are artificially veiled under Christian allusions; then the authentically Christian apocrypha infiltrated by Gnostic speculations; and lastly some half-dozen treatises of which some properly belong to Hermetic literature while others exhibit a curious transition between Hermetism and Gnosticism.[2]

Among these new finds, the treatise which has attracted far more attention than any other is the so-called Gospel of Thomas, a collection of sayings of Jesus, some of which appear in the form in which they are found in the Canonical Gospels; others seem to have been carefully edited (though how far the editing tended in a specifically Gnostic direction is a matter of dispute among scholars), a few were already known from sayings of Jesus that had turned up among the Oxyrhynchus papyri, and some were entirely new. Have we here evidence of a different tradition of the words of Jesus, outside of, and independent of, the tradition which eventually took shape in the Canonical Gospels? Some scholars say yes, and others say no. A great deal more detailed study will be needed before a definite answer can be given to these

[1] An excellent summary of what is now known about Mani and Manichaeism has been provided by G. Widengren in *Mani und der Manichäismus* (Urban Bücher 57, 1961).

[2] Op. cit. (1960), p. 146.

questions. For the moment we may content ourselves with the sober and measured judgement of Oscar Cullmann:

> If we do not arrive at completely assured results, still it remains true that these leaves, discovered by Egyptian peasants in an old cemetery, will for a long time occupy scholars in many different provinces: that of philology, that of the history of Gnosticism and of Jewish Christianity, that of the Synoptic problem, and of the exegesis of Jesus' words, and that of manuscripts (see the close relationship to Codex Bezae). They certainly give us new problems, but perhaps they may permit us to solve old problems, or at least to come closer to a solution.[1]

This new Gnostic material may thus come to be highly important in connexion with the history of the Church in the second century, and with that of the tradition of the New Testament. It can hardly bring us nearer to an answer to the question as to whether there was or was not a pre-Christian Gnosticism, on which the Gentile Churches leaned heavily for the working out of their theology.

It is partly a matter of definition. If we define Gnosticism sufficiently widely, we can affirm with certainty that it has a pre-Christian history. There was in the Greek-speaking world a widespread ethical pessimism, a tendency to think of the body as essentially evil, as the prison-house of the soul, that immortal being, the business of which on earth was to make itself as like to God as possible, and so to remain untouched and uncorrupted by that body with which it had come to be associated. There was in the East a widespread metaphysical pessimism in which the whole universe was interpreted in terms of the ceaseless warfare between the forces of light and the forces of darkness, with no assurance of a cessation of the conflict or of a final victory of the light. When these two met, as they did progressively from the time of the Roman conquests in the East in the first century B.C., the scene was set for that peculiar combination of elements from a variety of sources by which Gnosticism in all its forms was characterized. If taken in this very general sense, Gnosticism may well have been pre-Christian.

A number of attempts have been made in recent years to interpret Gnosticism as a phenomenon of more than local and temporal existence, and in terms which the modern world will readily recognize.

For Hans Jonas the clue to the understanding of Gnosticism is existentialism. The modern existentialist finds himself alienated from the world in which he lives, plunged in a false and artificial existence

---

[1] 'The Gospel of Thomas' in *Interpretation* (October 1962), an English translation of an article that originally appeared in the *Theologische Literaturzeitung* for May 1960.

which he did not choose and for which he is not responsible, challenged to recognize his own true being in freedom, and to make a firm decision in favour of authentic existence. The situation of man in the decaying ancient world was very much the same. The old orders of society, with their protecting educative power, had broken down. Man found himself in his world homeless, forlorn, and afraid. The physical world is orderly but unkind; it has been brought into being by malevolent powers for the enslavement of the human race. To be at home in such a world is to have sunk into forgetfulness, stupor, or drunkenness. The challenge of Gnosticism is that a man should recognize his own true being, and by the resolute assertion of his freedom should rise from the false and the transitory into the full reality of being, which is full of hope and promise. Opinions will differ as to the measure of the success with which this retranslation of the twentieth-century idiom of Martin Heidegger into terms of the ancient world has been carried out.[1]

A second attempt to interpret Gnosis generally, this time in the light of psychiatric experience, had been made by C. G. Jung—an attempt which deserves attention rather because of the eminence of the author than for any intrinsic merit in it. Once again, the setting is one of man's alienation from himself; as always in such a situation, man's deep inner self in its search for wholeness throws up images, and in the brilliant world-pictures of Gnosticism these images, though they are in reality only projections from the depths of man's own being, take on religious significance. On the whole Jung prefers Gnosticism to orthodox Christianity, as being truer to the natural realities, and as having found on the whole better symbolic expressions for the self. In our whole being we must take account of darkness no less than light, a point which had been earlier stressed by Jakob Boehme. Rather surprisingly Jung remarks:

The natural archetypal symbolism [of Gnosis] describing a totality that includes light and dark, contradicts in some sort the Christian but not the Jewish or Yahwistic viewpoint, or only to a relative degree. The latter seems to be closer to Nature, and therefore to be a better reflection of immediate experience. Nevertheless, the Christian heresiarchs tried to sail round the rocks of Manichean dualism, which was such a danger to the early Church, in a way that took cognizance of the natural symbol; and among

---

[1] Dr. Jonas's book *Gnosis und Spätantiker Geist* appeared in a revised second edition in 1954. His book in English, *The Gnostic Religion: the Message of the Alien God and the Beginnings of Christianity* (1958), sets out the same point of view as that expressed in the German book.

the symbols for Christ there are some very important ones which he has in common with the devil, though this had no influence on dogma.[1]

The correctness of such high speculations depends, of course, on the reliability of the evidence adduced, and on the verification of a multitude of details with which those who move at these altitudes cannot be expected to be familiar. It is when we descend from the heights to the often tedious but scientific work of verification that questions throng in upon us thick and fast.

We must ask, in the first place, where we encounter the Gnostic myth in the neat and simple form in which it has been summarized for us by Professor Bultmann. The surprising answer is: Nowhere at all. The myth is a synthetic product, pieced together from hints and shreds in different sources, many of them of uncertain date. We may maintain, if we will, that such a myth existed more or less in the form in which it is presented to us; but honest caution compels us to recognize that the evidence is far too slender for any confident affirmation to be based on it. Unfortunately, some scholars are less cautious than others; there is a tendency to suppose that when any Gnostic word or phrase occurs in any document that is available to us, the whole of the Gnostic myth must have been present in the mind of the writer whoever he may have been. Clearly, this is an assumption which is more readily made than proved. One can only echo the heart-cry of Professor Virginia Corwin in her work on Ignatius, where she complains of scholars of this school that

their primary interest is in individual figures and motifs of myth, which they find in different religions, but a difficulty arises because they tend to assume that the whole myth was known whenever a phrase suggests an aspect of it. That this is sometimes the case is of course true, but it is not always so, and it can never be assumed . . . Furthermore, the method is almost by definition atomistic, presenting concepts isolated from the total schemes in which alone they have meaning.[2]

As we have seen, in the later researches of Professor Reitzenstein much weight was attached to the books of the Mandaeans, that

[1] C. G. Jung, *Aion: Researches into the Phenomenology of the Self* (English trans., 1959), p. 196. See additional note on p. 190.

[2] V. Corwin, *St. Ignatius and Christianity in Antioch* (1960), p. 12. Professor H. Schlier, in his *Religionsgeschichtliche Untersuchungen zu den Ignatiusbriefen* (1929) attempts to show the extensive presence of the pre-Christian Gnostic myth in the writings of Ignatius; this is a view for which there is little to be said, and it has not met with general acceptance.

strongly anti-Christian Gnostic sect which still so strangely survives in Mesopotamia. To what extent is it possible to date these books, and how far is it possible to make use of them as evidence for the existence of a pre-Christian form of Gnosticism?

It is admitted that all the Mandaean manuscripts which we possess are late, probably not in any case earlier than the eighth century. This in itself proves nothing; a late manuscript may preserve for us what in itself is a very early work; a manuscript of the fourteenth century has kept alive for us the Roman poet Catullus who lived in the first century B.C. There is fairly wide agreement that the Mandaean books as we have them cannot be attributed to a period earlier than the fourth century A.D. This again proves nothing; a book compiled at that date might be made up, in part at least, of very much earlier material. We have to fall back on probability, and the nature of the texts themselves.

There is now reason to believe that some parts of the Mandaean texts draw on older material than had been generally supposed. A Swedish scholar, Dr. T. Säve-Söderbergh, has made a careful comparison of the Mandaean hymns with the Manichean hymns discovered in Egypt in 1931. He comes to the conclusion that the hymns preserved in the Mandaean books are the earlier and have been adapted by the Manichean writers. He is inclined to attribute the original writings to the second century A.D.[1] This, if correct, brings the Mandaean writings back to a venerable antiquity; but in the second century we are still only in the period of the developed and Christianized Gnosis of Basilides and Valentinus; no reason has yet been shown for supposing that these documents present to us anything that could be regarded as a pre-Christian Gnostic mystery, or that could be used as a clue to the interpretation of the development of the Christian faith in the New Testament period.

In the main we must accept as sound the verdict pronounced in 1953 by Professor C. H. Dodd:

Too often the documents cited are of quite uncertain date, and we wander in a world almost as timeless as the world of the myth itself. When some more precise chronology is possible, it always, or almost always, turns out either that the document in question belongs to the fourth century or later, or that it belongs to an environment in which the influence of Christian

---

[1] T. Säve-Söderbergh, *Studies in the Coptic-Manichean Psalm Book* (Uppsala, 1949). Säve-Söderbergh's view is accepted by Kurt Rudolph, who in *Die Mandäer* (1961) has written the fullest account we yet possess of the Mandaeans. Fresh Mandaean manuscripts have been brought to light and published by E. S. Drower, *The Canonical Prayer Book of the Mandaeans* (1959).

or at least of Jewish thought is probable, so that it is hazardous to use the document to establish a pre-Christian, non-Jewish mystery ... Alleged parallels drawn from this medieval body of literature have no value for the study of the Fourth Gospel, unless they can be supported by earlier evidence.[1]

It is certain that, over the next thirty years, the study of Gnosticism and its origins will be one of the major preoccupations of the interpreters of the New Testament and of Church historians; it may be hoped that in course of time certainty may be attained in areas which at present are a prey to total uncertainty. What has already been written has indicated something of the extent of this uncertainty. We may carry the matter a little further by raising once again the question of the origins of Gnosticism. It is clear that it was a flexible system that took into itself material from many sources. But, if we ask whence came the original impulse and the centre and heart of the doctrine, a whole variety of answers has been given and still is given. Harnack found the source of Gnosticism in the Greek spirit; for him the history of the early Church is to be explained in terms of the Hellenization of the Gospel— Gnosticism represents the abrupt and rapid Hellenization of Christianity, orthodox Christianity represents the gradual absorption by the Church of the Greek spirit; but heresy and orthodoxy alike are variants on a single theme. The school of Reitzenstein was convinced that Gnosticism, like Mithraism, came from the East; in it Iranian, Mesopotamian, and even Indian elements are traced, and these, it is held, gave its essential character to the complex whole. Quite recently a number of scholars have maintained, with force and learning, the position that the origins of Gnosticism are to be sought in Judaism, and in particular in the sorting out and readapting of Jewish eschatological hopes which was bound to follow on the disasters that had befallen the race in the destruction of Jerusalem.[2] At the present stage of the investigation, it is wise to say that we really do not know.

One question calls urgently for an answer. Where do we find the evidence for pre-Christian belief in a Redeemer, who descended into the world of darkness in order to redeem the sons of light? Where is the early evidence for the redeemed Redeemer, who himself has to be delivered from death? The surprising answer is that there is precisely no evidence at all. The idea that such a belief existed in pre-Christian

[1] *The Interpretation of the Fourth Gospel* (1953), p. 130.

[2] This view is upheld by R. McL. Wilson in *The Gnostic Problem* (1958) and by R. M. Grant in *Gnosticism and Early Christianity* (1959).

times is simply a hypothesis and rests on nothing more than highly precarious inference backwards from a number of documents which themselves are known to be of considerably later origin. Where, then, are we to look for the origin of the idea of the heavenly Redeemer, and of those redeemers who later were certainly believed in? Professor R. M. Grant, who affirms confidently that no trace of a pre-Christian redeemer has ever been found, sums up the problem, and a possible answer, with perfect lucidity:

In pre-Christian Graeco-Roman religion there was no redeemer or saviour of a Gnostic type . . . The most obvious explanation of the origin of the Gnostic redeemer is that he was modelled after the Christian conception of Jesus. It seems significant that there is no redeemer before Jesus, while we encounter other redeemers (Simon Magus, Menander) immediately after his time.[1]

Professor Grant is not alone in maintaining this view.

It is becoming increasingly clear that Gnosis in its essential being is *non*-Christian; the view that it was *pre*-Christian still awaits demonstration. Nothing will alter the fact that the people to whom these books belonged [the Nag Hammadi writings] did behave more or less as Christians, and must provisionally be regarded as Christian heretics. It is, however, clear that this Gnosis shows hardly a trace of inner connection with the historic events of Christianity, with the life and death of Jesus the Messiah.

Such is the judgement of one of the most learned students of Gnosticism in our time, Professor Gilles Quispel.[2] And Professor Quispel puts his finger on the central point of the whole debate. Whether we are right in saying that Gnosticism represents the outward projection of man's inner search for the unity of his own being, the protest of the deeper self against the tyranny of the intellect, or no, it is certain that for Gnosticism in all its forms man is at the centre of the picture; it deals with permanent and unchanging factors in the human situation, and to it history is a matter of supreme indifference. The

[1] R. M. Grant, *Gnosticism, A Source Book of Heretical Writings from the Early Christian Period* (1961), p. 18. Strong reinforcement may be found for this view in the thorough and careful study by Dr. C. Colpe, *Die religionsgeschichtliche Schule* (1962). He too holds that the existence of a 'pre-Christian Gnostic Redeemer' has never yet been proved. This is the first part of a three-volume study: the other two volumes will be eagerly awaited.
[2] *Gnosis als Weltreligion* (1951). It is interesting that Professor Quispel, like Lachmann and Reitzenstein before him, is not a theologian, but a classical philologist. In this admirable sketch of only ninety-five pages he makes a remarkably clear differentiation between Neo-platonism (late Greek philosophy), historic Christianity, and Gnosticism.

Christian Gospel is firmly rooted in history, in certain things that are believed actually to have happened.

At a later stage we shall have to consider again the significance of history and to take account of the extent to which mythological elements can be incorporated into a historical narrative. Here it cannot be too strongly insisted that history and myth belong to two different worlds. The myth, in this sense of the term, is the imaginative projection outwards of man's inner hopes, fears, or desires. It does not matter whether the events that are mythically represented ever really happened. Myth can quite contentedly take account of something which happens over and over again, as the mystery-religions incorporated into themselves the annual drama of the death of the world in winter and its rebirth in spring. History deals with that which happened once for all, at a recognizable time and place in this visible world, and which can never be repeated.

Gnosticism has to do with a God who is essentially and at all times unknowable, and of whom we can speak, if we speak at all, only in negative terms. No one is likely to deny that, if God exists at all, there is in him an unutterable mystery, which it is impossible for man to apprehend or to approach. For all that, the God of the Christians is not in the least like the God of the Gnostics. He is a God who can be known and loved; a God who is pleased to reveal himself and has revealed himself in history in the person of Jesus of Nazareth. This Jesus is no mysterious or mythological figure; he is a man who was born and lived at an identifiable time and place, was crucified once for all, and was raised from the dead never to die again. It is true that those who had believed in Jesus had to exercise their imaginative faculties to the utmost to find terms in which to express their sense of the dignity of the One in whom they believed God to have come to them. Nevertheless, this sense of historical once-for-allness runs right through the New Testament, being specially emphasized in the Epistle to the Hebrews, and distinguishes what it has to say from every Mediterranean myth.[1]

[1] This point has been strongly emphasized by Professor G. Stählin in his article on 'Myth' in Kittel's *T.W.N.T.*, vol. iii, pp. 769–803. His conclusion is that 'the Church of all ages has stood fast by the conviction that the Logos of the New Testament cannot be brought into any kind of relationship with myth'. It is interesting to note that Professor Stählin is one of the few contemporary New Testament scholars who has himself been a missionary. He would not maintain, nor would I, that there is no point of contact between Christian faith and these ancient expressions of human longing. We keep Easter at the season of the rising sap, the renewal of the earth; this suggests a deep acceptance by the

2. *The churches of the Gentiles*

With 'the Gentile churches', we have a rather easier task. We ask: Where is the evidence for the existence of these Gentile churches, developing on lines of their own, in almost total independence of their brethren in Jerusalem? In the latest discussion, the article of H. Conzelmann on *Heidenchristentum*, which we have summarized, the author admits twice over that there is no evidence in any of our sources for the existence of any such communities. This does not rule out the possibility that such Gentile communities may have existed. But everything that we say about them depends on more or less precarious inference. Yet we see the strange result that, in one of the most distinguished books of this century on New Testament theology, the work of Rudolf Bultmann, thirty pages are devoted to the message and teaching of Jesus, and a hundred pages to the exposition of the life and thought of these Gentile communities of which we cannot certainly know that they ever existed.[1]

If we take the picture given us by every single source on which we depend for our knowledge of early Christianity, even allowing fully for every variety of detail in the presentation, it is as different as possible from the imaginary picture given us by Bultmann and his disciples. Here are no isolated groups, forging their own theology in independence of what other Christians elsewhere might be thinking or doing. The picture is one of constant coming and going. It is not only Paul who travels; Aquila and Priscilla turn up at various places and various points of the narrative. They are typical of those mobile Christians, the anonymous founders of so many of the great churches of the Christian world. But always in the background is the mother church at Jerusalem; one of Paul's primary concerns is that there should be no schism in the body of Christ; and the aim of that great

---

[1] T. W. Manson rightly calls this the nemesis of a wrong method of work. 'I may remark in passing that the disseminated incredulity of Bultmann's *Geschichte der synoptischen Tradition* had its nemesis thirty years later in his *Theologie des neuen Testament*, in which a perfunctory thirty pages or so is devoted to the theology of Jesus himself, while a hundred or more are occupied with an imaginary account of the theology of the anonymous and otherwise unknown "Hellenistic Communities" ' (*Studies in the Gospels and Epistles* (1962), pp. 6–7). In point of fact all that really needs to be said about the Gentile Churches was said as long ago as 1928 by A. D. Nock in his study of the subject in *Essays on the Trinity and the Incarnation* (ed. A. E. J. Rawlinson).

Church of something very human and primitive; but this is very far from saying that Christian belief in the resurrection is derived from, or in any way deeply influenced by, pagan myths or mystery religions.

collection on behalf of the poor saints in Jerusalem, which he organized in all the Gentile churches and to which he gave so much of his time and strength in the concluding years of his active ministry, was precisely the demonstration of the unity of the body of Christ throughout the whole inhabited world.[1]

In point of fact, however, we are not left entirely to our own imagination to discover what a Gentile church was really like. We have a remarkably vivid picture of one in the Epistle to the Romans. This great letter is often misread and misinterpreted. Luther's tremendous experience of justification by faith, as mediated to him in the early chapters of the Epistle, has laid a heavy hand on exposition ever since; and the majority of expositors have concentrated on the first eight chapters, as though this was a great systematic doctrinal statement, to which everything else is an appendix. This is completely to misunderstand the situation. Romans, like all the other Epistles of Paul, is a real letter, a message of practical counsel to those who need the Apostle's help. Like all the others, it should be read backwards as well as forwards, if we are to understand what it is all about. This is a Gentile church. It is possible that there were a few Jews among the Christians; but in view of Paul's repeated references to 'you Gentiles', this must be regarded as doubtful. Here, as elsewhere, the church has come into being under the shade of the synagogue. Here, as elsewhere, there are at least two, and perhaps three, groups among the Gentile Christians. There may have been some who had actually been circumcised and so had pledged themselves to keep the whole law; there were many who had been hearers in the synagogue and who were familiar with the law of Moses but pledged only to its moral requirements; and there were some who had come in straight from paganism without the preliminary discipline of the law. These groups found it difficult to get on with one another. There were difficulties arising through differences of usage, the observance or non-observance of festivals and so on. These can be easily dealt with by the simple principle of mutual tolerance; the problem now is not that of the law, as it was in the days of the Epistle to the Galatians; it is that of the election of Israel. Is it possible that God should have cast off his people, and that the ancient election should have come to nothing? In the light

[1] Professor Henry Chadwick, in his inaugural lecture as Regius Professor of Divinity in the University of Oxford, *The Circle and the Ellipse* (1961), has drawn our attention again to the immense significance of Jerusalem in the early days as the centre of the whole Christian world.

of this formulation of the problem, it becomes clear that the difficult chapters 9 to 11, which are often treated as an awkward parenthesis between doctrine in chapter 8 and practice in chapter 12, are really the very heart of the Epistle; this, in fact, is what it is all about. Whether Paul has really proved his point may be arguable. There can be no doubt as to the point that he is trying to make—Israel remains the people of God; into that people the Gentiles have been grafted by a divine and miraculous act. So must they think of themselves, and in no other way. They are no new people, but the ancient people of God; since they have entered into the covenant-relationship with God through faith, they are heirs of Abraham, God's covenant with whom also was established on the basis of faith and on nothing else.[1]

It is sometimes affirmed that the original Christians had not supposed themselves to be adherents of a 'new' religion; and one of the changes alleged to have been introduced by the Hellenists is that of supposing themselves to be a 'new race', the third race as opposed to pagans and Jews. But this is an argument which will hardly hold water. The question as to whether Christianity was a new religion or not was not one that could be answered by the Christians; the answer was imposed upon them by their juridical situation in the Roman Empire. The Jews were a privileged people, and the law of the empire permitted the practice of their religion. Could the groups which gathered themselves round Jesus as Messiah or as *Kyrios* share in the privileges of the Jews? To this question the Jews returned an emphatic and resounding no. Israel as a race had rejected the Gospel; as the first century advanced, the Jews seem to have been moved by an almost fanatical hostility to the new movement. The Christians might claim to be the true Israel; the Jews would make it plain to them that the old Israel was very much alive and that Christians had no part nor lot in it. As so often, the form the Church took on was determined for it not so much by its own inner impulses as by the opposition from without in relation to which it had to take up its stand.

Even more significant than Paul's answer to the question relating to the election of Israel is his manner of handling the question. Throughout he argues from the Old Testament; he assumes that his readers will be familiar with it and that its authority will be unquestioned. And

---

[1] The argument of the Epistle to the Ephesians is very similar and thoroughly Pauline. Here, too, the unity of Jews and Gentiles is something brought about once for all by a single divine act, and not an empirical process which men can observe happening before their eyes. The verbs are all aorists!

here, more than at any other point, he strikes that which constitutes the unity of the early Christian communities. We have no evidence of any Christian community in the world which was not founded on the Old Testament. As yet the Christians had no Scriptures of their own; the Old Testament was their Bible. They had heard it read and expounded in the synagogue; now, almost certainly, they heard it read and expounded in Christian worship. The interpretation was new; everything was now understood Christologically, and the Old Testament was ransacked in order to discover the categories in which the reality of Jesus the Christ could be expressed, and to work out the parallels between the mighty acts of God on behalf of his people of old and those new and even mightier acts in which the Christian people felt themselves to be involved.

Some of the proof-texts were obvious. It did not take long for the Christian imagination to seize upon Psalm 16. 10: 'Thou dost not give me up to Sheol, or let thy godly one see the pit' as a foreshadowing of the resurrection. The picture of the Suffering Servant in Isaiah 53 clearly played a significant, perhaps even a decisive, role in helping Christians to understand what had been achieved by the atoning death of Messiah.[1] But there was also a possibility of much subtler exegesis, and the discovery of hints and pictures of the Christ in most unexpected places. The development of this kind of typological exegesis became almost a recognized profession in the Christian Churches. The function of the prophet in the early Church seems to have been not so much to foretell the future, though there were examples of this,[2] as to lead the congregation into a deeper understanding of the mystery of Christ through inspired exegesis of the Old Testament Scriptures. We are fortunate in having a remarkable example of Christian prophecy in the Epistle to the Hebrews.[3] The aim of the writer is to show the finality and all-sufficiency of Christ; this he does by drawing out the doctrine of the heavenly high-priesthood of Christ, a priesthood which is after the order of Melchizedek, and therefore different in kind, in order, and in permanence from that Aaronic priesthood to which the Jews were bound under the

[1] How far the mind of Jesus himself was influenced by the figure of the Suffering Servant is today a matter of controversy. Of its influence on the minds of the early disciples there can be no doubt at all.
[2] As, for instance, the foretelling of the famine by Agabus noted in Acts 11. 27.
[3] Not in the Revelation of St. John the Divine. This is the great Christian example of apocalypse, and this, as we have seen, is something that moves in a different world from that of prophecy.

law of Moses. This is a great and original epistle; the writer had a mind of extraordinary beauty, power, and penetration. As to his identity, and the identity of his original readers, we have scarcely a clue, though guesses are manifold. The presence of these great anonymous figures in the early Church is indirect testimony to the greatness of that Gospel by which they had been called into being.

The superscription of this Epistle 'to Hebrews' is almost certainly correct. The recipients were probably Jewish Christians who had failed to realize the full significance of that which was offered to them in Christ. But exactly the same process was going on in every Christian congregation throughout the Roman Empire. That the results varied a little from place to place need not be questioned; there would be differences of emphasis, according to the interests of both teachers and hearers in the various regions. But every congregation was familiar with the stories of the Exodus and the Passover, with the expectations of Messiah, with sign and psalm and prophecy. The idea that there were groups here and there who were unaffected by this relatedness of the Church to the Old Testament, and who worked out their doctrine of the Christ independently in Hellenistic terms and in categories that had nothing to do with the Old Testament, rests on no evidence whatever. That they used Greek words and borrowed terms and phrases from their neighbours has been readily admitted; but that the controlling influence was that of the Old Testament, interpreted in the light of what they had learned of Jesus of Nazareth, seems to me one of those basic truths to which the whole of the New Testament bears witness.

3. Early Catholicism

On the problem of 'early Catholicism', again, it is not necessary to dwell very long. It seems to arise in the main from a transposition of the problems of the Reformation period into the first century A.D. To an extent which it is hard for the Christian of the English-speaking world to realize, the mind of the continental Protestant has been fashioned by the running controversy with the Church of Rome which has gone on for more than four centuries. He has been taught to regard Catholicism as being at every point and in every respect a deformation of the Gospel. If there is anything even in the New Testament that seems to lend support to the Catholic position, that must at once be stigmatized as the beginning of the falling away of the Church from its true nature, a falling away which was almost complete by the second century and from which it was delivered only through the new revelation given by God through Martin Luther in the sixteenth century. Above all, no suspicion must be allowed to pass that the Church is in process of becoming a *Heilsanstalt*, an institution for the mediation of health and healing and salvation. If by this is meant that the Church comes to be regarded as an institution through membership of which salvation is automatically conveyed, without regard to faith or hope or the transformation of the life of the member, it may be stated at once that the Roman Catholic would be as resolute in repudiating that understanding of the Church as any Lutheran could be. But the idea that the institutional form of the Church is in itself and necessarily a falling away from the original truth and grace of the Gospel he would naturally be unable to accept.

But, through this anti-Catholic prejudice, a large group of continental scholars have been led to produce a fancy picture of the early Church, which does not correspond to any known reality. Let us take one single example. We know, as a matter of fact, extremely little about the organization of the early Church. It is the strange fact that we have no evidence of any kind that would enable us to say with certainty who was the celebrant (or even the celebrants) at the Lord's Supper in the first century. We may think that it was an apostle or a presbyter; but this is simply inference from later practice, an inference unsupported by any direct evidence. But, equally, in our evidence there is no place for that most familiar figure of continental Protestantism, the preacher, the man to whom is committed the *Predigtamt*, the office of preaching. It is not clear that preaching, in any contemporary sense of the word, played any part in the worship of the early Church; still less that there was any one person to whom the office of preaching was committed. It is probable (though this again is only inference, based on Acts 20. 7–10) that if an apostle or prophet was visiting a congregation, he would be invited to preach. But in the only description we possess of the earliest Christian worship, a rather disorderly kind of worship it must be admitted, in 1 Corinthians 14, we read: 'When you come together, each one has a hymn, a lesson, a revelation, a tongue, or an interpretation' (1 Cor. 14. 26). Paul recognizes this multiplicity of contributions; his concern is only that all should speak in succession and not all at once.[1]

---

[1] I think myself that at this point Paul is addressing the presbyters (though this is a word Paul himself does not use), and not the congregation as a whole; but this cannot be proved, and in any case does not affect the argument.

It is quite clear that there was no one single person, to whom alone was entrusted the task of preaching the word. Dr. Conzelmann's holders of the early *Predigtamt*, whose business it was to remind their hearers of the immediacy and the unconditional character of salvation, are the product of a lively Lutheran imagination in the twentieth century; they have no existence in any of the evidence that has come down to us.

Equally, those early believers of a period 'which recognizes no condition other than that of faith, and no means other than the Word' have no historical existence at all. If there is one thing more certain than another about these early churches, it is that admission to them was by faith *and baptism*. The New Testament knows nothing of membership in the Church by faith alone, without the accompanying act of obedience and confession. The Epistle to the Romans was probably written in A.D. 56, that is less than thirty years after the death of Christ; Paul takes it for granted that all his readers will have been baptized, and that the extraordinarily high and realistic doctrine of baptism which he presents to them is the familiar tradition of the Church and not a strange new doctrine which he has himself thought up under the influence of some Hellenistic tradition or other. Whether we like it or not, from the very beginning the Christian Church, which had grown out of the Jewish Church, had its institutional element. We may say, if we wish, that baptism was merely the outward expression of a living faith, and that faith was the all-important thing. This is true, but it does not alter the fact that, until faith had found its expression in baptism, the believer was not a member of the Christian community, the body of Christ. Non-sacramental Christianity, as it is to be found today in almost all the Protestant churches of the continent of Europe, is an invention of the rationalistic nineteenth century; it has little to do with the Christianity of the New Testament and cannot be made to square with it.

We none of us can escape our own presuppositions, or the background of the kind of Christian life that we have been brought up to live. The evidence of the New Testament is so rich, so complex, and so varied that it is quite certain that we shall none of us be able to do justice to it all. But we shall not be able to deal with it at all unless we are prepared to deal with it all, and to give due and unprejudiced weight to every part of it. There has been a tendency, on the part of many continental scholars, following the lines laid down by Baur more than a century ago, to affirm that the only completely genuine form of the

Christian faith is to be found in the four great Epistles of Paul, except in so far as even here Paul shows himself at certain points to have been corrupted by Hellenistic influences. The central doctrine is that of justification by faith, though Paul deals with this only in parts of two Epistles, and hardly mentions it in the other two—Paul's doctrine of the Spirit is far more central and characteristic than his doctrine of justification by faith. But a proclamation based on so narrow a foundation cannot be more than a thin and ineffective proclamation. One of the most distinguished members of the school which we are at present discussing, Heinrich Schlier, was led to question its adequacy. As he studied the New Testament more deeply, he became increasingly convinced that many of those things that had been rejected as 'accretions', as 'Hellenistic developments', and so forth, were in fact parts of authentic and essential Christianity. Eventually, to the astonishment and dismay of his friends, he announced his conversion to the Roman Catholic Church. If the only alternatives are the reduced Protestantism characteristic of so much German scholarship today and Rome, many would feel that the Professor had made the only choice possible to a man who is prepared to take seriously the whole of the evidence of the New Testament.[1]

For faith cannot be built on one narrow section of the Christian revelation without help from the other. Take, for example, the concept 'faith' itself. It is clear that the word is used with interestingly different connotations by Paul, by James, and by the writer to the Hebrews. The three in a broad general sense look respectively to the past, to the present, and to the future. In Paul faith means something like total surrender to God on the basis of the promises he has given to man in Jesus Christ. In James, faith means loving obedience to the commands of God. In Hebrews, faith means going forth boldly into the unknown, in the certainty that God is at the end of the journey as well as at its beginning. Clearly, each of these concepts is valid, Christian, and

---

[1] This point is dealt with by R. H. Fuller in *The New Testament in Current Study* (1962), pp. 137–8: 'It is becoming increasingly clear that the New Testament covers three phases in the emergence of Christianity: the ministry of Jesus, the apostolic and the sub-apostolic ages. Just as we are learning to see the apostolic age as the response to Jesus, in which what was implicit in him is now made explicit, so too it should become increasingly apparent that the sub-apostolic age, so far from being a corruption of its immediate predecessor, was the legitimate response to the apostolic age, in which what was implicit in the earlier period is now made explicit in the later. This would mean, ultimately, that the second-century achievements of catholicism— the creed, canon, episcopate, and liturgy—are the unfolding of what was implicit in the apostolic kerygma.' A typically Anglican point of view.

apostolic. Lacking any one of them our faith must be partial and one-sided.

The event of Jesus Christ is far too great to be caught and held in one interpretation and one only. Here was seen the wisdom of the Church in gathering together into the New Testament so many different streams of tradition and interpretation, rigidly excluding other streams which seemed to have become corrupted at the fount, but including all that could be genuinely called apostolic.[1] The startling thing about all these traditions is their unity; they all relate to one event, which must have been staggeringly great, and to one Person, who must have been unlike any other person who has ever lived. All the traditions are fragmentary and incomplete. No one would maintain that they are all of equal value; and all together they fail to answer a great many of the questions that we would like to ask. But, by their very richness and variety, they challenge us to go beyond them, to see how near we can come to that event and to that person.

Is it possible really to draw near to him at all? Can we of the twentieth century get anywhere near Jesus of Nazareth, and the event of his resurrection, or must we say simply that these things are hidden in mystery which we cannot penetrate? The attempt to answer this question must be the subject of a later chapter.

[1] The history of the Canon is a long and complicated business. The Church, or rather the churches, were never very clear as to what exactly they meant by apostolic; and in a considerable number of cases they did the right thing for the wrong reason.

Additional note: In the first printing of this book I accidentally omitted on p. 177 a reference to a valuable and suggestive article by Professor W. R. Schoedel on 'The Rediscovery of Gnosis', *Interpretation* (October 1962), pp. 387–401. I made use of this article in the final draft of my chapter, and much regret that an acknowledgement was not made at the time.

Chapter VI

RE-ENTER THEOLOGY

H ARNACK'S *What is Christianity?* marked the high point of the liberal interpretation of the Gospel. It must have seemed to many in 1900 that the reign of this school of thought was permanent and assured, and that no other interpretation of the work of Jesus Christ would ever be able to hold the field against it. Yet, almost as soon as the book appeared, there were signs that the Christian consciousness was not entirely satisfied. From the beginning Christianity has been a religion in which the personal relationship of the believer to Jesus Christ has been central. But, if Harnack is right, and the *Wesen*, the very essential heart of Christianity, is to be found in certain truths and principles, does any great importance attach to the person of the Revealer through whom these truths were made known?

The liberal view contained within itself the seeds of its own dissolution. The central message of the Gospels is not the teaching of Jesus but Jesus himself. It is impossible that this theological issue should be for long evaded; if disregarded, it will ere long reassert itself. And this is in fact what has happened in the twentieth century. In this chapter we take four men, of very different backgrounds and points of view, each of whom in his separate way has posed for us again the question: Who is Jesus of Nazareth, and how are we to think of him?

Albert Schweitzer (b. 1875)

Just about fifty years ago the learned world was astonished to learn that Albert Schweitzer was planning to go out to Central Africa as a medical missionary. It seemed that Schweitzer had the world at his feet. By the age of thirty he had won distinction in the two very disparate fields of music and theology. He was an acknowledged authority on the works of Johann Sebastian Bach and an organist of far more than ordinary merit; he was already the author of striking studies of the problems of the New Testament. It was known that he had since then qualified as a doctor of medicine. But high theology and missions do not seem always readily to go together; many thought that a year or two in the desolating climate of Lambaréné on the Ogooué River would prove quite sufficient, and that then Schweitzer would be back in his study in Strassburg. Nearly fifty years have passed; Albert Schweitzer has become one of the most famous men in the world, Nobel prizeman for peace, honoured by countless universities and learned societies. At the time of his death in 1965 he was still in Lambaréné, the service of humanity in its need giving him a satisfaction which he found nowhere else in the world. By many things he will be remembered; but perhaps his most abiding fame will rest on the book which he wrote when he was less than thirty years old, *The Quest of the Historical Jesus* (1906).[1]

This is indeed a tremendous book. Schweitzer has left on record some memories of the manner of its writing. Books were stacked everywhere in his room, including the floor, and those who came to see him had to edge their way perilously along the narrow waterways between the tall islands of books. Schweitzer had undertaken nothing less than a survey of the whole of the critical research on the life of Christ carried out in Germany (with a few glances outside) in the course of more than a century. In the process of doing so, he has given something like a brilliant summary of the development of the mind of man in one of the most creative of all the centuries of history. Two hundred and fifty-one writers are listed in the Index. It is quite certain that Schweitzer had not read all the works of all of these. But he has never been a man to pile up footnotes merely for the sake of effect; he had really read and pondered all the important books, and comments on them on the basis of full knowledge and penetrating insight. And this is far from being a dry-as-dust catalogue of names; Schweitzer carries on a running guerrilla warfare with the authors whom he is discussing; he sprouts metaphors, and at times his style is positively sprightly.

The book opens with some characteristically modest statements:

When, at some future day, our period of civilisation shall lie, closed and completed, before the eyes of later generations, German theology will stand out as a great, a unique phenomenon in the mental and spiritual life of our time. For nowhere save in the German temperament can there be found in

---

[1] This brilliant title seems to be due to the English translator. The German original appeared under the not very illuminating title *Von Reimarus zu Wrede*. Professor F. C. Burkitt, whom we have met in other connexions, was one of the first in England to become interested in Schweitzer's work. It was he who took the initiative in arranging for his great book to be translated into English.

the same perfection the living complex of conditions and factors—of philosophic thought, critical acumen, historical insight, and religious feeling —without which no deep theology is possible. And the greatest achievement of German theology is the critical investigation of the life of Jesus. What it has accomplished here has laid down the conditions and determined the course of the religious thinking of the future.[1]

Then begins the mighty catalogue of writers. They have come to the story of Jesus with every kind of point of view—faith, unfaith, half-faith. Their approach has been uncritical, critical, semi-critical, pseudo-critical. Hardly any of them have made a contribution of permanent value to the study, though some whose answers have been wrong have nevertheless rendered a real service by posing questions that subsequent study has not been able to evade. Schweitzer's book is itself a summary—usually fair, always alert, sometimes brilliantly illuminating—and a summary of a summary would be quite unreadable. The book itself must be read if the long procession of scholarly figures is to make on the mind of the reader the impression that the writer has intended.

Schweitzer is at his best on Renan, to whom he devotes a whole chapter; and this is right, since Renan's is by far the greatest of all the imaginative lives of Jesus. Ernest Renan (1823–92) was a great scholar, with a special knowledge of things oriental; he was also a consummate master of that admirable instrument of precise and lucid statement, the French language. With Renan, the problem of Christ and history emerged from the study of the scholar into the common ways of life. Eight printings of the *Life of Jesus* (1863) were required in three months; and the book will have readers until the world's end:

Men's attention was arrested, and they thought to see Jesus, because Renan had the skill to make them see blue skies, seas of waving corn, distant mountains, gleaming lilies, in a landscape with the Lake of Gennesaret for its centre, and to hear with him in the whispering of the reeds the eternal melody of the Sermon on the Mount.[2]

Renan's starting-point is that the supernatural is the unreal, and that miracles do not happen.[3] So what we are to see here is a purely human

---

[1] *Quest of the Historical Jesus* (reprint of 1961, New York), p. 1.
[2] Ibid., p. 181.
[3] To be precise, that no evidence in favour of a miracle which an historian could accept as conclusive has ever been produced.

life. The somewhat naïve Galilean peasant moves in a kind of magical glow of summer, surrounded by groups of his adoring female votaries. When he goes to Jerusalem in search of martyrdom, this is not due to any sense of vocation to effect the reconciliation of men with God through his death. Unwisely he has started to play a role which it is impossible for him to maintain; death is the only way through which he can escape from his problem without discredit. And so the story advances toward its moving conclusion. In Gethsemane, 'Did he remember the clear brooks of Galilee at which he might have slaked his thirst—the vine and the fig-tree beneath which he might have rested—the maidens who would perhaps have been willing to love him? Did he regret his too exalted nature? Did he, a martyr to his own greatness, weep that he had not remained the simple carpenter of Nazareth? We do not know!' And so the death after all is a victory: 'Rest now, amid thy glory, noble pioneer. Thou conqueror of death, take the sceptre of thy kingdom, into which so many centuries of thy worshippers shall follow thee, by the highway which thou hast opened up . . . Jesus will never have a rival. His religion will again and again renew itself; his story will call forth endless tears; his sufferings will soften the hearts of the best; every successive century will proclaim that among the sons of men there hath not arisen a greater than Jesus.'

What was wrong with Renan's work? A German scholar, Christoph Ernst Luthardt, gives the answer: 'It lacks conscience.'[1]

This, I think, is fair. Renan confuses rhetoric with profundity, and sentimentality with genuine religious feeling. Professing to work as an historian, he does not pursue with the needed seriousness the historical problems of the life of Christ; pretending to describe the beginnings of a religion, he has no clue to the challenge of faith or disbelief that is involved in any personal encounter with Jesus of Nazareth.

Many other examples of Schweitzer's precision and penetration could be given. And, when he comes to the end of his long survey, his conclusion is that all those who had set out to write a life of Christ had been engaged on a hopeless task. We simply have not the materials for anything like a biography in the modern sense. We can to some extent fill in the background from contemporary sources. We can estimate the reliability of different parts of the Synoptic tradition. But, for a psychological presentation of the development of the mind and

[1] *Quest*, p. 191.

thought of Jesus, there really is no foundation in the records. When we try to write his life, we are attempting to domesticate him within history as we ourselves understand it; to pull him out of his own time and setting into the modern world in order to make him intelligible to modern man. But Jesus will not obey our behest; he refuses to be domesticated, to be modernized; and it is for this reason that we feel that all the modern and liberal lives are falsifications rather than expositions of the records of the Gospel.

Even such consistency as has been attained in the modern lives has been possible only by reading into the records many things that are not there, by disregarding difficulties and contradictions, and by imposing on the materials a unity which is not to be found in them. But scientific criticism has reached a point of development at which it is no longer possible to play such tricks with the sources:

> Formerly it was possible to book through-tickets at the supplementary-psychological-knowledge office, which enabled those travelling in the interests of life-of-Jesus construction to use express trains, thus avoiding the inconvenience of having to stop at every little station, change, and run the risk of missing their connexion. This ticket office is now closed. There is a station at the end of each section of the narrative, and the connexions are not guaranteed.[1]

When the time arrives at which he has to work out his own constructive solution of the problems, Schweitzer is resolved to keep Jesus firmly in his own time and place, and not to use for the interpretation of him any modern categories. He finds the key in that element in the story which most expositors had tended to overlook or to underestimate—the sense of crisis, of judgement, and of the impending end of the world. He comes forward as the champion of what he calls 'thoroughgoing eschatology'.

It is unfortunate that Schweitzer chose to use the word 'eschatology' in this new and unfamiliar sense. 'Eschatology' is that which has to do with the last things; and traditionally the last things are death, resurrection, judgement, and eternal life. For the sudden intervention of God in the affairs of the world to put all things right and to bring history to an end, there is the appropriate word 'apocalyptic', and it is this word that Schweitzer should have used. But the damage is done and cannot be undone. 'Eschatological' is used by scholars in half a dozen

---

[1] *Quest*, p. 333. This is a good specimen of Schweitzer in lighter vein.

senses, often without definition, and the confusions are endless. The best that can be done is to state exactly what we do mean by the word, if we continue to have occasion to use it.

It is clear that there is an 'apocalyptic' element in the Gospels. There is the sense of crisis and of the end of the world. Some scholars have believed that the disciples lived in this world of fancy and imported it into the Gospel narratives, but that we should not attribute this outlook to Jesus himself. Others have thought that Jesus accommodated himself to the ideas and to the language of the time, but that this constituted no essential part of his teaching. Schweitzer takes the view that this is the very heart of the mind and message of Jesus, and that from no other point of view can we make sense of the records that we have.

In the Old Testament we find both prophecy and apocalyptic. When the prophet speaks, his gaze is directed to the contemporary situation and the immediate future; his language is that of high poetry, but it can usually be interpreted in relation to the situation from which he is speaking. When the visionary is looking to the end of all things, the language changes; because he is speaking of things that the human mind cannot compass, imagination changes to fantasy, and the landscape is filled with strange images of terror and darkness. The difference between the two can easily be sensed by comparing a genuinely prophetic passage with one in which the apocalyptic note begins to be sounded:

> For wickedness burns like a fire,
>   it consumes briers and thorns;
> it kindles the thickets of the forest,
>   and they roll upward in a column of smoke.
> Through the wrath of the Lord of hosts
>   the land is burned,
> and the people are like fuel for the fire;
>   no man spares his brother.
>
> (Isa. 9. 18–19.)

That is the genuine prophetic note. Apocalypse has a different accent:

> For the stars of the heavens and their constellations
>   will not give their light;
> the sun will be dark at its rising
>   and the moon will not shed its light.

Therefore I will make the heavens tremble,
 and the earth will be shaken out of its place,
at the wrath of the Lord of hosts
 in the day of his fierce anger.

          (Isa. 13. 10, 13.)

Prophecy is a call to repentance on the part of the people; apocalyptic gives the people assurance of safety, and perhaps of triumph, in the day of crisis when all things are dissolved. With the end of the canonical Old Testament the gift of prophecy died out, until it was renewed in John the Baptist. As the day of deliverance from foreign oppression seemed to be ever delayed, apocalyptic hopes and expectations seem to have developed in many parts of the Jewish world. The best-known apocalypse is, naturally, the Book of Daniel in the Old Testament, with its visions of the heathen kingdoms symbolized by wild beasts, and the true, human kingdom which is to be given to the people of the saints of the Most High (Dan. 7. 12–14, 26–27). But today we are able to study a whole range of these apocalypses, which have turned up in various languages and countries, with strange names such as the *Ascension of Isaiah*, and the *Assumption of Moses*. Among the most important is the *Book of Enoch*, which first became known at the end of the eighteenth century in the Ethiopic translation;[1] here we meet the mysterious figure of the Son of Man, through whom the purposes of God are to be accomplished.

What is the relation of this world of ideas to the preaching of Jesus? What was the kingdom which he proclaimed? Scholars, and their readers, had become accustomed to thinking of this kingdom as purely immanent, a new spirit or experience, brought in or established by Jesus, and then incorporated in the existence of the Church. An entirely contrary view was put forward in 1892 by a young scholar in a little book on the 'Preaching of Jesus concerning the Kingdom of God'.[2] Johannes Weiss (1863–1914), the son of a distinguished professor of theology, was a typical German prodigy of erudition and industry, who at his death at the age of fifty-one left behind an astonishing number of books of outstanding value. But none was more strikingly independent or influential than this brief study of one New Testament subject. Weiss took the view that the kingdom as Jesus proclaimed it is still

[1] Ethiopic manuscripts were brought home by the Scottish traveller James Bruce in 1773; a century later considerable portions of the book were discovered in Greek in Egypt.

[2] *Die Predigt Jesu vom Reiche Gottes*. The first edition contains only sixty-seven pages.

entirely future; its shadow already falls on the world in the presence of Jesus, but it will come, when it does come, only through the last great and cataclysmic act of God himself. Gradually it becomes clear to Jesus that the kingdom cannot come until the barrier opposed by the guilt of the people is taken away, and that this can be achieved only through the ransom-price of his death. After the price has been paid, the kingdom will come with power, and the time of triumph will begin.

It was this view, so revolutionary and so different from that which was current at the time, that Schweitzer took up and developed with the utmost rigour of consistent thought. The preaching of Jesus about the kingdom followed the general lines of contemporary apocalyptic; the one new factor was his overwhelming conviction that he was the one through whom the purposes of God were to be brought to fulfilment. Yet this truth is a secret that must be kept and not proclaimed. Jesus becomes convinced that he must die, and goes to Jerusalem with that intention. Upon his death the triumph will immediately follow—the kingdom will come and history will be brought to an end.

Jesus died. But history did not come to an end. What had gone wrong? Schweitzer does not tell us. His chapter on 'Thoroughgoing Scepticism and Eschatology' ends baldly with the words: 'At midday of the same day—it was the 14th Nisan, and in the evening the Paschal lamb would be eaten—Jesus cried aloud and expired. He had chosen to remain fully conscious to the last.'[1]

The implication is that from start to finish Jesus had been mistaken about himself, about his proclamation, and about the purpose of God—and was great enough to face with unclouded consciousness the realization of his mistake.

So the mystery remains unsolved. The concluding chapter on 'Results' ends with what have come to be almost the most famous words in modern theology:

He comes to us as one unknown, without a name, as of old, by the lakeside, he came to those men who knew him not. He speaks to us the same word: 'Follow thou me!' and sets us to the tasks which he has to fulfil for our time. He commands. And to those who obey him, whether they be wise or simple, he will reveal himself in the toils, the conflicts, the sufferings which they shall pass through in his fellowship, and, as an ineffable mystery, they shall learn in their own experience who he is.[2]

[1] *Quest*, p. 397.   [2] Ibid., p. 403.

Schweitzer has hardly had a single follower who has adopted his position in every detail. And indeed there is no difficulty in criticizing his views.

The evidence of the Gospels is so complex that it is quite certain that no single key will fit all the wards. Schweitzer, no less than those he criticizes, fails to do justice to many aspects of the story.

The ruthless logic of the dialectic of Jesus in his discussions with his enemies in the last week of his life does not in the least suggest the intemperate excitement of a fanatic.

Jesus is not after all so mysterious as Schweitzer would have us believe. It is quite true that 'the names in which men expressed their recognition of him as such, Messiah, Son of Man, Son of God, have become for us historical parables'; but it does not follow that 'we can find no designation which expresses what he is for us'.[1] Certainly we have no designation which expresses the whole of what he is for us— but neither had any other generation of the Church, including the first; hence the vast variety of names and titles for him in the New Testament.[2] But at all times Christians have used names and designations which they have known to be valid though incomplete; Jesus has never ceased to be the Good Shepherd and the Friend of Sinners.

Of the attitude of Jesus to his ministry and his death Schweitzer writes:

Jesus . . . in the knowledge that he is the coming Son of Man lays hold of the wheel of the world to set it moving on that last revolution which is to bring all ordinary history to a close. It refuses to turn, and he throws himself upon it. Then it does turn, and crushes him. Instead of bringing in the eschatological conditions, he has destroyed them. The wheel rolls onward, and the mangled body of the one immeasurably great man, who was strong enough to think of himself as the spiritual ruler of mankind and to bend history to his purpose, is hanging upon it still. That is his victory and his reign.[3]

This is as much rhetoric as anything that Renan ever wrote, though German rhetoric and not French. But it will not stand up under a moment's serious examination. Servants of God do not try to bend

[1] *Quest*, p. 403.
[2] Dr. Vincent Taylor has produced a valuable study of *The Names of Jesus* (1952). He makes the interesting point that later ages have added only one name or title, 'the Redeemer', to the fifty which are already to be found in the New Testament.
[3] *Quest*, pp. 370-1.

history to their purposes. There is no trace in Jesus, as presented in any of the sources, of that kind of arrogance which would rebel against the wise guidance of God and try to force his hand. A man of such slender spiritual resources as to be capable of such mistrust of the goodness of God could not have created that gigantic spiritual movement which we know as the Church of Jesus Christ.

And this leads on to the gravest weakness of all. When Jesus had died, apparently discredited and disillusioned, what was it that made the disciples so sure, in face of all the facts, that he had been right, and that in his death the kingdom of God had actually come? Historical causation is far more difficult to trace than physical; yet results must not be wholly incommensurable with alleged causes, or the student is entitled to judge that some essential factor has been mislaid somewhere along the way.

Schweitzer's chosen solution is inadequate and at certain points as weak as could be imagined. Yet his work has proved to be a turning point. We can never go back behind the recognition of apocalyptic as a real factor in the Gospel proclamation. We can never be content with a picture of Jesus as a rather civilized man of the nineteenth or twentieth century. We can never again separate 'the teaching of Jesus' from Jesus himself. In a new way the elemental power that is in the Gospels began to break out from them, and to present men with the challenge and the demand of a great mystery:

There was a danger that we should offer them a Jesus who was too small because we had forced him into conformity with our human standards and human psychology. To see that, one need only read the lives of Jesus written since the sixties, and notice what they have made of the great imperious sayings of the Lord, how they have weakened down his imperative world-contemning demands upon individuals, that he might not come into conflict with our ethical ideals, and might tune his denial of the world to our acceptance of it. Many of the greatest sayings are found lying in a corner like explosive shells, from which the charges have been removed. No small portion of elemental religious power needed to be drawn off from his sayings to prevent them from conflicting with our system of religious world-acceptance. We have made Jesus hold another language with our time from that which he really held.[1]

If we are less likely than our predecessors of a century ago to do all this, that is in large degree the measure of our indebtedness to Albert Schweitzer.

[1] *Quest*, p. 400.

Karl Barth (b. 1886)

Many theologians now living in the world could write their reminiscences under the title 'My encounters with Karl Barth'. The encounters may have been direct or indirect; personal or only through reading; favourable or bitterly hostile. But they will have been there. That has been the central importance of Karl Barth for more than forty years; he has been a touchstone, a sign, not infrequently a sign that has been spoken against.

One of the most eloquent utterances of those to whom Barth has been an offence and a stumbling-block is the passionate protest of Canon Charles Raven against the harm that he believed to have been done by Barth and the Barthians to the cause of scientific theology. Raven first pays a generous tribute to the liberation and enlightenment that came through Barth's teaching:

That in any case he did a great and wonderful work, that he brought to us all, even if we felt his emphasis to be one-sided and his strictures unfair, a deeper insight into the grandeur of religion, the miracle of God's grace, and the extent of our blindness and rebellion, and that even though we could not accept his denial of natural religion or his attitude to the Word of God, yet he stimulated, even by his negations, a vital interest in aspects of theology which had been neglected to our loss, all this remains an obligation which even his critics must thankfully acknowledge.

But on balance the loss is held to outweigh the gains. Liberalism in Britain, in the great traditions of F. D. Maurice, Hort, Gore, John Oman, Temple, and the rest, has never been anything like liberalism on the Continent. It was this true and necessary liberalism that Raven felt to have been threatened:

Theology had hitherto been concerned with the study of 'God and everything else together', and especially with restating the great doctrines: Creation, now regarded not as an act in the past, but as a continuing evolution; Incarnation, and its relationship to the creative process and to the indwelling of the Holy Spirit; Redemption and the light thrown by it upon the whole business of life through death; Community, and the relationship of individual to corporate well-being. To explore this restatement and its relevance to the life and thought of contemporary men had been the task laid upon every thoughtful Christian. Now theology was bidden to restrict itself to a rigidly specialised task, 'the study of Christian existence in history today', and told that concern with anything outside the Bible was 'vanity and

vexation of spirit'. The progress made since the abandonment of the con-
spiracy of silence was halted and condemned.[1]

This is a typically English reaction. It, and similar utterances which
could be collected from many sources, perhaps explain why there has
never been a strong Barthian movement in England. The situation has
been markedly different in Scotland and the United States of America,
and, needless to say, in Switzerland and on the continent of Europe
generally. The American translator of *Das Wort Gottes und die
Theologie*[2] has given a most interesting account of his own first encounter
with the Barthian world:

It was a generation ago that I ran across the German text, published under
the title *Das Wort Gottes und die Theologie* on the 'New Books' shelf in the
Andover-Harvard Theological Library in Cambridge, Massachusetts, near
which at the time I was serving as a parish minister. At first I glanced idly
through it for the chapter titles, then I found myself reading some of the more
arresting paragraphs, and presently succumbed so completely to the spell of
its passionate intensity and penetrating faith that I lost track of the passage of
time—not to be brought back to myself for two or three hours . . . To
question evolutionary modes of thought in that day was something like
questioning the Ptolemaic theory in the time of Copernicus, with the stupen-
dous difference that Copernicus seemed at first to shut the transcendent God
out of the world, and Barth seemed immediately to let him in.

The experience of discovering Barth was of the bitter-sweet variety,
producing an emotional dialectic which Barth himself would have prized . . .
There was undeniable exhilaration in rehearing and relearning that God is
God, that he *will* will what he will *will*, that he is not caught in the trammels
of the world he himself has created, and that men can produce him neither as
the conclusion of a syllogism, the Q.E.D. of an experiment, or the crown of a
civilisation.

My own experience slightly resembles that of Dr. Horton. In 1923
and 1924 I used to pass regularly through a long gallery of the Cambridge University Library to the little room in which I was writing a
fellowship dissertation. It was my habit to take up new books from the
shelves, as I passed by, and look at them. As I was specially interested
in the Epistle to the Romans, my eye was several times caught by
this new commentary by an entirely unknown writer named Karl Barth.

[1] C. E. Raven, *Science and Religion* (1953), pp. 213–15.
[2] Karl Barth, *The Word of God and the Word of Man* (English trans. by Douglas Horton: 1st ed., 1928, reprinted 1956).

I had not time to read the book; but I was interested by the comment of a German pastor, quoted on the dust-jacket, *Jetzt kann ich predigen*— 'Now I can preach'.

In 1928, in the course of a long and memorable conversation, that eminent Scottish theologian Hugh Ross Mackintosh advised me to read Karl Barth on the ground that I would find *much in him that was familiar and congenial*. I bought the book he recommended, *Das Wort Gottes und die Theologie*, and read it on board ship during my second voyage to India. I had never looked at the book since, until I started to write these lectures; it is interesting to recall the passages that made such a deep impression on me more than thirty years ago that I was able immediately to turn them up and recognize them. There was the famous passage about the expectancy of Sunday morning:

On Sunday morning when the bells ring to call the congregation and minister to Church, there is in the air an *expectancy* that something great, crucial, and even momentous is *to happen*... Do they know? Do they really know at all why they are here? In any case here they are—even though they be shrunk in number to one little old woman—and their being here points to the event that is expected or appears to be expected, or at least, if the place be dead and deserted, was once expected here.[1]

Then there is the notable passage in which Barth records his own spiritual ancestry:

Those who accept the thoughts I have brought forward as germane to the essential facts thereby acknowledge themselves descendants of an ancestral line which runs back through Kierkegaard to Luther and Calvin, and so to Paul and Jeremiah... I ought to add that our line does *not* run back through Martensen to Erasmus... and does *not include Schleiermacher*... In such a line the next previous representative might possibly be *Melanchthon*. The very names Kierkegaard, Luther, Calvin, Paul and Jeremiah suggest what Schleiermacher never possessed, a clear and direct apprehension of the truth that man is made to serve *God* and not God man. The negation and the loneliness of the life of Jeremiah... the keen and unremitting opposition of Paul to *religion* as it was exemplified in Judaism—Luther's break, not with the impiety, but with the *piety* of the Middle Ages—Kierkegaard's attack on Christianity—are all characteristic of a certain way of speaking of *God* which Schleiermacher never arrived at.[2]

The reference to Kierkegaard is, of course, highly significant. In

[1] *The Word of God and the Word of Man*, pp. 104-5. This address was delivered in July 1922.
[2] Op. cit., pp. 195-7: from an address delivered in October 1922.

1928 Kierkegaard was almost completely unknown in the English-speaking world. The only three theologians of an earlier date in whose works I have found allusions to him are the omnivorous Friedrich von Hügel (1852–1925), James Denney (1856–1917), and the equally omnivorous John Oman (1860–1939).[1] In 1928, the only piece of work on him available, and in print, in English was the article by Dr. A. Grieve in Hastings's *Encyclopaedia of Religion and Ethics* (1914), astonishingly good for its time; and not one single work had been translated into English. The flood of translations by Walter Lowrie, Alexander Dru, and T. F. Swenson was just about to begin.

More recent students have questioned whether the early Karl Barth had really understood Kierkegaard; of the effects on his thinking of Kierkegaard, as he had understood him, there can be no question. Kierkegaard had seen the significance of what he called 'indirect communication'. To suppose that religious truth can be communicated directly, as though it were mathematical truth or logical method, is a shallow blasphemy. All that religious truth can do is to present itself as a challenge, since the only way in which it can be apprehended is through faith. Hence Jesus Christ in the flesh is the 'divine incognito'; so far from proclaiming himself, he hides himself, since it is only the eye of faith that can discern who he really is. In his comment on Romans 8. 3, Barth quotes Kierkegaard with great effect:

If this be so, the mission of the Son is recognizable only by the revelation of God. We must therefore be on our guard against that 'fibrous, undialectical, blatant, clerical appeal that Christ was God, since he was so visibly and directly'! May we be preserved from the blasphemy of men who 'without being terrified and afraid in the presence of God, without the agony of death which is the birth-pang of faith, without the trembling which is the first requirement of adoration, without the panic of the possibility of scandal, hope to have direct knowledge of that which cannot be directly known ... and do not rather say that he was truly and verily God, because he was beyond our comprehension' (Kierkegaard) ... And it must needs be so. Blasphemy is not the stumbling-block that we all—some here, some there—discover in the life of Jesus. We stumble when we suppose that we can treat of him, speak and hear of him—without being scandalized.[2]

[1] Oman once told me that the only book in his life which he had been unable to finish was Karl Barth's *Römerbrief*! But equally it is reported that, when P. T. Forsyth began to be acquainted with the work of Karl Barth, he said: 'This is what Oman and I have been trying to say all along.'
[2] *The Epistle to the Romans* (English translation of the 6th edition by E. C. Hoskyns, 1933), pp. 279–80.

Characteristically Barth exaggerates by speaking of the 'impenetrable incognito' of Jesus Christ. The incognito was very far from being impenetrable; the whole point is that it was easily penetrable by those who came with humble and simple faith. But the principle that Kierkegaard states with regard to the communication of religious knowledge is vitally important and essential for an understanding of the Gospels. *Information* can be conveyed directly from mind to mind. Children can learn the Apostles' Creed by heart in half an hour; and then they *know* that Jesus Christ is 'his only Son our Lord'. But of what value is this knowledge, and what relation, if any, has it to religious faith? This is the complete answer to the problem that many inquirers have found so perplexing: Why did Jesus of Nazareth never declare himself openly and publicly to be Messiah and Son of God? The answer is that a man cannot convey true information about himself by making statements about himself. If I say 'I am a first-class cricketer', or 'I am an excellent singer', the statements may or may not be true; but in neither case are they interesting or relevant. All that I can really say is 'Give me a chance to play cricket with a good team', or 'Give me a chance to sing with a first-rate choir'—and *you shall be the judge*. With brilliant accuracy the Gospels have depicted Jesus as always refusing to answer questions, countering a question with another question. The scene of Peter's confession, where it is Jesus who asks the question: 'Who say you that I am?', is consistent with the whole of the rest of the Gospels, and with what we know of human nature. This is the way in which it could have happened; and it could not have happened in any other way.

But we have gone ahead a little too fast in our narrative and must turn back to place Karl Barth within the movement of his times.

Born in 1886, in 1917 he was pastor of the parish of Safenwil in the Aargau canton of German-speaking Switzerland. He was by conviction a theological liberal, and was closely in touch with the movement of 'Social Christianity'. Then came the cataclysm of the First World War; and the young pastor, sitting in his study in peaceful Switzerland, found that he had nothing to say to his people. The moral and spiritual consequences of the First World War were far more devastating than those of the second, since it burst on a Church and a world which were utterly unprepared for anything of the kind. It had been taken for granted, especially in Christian circles, that, though colonial wars might continue to be fought in remote parts of the world, war as an instrument of policy among the great nations of the world was unthinkable. The years between 1904 and 1914, like those since 1945, were a period of cold war, with Germany added to Russia as the chief provoking cause; but a number of crises had been passed through without explosion; it seemed likely that the procedure, though dangerously near to brink-manship, could be continued indefinitely. Then the explosion came. What had the Church to say? The evolutionary doctrine, to which most of the churches had committed themselves, was suddenly and horrify-ingly contradicted by the regression of great nations into barbarism. Moral platitudes and optimistic vistas now had nothing to say to people. Christian and non-Christian alike were plunged into perplexities, to which there seemed to be no answer, from which there seemed to be no way out. In this time of mental and spiritual disarray Karl Barth turned back to the Bible; he seemed to be reading it for the first time, as he discovered that the Bible is not a collection of the pious medita-tions of man upon God, but the clarion tones in which God speaks to man and demands his response.

The result was the publication in 1918 of the first edition of the commentary on the Epistle to the Romans—a bulky work of more than 500 pages, shapeless, confused, explosive, even violent, but with a passionate sincerity about it that at once attracted the attention of the world. The first edition was quickly exhausted; the whole book was completely rewritten for the second edition, which appeared in September 1921—tidied up a little, with some of its violence toned down. It is in this form that it has passed through edition after edition and remains one of the great theological works of the twentieth century. But it is really the first edition which is the most important; here in the brief Preface of little more than a page Barth has explained his purpose, and revealed something of the travail of spirit out of which the work was done: 'The reader will detect for himself that it has been written with a sense of joyful discovery. The mighty voice of Paul was new to me, and if to me, no doubt to many others also.' What has driven Barth to write has been the effort of listening to Paul himself, and not to the commentators:

The historical-critical method of Biblical investigation has its rightful place; it is concerned with the preparation of the intelligence—and this can never be superfluous. But were I driven to choose between it and the venerable doctrine of Inspiration, I should without hesitation adopt the latter, which has a broader, deeper, more important justification. The doctrine of Inspiration is concerned with the labour of apprehending, without which no technical equipment, however complete, is of any use . . . My whole energy of interpretation has been expended in an endeavour to see through and beyond history into the Spirit of the Bible, which is the Eternal Spirit.

These were provocative words and naturally Barth was before long engaged in a running warfare with half the scholars in Germany. He was accused of being a literalist, an 'enemy of historical criticism', of disregarding all the true canons of Biblical exegesis. Can there be such a thing as *interpretation*, which goes beyond the exact explanation of every word of the Greek? In view of the immense difference in time and background that separates us from Paul and the 'situation-conditioned' character of his writing, must it not be taken as certain that a great deal of what he has to say has no relevance at all for us today? Must not the attempt to make him speak at every point to the men of the twentieth century result in a wholly unscientific deformation of the original? This application of the text may be a useful occupation in the field of 'practical theology'; it has nothing to do with scientific exegesis.[1]

Barth has his answer ready. He has not neglected the field of historical and critical study. He has sat at the feet of the veteran scholars—Jülicher, Lietzmann, Zahn, and Kühl, and their predecessors Tholuck, Meyer, B. Weiss, and Lipsius.[2] But, when they have done their best, how little they have really done for the Epistle! All too often they dismiss parts of Paul's teaching as a purely Pauline point of view, or as something that can be illustrated by parallels from the literature of the time of Paul, instead of pressing forward to ask what it is that Paul is really concerned about, what it is that lies behind the particular form of words, often very difficult words, that he uses, and whether the concern of Paul is not also a very real concern of ours. Contrast with this the method of Calvin: 'how energetically Calvin, having first established what stands in the text, set himself to re-think the whole material and to wrestle with it, till the walls which separate the sixteenth century from the first become transparent'.[3] Calvin's *technical* equipment is inferior to that of a German scholar of the

[1] Some readers will recall the very odd division between 'Exegesis' and 'Exposition' in the *Interpreter's Bible*, that vast monument of American industry and scholarship.

[2] It is an interesting example of the 'provincialism' of which we have spoken that the commentary of Sanday and Headlam is not among those mentioned by Barth as an authority. In 1917 Barth knew no English. Since then, by diligent study of the speeches of Sir Winston Churchill, of detective stories, and of the sermons of John Donne, he has made remarkable progress in the language.

[3] *The Epistle to the Romans* (English trans., 1933), p. 7.

twentieth century; but his commentaries are works of *interpretation*, precisely the thing which the modern commentary so often fails to be.

Karl Barth's position, if freed from certain extravagances of language, is defensible. The New Testament is more than an archaeological collection of documents; it is a book by which men and women have lived, and in which century after century they have found the renewal of their faith. All Christians agree that the Bible is in some sense the Word of God;[1] it is the task of the interpreter to make that Word audible and relevant to the men of his own time. But interpretation of this kind can go forward on the basis only of exact and methodical exegesis of the text. The question is whether Karl Barth has really given the weight to the historical approach that is its due. I think the honest answer must be that for long stretches of the commentary he entirely fails to do so; his comments, vivid and arresting as they often are, have extremely little to do with the subject about which Paul is talking. Thus, for instance, in chapter 11 Paul is dealing with the problem of unbelieving Israel; Barth seems to have forgotten all about Israel, and to be concerned only with the problem of unbelief and election in the Church. Thus on 'the remnant according to the election of grace' (11. 6) he writes:

The election of men is by grace; this is the humiliation of the Gospel. But it justifies and saves because it humiliates. This is the Gospel of the remnant which verily exists, where light strikes *at this present time* in the misery and guilt of the Church. The one hope of the Church is that God should now justify himself and bear witness to his own oneness. And this is in fact the hope of the Church, because in Christ God is now revealing himself as the cause of our tribulation and of our guilt.[2]

This is both true and profound; but it is only by a somewhat violent wrench that what was written of unbelieving Israel is made to apply to the situation of a largely unbelieving Church. It is extended meditation, provoked by some of the thoughts of the Epistle, rather than exposition of it.

[1] Though many of them would find it extremely difficult to know exactly what they mean by the phrase that is so constantly used. One of the more valid criticisms of the Barthian position is that Barth has never succeeded in making quite clear what he does mean by the phrase 'The Word of God'.

[2] Op. cit., p. 397.

It often appears that Barth is not very much interested in the historical situation as such; if this is true, it may help to explain some of the ambiguities that run right through his work. What is history, and what is the relationship between history and revelation? Some comments made by Barth on D. F. Strauss and his *Life of Jesus* are illuminating at this point: enumerating the questions which Strauss has asked, and on which theology 'has not, right down to the present day, perhaps adequately declared itself', he formulates question 5 in the list as follows:

Is it not a fact that the goal of historical research can at best only be a historical Christ and that this implies a Christ who as a revealer of God can only be a relative Christ? Is it not a fact that such a Christ ... could on no account be the Word that became flesh, executing God's judgment upon us and challenging us ourselves to make a decision?[1]

What does this mean? The opposite of a historical Christ would appear to be a non-historical Christ. But could a non-historical Christ be a revealer of anything whatsoever? If by 'historical Christ' is meant one who is wholly absorbed by history, is identical with it, is wholly directed by its stream, the answer is that no human being is historical in this sense. To be human means precisely to be wholly in history, and yet at the same time to be in part independent of it, to transcend it, to criticize it, to live in continuously creative tension with it, and so in a measure to make history as well as to live it. Only a Christ who in this sense is completely historical can be the Revealer of God to men who live in history. A Christ who is in any way at all less than historical is not the Christ of the Gospels, or of the Church, or of faith, or of glory. The later work of Karl Barth suggests that he has gradually freed himself from this concealed docetism; in the earlier work it can hardly be overlooked.[2]

Karl Barth is a systematic theologian, and not a New Testament scholar. Yet all through it has been his aim that his theology should

[1] *Die protestantische Theologie im 19. Jahrhundert* (English trans., *From Rousseau to Ritschl*, 1959), p. 387.
[2] Walter Künneth (*Glauben an Jesus?* (Hamburg, 1962), pp. 198–9), states that this basic relativization of history is to be found at its strongest in Barth's discussion of I Corinthians 15, in his book *The Resurrection of the Dead* (*Die Auferstehung der Toten*, 1925). Barth storms against any kind of Easter-narrative which takes the form of a 're-counting of events'. But this involves in principle the elimination of the historical element in the *Kerygma*, and the incurring of a debt which in course of time has proved too heavy to be borne.

be thoroughly Biblical; *Kirchliche Dogmatik*, 'Church Dogmatics'—but this means the teaching of the Bible as understood in the Church, and lived out in the fulness of the Church's life. And throughout the long volumes of the *Dogmatik* he comes back and back to the interpretation of the Bible. At times the experts have been querulous and captious in their criticisms. It is undeniable that at times he neglects the finer points of scholarship and that his interpretation is wayward rather than exact; against such minor imperfections must be set the many passages in which his exegesis is solid, well based, and penetrating. The real weakness in his grasp of the Bible, in the creative works of his earlier period, relates not to details, but to far more general considerations; and this is important, since his weaknesses are precisely those which are most evident in large areas of German theology in the twentieth century.

In the first place, there are few signs of any clear or developed doctrine of the Holy Spirit. Romans 8 is one of the great New Testament sources of the doctrine of the Holy Spirit as the Spirit of the Risen Jesus. Karl Barth's commentary on it fills fifty-nine large pages; yet I am not sure whether at the end of all this the reader will have a clear idea of what it is all about. On page after page we are confronted with this kind of thing:

THE SPIRIT DWELLETH IN YOU. The Spirit is the truth . . . Truth is that redeeming subjectivity which secretly confronts every 'I' and 'Thou' and 'He', critically and immanently dissolving them by the objectivity which everywhere accompanies them. Truth permits no one to use it as a plaything; and it puts an end to all tragedy. Truth is far too merry and noble for us ever to justify our present life and address the present moment: 'Remain with me! Thou art so fair.' Truth is far too grim and terrible for us ever to desire to wrest it to ourselves, for example, by despairing and putting an end to our life.[1]

This may all be true and relevant; it is hard to see that it has much to do with the thought of Paul, or with the doctrine of the Spirit.

Secondly, in the early days up to and including the publication of the first volume of the *Kirchliche Dogmatik* (1932), Barth's concept of the Church was thin and inadequate. If we ask: 'When is the Church the Church?', the answer would seem to be: 'When a number of Christians are assembled in church on Sunday morning to listen to a sermon.' Barth himself is a preacher; as a Reformed theologian he

[1] *The Epistle to the Romans*, p. 257.

naturally and rightly exalts the sermon. But of the continuity of the life of the Church—that continuity which exists in the mystery of adoration and intercession, in the mysterious reality that since Pentecost there has never been a moment, day or night, in which the Church has not somewhere been engaged in prayer—he seems to be almost completely unaware.

Thirdly, and this defect is closely dependent on the other two, he is far less clear than we could wish him to be on the relationship between the Bible and the Word of God. When is the Bible the Word of God? Often we get the impression that the answer is: 'When it is being expounded from the pulpit by a preacher standing in the orthodox Reformed tradition.' Stated in this form, the answer is absurd, and it is hardly likely that this is what Karl Barth really means. Every day millions of Christians find that the Bible, laid open on the table in the privacy of their own rooms, lights up and becomes to them day by day the living Word of God. The *testimonium internum Spiritus Sancti*, the inward witness of the Holy Spirit, is a tremendous reality in the life and the continuity of the Church. This can be aided and encouraged by preaching, but is in no way dependent on it. To quote one notable example, the poet William Cowper, writing in 1764, tells us that

the happy period which was to afford me a clear opening of the free mercy of God in Jesus Christ was now arrived. I flung myself into a chair near the window, and seeing a Bible there ventured once more to apply to it for comfort and instruction. The first verse I saw was the 25th of the 3rd of Romans. Immediately I received strength to believe, and the full beams of the Sun of Righteousness fell upon me. I saw the sufficiency of the atonement he had made, my pardon sealed in his blood, and all the fulness and completeness of his justification. Unless the Almighty had been under me, I think I should have died with gratitude and joy. I could only look up to heaven in silent fear, overwhelmed with love and wonder. But the work of the Holy Ghost is best described in his own words—it is joy unspeakable and full of glory.

Cowper had been brought up from childhood in a Christian atmosphere, and had no doubt been familiar with the words of St. Paul long before their meaning so suddenly and dramatically flashed upon him. But similar experiences have been recorded in the case of non-Christians who, as far as can be traced, had never heard a word of the Bible, and at the very first reading of some portion of it have received an overwhelming impression of its truth and power. Coleridge defined the inspiration of the Bible in terms of its power to 'find' man, as no other book 'finds' him. It is this self-authenticating power of the written word, without the aid of any human intermediary, that lies at the heart of the conviction of the Church that the Bible is the Word of God. Contentions about the details of definition will continue until the world's end; the central conviction has stood unshaken through the centuries, and continues to be verified empirically today. The preaching of the Word in the assembly of the faithful is a great and wonderful thing; but any attempt to identify 'the Word of God' with this one particular form of its self-manifestation is bound to be self-defeating. At this point, perhaps, the views of Karl Barth need to be supplemented by the experience of Christians of traditions other than his own.

Yet, when we have said all that can be said in the way of criticism, Barth has rendered a great and notable service to Biblical study as well as to the renewal of systematic theology. The old liberalism on the Continent was almost wholly anthropocentric—man had become the measure of all things, including God: 'A hundred incidents are manifestly offensive: so much so that modern theologians blurt out and with touching simplicity: "Here we feel otherwise than Jesus felt"—a truth so desperately obvious that one would have thought it hardly worth while mentioning.'[1] Barth has reminded us in clarion tones that the Lord is a God of judgement and that by him actions are weighed. Man is put on trial, tested by the Word of God, shown up by the Word of God in the intricacies of his self-deception and his pride. The word of judgement can become the word of mercy only as man casts away all his defences and turns again to find his own true self in a restored relationship to the living God.

Edwyn Clement Hoskyns (1884–1937)

Edwyn Clement Hoskyns was in many ways curiously different from almost all the other theologians whom we are to encounter in our survey. His father was an Anglican bishop and was also a baronet; Hoskyns had grown up in that tradition of sober, upright, slightly austere High Church Anglicanism which was characteristic of what I have elsewhere called the 'country-house period' in Anglican history. After taking a not very distinguished degree at Cambridge, he had studied for a time in Germany, making the acquaintance both of Harnack and of Schweitzer. When in 1919 he returned to Cambridge

[1] *The Epistle to the Romans*, p. 280.

at the age of thirty-five as Fellow and Dean of Corpus Christi College, there was no reason to suppose that, in the eighteen years of life that remained to him, he would become a world-famous theologian, and would come nearer than any other theological teacher in individualistic England to creating a 'school'.

In technical equipment Hoskyns was inferior to many of his contemporaries in the Cambridge theological faculty. Unlike most of them, he had read History and not Classics, and had not that intimate knowledge of the Greek language that comes only with long years spent in reading and writing it both in prose and verse. To the end of his life he read Greek as a foreign language. But this was by no means wholly a disadvantage. The danger of the classical scholar reading the New Testament is that his mind glides over it too easily, that he takes too much for granted. Hoskyns took nothing for granted. He had an alert, restless, and inquiring mind, and came to the New Testament with an enviable freshness of disposition. This led him occasionally into surprising aberrations of exegesis. In Hebrews 4. 8, the reader of the Authorized Version is perplexed by the translation 'If Jesus had given them rest'. A little thought will show him that the reference is to the Joshua of the Old Testament, and that the translators with singular perversity have given the name in its Greek, and here most confusing, form. At one time Hoskyns was inclined to think that the reference in this passage really was to Jesus of Nazareth, who also as the human Jesus had not given his people rest. 'They won't consider it', he said, 'because of the Christ-ology it implies.'[1] This was an extreme case; but the capacity to hold all the possibilities, even the unlikely ones, before the mind is one that is of no small value to the scholar.

But the most important thing of all about Hoskyns was that, like Karl Barth, he was a converted liberal. I do not know exactly when the change took place; but it was certainly before his return to Cambridge in 1919. Nor do I know when he first made the acquaintance of the writings of Karl Barth. Canon Charles Smyth once told me that Barthian echoes were to be heard in Hoskyns's lecture room not later than 1923, at a time when few students in England had even heard the name Karl Barth.[2] Certainly Barth was one of the formative influences in the

[1] As far as I know Hoskyns never put this eccentricity of interpretation into print. I recall very vividly the conversation in which he set his ideas before me.
[2] See also his biographical sketch, in E. C. Hoskyns, *Cambridge Sermons* (1950), pp. vii–xxviii.

214 THE INTERPRETATION OF THE NEW TESTAMENT

mind of Hoskyns. One of his greatest literary memorials is the translation of the Commentary on the Epistle to the Romans (1933), a
work which cost him eighteen months' hard labour, and in which he
manifests in the highest degree that sympathetic understanding of the
mind of his author which makes possible translation as interpretation,
and not simply as the mechanical transference of thought from one
set of words to another.

It was this sense of mission, mission to replace the current liberalism
by something nearer to the truth of the Gospel, that produced in
Hoskyns's lecture room the electric atmosphere of excitement and
expectation that has been so well described by a number of his pupils.
It was as a teacher and inspirer of others that Hoskyns was great. He
did not much care for the endless labour of writing; apart from the
translation of Barth's *Romans* and the great commentary on the
Fourth Gospel to which we shall come later, and which was still
unfinished at the time of his early death, his writings are limited to one
book, *The Riddle of the New Testament*, to a collection of his Cambridge
sermons, and to a few articles in periodicals and composite works
It was in the face-to-face contact with living individuals that he
came alive and was able to communicate something of that life to
others.

It would be a mistake to think of Hoskyns only as a controversialist.
Yet liberalism was to him, in a very real sense, the enemy. He believed
that it was not founded on careful and accurate scholarship; and he was
convinced that it must in the end have disastrous consequences in the
life of the Church of Christ. Like many other Cambridge scholars,
Hoskyns gave some of his time to the correction of the examination
papers of boys and girls in the public and state schools of the country;
as he read the answers to the New Testament papers, he was horrified
to discover the extent to which the whole religious teaching in schools
had come to be dominated by a liberal presentation—a Bible from
which the supernatural had been carefully excluded, a calmly rational
presentation of the miracles, a Jesus of Nazareth who was admirable
as teacher and example, but from whom all messianic and divine
attributes had been pared away.[1]

This particular brand of liberalism rested on two main pillars. The
first was the conviction that the real founder of Christianity, in its
traditional form, was not Jesus but Paul. Paul was the evil genius who

[1] It is interesting to note that two such very different men as William Temple and
Hensley Henson, both far more liberal in the ordinary sense of the word than Hoskyns,

had changed the simple Gospel of Nazareth and Judaea into a complex theological system of redemption and salvation; to find the true doctrine we must get behind the Pauline presentation to the simplicities of the real Gospel. The second pillar was the belief that the increasing complexity of the Christian beliefs about Jesus is characteristic of the later stages of the tradition; if we go back from Matthew and Luke to Mark, now known to be the earliest Gospel, we shall find the tradition in a simpler form—indeed, we may be able to go back to an even simpler form, if some elements that are present even in the Marcan tradition can be removed. The New Testament writers present the life and death of Jesus as a drama of salvation; if we can get rid of these dramatic or dogmatic elements, we shall be on the way to discovering the realities of the historic Jesus:

Such evidence would suggest that the historical Jesus was unencumbered with this heavy significance. The claim has been made that it is precisely this discovery which results from the application to the Gospels of modern methods of historical and literary criticism. It is claimed that historical criticism rids the Jesus of history of any redemptive significance, and in particular rids his death of that peculiar importance which primitive Christian piety attached to it. This removal of the encumbrance with which the writers of the New Testament and the Church are supposed to have loaded the Jesus of history gave the sanction of critical scholarship to the modern distinction between Jesus and the Church, and set modern writers and modern preaching free to place him in the context of humanitarian idealism or in the context of popular ideas about evolution.[1]

It was this idea that Hoskyns was determined to destroy. The whole of his book *The Riddle of the New Testament* (1931: 2nd ed., 1936) is a series of hammer blows, at what, thirty years ago, was a widespread understanding of the Gospels.[2]

[1] *The Riddle of the New Testament* (1st ed., 1931; I quote from the edition of 1947), pp. 60–61.

[2] Earlier sketches of his position had been put out by Hoskyns in his essays 'The Christ of the Synoptic Gospels' in *Essays Catholic and Critical* (ed. E. G. Selwyn, 1926) and on 'Jesus the Messiah' in the composite work *Mysterium Christi* (1930).

---

were perturbed about the same problem at about the same time. See an extremely interesting letter of William Temple, then Archbishop of York, to the Headmaster of Rugby School, dated 16 July 1934. Referring to three books written for use in schools he writes: 'What I personally miss throughout is all sense of a great historical movement characterized by a sense of divine mission ... It is not legitimate to write about the Old and New Testaments without explaining that these present themselves, not primarily as a record of men's thoughts about God, but of God's acts in dealing with men.' See the *Life* by F. A. Iremonger (1948), pp. 139–40.

The results of the critical study of the Gospels, as set out in chapter III, provide us with the instruments which we need to pursue our researches further on the lines which Hoskyns is about to' propose. We hold with some confidence that Mark is the earliest of the Gospels and that both Matthew and Luke used him in the composition of their Gospels. If there is any tendency to heighten the drama, to complicate the simple narrative of Mark with extraneous theological matter, we shall certainly find it in those points at which Matthew and Luke differ from Mark. Do we in fact find that this is the process which has taken place? After a careful survey of the evidence Hoskyns answers in the negative. Matthew and Luke have far more material than Mark, particularly in the matter of words and discourses of Jesus. Each is an author and artist in his own right; the picture he gives of Jesus is his own, and is not merely derivative. Each uses freely the material given in Mark; each tends to correct Mark's rather provincial Greek, to explain what he has left obscure, to bring events into a more intelligible order. But essentially the representation of Jesus is the same, and, if there is any tendency, it is not towards heightening the majesty and the mystery of Christ; it is rather in the opposite direction—Jesus is a little tamed, a little softened and brought a little nearer to the ordinary categories of human existence:

But in the whole of this process of editing they nowhere heighten Mark's tremendous conception of Jesus. No deifying of a prophet or of a mere preacher of righteousness can be detected. They do not introduce Hellenistic superstition or submerge in the light of later Christian faith the lineaments of Mark's picture of Jesus. They attempt to simplify Mark. He is more difficult to understand than they are . . . All three evangelists record the intervention of the living God in the heart of Judaism at a particular period of history in the words and actions and death of Jesus of Nazareth; all three describe this intervention in the context of Old Testament prophecy; and all three regard these happenings as one great act of God by which his rule is inaugurated on earth and as a result of which those who believe are enabled to do the will of God, are freed from the powers of evil, are forgiven their sins, and are given a confident hope that they will share in that life which belongs to the era that is to be.[1]

So far so good. But the critical analysis of the Gospel documents has revealed to us a number of sources, now lost to us except in so far as they have been preserved in our Gospels. There is the celebrated Q,

[1] *The Riddle of the New Testament*, p. 104.

that collection of the Sayings of Jesus, which, if it existed in written form, was one of the very earliest manifestations of the Christian desire to write down and to preserve the record of the Son of Man. There was L the special source of Luke, and M the special source of Matthew. If we look critically at these, may we perhaps find in them the lineaments of the simple preacher of righteousness, the teacher of the new Law, who was willing to die rather than betray his loyalty to God, but never supposed that his death was fraught with eternal consequence for the human race? With this question in mind, each of these sources is again put through the sieve and carefully investigated. In each case the result is the same; at no point is there any evidence of a period of purely historical understanding of Jesus Christ, which has later been overlaid with the theological incrustation.

How, then, are we to think of the theologians, Paul, John, and the author of the Epistle to the Hebrews? Here everything seems to be concentrated on significance, and the original history sinks into the background. It is startling that Paul, living in a world in which there must have been constant talk of Jesus and his history, hardly ever refers to that history; he seems to be so absorbed by the Christ of his preaching as to have no need any more of 'Jesus after the flesh'. The writer of the Fourth Gospel does, indeed, clothe his ideas in the form of a Gospel, a 'life' of Jesus; but is this more than outward clothing for ideas which in reality are independent of their form? Hoskyns penetrates beyond this rather superficial question to the reality underneath; what is it with which these theological writers are most deeply concerned? The answer must be that it is with one who was manifest *in the flesh*. In a pregnant passage he indicates the real difference between knowledge after the flesh and knowledge after the Spirit:

This spiritual knowledge [of his friends] is a knowledge of living men, of men of flesh and blood. The difference between a carnal and a spiritual knowledge consists in a difference of judgement. So the change from a carnal to a spiritual knowledge of Christ does not mean that the object of his knowledge has changed from the Jesus of history to the Spirit-Christ. To suppose this would be to make nonsense of his epistle . . . His description of these Christians as 'in Christ' can be explained only on the supposition that conversion, if it is to be fruitful, must bring with it comprehension of the earthly life of Jesus in the flesh and an actual sharing in his obedience to the will of God.[1]

[1] Op. cit., pp. 160–1.

So the conclusion of this study is that there is a real unity in the New Testament documents. The Gospels bear witness to a history *in which an eternal significance is present*; the theologians bear witness to *a history* in which an eternal significance is present. The believers in Jesus did not read into him, from the Old Testament, a significance which was not really there; they recognized a significance which really was there. Jesus himself lived in the categories of the Old Testament, which is the record of the great acts of God in history; he was aware that he himself was the greatest act of God in history; in him and by him the destiny of men would stand and fall. The Riddle of the New Testament is Jesus Christ himself. History can go so far as to define the riddle, to formulate precisely the terms in which it presents itself to the human race; but it remains a riddle of the Sphinx until another dimension than that of history is called in to aid in its resolution.

In consequence, though the writers[1] affirm with rather surprising confidence that 'the historical problem has been solved', they point to other problems which lie beyond the limits of the purely historical method:

The book ends, as it must end, in an unresolved tension between confidence and helplessness. It ends confidently because the historical problem has been solved, and yet the solution of the historical problem does nothing either to compel faith or to encourage unbelief . . . The historian can help to clarify the issue, but no more. He is unable to decide between faith and unbelief, or between faith and agnosticism . . . Upon the ultimate question of truth and falsehood he is unable, as an historian, to decide . . . Here, then, the historian is driven to lay down his pen, not because he is defeated; not because his material has proved incapable of historical treatment, but because, at this point, he is faced by the problem of theology, just as, at this same point, the unbeliever is faced by the problem of faith.[2]

Hoskyns had provided a notable example of what it is now customary to call 'Biblical theology'. The three principles on which such a theology may be said to be based are: the recognized unity of all the New Testament witnesses, amid all their great variety in detail; the distinctiveness of the New Testament witness, as against everything which surrounds it in both the Jewish and the Gentile worlds; and the

---

[1] In this book Hoskyns was helped by his friend and pupil Noel Davey.
[2] Op. cit., pp. 179–82.

essential relationship between Old and New Testaments, the deep
penetration of the New Testament not only by the words but also by
the concepts and categories of the Old Testament, so that the New
is essentially a Hebraic and not a Hellenistic book.

The Riddle of the New Testament has great and abiding value. It
puts in clear form almost all the problems which have to be dealt with
in the interpretation of the New Testament. The book at once made a
deep impression in England, just because it was launched as a challenge
to so much that was current and accepted in English theology at the
time. But its influence extended beyond Britain. It is one of the very
few works of British theology which has been translated into French,
German, and Dutch, and is widely known to continental scholars.
The editor of the German translation remarks, perhaps a little over-
enthusiastically, that 'in no other work do we find so compact and
impressive an exposition of the present state of New Testament
science after a century of critical and historical investigation'. But not
all the positions of Hoskyns have proved acceptable without further
investigation. As Professor Kümmel says in a by no means unfriendly
summing up of his work:

Many of the historical propositions put forward by Hoskyns are open to
serious criticism; and, even though the central position maintained by him,
that the personal claim and the reality of Jesus Christ form the historic roots
of the New Testament proclamation, be accepted, it cannot be denied that the
three later theologians of the New Testament, and indeed the writers of the
Synoptic Gospels, attached to the oldest form of the proclamation interpretations which have been influenced by new and alien ideas, such as do not
lend themselves in every respect to a single unified presentation of the
New Testament proclamation of Christ. The unity of the New Testament
presentation is self-evident on the basis of belief in the inspiration of the
canonical Scriptures as a whole; but it cannot be maintained as self-
evident on the basis of strict historical investigation; and no method which is
free from objection is available to the student other than that of the separate
investigation of each individual book of the New Testament, and of each
strand of tradition.[1]

That this is true cannot be questioned by any serious student

---

[1] W. G. Kümmel, *Das neue Testament* (1958), p. 519. See a valuable reconsideration of
The Riddle by Professor C. F. D. Moule, in *Theology*, vol. lxix (1961), pp. 144–6. I
agree with his conclusion that, when later criticism has done its worst with *The Riddle*,
'it remains not only a far more readable book than most, but better than many for putting
in the hands of an enquirer'.

of the New Testament; that such further investigation will seriously modify the position taken up by Hoskyns may be doubted by those who feel that he has well and truly established his main positions.

The later years of the life of Hoskyns were occupied with his work on a large commentary on the Fourth Gospel. The work had, indeed, been started in early years; he was already engaged on it not later than 1924. It had been planned as one of the volumes in the Westminster Commentary Series; but, as it grew beyond the limits of this plan, it was decided that it should appear as a separate work. Hoskyns wrote and rewrote; new ideas were constantly coming to him, and he could not be satisfied that what he had written was exactly what he intended to convey. Eventually the work was practically finished; in the last year of his life, when he was already suffering from the grave malady which carried him off at the age of fifty-three, he was copying and revising the draft for the last time, and destroying the earlier draft as the rewriting progressed. It is believed by some of his friends that at this time his mind was not working at full pressure, and that the draft which was destroyed might have proved to be even more valuable than that which has survived. When Hoskyns died, the manuscript was not quite complete; it was edited with sedulous care and devotion by his friend and pupil Noel Davey, and saw the light in 1940.

Work on St. John's Gospel was peculiarly congenial to the mind and temper of Hoskyns. He was capable of careful and sustained work on matters of textual and linguistic criticism—one of his favourite methods was to show by careful comparison the way in which St. Luke, without quotation but by his exact choice of words, indicates the points at which he is interpreting the narratives of the life of Jesus in the light of narratives in the Old Testament. But, as is evident from one of the quotations we have already given from *The Riddle of the New Testament*, his mind was always pressing on to the urgent questions of faith and unbelief. The New Testament was not written as an academic text-book for professors to exercise their wits on; it was written out of a burning experience of the reality of God as made manifest in Jesus Christ, and as a means by which a like experience could be communicated to the readers. Through all the years in which Hoskyns was working on his commentary, he was also Dean of a College and preacher in its chapel, concerned to make the words of the Gospel a living reality to the young men under his charge. It was the issue of faith and unbelief that was ever prominent in his mind.

This is the central issue in the Fourth Gospel. As we have seen, at a comparatively early date scholars gave up the attempt to treat the Fourth Gospel as though it was literal history and to fit it into the Synoptic pattern. But, if it is not literal history, what is it? The answer is that it is a theological reconsideration of the life of Jesus of Nazareth, in the light of the deepest problems raised by that life, and in such a way that the theological problems cannot be evaded by any reader who devotes even a minimum of attention to the work. The dramatic quality of the Gospel is very high. Chapters 3 to 13 are, in fact, a delineation of the growth of faith and unbelief, and of their gradual separation out from one another, until the final conflict of the Cross and passion is seen to be inevitable.

This exactly suited Hoskyns's method. In the Introduction and throughout the commentary, he is constantly underlining the theology of the Gospel. Here is confrontation and challenge; here the ultimate issues of life and death have to be decided. The whole great work is little more than a variant on this one single theme.

The weakness of the method of Hoskyns is that it pays too little attention to the historical issue. 'What really happened?' This is the naïve but inevitable question of the theologically unsophisticated reader. It seems at times that Hoskyns is prepared to reject the question altogether, or at least to push it into the background. That is the question that you must not ask. It is irrelevant, and distracts us from the main issue of faith or unbelief. The Lord meets you in his Word. You are called to stand and deliver, to commit yourself, or to refuse to commit yourself, in this great battle between the classic Johannine opposites of light and darkness, life and death.

We may be prepared to go a long way with this argument. But the naïve historical question will not be stilled. What really happened? It may be that the final answer will be that we do not know. But this is a conclusion that may not be reached until every particle of evidence has been most carefully and particularly weighed, and until the fullest significance has been attached to it. For the story of Jesus of Nazareth, according to all traditional Christian understanding of it, is the story of the intervention of God in history. Though some scholars, and many Christians, are impatient in the face of such assertions, it seems to be the case that the faith of the Church stands or falls with the general reliability of the historical evidence for the life and death of Jesus Christ.

Rudolf Bultmann (b. 1884)

One can write of Rudolf Bultmann only with respect, and even with affection. At seventy-eight he is one of the great father figures of Western theology. There is hardly a subject connected with the New Testament which he has not touched; and, as with Karl Barth, whatever one's disagreements with him may be, it is necessary to wrestle with him, to take account of all that he represents, to adopt a position in relation to what is still the most powerful contemporary movement in New Testament interpretation.

Through all the fifty years of his writing career, Bultmann has maintained a kind of massive immobility. That he has learned much and changed his opinions on many matters no one would venture to deny. Yet the structure of his thought was early fixed, and seems to have undergone no fundamental modifications through the years. We commented earlier on the fact that no ghosts are ever laid in Germany. In the writings of Bultmann we encounter the full procession of the ghosts. Here is Strauss telling us that the life of Christ cannot be written because the connecting thread between the individual events has been broken. Here is Baur, insisting on the radical difference between Jewish and Gentile Christianity. Here is Schweitzer, happily a still living, powerful ghost, teaching us that Jesus of Nazareth supposed that the great act of God in him would mean the end of human history. Here is the radical scepticism of Wrede. Above all, here is the tradition of the religio-historical school as it was in Marburg in its flourishing days of forty years ago.

As a result, Bultmann can write today things which are quite astonishing in the climate of contemporary theology. For instance, in a recent essay on 'Changes in the Church's understanding of itself in the early days of Christianity', we are told that Paul changed overnight from an understanding of the *Ekklesia* which was based on the Jewish tradition of the Old Testament to a Hellenistic concept based on the Gnostic understanding of the body of Christ, and that neither he nor his followers at the time noted the inconsistency.[1] The essay bears the wrong date; it should be 1925, not 1955. Forty years ago, in what was perhaps a less critical age, statements of this kind met with fairly ready acceptance. Today it is impossible to accept the idea that

---

[1] 'Die Wandlung des Selbstverständnisses der Kirche im Urchristentum' in *Glauben und Verstehen*, vol. iii (1960), pp. 131–41. 'Paulus hat hier keinen Widerspruch empfunden'; 'Der Widerspruch konnte verborgen bleiben', p. 137.

a man whose intellect was powerful enough to shake the world, and whose letters are still sacred Scripture to millions of people, was so unintelligent as to make a major revolution in his thinking without even noticing that he was doing it.[1]

In another even more recent essay Bultmann tells us that Thucydides was the first of the great Greek historians. Alas for poor Herodotus, the father of history! But, apart from this possible rivalry between great names, we are further told that the Greek historian was primarily concerned with ascertaining what had happened in the past and did not reflect on this or that possibility in the future. In consequence, 'the Greek historians did not pose the question as to the meaning of history, and as a result no philosophy of history came into existence in Greece'.[2] So Bury in his prosaic way, and Cornford in his highly imaginative way, have both written in vain.[3] The fact is, of course, that the Greeks with their cyclic view of time believed that the future was already foreshadowed in the past, and that the study of history could be of the greatest value 'existentially', as we now say, to the statesmen and the men of affairs. This was the view of a later and much less great writer, Plutarch; and this classical view remained hardly challenged until the eighteenth century.

What is it, then, that makes Bultmann outstanding? Why do we still continue to read him, in spite of so much that was long since out of date and open to damaging criticism on many grounds? It seems to me that there are two reasons.

In the first place, Bultmann really knows Greek. He is one of the comparatively few New Testament scholars who has kept up the reading of classical Greek. He understands much of Greek literature and can quote it with affection, as in the chapters in *Primitive Christianity*,[4] in which he deals with the Greek heritage, adorning his pages with appropriate quotations from Aeschylus and Aristophanes.[5] As we have had occasion to remark elsewhere, the difference between

---

[1] It is also noteworthy that in this essay there is not one single word about the missionary outreach of the Church. But if there was one thing more than any other which characterized the early Church, surely it was the sense of being a *missionary* Church. Omission of this element is bound to result in distortion.

[2] *Glauben und Verstehen*, vol. iii, p. 92.

[3] J. B. Bury, *The Ancient Greek Historians* (1909); F. M. Cornford, *Thucydides Mythistoricus* (1907).

[4] Edition of 1956, pp. 103-45.

[5] Note also the impressive study of '*Polis* and *Hades* in the Antigone of Sophocles' which he contributed in 1936 to the *Festschrift* for the fiftieth birthday of Karl Barth, republished in *Glauben und Verstehen*, vol ii, pp. 20-31.

classical Greek and New Testament Greek is much less than is often supposed; and few things are more valuable for an expositor than a really intimate knowledge of Greek classical literature. As a result of this acquaintance, when Bultmann speaks on a point of philology, he speaks with authority. His articles in Kittel's great *Wörterbuch* are among the best. Some of the young men who have been commissioned to do articles give the impression of having dug up their information from lexicons and indexes, and of having little real command over the material that they are handling; Bultmann speaks of that which he knows, and his words carry conviction.

In the second place, Bultmann is intensely and passionately concerned about the *theology* of that which is contained in the New Testament. When critical analysis has done its utmost (and when Bultmann has done his utmost some readers have the impression that what is left is just a pile of shreds), the work is only in its beginning; this is a Gospel that has to be preached, to be made intelligible to modern men in terms of challenge and consolation. The pastoral concern which runs through all Bultmann's work is unmistakable; and one who does not know him as a preacher is likely to be mistaken in his estimate of the work of the man as a whole.

A single quotation must suffice to illustrate Bultmann's quality as a preacher. He is speaking to students at the University of Marburg, in the closing service of a semester, on the text Mark 13. 31–33: 'Heaven and earth shall pass away, but my words shall not pass away.' Towards the end of the sermon, he asks:

And what of the time that has not merely passed away, the time which we squandered or misused? Those moments of which we are ashamed? Do they not lead us to the awareness that the gift of eternity is the gift of forgiving grace? Must not such memories bring home to us in the plainest possible manner our helplessness in the presence of God, that helplessness in which alone we can receive the grace of God? And then, is not the distress of such recollections turned into thanksgiving? Even in the hours of that which was evil and mean God's hand has upheld and humbled us, and we apprehend his prevenient grace, that is willing to turn them into a blessing to us.[1]

It seems to me likely that many readers, faced with this quotation, and with the illustration from Marcel Proust's *A la recherche du temps perdu* in the paragraph which follows it, would not readily identify

[1] *Marburger Predigten* (1956), p. 225.

the author, if the name had not been already given. As a preacher
Bultmann usually attains to the perfect lucidity which is not always
granted him in his more theological writings. Karl Barth has written a
notable pamphlet under the title *Rudolf Bultmann: Ein versuch ihn
zu Verstehen*—'Rudolf Bultmann: An Attempt to Understand Him'.[1]
If one great theologian has to take all this trouble to understand
another, where shall the ordinary layman appear? But it is in these
passages of pastoral lucidity that we shall find the clue to much of
Bultmann's thinking, and in particular to that which has made the
greatest stir in the learned world and beyond it—the demand for the
radical 'demythologization' of the New Testament.

Bultmann asked himself the question: 'How can the New Testament
be preached to modern men?' He came to the conclusion that the
task was made much more difficult by the mythological language in
which the teaching of the New Testament is expressed, and which
has been taken over rather uncritically by the Church. He advanced to
the fray in a celebrated pamphlet, which first saw the light in 1941 during
the dark days of the war, under the title *New Testament and Mythology;
the problem of eliminating the mythological elements from the proclamation
of the New Testament*. Bultmann enters boldly into the attack; the
general world-picture of the New Testament is one that can only be
described as mythological:

The world is like a three-storeyed building. In the middle is the earth;
above it is heaven, below it is the subterranean world. Heaven is the dwelling-
place of God and of the celestial beings, the angels; the lower world is hell,
the place of torment. But the earth itself is not simply the scene of natural,
everyday events, of forethought and of labour, in which it is possible to
reckon with a regular and unchanging order; this earth too is the scene of
the action of supernatural forces, of God and of his angels. These supernatural forces intervene in natural events, in the thoughts, in the will, in the
actions of men.[2]

---

[1] It is not difficult to understand how it came about that at one period Barth and Bultmann felt themselves to be allies in a single cause. Barth refers to the qualified rejection of
his work on Romans by Schlatter, and the qualified acceptance of it by Bultmann—
in spite of Bultmann's merciless criticism of Barth's failure, as it seemed to him, to take due
account of the true canons of critical exegesis. And even in later years, when divergent
theological tendencies had carried them far apart, one can see how the fundamental
pastoral concern of both produces similarities even amid the differences. An English
translation of Barth's pamphlet is now available in *Kerygma and Myth*, vol. ii. (1962),
pp. 83–132.

[2] *Kerygma und Mythos*, vol. i (1948), p. 15 (English trans., 1953, pp. 1–2).

So much for the outward picture of the world. The representation of the revelation in Christ is, according to Bultmann, equally mytho-logical:

'When the time was fulfilled', God sent forth his Son. This Son, who is a divine pre-existent being, appears upon earth as a man; his death on the cross, the death of a criminal, makes expiation for the sins of men. His resurrection is the beginning of that cosmic catastrophe, as a result of which death, which was brought into the world by Adam, is annulled; the demonic powers have been deprived of their authority. The Risen One is exalted to heaven, where he sits at the right hand of God. He has been made Lord and King. He will return on the clouds of heaven to perfect the work of salvation; then the resurrection of the dead and the judgment will take place; finally sin, death, and all suffering will be brought to an end.[1]

Such a mythological presentation is, it is maintained, completely unintelligible to the modern man:

The concept of a Christ who pre-existed as a heavenly being, and the corresponding concept of man's own translation to a heavenly world of light, in which the self is destined to receive a celestial nature, a spiritual body, are to him not merely inapprehensible by any rational process, they are totally meaningless. For he cannot understand how it could be that salvation could take the form of the attainment of such a condition, or that in it he could reach the fulfilment of human life, and of his own authentic character as a personal being.[2]

Now it is not enough to answer that all great literature, whether it be Aeschylus or Shakespeare, is expressed in its own idiom, and that anyone who wants to understand it must be prepared to take a certain amount of trouble to master the idiom.[3] The problem lies deeper; when we have mastered this to us unfamiliar terminology, what does it really convey, and in what sense are we required to accept that which it conveys as the truth? This is a question which we must not attempt to dodge:

[1] Op. cit., pp. 15–16 (English trans., p. 2).
[2] Op. cit., p. 21 (English trans., p. 8).
[3] Bultmann is perfectly prepared to recognize that the Gospel can never be congenial to the modern man—there is, as Kierkegaard so clearly saw, always an 'offence'. In one of his most recent essays, 'Das Befremdliche des christlichen Glaubens' (1958) in *Glauben und Verstehen*, vol. iii (1960), Bultmann identifies the two-fold offence as the idea that an event in history can be accepted as 'the eschatological event', and the Cross of Christ (op. cit., p. 211).

At this point absolute clarity and integrity are demanded of the theologian and the preacher. This is a duty that they owe to themselves, to the Church, and to those whom they desire to win into the fellowship of the Church. The preacher in his sermons must not leave his hearer in any uncertainty as to what he requires them to believe to be true, in the strict sense of that term. Above all he must not leave the hearers in any uncertainty as to what he himself has quietly suppressed; and in this regard he is bound to be completely honest with himself also.[1]

No one who has ever had to preach on Ascension Day is likely to doubt that this is a challenge that has to be taken extremely seriously. And the challenge has been made by Bultmann on behalf of the Gospel, on behalf of the honesty and integrity of proclamation.

It is to say the least of it unfortunate that in this essay, which caused such a theological furore, and which is still a lively subject of discussion in theological circles, Bultmann never made clear what he meant by the word 'myth', or what exactly it was that he wanted to eliminate from the proclamation of the Gospel.

The word 'myth' can be used in a whole variety of senses; it is indeed one of those words which, like 'eschatological', would be far better banned from all decent theological usage.

Some would use the word as denoting a tale which corresponds to nothing which ever really happened at all. There are some who use the term the 'Christ-myth' to express their conviction that what we are told of Jesus Christ does not correspond to any historical reality whatsoever. And some would feel that this does not greatly matter; the stories have value, quite regardless of whether there is in them any 'objective' truth or not. This seems to be the position taken up by the philosopher R. B. Braithwaite; he writes:

A man is not, I think, a professing Christian unless he both purposes to live according to Christian moral principles and associates his intention with thinking of Christian stories; but he need not believe that the empirical propositions presented by the stories correspond to empirical fact ... And in many people the psychological link is not appreciably weakened by the fact that the story associated with the behaviour policy is not believed.[2]

This is a rather unusual view, and might seem to offer support only for a rather tenuous kind of faith.

[1] Op. cit., p. 21 (English trans., p. 9).
[2] R. B. Braithwaite, *An Empiricist's View of the Nature of Religious Belief* (1955), pp. 22–31, quoted in J. Baillie, *The Sense of the Presence of God* (1962), p. 142.

But this is emphatically not the view of Bultmann. He holds that something did happen, and that faith is necessarily and irrevocably linked to that happening.

What was it, then, that happened? When we have got rid of all the mythology, what will be left? We can quite easily dispense with the three-storeyed universe. There was a time when the Copernican understanding of the solar system caused grave disturbance, but more to the philosophers than to the theologians, since the philosophers were committed to an Aristotelian view of motion which really was wholly irreconcilable with the mathematical discoveries of Copernicus, Kepler, and Galileo.[1] But theologians have long since emancipated themselves from the idea that primitive concepts of the visible world stand in any essential relationship to the Christian Gospel; and one may suppose that the theologian has been followed by every intelligent reader of the Gospels. And both theologian and layman may be excused if they hold the view that the ancient language, if not taken with absurd literalism, is the best that could be found to express certain great religious ideas. When the layman hears the splendid words:

> For thus says the high and lofty one
>   who inhabits eternity, whose name is Holy:
> I dwell in the high and holy place,
>   and also with him who is of a contrite and humble spirit,
> to revive the spirit of the humble
>   and to revive the heart of the contrite
>
> (Isa. 57. 10)

it is hardly likely that he imagines to himself God dwelling at the top of a pinnacle of light. It is probable that some children are still condemned to sing

> There's a friend for little children
> Above the bright blue sky;

but no intelligent child takes this literally any longer than it takes literally the view that Santa Claus comes down the chimney on Christmas Eve.

[1] On all this see the very interesting account in J. Dillenberger, *Protestant Thought and Natural Science* (1960), pp. 21–103; and see also a suggestive note on pp. 281–2, in which Dillenberger discusses the significance of mythical and mythopoeic language.

It appears, however, that Bultmann would extend the term 'myth' much more widely, and would include under it almost the whole of the traditional formulation of the Creed. The idea of Christ as a divine being who entered into human life is Gnostic and cannot be accepted; and so on. And yet Bultmann is desperately concerned about the *Kerygma*, the proclamation of new life for men in Jesus Christ. What is the *Kerygma*, and how is it to be proclaimed?

The answer is to be found in Bultmann's acceptance of the existentialist philosophy, particularly as this is set forth in the writings of Martin Heidegger. This is a familiar procedure. The theologian takes that form of philosophy which is dominant in his day and reinterprets the Christian faith in the terms and categories of that philosophy. This is what Thomas Aquinas did with the Aristotelian system of his time. We have had occasion to note the influence of the Hegelian philosophy on German theology of the nineteenth century. And now it is the turn of Heidegger. The danger, of course, in all such adaptations is that they make theology living and relevant for a time, but when the philosophical climate changes, the theology which was attached to an outworn philosophy simply disappears. The interesting thing about Bultmann is that he is not a systematic theologian, but an interpreter of the New Testament; he frankly and openly brings his philosophical convictions to bear on his interpretation of the New Testament.

There is a great deal to be said, much more than some critics will allow, in favour of Bultmann's choice of the philosophy of existence as the form within which he will work out his interpretation of the New Testament. This philosophy does not deal with theories or generalizations; it starts from the particular man, in his existence, in the situation in which he finds himself, with all its turmoil and all its uncertainties. Here am I, and here are you. We have been flung into existence without our knowledge or consent; we have to make the best of it, as best we may. There are two possibilities before us—to sink down into mere existence, or by a resolute and repeated act of decision to rise to the height of authentic existence.

The man who merely exists is full of anxiety:

That which is visible and tangible is transitory; and therefore any man who bases his life upon it has fallen under the power of transitoriness and death . . . One who tries to use the tangible as the basis for his own security is thereby driven into conflict with 'the other'; he has to assure himself against the possibility of aggression on the part of 'the other'. From this arises on the one hand jealousy and anger, rivalry and conflict; and on the other treaties and conventions, conventional judgments and every kind of compromise . . . This is the source of man's bondage to the fear, the anxiety (Rom. 8. 15) which weigh so heavily upon him. Every man strives to cling on to his own existence and to his possessions, all the time with the feeling that everything, even his own life, is slipping away from him.[1]

This is inauthentic existence; here a man does not really exist, he is merely part of his surroundings, at the mercy of others and a constant prey to fear. In Jesus Christ (and here Bultmann is adding what is not to be found in any existential philosophy) God meets man with challenge and promise. If a man hears and decides in favour of authentic existence, he is set free from anxiety, and able to rise to a wholly different level of existence in which he is open to the future:

The man who opens his heart to grace receives the forgiveness of sins, that is, he is set free from the past. This is also the meaning of the word 'faith'— to open oneself freely to the future. Such faith is also obedience, since it involves man's turning away from himself, his surrender of all security, his abandonment of the effort to gain significance . . . it involves a total self-surrender to God, which expects everything from God and nothing from itself; and consequent on this, deliverance from everything tangible and worldly, an attitude of detachment from the world and so of freedom.[2]

Such decision is not one single act made once for all; it is to be regarded as an attitude, as the occasion of repeated encounters with God in Christ, in which 'eschatological existence' is reaffirmed, and freedom from the world is made the great reality.[3]

All this is admirable, and every statement can be supported by quotations from the New Testament. Perplexity begins when we inquire as to the foundation on which all this rests; a little further inquiry reveals why it is that one section of opinion regards Bultmann as the prophet of the new age, and another regards him and his

[1] Op. cit., p. 30 (English trans., pp. 18–19).
[2] Op. cit., p. 29 (English trans., pp. 19–20).
[3] Other aspects of Bultmann's work are noticed elsewhere in this volume. The publication of Bultmann's essay provoked an immense international controversy, which still continues; the successive layers are to be found in the five volumes of essays *Kerygma und Mythos* (ed. H. W. Bartsch), a number of which have been translated into English. I still regard as unsurpassed the general survey of Bultmann's thought provided by Giovanni Miegge, in a book which I translated from the Italian under the title *Gospel and Myth in the Thought of Rudolf Bultmann* (1959). Many echoes of Bultmann's thought will be found in the highly controversial volume *Honest to God* by Dr. J. A. T. Robinson, the Bishop of Woolwich, which appeared while this chapter was being revised.

doctrine as the gravest threat to the continued existence of Christian faith in a troubled world. Who is Jesus Christ, and in what sense is it true that God meets me in him and in his death?

Two points in Bultmann's exposition are likely to prove perplexing to the English reader who is not familiar with the whole background of Bultmann's thought.

He is constantly girding at anything like an 'objectivizing' attitude towards God. The words 'objective' and 'subjective' have changed their meanings so often in the course of the development of Western thought that we always do well to regard them with suspicion. In English, the word 'objective' is usually a good word; to be objective is an admirable quality—it speaks of impartiality, reason, and a reduction of the personal equation to a minimum.[1] It is, therefore, strange to us to find 'objectivity' condemned or rejected.

Kierkegaard was fond of saying that 'subjectivity is all'. By this he was not, of course, defending a kind of solipsism, in which I alone exist and everything is real only in so far as it exists in relation to me. What he was doing was to protest against an attitude of cool and rational detachment and the supposition that knowledge of a truth of any importance can be attained in this way. Truth is truth for me only when I have taken it into myself, only when I am engaged, when it has become a matter of life and death to me. In this sense God can never be an 'object'; this, I think, is what Bultmann means when he protests against the 'objectivizing' of God.

Confusion arises from another source. Idealists are inclined to say that God can never be object, since he is always subject. This may be true of the Absolute of philosophy, since all experience is in some way the experience of the Absolute coming to self-consciousness. It is emphatically not true of the God and Father of our Lord Jesus Christ. This God is emphatically object. It is not simply the grammatical fact that in the New Testament the word 'God' is constantly found in the accusative case—God is the *object* both of human knowledge and human love. The whole structure of the Christian revelation culminating in the Incarnation is based on the fact that God has put

[1] Though he does not use the word, Bultmann has very interesting things to say along this line in a paper with the title 'Is Exegesis without Presuppositions Possible?' (1957), *Glauben und Verstehen* (1960), pp. 142–50. He starts off: 'To this the answer must be Yes, if "without presuppositions" is taken in the sense that the *results* of exegesis are not presupposed. In this sense, exegesis without presuppositions is not merely possible; it is obligatory.' He goes on to show that in another sense such 'objectivity' in relation to the text is not possible.

himself into a relationship with men in which he is both subject and object, he knows and is known. This is mysterious. But it is implicit in the doctrine of creation. God *was* related to nothing but himself. God is now related to something outside himself, and, as the Cross of Jesus shows, he is prepared to follow out the implications of that fact to the very last limit. To none of this, I think, would Bultmann raise any objection, though he might not feel readily at home with our English terminology, any more than the English reader is readily at home with his.

What, then, is he objecting to? It is the reduction of God to a series of propositions which can be rationally apprehended, to an 'it' with which we can play as we will. God is always active. I know nothing of God as he is in himself—he is always God turned towards me, God who comes towards me in challenge and demand. We are reminded of Martin Buber's doctrine of 'I' and 'Thou'; if I think otherwise of him, I am not thinking of God at all.

Secondly, Bultmann is conditioned by a violent hostility to any tendency to reduce the Gospel to history. In contrast to a number of scholars, who would be prepared completely to volatilize the narrative elements in the Gospels, Bultmann would be the last to deny that 'something happened'. As we shall see elsewhere, he holds that we know very little of what happened; but the *Kerygma*, the message of Jesus Christ, is concerned with something that actually happened in time. His hostility is directed not against those who hold that there is a historical basis for Christian faith, but against those who imagine that the truth of the Christian Gospel can be demonstrated by the verification of historical evidences. Nothing in this field can be *demonstrated*. The acceptance of the Gospel is a matter of faith and nothing else; in this sense Bultmann has some grounds for the claim that he makes to be the restorer of the true Reformation doctrine of justification by faith. No man was ever saved by accepting the truth of certain historical facts. Faith belongs to a different dimension altogether.

As is well known, Bultmann makes a convenient distinction between the *historisch*, the thing that merely happened, and the *geschichtlich*, the historic event that becomes significant. Things are happening all the time; but most of them are no more significant than the falling of leaves from the tree outside my window. Only that is history for me by which I am challenged, in relation to which I have to act, in which I find the existential moment. So Bultmann concludes his Gifford Lectures on 'History and Eschatology' with a fine and moving passage on the significance of history:

The meaning in history lies always in the present, and when the present is conceived as the eschatological present by Christian faith the meaning in history is realised. Man who complains: 'I cannot see meaning in history, and therefore my life, interwoven in history, is meaningless', is to be admonished: do not look around yourself into universal history, you must look into your own personal history. Always in your present is the meaning in history, and you cannot see it as a spectator, but only in your responsible decisions. In every moment slumbers the possibility of being the eschatological moment. You must awaken it.[1]

But we are still faced by the inescapable problem that Jesus of Nazareth remains obstinately and irrevocably in the past; nineteen hundred years have sped away since he lived among men. How then are we to make him present? How is the challenge implicit in the *Kerygma* to become a living and existential challenge to me?

The whole work of Bultmann can be summed up as a gallant attempt to solve the problem, to make the challenge existential— without belief in the resurrection of Jesus Christ as something that actually happened, and without a doctrine of the Holy Spirit.

Bultmann does not believe that the resurrection of Jesus Christ was *historisch*, historical in the sense of having actually taken place. We cannot get beyond the faith of the first disciples; they came to believe that Jesus was alive, and so he was alive for them; and just so he can become alive for us:

The truth of the resurrection of Christ cannot be understood until that faith which acknowledges the Risen One as Lord has sprung up in us . . . Christ is present in the *Kerygma*, not as a great historic personage is present in his work and in its effect in history . . . What we are concerned with is the fact that an historical personage with his own personal destiny has been raised to the level of the eschatological event . . . If a man accepts the word as directed to himself, as the word which offers to him death and life by means of death, he has believed in the Risen One.[2]

On this Giovanni Miegge has commented:

True Christians in every generation have thought exactly in this way. But

[1] *History and Eschatology* (1957), p. 155.
[2] *Theologie des Neuen Testaments* (1948–53), pp. 300–1 (English trans., vol. i, pp. 305–6).

they have never supposed that the power of the resurrection can be experienced, except as it comes to us from a supernatural event that has really happened; they pass without difficulty from the 'merely' historical fact of the resurrection of Christ to the power of his resurrection as it is perpetually renewed in the believer. Is it possible to separate the two things, as Bultmann would do? Is it possible that faith in the resurrection should become incarnate in a man, unless he believes that on Easter morning Jesus of Nazareth really left the sepulchre empty and appeared before the eyes of his disciples, astonished, doubtful, and reluctant to be persuaded as they were?[1]

This seems to me unanswerable. The distinction between *historisch* and *geschichtlich* is useful and valuable. It is just the fact that not everything that 'merely happened' can become significant. But can anything become *geschichtlich* which was not first *historisch*? Can anything become historically significant, if it did not first actually happen? If words mean anything, the answer must be No. Can Christ effect in me life through death, victory and deliverance from transitoriness, if he was not himself first raised from the dead, literally and in the completeness of his manhood, by the glory of the Father? (Rom. 6. 4.) This is the burning question which will not stay for an answer.

How, to put the question once again, is the challenge of Jesus Christ made contemporary with me? The answer of Bultmann is that it comes to me in the *Kerygma*,[2] in the preaching of the Church, which itself is part of the eschatological event:

Revelation does not reach us as the communication of an idea of God, or of the idea of divine grace; it touches us in an individual, in a historic figure, and it renews itself from moment to moment in the preaching delivered by other definite historical figures who ... 'on behalf of Christ, as though God did beseech us by means of them' proclaim God to me as the God who can moment by moment be realized as my God.[3]

---

[1] *Gospel and Myth* (1959), p. 50.

[2] For Bultmann the reality and validity of the *Kerygma*, the proclamation and the thing proclaimed, is central. Objection to precisely this point is taken by the Swiss liberal theologian Fritz Buri, Professor in the University of Basel. The New Testament, we are told, needs to be not only demythologized, but also 'dekerygmatized', since the *Kerygma* itself, as Bultmann understands it, still contains many irrational elements, which make it unacceptable to modern man in his purely rational world (F. Buri, 'Theologie der Existenz' in *Kerygma und Mythos*, vol. iii, ed. H. W. Bartsch (1954), pp. 81–93). Professor Buri is nearing the completion of a major work on dogmatic theology which has been described as the first liberal dogmatics to be produced for thirty years; two volumes have so far appeared—*Vernunft und Offenbarung* (1956), and *Der Mensch und die Gnade* (1962).

[3] *Glaube und Verstehen*, vol. ii, pp. 258–9 (English trans., *Essays*, p. 287).

It must strike an English reader as strange that, at this point, there is no reference whatsoever to the work of the Holy Spirit. Bultmann parts company with the New Testament in the same way as Barth and for the same reason. There is the same exaggeration of the significance of preaching, which is characteristic of continental Protestantism; and there is the same lack of a theology of the Holy Spirit, as the One through whom time and distance are annihilated, and through whom the Word of Jesus becomes the living and contemporary word, whether preached by the eloquent orator in the great cathedral or read by the simple fishwife by the light of a guttering candle in her lonely room.

But who shall cast a stone? Polite references to the Holy Spirit at suitable intervals are to be heard in the preaching and worship of all the denominations. But who has developed a theology of the Holy Spirit that really does justice to the part that he plays in the whole New Testament revelation? Bultmann is right. The message of the Gospel is always *Kerygma*—it is always contemporary, and it is always challenge. For this reminder we shall always be profoundly indebted to him.

We can make our own the comment of a Roman Catholic scholar, who writes:

Though many reservations in relation to the theology of Bultmann may be regarded as justified, we ought to lay ourselves open to the immense spiritual potentialities which have been released through it, and which help us to have 'fellowship with God' as truly believing, hoping and loving Christians. The powerful effects which have followed upon the teaching of Bultmann would be almost inexplicable, unless he had discovered at least one key, which really fits, and opens up to the understanding of faith whole new dimensions of the holy Scriptures.[1]

[1] Thomas Sartory, o.s.b., *Mut zur Katholizität* (1962), p. 471, n. 94.

Chapter VII

THE GOSPEL BEHIND THE GOSPELS

To write a history of views and opinions clearly held is no very difficult task. Important books have to be identified and analysed, considered in chronological order and related to one another; and then after a fashion the work is done. It is much more difficult to trace the mysterious process by which a whole climate of opinion changes, current solutions no longer satisfy, old forgotten searchings are unearthed anew, and a range of fresh questions is asked about familiar themes. Such a change never takes place suddenly; a certain restlessness prevails; a feeling of frustration, a sense of having reached the limit beyond which certain lines of investigation are no longer fruitful, perplexes the thinker. Then some hand touches a switch; a new door is opened, new perspectives of thought open out; study and investigation renew their vigour and can be prosecuted with hope of fresh illumination. Again and again it proves to be the hand of a young man which finds the right switch, and opens the door to a new period of adventurous discovery.

As we have seen, it is not possible to say exactly at what date the priority of Mark to the other two Synoptic Gospels came to be generally accepted as the central key to the investigation of the Synoptic problem. By about 1890 acceptance of the principle had become almost universal, and for the next thirty years documentary study, the attempt to trace and identify the written documents which lie behind our Gospels, was the main preoccupation of scholars engaged in the exact and scientific study of the Gospels. There was a tendency to think that, once all these documents had been identified, their contents at least approximately worked out, and their relation to our Gospels in principle determined, all the major problems of Gospel criticism would have been solved. No scholar doubted that before anything at all came to be written down, there had been an earlier period of oral tradition during which the stories of the words and works of Jesus circulated among the believers in Aramaic; but it was thought that this period was now inaccessible to us, and that to attempt to get behind the first written records into this still older period would land us in a dream-world of unverifiable speculation.

It was exactly at this point that the new questioning began to arise. Is not the period before the beginning of written records the most crucial of all for the formation of the Gospel tradition? Is it quite certain that we are excluded by the lapse of time from all knowledge of it? Old Testament scholars had begun to work their way back behind the documentary hypotheses of the origin of the Hebrew books to the oral traditions which must have underlain them. Is there not at least a chance that the application of similar methods to the New Testament may carry us back one stage further towards the saving acts of God in Christ? If so, and even if success should be no more than limited, is not the attempt well worth making?

It is not possible to say just when these questionings began to stir in the minds of scholars. Perhaps, indeed, they had never really ceased; perhaps, even in the intense concentration of many minds on documents, existing or hypothetical, the sense of a mysterious and seductive 'beyond' had never died out. We can, however, date with almost exact precision the point at which these concerns were crystallized in clear form, and at which the new questions were first put in challenging form before the world of scholarship. A new epoch in the study of the Gospels opened in 1919 with the publication of a book *Der Rahmen der Geschichte Jesu* ('The Framework of the Story of Jesus') by Karl Ludwig Schmidt, at that time twenty-eight years old, and a teacher (not yet professor) in the theological faculty at Berlin. Schmidt continued to do valuable work in various directions; of his later works, the best known to English readers is probably the article on *Ekklesia* in Kittel's *Wörterbuch*, which has been translated as one of the 'Bible Key-words'. But it was the first book which established his reputation; he never perhaps quite equalled again the brilliance and originality of his first notable contribution to theology.

As is clear from the title of his book, Schmidt has directed his attention primarily to the framework within which the life of Jesus has been set by the evangelists. The Gospels consist for the most part of a series of short episodes, of which Jesus is the subject. In the majority of cases each episode is complete in itself, compact, vivid, and distinct. Few of the stories contain within themselves any clear indication of time or place. Of only a few of them is it possible to say with certainty that they must belong to one period rather than another in the ministry of Jesus.

No one doubts that the stories which are related by Mark, our earliest evangelist, had come to him from a variety of sources. Mark has linked these together by a series of bridge passages. He has provided chronological order, and a scheme by means of which we are able to follow the ministry of Jesus from the preaching of John the Baptist to the crisis of his arrest and crucifixion. Many scholars had accepted the view that Mark's Gospel is genuine 'history'; he has arranged his material in a certain way because this is the way in which things happened; his chronology is reliable and corresponds closely to the events of the ministry of Jesus as they actually took place. As we shall see later, this view had not remained unchallenged. Schmidt takes up the question again, and asks, in the light of detailed and careful study, whether it is really possible to regard Mark as 'history' in the sense in which this word is generally understood.

When we study the 'bridge passages', we find that they are often vague and dim, in contrast to the clarity and definiteness of the events and sayings which they serve to link together. The data of time and place which they supply are in many cases not clearly related to the episodes to which they refer; in all probability they formed no part of the original tradition. Many years earlier David Friedrich Strauss had likened the stories of Jesus in the Gospels to a handful of pearls of which the connecting string had been broken. Schmidt takes up the same idea. The connecting string, the framework, has been supplied by the evangelist himself to give unity to his narrative in the light of his own interests and preoccupations. His work will prove to be of great importance, when we come to consider it as evidence for the life and thought of the early Church at the time at which he was writing; if our aim is to come nearer to the events as they actually happened, we may almost wholly disregard the framework, the historical value of which is now seen to be considerably less than had been previously supposed.

We are thus brought back to the earliest stage of the formation of the Gospel tradition. Originally the episodes, and the accompanying words, circulated singly among the believers. At a very early date some of the single traditions may have coalesced, through similarity of subject, or through mere verbal correspondence.[1] For the most part this tradition is oral—the stories pass from mouth to mouth; but quite soon after the death of Jesus the first steps towards writing may have been taken:

It is not difficult to imagine how self-contained units of Christian teaching came to be hammered out, first orally, then as written fly-sheets or tracts—

---

[1] A clear example of this process is Mark 9. 49–50, where three quite separate sayings have been brought together, the link being the occurrence in each of them of the word 'salt'.

often in several differing though related shapes, according to the contexts in which they were used. When therefore John Mark (for example) sharpened his reed pen and dipped it in the ink to write, he had already behind him a considerable tradition of Christian speaking and possibly writing, by Peter and many others—recognized patterns of argument and exhortation, of defence and attack, of instruction and challenge—from among which he might select his narrative material and his sayings. The earliest Christian writers were probably already heirs to a considerable body of tradition.[1]

To what do we owe the preservation of these stories? There can be only one answer; they belong to the history of the community, and particularly to its character as a worshipping community: 'If it is the case that the rise of the Christian faith can be understood only in terms of the development of Christian worship—a view which has won increasingly wide acceptance in recent years—it is clear that the rise of Christian literary activity must also be understood in relation to the experience of worship. In my opinion, the significance of the early Christian tradition of worship for the process by which the literature of the Gospels came into being cannot possibly be exaggerated.'[2] If this view is correct, it seems to follow naturally that those events were repeated and remembered which were of interest to the worshipping community, or of significance for its life, in relation to its practical, or pastoral, or missionary work. In every case we are entitled to ask: 'To what situation in the life of the early Christian Church does this episode or saying correspond? Why was it repeatedly told? Why was this saying of Jesus felt to have continuing significance for the life of the worshipping Church?'

To this analysis of the Gospel into its original constituent fragments there is one major exception. The narrative of the Passion seems to have reached something like its present form at a very early date. There are many details in this narrative which seem to have in themselves no significance either for the Christian at worship or for the task of Christian apologetic; they are retained because at an early stage they had become part of a larger whole, which in all its main lines remained unaltered by the later developments of the tradition.

It would be difficult to improve on the summary given by Professor W. G. Kümmel of all the various elements which go to make up the picture as Schmidt has presented it:

J. G. Herder's thoughts on the individual forms of the oldest traditions of

[1] C. F. D. Moule, *The Birth of the New Testament* (1962), p. 55.
[2] K. L. Schmidt, *Rahmen*, p. 31.

the Gospels, and their character as *testimony*; the insights of F. Overbeck into
the nature of 'primitive Christian literature', which is distinguishable from all
later Christian literature and is recognizable by its own special characteristics;
A. Deissmann's recognition of the popular character of the original Christian
writings; the attention drawn by J. Wellhausen to the doctrinal interests by
which the selection of the materials brought together in the Gospels has been
influenced, and to the part played by the evangelists themselves in providing
the connecting links by which the Gospels are held together in unity; the
observation recorded by P. Wendland and W. Bousset that from the beginning a distinction existed between the single-episode narratives of the Gospels
and the connected story of the Passion—all these ideas had prepared the way
for the 'Form-critical' handling of the Gospel traditions. But the strongest
impulse of all . . . came from the work of Hermann Gunkel, one of the
founders of the 'religio-historical' school, who had in later years devoted
himself to the interpretation of the Old Testament. In dealing with, in
particular, the sagas of the patriarchs and the songs of the Old Testament,
Gunkel had developed the method of trying to establish the original oral
traditions of individual events, and the mental presuppositions (*Sitz im Leben*,
life-situation) by which the formation of this tradition had been conditioned.
This work of Gunkel played a decisive part in preparing the way for the
investigations of the Gospel-traditions carried out by K. L. Schmidt and the
other members of the 'Form-critical' school.[1]

It is important not to exaggerate the originality of K. L. Schmidt,
considerable though this was. Contemporaneously with him two
other scholars were working independently on very similar lines. Also
in 1919, Martin Dibelius (1883–1947) published his book *Die Formgeschichte des Evangeliums* (English trans., *From Tradition to Gospel*,
1934). This was followed by the *Geschichte der synoptischen Tradition*
(1921) of Rudolf Bultmann, of whom we have had much to say in other
connexions. These three together may be regarded as the founders of
what has come to be known in English, rather inaccurately, as 'Form-
criticism', though in German its title is the *formgeschichtliche Methode*,
the scientific study of the history of literary forms.[2]

At the outset of his elaborate study of the forms of the Gospel
tradition, Dibelius makes two general statements which have a deter-
minative effect on all that is to follow.

[1] W. G. Kümmel, *Das neue Testament*, pp. 422–3.
[2] It is almost certain that Dibelius took over this expression from the sub-title of a book
very well known in its day—Eduard Norden's *Agnostos Theos: Untersuchungen zur
Formgeschichte religiöser Rede* ('The Unknown God: Inquiries into the History of the
Forms of Religious Utterance', 1913).

He starts by making a distinction between 'literature in a high or classical style', and *Kleinliteratur*, literature for popular consumption. Up to a certain point this distinction can be justified. Certainly the writers of the Gospels did not follow the classical rules of composition, as elaborated by contemporary rhetoricians, and their style, as we have seen, belongs to the tradition of the *Koinē* and not to that of the classical writers of ancient Greece. When we look more closely, however, the generalization may seem to be more misleading than illuminating. The Gospels may not be classical; but they are not in the least like the pathetic and almost illiterate manifestations of popular writing so many examples of which are available to us in the papyri. They are literature; this is the operative word, and the gap which divides them from the greatest of classical writing is far less than that which divides them from the world of the popular and uncultured. The distinction is, in any case, one which is very difficult to sustain. To take an example from English literature, to which class does John Bunyan's *Pilgrim's Progress* belong? From one point of view it is certainly 'popular literature', written by a self-educated tinker for largely uneducated readers; yet it is one of the great and abiding classics of English literature.

Secondly, Dibelius affirms that the writers of the Gospels are to be thought of as compilers rather than authors:

> The literary understanding of the Synoptic Gospels begins with recognition of the fact that they are made up of collections of traditional material (*Sammelgut*). Only in the smallest degree are the writers of the Gospels authors; they are in the main collectors, transmitters, editors. Their activity consists in the handing on, grouping and working over of the material that has come down to them, and their theological apprehension of the material, in so far as one can speak of an apprehension at all, finds expression only in this secondary and mediated form. Their attitude to their work is far less independent than that of the author of the Fourth Gospel, far less than that of the writer of the Acts of the Apostles.[1]

Here, once again, the over-confident affirmation of a general principle is likely to prove, and has proved, gravely misleading, unless it is immediately balanced by the statement of supplementary considerations.

No writer writes completely out of the blue. Even the lyric poet of the purest inspiration is in point of fact dependent on a long tradition, and the skilled critic can often identify the influences that have made

[1] M. Dibelius, *Die Formgeschichte des Evangeliums* (3rd ed., 1959), pp. 2, 3.

him what he is. Far more than the poet, the historian or the biographer[1] is dependent on the past. By the choice of his medium each has cut himself off from the realm of pure invention. But only the very poorest of historians or biographers are mere 'collectors, transmitters, editors'. We may well admit that the writers of the Gospels invented nothing; they lived by a tradition and they were faithful and careful recorders of it. Yet I am inclined to think that if a reader, trained in the art of literary criticism in fields other than those of the New Testament, were to come fresh to the Gospels, the immediate and overwhelming impression that he would receive would be that each of the evangelists is an author, and an author of genius, in his own right.

Just when and how this peculiar form of literary composition which we call a Gospel first came into being is a question that we cannot regard as having been as yet definitely settled. Was Mark the first to achieve success or had he predecessors in the art? We cannot say for certain. However that may be, it is clear that each of the evangelists was faced with a literary task of the gravest difficulty. Within the narrow compass of a papyrus roll, he had to set down for the benefit of his readers and of the future all that was essential in the Church's memories of Jesus Christ. Each had large quantities of material, written and unwritten, on which to work. Each Gospel is the product of extraordinary skill in selection and arrangement. We shall later consider the particular theological principles and interests which influenced the evangelists as they set their hands to the work; for the moment we are concerned only with the astonishing skill with which a most difficult task has been achieved.

Mark's Gospel can be read through without haste in not more than forty-five minutes. For the Fourth Gospel about an hour is required, and naturally a little longer for Matthew and Luke. It is to be regretted that Christians do not more often read through a Gospel at a sitting; only then does the splendour of the evangelists' achievement become apparent. It is a great advantage to us that we have four Gospels. Yet if three Gospels had perished and only one had survived, whichever of the four had been the survivor, we should still have had an astonishingly complete presentation of the manifestation of the Word of life among men. In much that follows in this chapter, we shall be concerned with details; unless the details are seen against the background of the larger whole, we are liable to be seriously misled.

[1] We shall consider later in what sense, if in any, it is right to speak of the Gospels as biographies.

We shall, then, find it necessary to keep our eyes open as we read the 'Form-critics', and to exercise on them that critical spirit which they exercise on the Gospels. But it is impossible that all the careful study they have directed to the Gospels should prove to be without value; and, provided that we keep certain critical reservations in mind, we are likely to find that they have much that is profitable to teach us.

II

We have already alluded to the first point at which the methods of the 'Form-critics' prove themselves to be of value—the study of the forms in which the various traditions about Jesus of Nazareth have come down to us.

We may start with a remark of quite general bearing. As the origins of the tradition are to be sought on Palestinian soil, we shall not be surprised to find in the Gospels a parallel to a distinction which is deeply marked in the whole tradition of Jewish literature. On the one side stood the *halākhā*, oral transmission in the schools of the Rabbis, by means of which the words of the wise on matters of ethical concern were passed on from generation to generation. Here great attention to verbal accuracy was demanded, and every attempt was made to ensure that the tradition, as it was handed on, correctly reproduced that which had been received from the past. The *haggādāh*, the edifying literature, covered a very wide range of subjects—folk-lore, homiletics, magic, astrology, and others besides. This was never regarded as authoritative in the same way as the *halākhā*; greater liberty was permitted, and there was much less rigidity in the reproduction of a fixed tradition. In the New Testament, the actual sayings of Jesus corresponded to the *halākhā*; the words were treated with great reverence, and care was taken to pass them on, as nearly as possible, allowing for problems of translation, in the form in which Jesus himself was believed to have spoken them. In the reporting of *incidents*, where Jesus was the principal actor, considerably greater freedom was allowed.

Within this general framework, we now come to the question of the forms or types of tradition which are to be encountered in the New Testament, and particularly in the Gospels. Many of the 'Form-critics' believe that there are laws according to which oral traditions shape themselves, and that these are observable and verifiable in spheres of tradition other than the New Testament. Here work on the

Old Testament, and notably that of Hermann Gunkel, has proved valuable. By careful attention to the Old Testament text, it is possible to work out the *Gattungen*, the types and forms of tradition in which the material was shaped before it ever came to be written down, and which have left their clear traces on the final form in which the books are preserved for us in the Hebrew Old Testament.

No careful reader will find any difficulty in doing a certain amount of elementary work on these lines himself. At a first reading of the Book of Judges, he becomes aware of the difference between the magnificently original Song of Deborah in chapter 5 and the prose account of the same affair in chapter 4, which is also impressive in its own way but differs a good deal from the poem both in detail and in the manner of presentation. The great sagas of Gideon and Jephthah are accompanied by the terse annalistic sections in which no vivid details are given and by the homiletic sections in a style rather like that of Deuteronomy; the whole is held together by the scheme—peace, sinfulness, oppression, deliverance through a judge, and then again peace. Another field in which the study of the *Gattungen* has proved to be of great value is the Psalms. Here again it is possible to identify certain clearly defined types—the royal Psalms, the Psalms of historical narrative and proclamation, the hymns of praise probably associated with the worship of the Temple, and so forth.

The method has its dangers as well as its uses. There is a tendency to go on inventing types and varieties, headings and sub-headings, until there are almost as many classifications as there are pieces of literature to classify. Then, in this excessive interest in systematization, we all too easily forget that tradition, whether literary or pre-literary, is a living thing and far too flexible ever to be satisfactorily reduced to system. Whatever form of classification we adopt, we are likely to find that the exceptions are as numerous as the items which fit into our scheme. The traditional division of the plays of Shakespeare into Tragedies, Histories, and Comedies has its uses; but how many of the plays in point of fact escape from the tidy limits of this classification!

It is obvious that, if this method of literary analysis is applied to the sayings of Jesus in the Gospels, a variety of systems of classification can be adopted.

Dibelius distinguishes five main types—'Paradigms', Short stories (*Novellen*), Legends, Edifying utterances (*Paränesen*), and Myths. None of these terms is likely to be clear to the reader without a word of explanation.

The Paradigm, or Pronouncement-story, is a brief episode, often controversial in character, in which the culminating point of the story is a pregnant utterance of Jesus, in which some truth is decisively conveyed: 'They that are whole have no need of the physician, but they that are sick' (Mark 2. 17).

The *Novelle* is a longer narrative in which a good deal of detail is given, but which does not lead up to any decisive utterance. The story seems to be told for its own sake. The best example is perhaps the healing of the Gadarene demoniac, who said that his name was Legion (Mark 5. 1–20). A notable word is spoken to the man who has been healed; but no fundamental principle is stated. There are fairly close parallels to this type of story in ancient sources outside the New Testament and the Christian sphere.

The term 'Legend' Dibelius deliberately takes over from the later Christian vocabulary; legends of the saints make up a large part of the edifying literature of the later Christian centuries. The term 'Legend' does not necessarily imply that what is recorded is untrue or unhistorical. What is important is the point of view of the narrator— the story is told to reveal the moral or spiritual excellence of the one of whom the story is told. In the Gospels, Dibelius picks on the story of Jesus in the temple when he was twelve years old (Luke 2. 41–52) as a highly typical example of this kind of narrative.

'Edifying material' covers the greater part of the words of Jesus addressed to the disciples, in which the new life of the believer is set forth as it has to be lived in a hostile world. Here the material is so rich that a further five-fold division is suggested—picture-utterances (*Bildwort*), actual parables, the prophetic call or challenge, brief commands, and more extended instructions by way of command.

'Myth' is to be recognized when a story breaks loose from the ordinary limitations of time and space in such a way that the supernatural is seen breaking in directly upon the human scene. Dibelius takes the view that the mythical element in the Gospels is very small.[1] One of the principal points at which he regards it as being clearly present is the story of the Transfiguration. Here we move in a world very different from that of the rest of the Gospels; the transcendent, which elsewhere is latent, at this point breaks through, and is vividly brought to our attention; the participants in the scene include Moses and Elijah, who are no longer living in the world of men.

---

[1] It will be noted that he is using the term 'myth' in a much more limited sense than Bultmann.

Bultmann's approach is somewhat different. What Dibelius calls paradigms he calls 'apophthegmata'; he, too, recognizes the same phenomenon of the brief story, often polemical in character. He almost apologizes for including these narratives in his studies, since his main concern is with the words of Jesus; but he justifies this proceeding, rightly in my opinion, on the ground that the whole point of the story is in the word with which it ends. These stories are not primarily biographical; they are theological, told for the sake of the utterance in which the presence of the Lord is made plain. Bultmann then goes on to make a five-fold analysis of the sayings of Jesus, and here the correspondence with the view of Dibelius is less noticeable. His five groups are *Logia*, utterances in which Jesus is presented as the great teacher of wisdom; Prophetic and apocalyptic sayings, in which the future is brought near; words of Law, and rules for the life of the community; 'I-words', in which Jesus speaks in the first person, on his own authority, and reveals who he is; Parables, and similar utterances of a pictorial type.

No one is likely to deny that there is value in the classification of material. The question at once arises, however, whether the classification really arises out of the material itself or whether it has been imposed upon it. The fact that various scholars analyse the words of Jesus in different ways suggests that not all is perfectly clear, and that the categories of which use has been made are not so much inherent in the New Testament itself as arrived at by other methods and imposed upon the material from without. Many of the words of Jesus could readily be assigned to more than one of the suggested categories; others do not seem to fit easily into any of them. Unless we are careful at all times to maintain the flexibility of mind without which literary analysis cannot be successfully carried on, we may find that what gave promise of being a useful tool has turned out to be a cramping suit of armour. Even a term like 'parable' cannot be used as though it meant only one single thing; there is a considerable difference between such brief comparisons as that of the man who built his house upon a rock, the brief nature parables such as that of the seed growing secretly, and the extended stories of the Unjust Steward and the Prodigal Son.

Nevertheless, with these reservations, the method can be accepted as helpful, as a means to the study of the Gospel tradition in its formative period. We picture the early Christian groups at a time when no written New Testament Scriptures existed. We see the three types of servants of the Church, preachers, teachers, and narrators, at work.

This is the kind of material upon which they were at work. Amid many uncertainties, we may hope rightly to have detected something of the kind of thing that was going on in a period of which we know very little directly, but regarding which we can infer a good deal by working backwards from the later and well-established results.

Once we have established the general lines of the development of the tradition, the second step in 'Form-criticism' is the attempt to determine the *Sitz im Leben*, the life-situation to which each of the separate sections in the Gospels is related. Here the reference is in part to the situation in the life of Jesus but even more to the situation in the life of the Church. These traditions have come down to us because the believers of the first generation found them relevant to their own situations. They were not antiquarians, jealously gathering together every scrap of information about a not very distant past; they were believers, living a difficult life of adaptation in hostile surroundings, and needing at every moment the guidance of the living Lord as mediated to them through the living voice of tradition. Relevance might naturally be of very different kinds; it could relate to problems of the inner life of the Church, to apologetics, to polemical encounter with the enemies of the faith, to the instruction of the newcomers to the community, to direct missionary proclamation. It may be supposed that different areas would have different interests, and that there would be a rather marked distinction between Gentile Christians and those of Jewish origin.

To attempt to get behind the traditions in their present form to the situation in which they were first formed and to which they seemed immediately relevant is a perfectly legitimate exercise of the critical art. It must, however, be said at the outset that the practice of it is very far from easy, and that unless the critic is exceedingly cautious he is likely to stray out of the narrow pathway of scientific theology. Only in rare cases can we hope to establish more than probability. Much depends on the personal equation and on the particular approach of the individual critic—as is evident from the sharp differences among the critics in their estimate of particular episodes. Why, we may ask, was the simple and touching episode of the blessing of children by Jesus reported? It is just conceivable that the question whether children of Christian parents should or should not be baptized had already raised its head in the Churches of the earliest Christians.[1] It is much more

---

[1] Some representatives of the Form-critical school simply *assume* that the reference here is to the baptism of infants; but this is exactly the kind of assumption that must never be made.

likely that these Christians were exercised by the problem of the status of the children of mixed marriages, where only one parent was Christian. In 1 Cor. 7. 14, Paul gives the ruling that, in that case, the children are 'holy', called by God's grace, since the prevailing influence was that of the believing parent. But the story of Jesus and the children may have been told because Christians, whose conscience had been newly awakened by their faith, had become disturbingly conscious of the shocking neglect of children which was characteristic of the Roman world; a little later the Roman satirist Juvenal, moved by the same lack of concern on the part of parents for their children, was to write *Maxima debetur puero reverentia*. Or it may be that the Christians who handed on the story were thinking not so much of the children as of the childlike quality of the faith demanded of the Christian, which is often directly emphasized by the Lord himself, and without which the believer cannot enter into the kingdom of heaven. Here are four possibilities. Who is to decide between them? Now, as we have seen more than once, to treat a possibility as though it were a probability, and then a little later to treat it as though it were a certainty, is an offence against the basic canons of critical and scientific work. None of us is, perhaps, entirely guiltless in this matter.

III

So far we have considered two characteristics of 'Form-criticism', and have concluded that it provides useful, though somewhat dangerous, tools for the study of the Gospel traditions. Its third characteristic has been an extremely negative attitude towards the historical validity and reliability of those traditions, so much so that it has been possible for Rudolf Bultmann to reach the conclusion that of Jesus of Nazareth, as he actually was in history, we know hardly anything at all. Whence comes this very negative attitude?

One of the ghosts that it has been hardest to lay in Germany is the ghost of Wilhelm Wrede. In 1901 Wrede wrote a little book, *Das Messiasgeheimnis* ('The Secret of the Messiahship'), which has had an influence out of all proportion to its size.[1] It had usually been taken for granted that Jesus in some sense claimed to be the Messiah. Thus

---

[1] This is one of the brilliant German books that has never been translated into English. This may be because Wrede almost immediately met an English foeman worthy of his steel. In *The Life of Christ in Recent Research* (1907), William Sanday said all that really needs to be said about Wrede. Schweitzer, who did not agree with him, devotes a long section to his work (*Quest*, chap. xix).

Harnack in *What is Christianity?* expressed his opinion on the subject in no uncertain tones:

We shall never fathom the inward development by which Jesus passed from the assurance that he was the Son of God to the other assurance that he was the promised Messiah ... What a moment it must have been for him when he recognised that he was the one of whom the prophets had spoken; when he saw the whole history of his nation from Abraham and Moses downward in the light of his own mission; when he could no longer avoid the conviction that he was the promised Messiah... The idea of the Messiah became the means—in the first instance for the devout of his own nation—of effectively setting the man who knew that he was the Son of God, and was doing the work of God, on the throne of history.[1]

Wrede took a very different view. The life of Jesus was not messianic, and Jesus himself never made any claim to be Messiah. It was only the resurrection that convinced the disciples that Jesus was the Messiah. Having come to this conviction, they then realized that he had been the Messiah all along; they therefore proceeded to read back the Messiahship into the life of Jesus. But, if Jesus was actually the Messiah all the time, how did it come about that the disciples were unaware of the fact throughout the ministry? How did it come about that the Jews went so far as to crucify the one who was actually their promised deliverer? To account for this, the tradition, or perhaps it was the author of Mark's Gospel himself, ingeniously invented the idea of the Messianic Secret—they did not realize that he was the Messiah, because Jesus himself carefully concealed the fact from them; to the end they were unaware of it. The story of Peter's confession, his great utterance 'Thou art the Christ', is a reading back into the time of the ministry of what was in reality a post-resurrection appearance of the risen Christ, and of the recognition by Peter of his messianic character.

This is not the place for a detailed discussion of Wrede's views. The influence of them is to be seen in the contrast between Harnack and Bultmann. Harnack confidently affirms that Jesus claimed to be Messiah; Bultmann tells us that we must regard it as very doubtful whether Jesus ever made any messianic claim at all.[2] But the influence of Wrede

---

[1] *What is Christianity?*, p. 141.

[2] *New Testament Theology*, pp. 26–33. Here Bultmann follows almost exactly the lines laid down by Wrede in 1901, and rejects the more positive reconstruction of the thesis of Wrede, which was the work of Julius Schniewind (1893–1948).

goes much deeper than this. To put it quite crudely, it is the old question of the hen and the egg. Did the tradition create the Christian community? Or did the Christian community create the tradition? It had usually been supposed that the tradition created the community. Now Wrede affirms that at one point of crucial importance the community created the tradition, and read back into the life of Jesus something that had never been there at all. This creative quality of the Christian community is taken almost as an axiom by the majority of the supporters of the Form-critical school.

No one is likely to deny that a tradition which is being handed on by word of mouth will undergo modification. This is bound to happen, unless the tradition has been rigidly formulated, and has been learned by heart with careful safeguards against the intrusion of error.[1] Most of us would, I think, be inclined to agree that, in the story of the coin in the fish's mouth, and of Peter walking on the water in Matthew 14, an element of imaginative enlargement has at some point or other been added to the original tradition. Again, the variation of the forms in which sayings of Jesus appear, as between one Gospel and another, suggests that there was a freedom of interpretation, even in this most sacred area of the tradition, which did not demand exact verbal fidelity. But there is a vast difference between recognition of this kind of flexibility, of this creative working of the community on existing traditions, and the idea that the community simply invented and read back into the life of Jesus things that he had never done, and words that he had never said. When carried to its extreme, this method suggests that the anonymous community had far greater creative power than the Jesus of Nazareth, faith in whom had called the community into being.

At this point, once more, it is most difficult to attain to objectivity. For example, Bultmann holds that the story of the temptation of Jesus is the fruit of the inventive power of the community.[2] This story is

[1] But this is exactly the way in which tradition was handed on among the Jews. It is precisely on this ground that the Scandinavian scholar H. Riesenfeld, in an essay entitled *The Gospel Tradition and its Beginnings* (1957), has passed some rather severe strictures on the whole 'Form-critical' method. On Riesenfeld, see also M. Dibelius, *Die Formgeschichte des Evangeliums* (3rd ed., 1959), Appendix by Gerhard Iber on *Neuere Literatur zur Formgeschichte*, pp. 308–9; and add Birger Gerhardsson, *Memory and Manuscript* (1961).

[2] *New Testament Theology*, p. 27: 'The story of the temptation is a legend which arose out of reflection on the quality of Jesus as Messiah, or rather on the nature of the Christian belief in Jesus as Messiah.' Bultmann simply states his view, without any supporting arguments.

highly poetic and imaginative in form. In a few verses, it sums up in picturesque fashion the great problems of the kingdom of God as seen in the light of the ministry of Jesus. To sum up so much spiritual truth so simply, so briefly, and in such unforgettable images demands creative genius of the highest possible calibre. Who in the early Christian groups had such genius? Paul, on occasion, is capable of flights of lyric splendour; but he has not a plastic, visual imagination of the kind that expresses itself in such forms as the story of the temptation. In the first century we know of one man, and one only, who had that kind of imagination, and that kind of power over words. His name was Jesus of Nazareth. Now it is just within the bounds of possibility that, through long meditation on the nature of the kingdom, the community arrived at a particular understanding of its own problems as it faced a hostile world; and that some unknown genius then gave that understanding pictorial form. But the probability is immensely the other way—that Jesus, wishing to communicate to his disciples the mystery of his own relationship to the kingdom of God, found for that mystery this perfect expression and passed it on to them in a form that they could not forget. Let it be stressed that there is no question here of evidence; the story of the temptation belongs to one of the earliest strata of the tradition. It is simply one man's judgement of spiritual and literary possibilities against another's; we have passed from the realm of science into that of poetry, from objective reasoning to the personal equation of individual literary judgement.

IV

On the whole Form-criticism has not had a very good press in England. One of the first British writers to make a general survey of the new movement was the Methodist Professor Vincent Taylor. In his book *The Formation of the Gospel Tradition* (1933), Taylor was rather hard on the negative and unscientific elements in it and indicated its limitations as a method of approaching a period nearer to the ministry of Christ than our Gospels and the documents which underlie them. In this Taylor was not untypical of the world of English theology. It is not to be supposed that 'Form-criticism' was universally and enthusiastically welcomed everywhere in Germany; but on the whole its influence has been deeper and more general on the Continent and in America than in Britain.

'Form-criticism' was destined, however, to find a champion and a powerful expositor in the University of Oxford. R. H. Lightfoot (1883–1953) learned German, became acquainted with the work of that accomplished scholar Ernst Lohmeyer (1890–1946)[1] who had extended the use of the 'Form-critical' method from the Gospels to the Epistles of St. Paul, became convinced that this was important, and set himself to become the channel through which this new approach to the Gospels should become familiar to the English-speaking world. Lightfoot was in reaction against the school of Headlam and others, which, as we have seen, was inclined to think that in Mark's Gospel we have history in an almost pure form. The title of his Bampton Lectures, *History and Interpretation in the Gospels* (1935), indicates the approach that he was determined to recommend. In the Gospels, he maintained, there is no such thing as pure history; history and theology are always intermingled, even in Mark's Gospel, and we shall be wholly unable to understand the history, unless we are prepared also to take seriously the theology.[2] Among the insights of Lohmeyer to which Lightfoot paid special attention was the observation that places and place-names in the Bible often have more than their obvious significance. Lohmeyer in his book *Galiläa und Jerusalem* (1936) draws attention to this possibility. Lightfoot goes further in working out the details. To Mark, Galilee is the sphere of redemption, of the divine operation; Judaea is the world of hate, misunderstanding, opposition, and finally disaster. In the Fourth Gospel, the situation is almost exactly reversed; Jerusalem is the centre of the stage, on which the divine drama of redemption is to be worked out. It is here that both faith and unbelief will be revealed, the slowly dawning faith of the disciples, the unbelief of 'the Jews', who in this Gospel are always the enemy. Judaea, not Galilee, is in this Gospel the *patris*, the native country, of Jesus; it is only as it were by chance that he is a Galilean.[3] There can be no doubt that there is value in this line of study; in reading the Gospels we must be prepared at every point for the presence of theology, underlying even the apparently simplest statements. It is part of our prudence as students to be on the

[1] Lohmeyer is one of the many German scholars whose works have never been translated into English. His more technical writings have been interpreted by Lightfoot and others; I think that his scholarly exposition of the Lord's Prayer, *Das Vaterunser* (2nd ed., 1954), would well repay translation.
[2] This, it will be remembered, was exactly the position reached by Hoskyns at about the same time, and through the use of methods very different from those favoured by Lightfoot.
[3] This is worked out in detail in Dr. Lightfoot's second book, *Locality and Doctrine in the Gospels* (1938).

alert for this theology, even though we cannot always be certain that our interpretation of the theology is the right one.

Dr. Lightfoot concluded his first book with the words: 'It seems, then, that the form of the earthly no less than the heavenly Christ is for the most part hidden from us. For all the inestimable value of the gospels, they yield little more than a whisper of his voice; we trace in them but the outskirts of his ways.'[1] Lightfoot had overestimated his readers' knowledge of the text of Holy Scripture; his words were very generally misunderstood in the sense of Bultmann, that in reality we know hardly anything at all of Jesus Christ. No one who knew Dr. Lightfoot, or had heard him preach, could have fallen into this error. The passage of the Book of Job to which he is referring reads as follows:

Lo, these are parts of his ways:
    but how little a portion is heard of him?
    but the thunder of his power who can understand?
                        (Job 26. 14.)

From Lightfoot's own later utterances,[2] it is clear that what he meant was something like this: 'Everyone is agreed that, with the frailty of our mortal senses, we are utterly incapable of beholding the glory of the heavenly Christ. But perhaps, contrary to what is often supposed, the same is true of the earthly Christ as well. The mystery even of his earthly life is too great for us. We have been given as much as is good for us; and even that little has been enough to set the earth in a blaze for nineteen centuries.'

Dr. Lightfoot has had a number of followers, especially in the University of Oxford. These have been at one with the Form-critics in Germany in holding that the primary phenomenon with which we are concerned, and beyond which in a very real sense we cannot go, is the faith of the disciples. Since Jesus Christ himself wrote nothing and we have therefore no direct evidence such as we have for Julius Caesar,[3] this affirmation is something of a platitude; but a platitude that needed to be insisted on, in view of the almost slavish devotion to the

[1] R. H. Lightfoot, *History and Interpretation in the Gospels* (1935), p. 225.
[2] See especially *The Gospel Message of St. Mark* (1950), p. 103, n. 1.
[3] But it is just with the fact that we have the *Commentaries* of Julius Caesar that our difficulties begin. Here we have Caesar as he wished to present himself to the world; but what relationship, if any, existed between this Caesar and Caesar in his nightgown?

historicity of Mark by which an earlier period had been marked. But this
group of students are not, in fact, inclined to the extreme scepticism of
the German school; they are concerned to go beyond the tradition
as we have it to that which lies behind it. To take up an earlier epigram,
they are on the whole convinced that it was the tradition that created
the Church, that in this tradition we can see, though as it were at one
remove, that historical phenomenon of Jesus Christ through which the
Church came into being.[1] There are naturally differences of opinion
within the group; but it can be said that on the whole their results are
less negative than those of their German colleagues.

Oddly enough, the British scholar who has done the most remarkable
work on the Gospel behind the Gospels, on those traditions which lie
behind the Gospels in their present form, is one who would certainly
not class himself as a member of the Form-critical school—Professor
C. H. Dodd (b. 1884). In two short books, as remarkable for their
brevity as for their contents, Dr. Dodd has asked, and in his own way
answered, two fundamental questions.

In one, *The Apostolic Preaching and its Development* (1936), he
raised the question as to the nature of the proclamation, the *Kerygma*,
which was made by the earliest followers of Jesus. What did they
actually tell their listeners? It is clear that they did not, as Harnack had
supposed, tell them of the Fatherhood of God and the infinite value of
the human soul. By an ingenious combination of the evidence of the
speeches in the Acts of the Apostles, 1 Peter, the letters of Paul, and
other parts of the New Testament, Dodd reaches the conclusion that
the earliest preaching was a declaration of the mighty acts of God in
Jesus Christ, a little reminiscent of the recital of the mighty acts of
God in relation to Israel, such as we find in Joshua 24 and the historical
Psalms. The burden of it all is 'This has God *done*'—and on this follows
the challenge: 'Therefore this must *you do.*' This is the *Kerygma*,
the task of the herald—not to teach or to edify, but to bring *news*. At a
later stage there will be *Didache*, teaching, the instruction of the converts in what it means to be a Christian; the second half of a Pauline
Epistle is in most cases taken up with instruction of this kind.

In the slightly earlier and no less important book, *The Parables of the*

[1] A general view of the findings of this group may be encountered in the volume of
Studies in the Gospels (1955), edited by Professor Dennis Nineham, which was to have been
presented to Professor Lightfoot, but which, because of his early death, could only be
published in his honour. I would further specially recommend a series of articles by Professor Nineham, on the role of the eyewitness in the early Church, published in the *Journal
of Theological Studies*, N.S. (1958), pp. 13-25, 243-52.

Kingdom (1935), Dodd tries, with notable success, to get behind the parables as they now stand to the parables as originally spoken. In their present form a number of the parables seem to set forth general truths or problems of the Christian life which are the same at all times and in all places; the traditional interpretation, such as that of the parable of the Sower in Matthew 13, rather supports this view; and this in its turn has been strengthened by the allegorical interpretation of the parables, which was in honour almost to our own day.[1] Can we get behind the incrustation of the tradition and nearer to the original? Dodd is of the opinion that we can. We can, in fact, trace the Church's understanding of such a parable as that of the Sower, in three successive stages. There is the late stage, in which the parable has been generalized ('There are men and women of different types in every congregation'); the intermediate stage, in which the waiting Church applies the parable to its own necessities ('Why is the progress of the Gospel in the world so slow?'); and behind this is the situation in which the parable was originally spoken—that situation of incredible urgency, in which the message of Jesus faced Israel with a decision which was literally a decision of life or death.

Dodd, here disagreeing radically with the position maintained by Albert Schweitzer, holds that in Jesus the *Eschaton*, the last word of God to men, is already here. The kingdom is not just a future reality—it is something that is already here, and by their reaction to it men will be judged. In working over the words of Jesus, in what came to seem to them a very long interval between the resurrection and the expected triumph, the disciples tended to refer many sayings to the future, to the as yet unfulfilled. But Dodd maintains that this was not the original reference; that reference was to the Son of Man who is already present, and whose challenge is a matter of immediate urgency. For this view Dr. Dodd invented the not very happy expression 'realized eschatology'.[2] His earlier statement of his views seems almost wholly to exclude the future, and that genuine eschatology which is concerned with the real end of all things, when God has finished all his purposes with the visible universe, when time is no more and eternity alone remains. Everything is concentrated in the present, in the decisive

---

[1] It is obvious to the typologist that the inn to which the Good Samaritan brings the wounded man is the Church, and that the two pence with which he pays the costs of the unexpected visitor are the two sacraments of the Church.

[2] A German scholar, criticizing Dodd's term as unsatisfactory, invented the even worse expression 'sich realisierende Eschatologie', eschatology which is in process of realizing itself!

challenge of the immediate 'Now'. The parable of the wise and foolish virgins had been almost universally interpreted of the 'second coming' of the Son of Man; we now see it in the light of the presence of the Son of Man among men, and the extreme peril that awaits those who fail to realize what hour of the day it is, and what demands are being imperiously made of them.[1]

It is only rarely that one great scholar builds directly on the work of another. We have this fascinating and unusual spectacle in the works on the parables by, respectively, Dr. C. H. Dodd and Professor Joachim Jeremias of Göttingen. To Dodd's work Jeremias pays this notable and large-hearted tribute: 'In this extraordinarily important book the attempt has actually been made for the first time with success to relate the parables to their situation in the life of Jesus, and thereby to open a new epoch in the interpretation of the parables.'[2]

But Jeremias believes that it is possible to go a good deal further than Dodd has gone, and that the attempt has almost unlimited promise in it: 'Back to the very words of Jesus—that is the task! What a great gain it will be if we succeed in finding here and there behind the veil of primitive understanding the face of the Son of Man!'

What place, then, did the parables play in the teaching of Jesus? Here the suggestion of Jeremias is extraordinarily interesting and fruitful— the parables are not kindly words of good advice to the poor and needy; they are part of the polemic of Jesus—a vigorous and at times almost embittered polemic—against his enemies:

The parables which have as their theme the gospel ... are, apparently without exception, addressed not to the poor, but to Christ's opponents. That is their special character, their place in life. They are not primarily the offer of the gospel but the defence, the justification of the gospel, weapons in the conflict with the critics and enemies of the gospel. How did Jesus justify the gospel to his critics?[3]

So the panorama passes before us, and we see how parable after parable is related to the daily life of the time of Jesus, and to the terrifying challenge to decision which he presents to his contemporaries. The work of Jeremias, like all other notable works of theology, is

---

[1] Dr. Dodd's views have not proved universally acceptable; and it is to be noted that in his later writings he gives greater recognition to the fact that in the Christian tradition there must always be a place for the future as well as for the present.

[2] J. Jeremias, *The Parables of Jesus* (1947, English trans. 1954).

[3] Ibid., p. 85.

susceptible to criticism at certain points; as a whole it reveals in a positive form the value and the possibilities that we owe to the 'Form-critics' and their new ventures into the field of Gospel criticism.

Room must be found for one more recent and notable example of the use of the 'Form-critical' method for constructive purposes. *The Birth of the New Testament* (1962) by Professor C. F. D. Moule is not quite like any other book ever written about the New Testament. The writer himself states (p. 3) that the general approach is that of 'Form-criticism', though the conclusions reached are more conservative than those that are generally typical of this approach. Like Dibelius and others, Moule is concerned to penetrate behind the New Testament into that dim period when no New Testament as yet existed. But he is not interested in the minute analysis of traditions and the careful weighing of the authenticity of this or that particular word or episode. He asks another set of questions. What were the earliest Christians concerned about? How did they live? What were the problems that lay heavy on them? So we take a look at these early Christians as they exercise themselves in worship, as they learn to distinguish themselves from the Jewish people, as they wrestle with the interpretation of the Old Testament, and so on. Not everything is certain in the picture; yet we do gradually come to a convincing delineation of a perplexed, enthusiastic, adventurous people, hewing out for themselves an extra-ordinarily difficult way into an unknown future. And the book is full of unexpected and interesting sidelights, drawn from a most extensive acquaintance with the whole background of the New Testament. Of these one single example must suffice:

It seems fair to assume that, broadly speaking, the average Jew was better educated than the average Gentile, if only because Jewish family life was the soundest in the empire, and also the education which Jewish children received in the synagogue school was, within its limits, probably more con-scientious and thorough than the teaching given by Gentile schoolmasters who had not necessarily the intensity of vocation belonging to a devout teacher of the Torah.[1]

V

By constant reiteration certain affirmations come to be treated almost as axioms. The uncritical acceptance of any unproved axiom makes

[1] C. F. D. Moule, op cit., p. 157. The reader of a comparatively simple book may be assured that it is based on an immense range of learning. In the Index, references are given to the work of no less than 291 modern scholars; Schweitzer was content with 251!

further scientific work almost impossible. Nothing is more important
than that every axiom should constantly be put to the test and verified
in every possible way.[1] Four quasi-axioms of the 'Form-critics'
need specially to be passed through the fires of criticism.

The first is that the early Christians, and those who first reduced the
Christian traditions to writing, were not interested in history. For instance, Dr. H. G. Wood quotes from Erik Sjöberg the categorical
statement that 'there is not a single word of Jesus, not one single
isolated story in the Gospels, which can be regarded as having been
handed down from a purely historical interest'.[2] Here everything
depends on the exact meaning one attaches to words. *Rein geschicht-
liches Interesse*, 'pure historical interest', is a loose and inaccurate
phrase, hardly susceptible of exact interpretation. If by it is meant that
kind of history which is pure recording, without interest or engagement
on the part of the recorder, I suppose that no one has ever supposed
that the Gospels were in that sense history. The pure and passionless
history of which the late Lord Acton approved, and which he tried to
impose on his collaborators in the *Cambridge Modern History*, was an
invention of the late nineteenth century.[3] There is not a trace of it in
the Old and New Testaments—and very little, it may be added, in the
literature of Greece or Rome.

Dr. Sjöberg, like Lord Acton, is not quite consistent. Having said
keine Einzelgeschichte, 'not a single individual incident', he then
admits the exception which proves the rule, in this case the episode of
the young man who fled away naked by night (Mark 14. 51 ff.). Dr.
H. G. Wood, one of the very few New Testament scholars who is[4]

[1] Cf. C. F. D. Moule, *Journal of Theological Studies*, N.S. vol. xiii (April 1962), p.
143: 'That the Christian writings sprang from preaching, not from any historical or biographical concern is, as we know well, an axiom of *Formgeschichte*. But ought it to be
treated as axiomatic? Once disallow it, together with some allied axioms about *ideo-
logische Geschichtstheologie*, and some of the clear-cut (and cavalier) decisions about
sources and motives become less cogent.'

[2] H. G. Wood, *Jesus in the Twentieth Century* (1960), p. 148, quoting Erik Sjöberg,
Der verborgene Menschensohn in den Evangelien (1955), p. 216. This kind of categorical
statement must always be regarded with profound suspicion. One of the earliest lessons
we all learned in our study of philosophy is that it is impossible to prove a negative; any
statement which begins 'Es gibt kein Jesus Wort, keine Einzelgeschichte' will put every
serious student on his guard.

[3] And even Lord Acton did not manage to be consistent. He sharply criticized his
friend, Bishop Mandell Creighton, because in the first volume of his *History of the Papacy*
Creighton had not been nearly severe enough on the medieval persecutors, of whom Acton
himself so profoundly disapproved.

[4] 'Is' when this section was written, now alas! 'was'; Dr. Wood died full of years and
honour in March 1963.

also in his own right a trained and professional historian, adds quite a number of others. The most obvious is the allusion to Simon of Cyrene as the father of Alexander and Rufus (Mark 15. 21); unless we are going to look for obscure typological or allegorical meanings in these names, it seems sensible to suppose that the family of Simon of Cyrene was known to the readers of the Gospel, and that the writer puts in the names to remind them of this interesting connexion between people they knew and the actual events of the crucifixion.[1]

We come back to the question as to what is meant by history. If by the word we mean 'mere historicity', the endless ebb and flow of events without meaning, then of course we shall look in vain in the New Testament for history. But all the early Christians, as we have seen, were profoundly influenced by the Old Testament; and the Old Testament is the record of a revelation of God which moves forward *through the history* of a chosen people. Christians believed themselves to be the recipients of the tidings of the new 'saving acts of God', akin to his acts of old—the interpretation of salvation in terms drawn from the Book of Exodus runs right through the New Testament; it was of immense importance to the Christian that the later acts of God, like the earlier, were acts of God *in history*. They had been led to depend for their salvation not on 'cunningly devised fables' (myths, 2 Peter 1. 16), but on events which had actually occurred. To them history in the true sense of the term, so far from being a matter of indifference, was all-important.

Secondly, it is again and again repeated that the Gospels are not biographies. Here again everything depends on definition. If we mean by biography either the three-volume Victorian variety, with copious quotations from the subject's letters and speeches; or the acute psychological analysis carried out by Lytton Strachey and his successors, purporting to show the subject's inner development from the cradle to the grave and his reaction to the various influences that were brought to bear upon him; it is quite clear that the Gospels are not 'biographies'. But if it is the aim of biography to give succinctly a living and vivid impression of someone who really lived, it is hard to see into what other category the Gospels are to be placed. After all, the

---

[1] It is, of course, the interesting fact that the name Simon is Hebrew, Alexander is Greek, and Rufus is Latin; the writer of the Gospel cannot have been unaware of the parallel with the three languages of the superscription on the Cross; but it is hardly necessary to suppose that this was the *reason* for which he put in the names, still less that he invented them for this purpose.

Lives of Izaak Walton and Johnson's *Lives of the Poets* are also biographies. New Testament scholars might, perhaps, with advantage to themselves, have paid greater attention to the work of the greatest of ancient biographers who was almost a contemporary of the apostolic writers.[1] Plutarch of Chaeronea has left us a remarkably clear account of what he understood his vocation as a biographer to be:

I am not a writer of histories but of biographies. My readers therefore must excuse me if I do not record all events or describe in detail, but only briefly touch upon, the noblest and most famous. For the most conspicuous do not always or of necessity show a man's virtues or failings, but it often happens that some light occasion, a word or a jest, gives a clearer insight into character, than battles with their slaughter of tens of thousands and the greatest array of armies and sieges of cities. Accordingly as painters produce a likeness by the representation of the countenance and the expression of the face, in which the character is revealed, without troubling themselves about the other parts of the body, so I must be allowed to look rather into the signs of a man's character, and by means of these to portray the life of each, leaving to others the description of great events and battles.[2]

This is a notably modest account of the task that he has taken in hand; yet, even at a first reading of this passage, certain similarities between Plutarch's objective and that which the evangelists had set before themselves strike upon the mind. Naturally Plutarch used sources; he had a wide acquaintance with the historical writers who had preceded him. But he uses these sources freely as he needs them for his own purpose; and he is careful not to claim for himself the character of historian. In point of fact, when he can be compared with his sources, he reveals himself as sometimes careless and inaccurate.[3] Yet he is an honest and sincere writer, and, where he is our only authority, as he is for one of the noblest and most picturesque episodes in the whole of Greek history, the career of Timoleon in Sicily, every historian of Greece accepts him as being on the whole a reliable witness to the

---

[1] I am not directly acquainted with the book of H. Almqvist, *Plutarch und das Neue Testament: Ein Beitrag zum Corpus Hellenisticum Novi Testamenti* (1946).

[2] *Vita Alexandri*, 1, 1.

[3] One of Plutarch's modern editors complains that 'among the faults of Plutarch's *Life of Themistokles* must be reckoned his disregard of chronology—the natural consequence of the purely ethical aim of his biographies' (H. A. Holden, *Plutarch's Life of Themistokles* (1881), p. xliii). Yet Dr. Holden has no hesitation in accepting Plutarch's work as a valuable supplement to the considerable amount of information we have about Themistocles from Herodotus and other ancient authors.

events which he records. And this charming man was influenced by far more than mere intellectual curiosity. His writings reveal a great deal of the old-world piety of the Greek village and an intense ethical concern. He writes his lives of the noble Greeks and Romans to show the young what is to be admired and what is to be avoided; he is not afraid of the simple categories of good and evil.

Now, admittedly there is a great difference between the admiration for the heroes of old which it is the purpose of Plutarch to inculcate, and the faith in Jesus Christ which is the concern of the Gospels. But, when it is suggested that there is nothing in the literature of the ancient world that in the least resembles them, it is time that a protest was entered.

Thirdly, it is commonly claimed by writers of the Form-critical school, that every single unit of the tradition can contain within itself the whole of the Gospel, and can convey that challenge which is the essence of the Gospel. It is rather fashionable to quote a considerably earlier writer, Martin Kähler (1835–1912), to the effect that 'in every drop in the dewy meadows, the sun's light is mirrored and reflected; so in each little episode the entire person of our Lord encounters us'.[1] On this Dr. Heinz Zahrnt comments: 'Evidently the smallest unit of the tradition, the shortest scene and the briefest saying comprehend within themselves and reflect the totality of the person and the mission of Jesus. Is the sun divided, because its light is reflected back from countless dew-drops?'[2] Now the picturesque illustration is illuminating under one aspect and self-evidently misleading under another. It is indeed the sun, and the sun only, which is reflected back from the dewdrops. It is Jesus, and Jesus only, whom we meet in the Gospel tradition. But it is simply not the fact that we can find the whole of any man's character or destiny in one word or episode or saying.[3] There are many recorded remarks of Samuel Johnson of which we feel that he alone could have

---

[1] Martin Kähler, *Der sogenannte historische Jesus und der geschichtliche, biblische Christus* (1892 and several times reprinted), pp. 60 ff.

[2] H. Zahrnt, *Es begann mit Jesus von Nazareth* (1960, p. 83. English trans., *The Historical Jesus*, 1963).

[3] This point is well made by Professor Otto A. Piper in a review of Bornkamm's book *Jesus von Nazareth*: 'He emphasizes that what can be discerned historically from the Gospels are but isolated stories and sayings. One is therefore surprised to be told that "each story in itself contains the person and history of Jesus in their entirety" (p. 25). To this reviewer it would appear that the materials forming the Gospels are enigmatic and ambiguous, when taken by themselves, and that it is only in the light of an underlying pattern of the Gospel story that they can be understood as presenting a common message' (*Interpretation* (October 1961), p. 476).

made them, and that in each his quintessential character is made plain. But it is only through the slow ingestation of all that Boswell has collected about him that we come to know that great man in all the absurdity and all the grandeur of his character. Similarly, in every incident of the record we meet the authentic Jesus. But it is only through the accumulation of the evidence of all four Gospels that we know him as he is; it was precisely because the early Christians realized that this and that episode did not tell them all that they needed to know that from such a very early date collections of the traditions began to be made.

Fourthly, we are told that the early Christian communities made little distinction between the history of Jesus before the Resurrection and his history after the Ascension, between the words that he was believed to have spoken in the days of his flesh and the words that he continued to speak in the Spirit in the Church through the lips of inspired teachers and prophets. This seems, in point of fact, to run counter to all the evidence that we have. All the evidence makes it plain that 'the doctrine of the Ascension', to use a much later phrase, was firmly held in the early Church. For a certain period manifestations of the risen Lord occurred; after that no such manifestations occurred. No confusion between these two periods was possible. The only post-ascension utterances of the risen Christ in the New Testament (apart from a few brief words reported as having been spoken to St. Paul) are the letters to the seven churches in the book of Revelation. It is hard to imagine anything more different than these from the traditions of the Gospels; in them everything is related to the contemporary situation of the churches, and nothing is read back into an earlier period of the existence of the Son of Man in Palestine. In the Epistles of Paul we have a great many inspired words which could easily have been read back into the Gospel; in no single case has this happened: at no point is there any confusion between the word of the Lord and the word of the Apostle speaking in his name. As early as the first Epistle to the Corinthians, Paul draws a distinction between those matters on which he is able to cite an authoritative word of the Lord (1 Cor. 7. 10), and those many others on which he has laboriously to reach a conclusion through the exercise of his own faculties under the guidance of the Spirit (1 Cor. 7. 12).

VI

At point after point the affirmations of the Form-critical school, especially in its German form, have failed to carry complete conviction.

The time had come for a thorough investigation and reassessment of the principles of this school. It seems that the reaction is now on the way.

The first point gained is the recognition that the evangelists were not, as Professor Dibelius maintained, mere compilers, but were authors and theologians in their own right. It is in this connexion that the studies of Dr. Austin Farrer are seen to be of great importance; he maintains with considerable vigour and ingenuity the thesis that the Gospels must first be considered as wholes, and that only when this consideration of the wholes has been accomplished can the significance of the parts be seen:

Form-criticism is concerned with small patterns, the patterns of the parts; we are concerned with a large pattern, the pattern of the whole. What is the relation between the large pattern and the small? The study of the large has the priority . . . The pattern of the whole comes first. Every sentence of a book is formulated by the mind which writes the whole. The parts, of course—the paragraphs, let us say—have a sort of independent and interior life of their own, for otherwise the book will be unreadable . . . But we clearly cannot go on to say: 'Therefore in the case of a well-written book we can practise the wholly autonomous art of paragraph-criticism; we can examine the form of any given paragraph in and by itself, confident that no stroke of arrangement in it is due to the pattern of the whole work, or to what the author wants in the end and in general to say. The pattern of the whole merely arranges the paragraphs, it does not in any way constitute them.' To talk like this would be absurd. It is patently false that paragraph-criticism is autonomous.[1]

That Dr. Farrer is right must be self-evident to anyone who has ever written a book. If the book is to be readable and convey meaning, the first page cannot be written until the whole is in view; two-thirds of the agony of composition is endured in the period of labour before the pattern of the predestined book emerges.

What has all this to say to the Form-critical method?

Some of Dr. Lightfoot's readers may have felt that under his guidance they were rediscovering the evangelist and losing the facts of the evangel. Whatever the loss may be, the gain is solid and unmistakable—by Dr. Lightfoot's aid we find ourselves in touch with St. Mark, a living Christian mind, and a mind of great power. And this discovery comes like water in the desert to

[1] A. M. Farrer, *A Study in St. Mark* (1951), pp. 22–23.

men who have been trained to see in his gospel a row of impersonal anec-
dotes strung together by a colourless compiler . . . The solid gain of the
theological interpretation is that it restores to us the unity of the Gospel. The
Gospel is a genuine, and profoundly consistent, complex act of thought. This
means that we are no longer reduced to making what we can of the parts.
We may hope to make something of the whole, for there is a whole after all.
Not at first sight what we should call an historical whole; the unity seems to
date to be one of doctrinal and symbolical development. But if we sift this
complex unity to the bottom, and master it as fully as we can, we may find that
it speaks history to us.[1]

As is the case with many other writers, Dr. Farrer's success in the
working out of his principles is not as great as in the formulation of
them. The weakness of his work here, as in others of his writings, is an
over-elaborate ingenuity, as a result of which really valuable observations tend to be lost in a maze of secondary and ill-established imaginings.[2] But the enunciation of the principles was well worth while;
we must deal with the Gospels as wholes, and with the evangelists as
authors and not as mere compilers.

Dr. Farrer is not alone in this conviction. The most striking work
along these lines so far, all the more striking because it comes from the
heart of the Form-critical school, is the book of Hans Conzelmann, *Die
Mitte der Zeit* ('The Midst of Time' (1954; 3rd ed., 1960)), of which the
English translation bears the title *The Theology of St. Luke* (1960).[3]
Dr. Conzelmann sees that Luke has a very definite point of view
of his own, that in the light of this point of view he has rewritten
the entire story of Jesus, and that he has added as a supplement to
that story the first volume of a history of the Church. The whole of
Dr. Conzelmann's work is devoted to an elucidation of the Lucan
point of view.

Conzelmann's study is extremely careful and thorough; but at times
he seems to impose his theories on the facts instead of letting the
facts determine the theories. For instance, he lays great stress on the
idea that for Luke the period of the ministry of Jesus is the time of
present salvation, in which the great adversary has for the time being

[1] A. M. Farrer, op. cit., pp. 7–8.
[2] So much so is this the case with *A Study of St. Mark* that a few years after its publication Dr. Farrer himself withdrew it and substituted for it another book, a study of both
St. Matthew and St. Mark (1954).
[3] Professor C. K. Barrett, with his usual erudition and acumen, has summarized for us
recent continental work on St. Luke in a neat little book entitled *Luke the Historian in
Recent Study* (1961).

lost his power. In support of this view, he makes use of the statement at the end of the story of the temptation, 'the devil . . . departed from him for a season', which he interprets as meaning that 'the devil left him till the appointed time', that is, the time of the passion. But in point of fact the Greek words ἄχρι καιροῦ mean simply 'for a short period', and cannot be made to mean anything else; the argument based on a mistranslation of them falls to the ground.

But it is necessary to take very seriously Dr. Conzelmann's central contention. The early Church had to wrestle with the problem of the delay in the coming again of Jesus; they had thought that the time between 'the Ascension' and 'the Parousia' would be very short; but he did not come again, and the Church had to rethink its whole theology in the light of this disillusionment. Luke was one of those who took in hand this essential task:

> Luke sees salvation already in the past. The time of salvation has become historic, a period of time which certainly determines the present, but as an epoch is past and closed . . . This signifies neither more nor less than the conception that the time of the End (*Endzeit*) did not break in with Jesus. Rather, the future time of salvation was portrayed in advance in the middle of the *Heilsgeschichte* (history of God's saving acts) in the life of Jesus . . . The good news is not that the kingdom of God has come, but that through the life of Jesus the hope of the coming kingdom has been established. Its nearness thus becomes a secondary factor.[1]

It is clear that for Dr. Conzelmann Luke's portrayal is a distortion, indeed almost a betrayal, of the original Gospel. Indeed, one of the leading members of the Form-critical school has been heard to refer to Luke in a lecture as 'this falsifier of the Gospel'.

In the passage just quoted there are far more points for discussion than can be handled within the limits of this chapter. At the outset the discussion is made difficult, as so often in theological writing, by a certain lack of precision in the use of terms. What exactly does it mean that 'the time of the end', the *Endzeit*, came, or did not come, in with Jesus of Nazareth?

There may have been some among the early Christians who thought that the coming of Jesus meant absolutely the end of history, in the sense that nothing more would ever happen—God would bring all the happenings of history to an end, and the present heavens and earth

---

[1] Op. cit., p. 27.

would pass away once and for all. If any among the early Christians held this view, they must have been very few, and they have left hardly any trace on the New Testament record. Albert Schweitzer thought that Jesus himself understood 'eschatology' in this way and therefore died in the midst of the total disappointment of his hopes. But there is in fact hardly any evidence in the New Testament that tells in favour of this view, and a great deal that tells against it. The problem of the early Church was in fact entirely different; or, rather, there was a whole range of problems that had to be faced. The first Christians did not imagine that nothing would ever happen again; they thought that they knew very well what would happen; and they found that what happened was entirely different from what they expected.

As good Israelites, they believed that the kingdom of God would mean the deliverance of his people from captivity, and the setting up of the visible authority of God in Jerusalem, the holy city. From Jerusalem the law of the Lord would stream out into the world; the Gentiles would flow together to Jerusalem to receive the holy law, as in fact the Church had seen them flow together on the day of Pentecost.[1] This was the common ground of Jewish expectation. The Christians knew two things in addition to this general expectation. They knew the identity of the One through whom God would exercise his kingly authority—Jesus of Nazareth. And they were convinced that he who had been briefly withdrawn from their eyes would return very soon indeed to establish his kingdom with power. Then would come 'the times of refreshing', the period of the restoration of all things to that which according to the will and purpose of God they ought to be.[2] But history went on; things happened; and they were not at all the kind of things that ought to have happened. The Church was faced by three gigantic theological problems. In the first place, in spite of the preaching of the Resurrection, the Jewish people as a whole were not converted. Tension between Church and synagogue went on increasing, until by the end of the first century 'the Jews' are the enemy. It is clear that the term 'the people of God' has radically changed its meaning; it is not through the ancient Israel that the purpose of God will be ful-

[1] The only account of the day of Pentecost which we possess, that in Acts 2, works out very carefully the parallels and the contrast with the story of the tower of Babel in Gen. 11. The writer is specially careful to include in his list of nations representatives of the traditional division of the nations among the sons of Noah—Ham, Shem, and Japheth.

[2] I take the view, which is not shared by all scholars, that in the early chapters of Acts, Luke is using good authorities and depicts for us with considerable accuracy the kind of ideas that were entertained by the early Christians.

filled. In the second place, the interval between the resurrection and the *parousia*, the coming again of Christ in glory, is seen to be far greater than had been originally expected. Some among the Christians had died, and therefore would not be there to greet the Lord on his return.[1] Thirdly, the pressure of events made it plain that the movement of the Gospel would be exactly the opposite of that which had been expected. The Gentiles would not come to Jerusalem to hear the Word of the Lord; the Word of the Lord would go out to the Gentiles, until it had reached the utmost limits of the known world. Jerusalem would continue to be the mother-church; but the Church of God would be the same everywhere, and the proclamation of the Word must go forward until it filled the world.

Paul had understood his own mission as far more than simply the conversion of a certain number of Gentiles in a number of cities in the Mediterranean world; his work is an essential part of revelation—the revelation that Christ is the door for Jews and Gentiles alike, and that Gentiles have full citizen-rights in the city of God on the basis of faith in Jesus alone; it is also an essential part of the divine purpose—the pouring out of the Spirit on the Gentiles declares that this is in reality the 'time of the end', but that 'end' cannot come in its finality until the fulness of the Gentiles has come in.

Luke stands a little further back from the events than either Peter or Paul. Combining in his own person the gifts of a great historian and a great theologian, he brings history and theology together. From the point of view of some scholars this is the great and unpardonable heresy—the Gospel, as they have understood it, breaks into history, shatters it, and brings it to an end; and so any attempt to 'historicize' the Gospel, to bring it into relation with history, of necessity robs it of its essential character. Of course, this depends on the interpretation that we give to the word 'history'. We may put the problem in another way. What is the relation between *Heilsgeschichte*, salvation-history, the record of the mighty acts of God, and ordinary history, those banal things that happen from day to day? Some would answer: 'There is no connexion; these are two separate streams which flow in parallel lines and never meet.' Luke, naturally, had never heard these modern expressions; but his answer to the question is perfectly clear; *Heilsgeschichte* and secular history are the same history; each from a different

---

[1] 1 Thessalonians shows us vividly the dismay felt by a new group of Gentile Christians, filled with eschatological expectations, when one or more of their number died and the *parousia* had not yet taken place.

point of view is the story of God's providential government of the nations, all of which he holds in the hollow of his hand. It is for this reason that, at the outset of his Gospel, he so carefully relates the ministry of Jesus to the rulers of the secular and the religious worlds (Luke 3. 1–2). For him, the world since Pentecost is the scene of the new mighty acts of God in history. History can be understood in no other way; it is the scene of the forward march of God among the nations, as God goes out through his Word to gather out from all the nations a people acceptable to himself. For this reason the Church is all-important, since it is only through the Church that the march of God among the nations can become manifest.

Is Luke the great creative theologian of the Church, or is he 'this falsifier of the Gospel'? A missionary, who is also a theologian, has great advantages in making the attempt to understand the New Testament, since, far more than the scholar in a Western Church, he stands in a relationship to the original facts which greatly helps to make them intelligible. The missionary is completely immersed in history— not of course in what the Germans call *Geschichtlichkeit* or *Historismus*, the mere arid succession of the things that come and go. He is engaged the whole time in making history, divine history. Things are happening today which have never happened before. In the mysterious providence of God, peoples which have never heard the Word of God, and were therefore without hope and without God in the world, are today hearing and believing. In this village and that, the first baptisms have taken place; for the first time since the foundation of the world the table of the Lord has been spread, and the faithful have gathered, as the early Christians did, in the assurance that *Kyrios Christos* is in their midst. These things are not epiphenomena of the Gospel, secondary accretions of little importance. They *are* the Gospel. It is only when these things are taken seriously that it is possible to understand what Paul is talking about in his Epistles; or, to go further back, to understand what Jesus Christ means when he claims to be the One in whom uniquely God speaks to all men—'but I say unto you...'

VII

The problem of history will not for ever be denied. There was a time at which even the suggestion that a return to the 'Quest of the Historical Jesus' might be possible was too far-fetched to be taken seriously. To one who has lived through that period, it is almost startling that one of the most notable trends in contemporary theology is precisely 'The New Quest of the Historical Jesus'.[1]

If a starting-point for the new quest has to be fixed, one might be inclined to pitch upon an address on 'The Problem of the Historic Jesus', delivered by Ernst Käsemann, at that time Professor of the University of Göttingen, on 20 October 1953, and printed in the Zeitschrift für Theologie und Kirche in 1954.

Käsemann's reputation stands deservedly high in the theological world. He is a man of great perceptiveness, patient diligence, and sterling integrity; always ready to strike out beyond his past conclusions to new adventures of thought, and above all, like Bultmann, deeply concerned that the Gospel should be preached as a divine challenge to which the response of men is demanded. Throughout his career he has been a champion of the 'Form-critical' tradition, and tends to move within the limits of its accepted categories. As Professor Moule remarks, in a brilliant review of Käsemann's collected essays, Exegetische Versuche und Besinnungen (1960): 'The probing acuteness of Dr. Käsemann's mind compels admiration and starts exciting hares ... But the ruthless tidying leaves an uncomfortable impression of a topiary sort of gardening, with familiar formgeschichtlich shapes.'[2]

We had been told by the 'Form-critics' that the early Church was not interested in history, that the glorified Kyrios Christos had practically swallowed up the Man of Nazareth, and that the events of the earthly life of Jesus had but little interest for those Gentile believers who lived in the period after the resurrection. And yet we are faced with the plain fact that our New Testament contains no less than four Gospels, in which a great deal is related about the earthly life of Jesus. If there was so little interest in history and historical recollection, why did the Church ever come to write Gospels, why were they generally accepted in a great variety of churches, and read with veneration as an indispensable part of divine revelation?

It is this question with which Professor Käsemann sets himself to

[1] This is the title of an interesting book by a young American theologian, J. M. Robinson (1959), now a devoted follower of the Form-critical method. In a recent number of the Zeitschrift für Theologie und Kirche (June–July 1962) two writers learnedly discuss the question whether the 'New Quest' is really as new as Robinson thinks; they are inclined to hold that it has been present implicitly if not expressly in the work of Rudolf Bultmann from the beginning. They may be right; yet it can hardly be denied that a new movement of thought, surprising and welcome to those accustomed to the highly negative utterances of the Form-critical school, has been gaining in strength over the last ten years.

[2] Journal of Theological Studies, N.S., vol. xiii (April 1962), p. 144.

deal in his extraordinarily interesting and valuable essay, all the more valuable in view of the tradition of scholarship to which the writer belongs. It is not possible to do more than give one or two extracts, to illustrate the acuteness of Käsemann's mind and the nature of his approach:

If the earliest Christians identified the humiliated with the glorified Lord, at the same time they proclaimed that it was impossible for them, in their delineation of his history, to abstract from their faith. On the other hand, they also proclaimed that they were not willing to let a myth take the place of history, or to substitute a heavenly being for the man of Nazareth. So they were contending practically on the one hand against an 'enthusiastic' docetism, and on the other against an historicising doctrine of *Kenosis*. Quite clearly they held the opinion that the earthly Jesus can be understood only in the light of Easter, and of his dignity as the Lord of the Church; but, conversely, that Easter cannot be adequately understood, unless account is taken of the earthly Jesus. The Gospel is always engaged in this warfare on two fronts.[1]

Dr. Käsemann then goes on to select certain sayings of Jesus which he regards as unmistakably authentic, partly because they stand in such sharp contrast to anything that could be expected in the Jewish surroundings of the time of Jesus, partly because the earliest Christians, though they so faithfully kept these sayings on record in the traditions, seem already to have been unable to understand them; and then asks what impression we can form of the proclamation and person of Jesus Christ, in their integrity, and before the fashioning-process of the community-mind had begun to work upon them.

He ends his essay with the words:

The Gospel itself is not anonymous, or it would lead to moralism and mysticism. The Gospel is firmly bound to the one who both before and after Easter revealed himself to his own as the Lord, inasmuch as he brought them into the presence of the God who is not far off, and so into the liberty and the responsibility of faith. He does this without any demonstrable legitimation, without making the claim that he himself is the Messiah, and yet he does it in the full authority of the one to whom the Fourth Gospel refers as the only-begotten Son. For this reason it is impossible to fit him, in the last resort, into religio-historical, or psychological, or historical categories. Here, if anywhere, the fact of historical contingency must be recognised. The problem of the historical Jesus is not something that we have invented; it is the riddle with

[1] E. Käsemann, *Das Problem des historischen Jesus* (1954), p. 134.

which Jesus himself confronts us. The student of history can affirm the existence of this riddle, but he cannot find a solution for it. The solution can be found only by those who, since the time of the Cross and the Resurrection, confess that he is the one who, when on earth, he did not claim to be and yet already was, that is to say the Lord, the One who brings the freedom of the children of God, which is the obverse of the sovereignty of God. For the contingency of his history finds its answer in the contingency of faith, for which the history of Jesus renews itself as event, now as the history of the exalted Lord who is the subject of the proclamation, and yet now as then an earthly history, in which men are encountered by the Gospel in its utterance to men and in the claim which it makes on men.[1]

This is, indeed, a break-through. In 1929 Rudolf Bultmann wrote, in an essay on 'The Significance of the Historic Jesus for the Theology of Paul', that

it is not permitted to go beyond the 'proclamation' (*Kerygma*), using it as a 'source' in order to reconstruct the 'historic Jesus' with his 'messianic consciousness', his 'inwardness' or his 'heroic character'. This would be precisely the Χριστὸς κατὰ σάρκα (Christ according to the flesh) who belongs to the past. It is not the historic Christ who is the Lord, but Jesus Christ as he is encountered in the proclamation.[2]

These words, and others like them, had been regarded as almost canonical for a quarter of a century, in all the circles influenced by the 'Form-critical' tradition of New Testament interpretation. Now in those very circles a different voice begins to be heard. 'Who shall forbid us to ask the question concerning the historic Jesus?' asks Gerhard Ebeling, now professor at Zurich. 'This defeatism has no justification ... either as regards the state of the actual historical sources available to us or in relation to the possibility of historical understanding in general.'[3] Even more precisely Günther Bornkamm of Heidelberg presses the question: 'How is it possible for faith to be content with mere tradition, although that tradition be set down in the Gospels? Faith must break through, and ask the questions that lie behind the tradition. It is impossible seriously to suggest that the Gospels and the traditions contained in them forbid us to ask the question regarding the historic Jesus. They not merely permit the attempt; they positively require it.'[4]

---

[1] E. Käsemann, loc. cit., pp. 152–3.

[2] Reprinted in *Glauben und Verstehen*, vol. i (2nd ed., 1954), p. 208.

[3] In *Zeitschrift für Theologie und Kirche* (1959), Additional number, p. 20.

[4] G. Bornkamm, *Jesus von Nazareth* (1956), pp. 5, 20—a book to which we shall return later on. There is an excellent chapter on this subject, 'Die Wiederentdeckung des historischen Jesus' in H. Zahrnt, *Es begann mit Jesus von Nazareth* (1960. English trans., *The Historical Jesus*, 1963), pp. 104–17, with many relevant and apt quotations.

The break-through into this new area of study has naturally resulted in a tremendous spate of books and articles in Germany, with repercussions in America, and to a certain extent in other countries also. Almost every accredited theologian has felt it necessary at some point or other to indicate his attitude to the problem; the debate continues to be exceedingly lively, and is likely to continue for a number of years.[1]

In all this flood of literature, and in all these various attempts to answer the question why the early Church was so resolutely determined to keep the records of the earthly life of Jesus alive in the tradition, and later in the Scriptures of the Church, there is one point to which perhaps adequate attention has not been directed—the essentially missionary character of the greater part of the work of the Church in the period before, during, and after the writing of the Gospels. Here an illustration from modern missionary experience may not be out of place.

The first great Indian bishop of the Anglican Church, Vedanayakam Samuel Azariah, when asked where you should start when preaching the Gospel to those who have never heard it, used to answer without hesitation: 'You must start from the resurrection of Jesus; what they need to know is that there is a living, loving Saviour, and that he is not far from them.' Here in the strictest sense of the term is *Kerygma*, proclamation of the thing that has happened, of the mighty acts of God in Christ. The parallel with the Acts of the Apostles is self-evident; this was the starting-point of the apostolic preaching, and even in sophisticated Athens the burden of Paul's preaching was 'Jesus and the resurrection' (Acts 17. 18). But, as soon as this message of salvation has been apprehended, a two-fold process is set in motion. The one who has received salvation must learn to live according to the principles of the new world of salvation; hence the need for that *Didache*, instruction in virtue, which fills so much of the Epistles. But also the convert is filled with an intense desire to know more about the Saviour in whom he has come to believe, and who, he is assured, lived a very ordinary human life among men upon our familiar earth. Who is the One to whom he speaks in prayer? Who is the One who is present in the Holy Communion? The outline 'Cross and Resurrection' needs to be filled with living content. Every kind of question is asked; some of them, such as the question that endlessly recurs in India: 'Was Jesus married,

[1] A progress report on a large scale is to be found in H. Ristow and K. Matthiae, *Der historische Jesus und der kerygmatische Christus* (1961), a composite volume to which no less than forty-eight scholars from twelve countries have made contributions.

and, if not, why not?', questions the answer to which, if it could be given, would tend not so much to edification as to the satisfaction of merely human curiosity. The apocryphal Gospels are there to show us at a later date how ready anonymous writers were to supply legendary material to minister exactly to this spirit of curiosity. But the spirit of questioning seems to have arisen much earlier, and legitimately. As long as the preaching was in Palestine, where the events of the life and death of Jesus of Nazareth were widely familiar, little was needed beyond the *Kerygma*. As soon, however, as missionary work moved out beyond these narrow limits to Caesarea and Antioch in Pisidia and Ephesus and Rome, almost of necessity the *Kerygma* of the Cross and Resurrection had to take a step backward in history, and to deal with the preaching of John the Baptist, and the ministry of Jesus, 'who went about doing good, and healing all that were oppressed of the devil; for God was with him' (Acts 10. 35). This is just the way in which the writer of the Acts of the Apostles has represented things. We could almost have inferred from contemporary experience that it would be so; and we can see how important it was that from the start the preacher of the Gospel should be able to answer the questions that really were related to the essence of the Gospel, but that at the same time the figure of Jesus should be safeguarded against the intrusiveness and irreverence of the all too active human imagination.

The missionary clue to the background and the writing of the Gospels can perhaps be followed up a little further. Clearly, the missionary work of the Church entered on a period of serious crisis about thirty years after the events with which the proclamation was concerned. During this first generation the work of proclamation was carried on in the main by eyewitnesses of the events or by those who had been in direct contact with them. From the start a distinction was recognized between those who 'lived of the Gospel' and those who, without official accreditation, spread the word abroad and were the anonymous founders of those churches which later, often without historical authentication, claimed Apostles as their founders. During this period, with the constant coming and going between the Churches of which we have so many notices in the Epistles of Paul, there were a number of safeguards against eccentricity in the proclamation. Yet the New Testament itself is evidence that, even in this earliest period, there was great variety of emphasis in the proclamation, and that from the earliest times there was the possibility of what was later to be stigmatized as error.

But, in the second period, the situation was entirely different. The eyewitnesses and their immediate disciples died off one after the other, and the work of proclamation came more and more into the hands of those who stood in an increasingly remote and tenuous relationship to the historic events of the Gospel. With the rapid extension of the Church any kind of control became increasingly difficult. The fact and the threat of persecution by the Roman power made it necessary for the Churches to reckon with the possibility that communication between them might for a time become impossible. The destruction of Jerusalem and the scattering of the members of the original Church meant that the Christians no longer had any local centre to which they could look as the guarantee of continuity with the earliest days of the Gospel. It is in circumstances such as these that the necessity of a written record becomes evident; only so can the preacher of the Gospel be assured that his preaching is in accord with the original revelation, and that the answers he gives to the innumerable questions that he will be asked will be in accord with the mind of the Lord and of his followers. The original aim of Gospel-writing seems to have been not so much the edification of the Church (though Gospels were soon found to be indispensable for this purpose as well) as the maintenance in its purity of the original missionary proclamation.

If this appreciation of the situation is correct, we may hope to approach the Gospels *historically*, with some understanding of what they are, and of what it is that they are trying to do.

When the historian approaches the Gospels, the first thing that strikes him is the extraordinary fidelity with which they have reproduced, not the conditions of their own time, but the conditions of Palestine in the time and during the ministry of Christ.[1] For instance, the preaching of Christ is the proclamation of *the kingdom*; after the Ascension the kingdom is hardly mentioned. The Church undoubtedly adapts the message to its own time; yet it faithfully records the controversies of Jesus on such subjects as the observance of the Sabbath day, or the Jewish law of Corban. Only those who have tried to do it can have any idea of the enormous effort of historical imagination required to project oneself back into the conditions of a period that has for ever passed away.

Mark gives evidence of being a catechist's manual—a brief summary of Christian history for preachers, especially in relation to the kind of

---

[1] This does not exclude the possibility that at certain points the evangelists may have been ill-informed, or may have misunderstood the evidence before them.

questions they will be asked by those to whom they go. It is a book of extraordinary dramatic intensity. For many years it has been my custom, at the beginning of Holy Week, to read Mark 10–15 straight through at a sitting. I cannot imagine any reader doing this without becoming aware of the mounting tension in the mind of Jesus himself and of those who followed him, tension which reaches the point of agony, because Mark is writing from the point of view of a time *at which the result is not yet known*. It is often said that the Resurrection casts its light back on the Gospel narratives. In Mark this is only to a minimal extent the case. If we read with imagination, we can walk with the Son of man in his way, as he himself discovers painfully and humbly what that way is to be.

Traditionally, Mark's Gospel is associated with Peter and the Petrine tradition of the life of Christ. It falls outside the scope of this book to discuss the nature and validity of that tradition; it falls within it to note one peculiarity of St. Mark's narrative, recognition of which we owe to the minute and careful studies of the style of Mark carried out by Professor C. H. Turner of Oxford. He observes that in passage after passage we start with a third person plural, which suddenly changes into a third person singular. For instance, in 1. 21, 'they enter Capernaum; and at once he taught on the Sabbath in the synagogue'; 11. 17, 'and they came again to Jerusalem; and as he was walking in the temple ...'; 14. 32, 'and they came to ... Gethsemane, and he saith to his disciples ....'[1] Turner comments that 'a sentence commences with the plural, for it is an experience which is being related, and passes into the singular, for the experience is that of discipleship to a Master ...' If the reader will now take one step further and put back Mark's third person plural into the first person plural of narrative, he will receive a vivid impression of the testimony that lies behind the Gospel; thus in 1. 29, 'we came into our house with James and John: and my wife's mother was ill in bed with a fever, and at once we tell him about her'.[2]

It is wise not to lay too much stress on a single point of this kind; but it confirms the impression we have received of the extraordinary

[1] The most notable thing is that in none of these cases does either Matthew or Luke retain the plural. The complete list of these 'Petrine' plurals is as follows: 1. 21, 29; 5. 1, 38; 6. 53, 54; 8. 22; 9. 14, 30, 33; 10. 32, 46; 11. 1, 12, 15, 20, 27; 14. 18, 22, 26, 32.

[2] In *A New Commentary on Holy Scripture*, Part III, pp. 48, 54. See also the use made of this point by T. W. Manson in *Studies in the Gospels and Epistles* (1962), pp. 40–45. Between 1923 and 1928 Turner published in the *Journal of Theological Studies* ten minutely careful articles on 'Marcan Usage: Notes Critical and Exegetical on the Second Gospel', in each of which observations of the greatest value are to be found.

success of the writer in going behind the Resurrection, and recording
the events of the ministry of Jesus as they were understood by those
who shared them at the time. Only so was it possible to make plain to
Gentile converts, who were likely to have a very different understanding of the relationship between time and eternity, that the Gospel
which they were called to believe was most firmly rooted in history,
and in the history of one particular man.

Of Luke it is hardly necessary to say more than we have already
said. Here, too, the relationship to missionary proclamation is self-
evident. We have no means of identifying the 'most excellent Theo-
philus'; but the natural inference from the Gospel and the Acts is that
he is an intelligent Gentile convert who needs just that enlargement of
his faith which such a document as the Gospel is well calculated to
supply. Luke writes from the post-Resurrection point of view. As has
been remarked, there is in Luke no *theologia crucis*. There is none of
the agonizing suspense of the Marcan narrative, since the end is
already known; all things are seen as appointed by the providence of
God; and those things which might make it difficult for Gentile readers
to understand are either explained or quietly suppressed.

The Fourth Gospel is expressly missionary in its purpose. 'These
things are written that ye might believe.' This is the Gospel of the
mission of Jesus; the words 'he that sent me' occur with almost
monotonous iteration.[1] Twice over, the mission of the disciple is set
forth in the solemn words: 'As the Father has sent me, even so I send
you', 'As thou didst send me into the world, so I have sent them into
the world' (John 20. 21; 17. 18). The mission continues. It is not clear
who the recipients of the Gospel are. Dr. C. H. Dodd, who in his
book *The Interpretation of the Fourth Gospel* has made use of the
researches of thirty years to lay a sound foundation for the understanding of this Gospel, has suggested a group of thoughtful and
educated Hellenists in one of the great cities of Asia Minor.[2] We
simply do not know. What is clear is that the delineation of the great
drama of faith and unbelief, with which the greater part of the Gospel
is filled, is existential in character; here the readers are to see themselves,

[1] Two Greek words, πέμπω and ἀποστέλλω, are used; I have not been able to find that
there is any difference in meaning between them.
[2] Others might think of a group of deeply Hellenized Jews, the same kind of group,
mutatis mutandis, which first received the Epistle to the Hebrews. In this sense see
J. A. T. Robinson, 'The Destination and Purpose of the Fourth Gospel' in *Twelve New
Testament Studies* (1962), pp. 107 ff., and W. C. van Unnik, 'The Purpose of St. John's
Gospel' (1957) reprinted in *The Gospels Reconsidered* (1960), pp. 167 ff.

and to know that that judgement, which is another characteristic feature of the Gospel, is being passed upon them as they read.

Matthew is the one Gospel which does not fit into the missionary pattern. It seems clearly to be written for Christians. Dr. Alexander Nairne used to call it the liturgical Gospel; certainly its lapidary, architectonic structure makes it very suitable for reading aloud in church.[1] But this, more than any other, is a Gospel of warning and judgement. It is written for a Church, perhaps in Syria, which has lost its first love, and needs to be called back to the austerity of the true faith. 'It happened to the Jews; it could happen to you.' This is the constant refrain. Matthew is the Jewish Gospel only in the sense that it shows more clearly than the others the judgement and rejection of the Jews, who ought so easily to have been able to recognize their king. Right at the outset of the Gospel we are confronted with the story of the wise men from the East. It is surprising that so few commentators have grasped why, in this most carefully constructed Gospel, this story meets us at the outset. The point is not so much that the wise men found the Redeemer, as that the Jews, who had the Scriptures and could give all the right answers, failed to find him. 'It happened to them; it could happen to you; without are the weeping and the gnashing of teeth.' We can see at once the close parallel with the letters of warning in the first three chapters of the Book of Revelation.[2]

VIII

So, we have our four Gospels. We are beginning to read them again as wholes, to understand their theology, to see why each is as it is, and what principle governed the selection of their material. We no longer think of the evangelists as unskilled fitters-together of rags and patches. But taking these four Gospels critically, and remembering the kind of influences which have formed the traditions that underlie them, is it possible, synthetically, we will not say to write a life of Jesus of Nazareth, but at least to give an impression, a sketch of him as historically he was, in the years between about 6 B.C. and A.D. 29, in Judaea and in Galilee of the Gentiles? Only a few years ago the answer of many theologians would have been an uncompromising No. It is

[1] This idea has been further developed by G. D. Kilpatrick, *The Origins of the Gospel According to St. Matthew* (1946). An important study by G. Bornkamm, G. Barth, and H. J. Held is *Überlieferung und Auslegung im Matthäusevangelium* (1960).

[2] Yet Matthew, too, is concerned with the missionary dimension, and with the recovery of the missionary vocation of the Church; see especially chapter 10 of the Gospel.

all the more remarkable that in 1956 Germany gave convincingly, though cautiously, the answer Yes.

In that year, the publishing firm of W. Kohlhammer in Stuttgart published in its series of serious paper-backs a little book called *Jesus von Nazareth* by Günther Bornkamm, Professor of New Testament Exegesis in the University of Heidelberg.

The appearance of this work was widely hailed as an event in Christian history, and not without reason. For the first time a leading representative of the 'Form-critical' school set to work to produce, if not a life of Jesus, at least a synthesis of all that, according to the principles of this school, it could be held that we know about him. In view of the often extremely negative character of the conclusions of this school, readers were astonished that Professor Bornkamm could find so much that was positive to say, could admit so much of the tradition as genuine, and could assure us that, for all the weaknesses and uncertainties in the evidence, we still can have before our minds a living and reasonably full picture of Jesus of Nazareth as he actually was. 'Understood in this way', he says, 'the primitive tradition of Jesus is brimful of history.'[1]

The method, as may be supposed from what has been already said, is to attempt to get back to 'those facts which are prior to any pious interpretation and which manifest themselves as undisturbed and primary' (p. 53). This means the exclusion of a great deal in the Gospels as we now have them: 'We can say with certainty wherever in the tradition the word "faith" refers to the message of salvation and to Jesus as the Messiah, or where the word "faith" is used in this sense absolutely without any addition, we have to do with the usage of the later Church and her mission' (p. 129). Yet, even when so much has been excluded, in the stories of controversy, in the parables interpreted in the light of their original setting, in the proclamation of the kingdom as the great act of God, in the steady movement of the story to its climax in the Cross, we feel that we are able to reach out beyond the early Church and its interpretations to the primary and authentic, to the majestic and challenging figure of Jesus of Nazareth himself.[2]

[1] *Jesus of Nazareth* (English trans., 1960), p. 26.

[2] I have given a good deal of space to this work of Professor Bornkamm, because it is readily available in English, and also because it is the first attempt, on the principles of the 'Form-critical' school in its later development, to present something like a complete picture of Jesus. Many other scholars, however, are engaged in this 'new Quest of the Historical Jesus', and some, like Professor G. Ebeling of Munich, and Professor H. Fuchs of Berlin, seem willing to go further than Professor Bornkamm in a positive direction. A very useful summary of these more recent developments is provided by J. M. Robinson in *Interpretation* (January 1962), pp. 76–97: 'Basic Shifts in German Theology'.

A great deal can be said in praise of Bornkamm's book. It is the work of a man of unexceptionable candour and honesty. And there really was no need for the disclaimer in the Preface: 'Also I may assume that only the foolish will miss "edification" and personal testimony, and confuse the objectivity proper to a scholarly exposition with an indifference incompatible with the experience of the Emmaus disciples: "Did not our hearts burn within us while he talked to us on the road?".'[1] This is the work of a humble and believing man.

Yet, with all the grounds for commendation, there are also aspects of the book which must make us hesitate before passing an entirely favourable judgement. For, though the book presents itself as a piece of historical research, it is not the work of an historian.

We have already commented on the immense difficulty of the work of the theologian, in that he should be perfectly at home with the principles and methods of three separate and to some extent mutually exclusive disciplines—philology, philosophy, and history. Bultmann and his followers are strong in the field of classical philology, though hampered in their work by their limited knowledge of the Semitic languages and the Semitic background of so much of the New Testament. All have drunk deeply at the fount of German philosophy and are familiar with the use of philosophical categories for the elucidation of theological truth. But none of them shows signs of having had training in the hard school of the historian. Historical research is always a difficult and delicate business. The difficulty is immensely increased, if the object of historical research is, as in the case of the New Testament documents, also the concern of faith. The only way to become an historian is through the handling and weighing of historical evidence. It would be an excellent thing if every scholar who wishes to approach the New Testament in the light of history could be required to win his spurs elsewhere in the wide fields of ancient history, and, only when his competence has been proved in the less difficult areas, to advance to the supremely difficult task of the historical reconstruction of the life of Jesus and of the story of the early Church.

For it is hardly possible to imagine a greater difference than that between the temper of the historian and the temper of the philosopher. The philosopher is concerned with universals; his aim is to bring as many phenomena as possible under one single law—in this he is akin

---

[1] Op. cit., p. 10. It is to be noted that, on the view of Professor Bornkamm, the experience of the disciples on the Emmaus road is purely legendary.

to the physical scientist. He seeks for one single standpoint, from which he may be able to survey the whole of time and eternity, to penetrate the inmost secrets of being, and in a measure to grasp the ultimate pattern of reality. The historian, if he is a true historian, knows that there are no rules. What he deals in is the unique, the unrepeatable, and the unpredictable. Generalization is always hazardous, and he can hope for no more than approximation to a truth which is in point of fact an ever-vanishing horizon. For this reason the historian as such tends to be always in bad odour with the philosopher. Lessing, in *Die Erziehung der Menschengeschlechts* (1780), laid it down in the eighteenth century that 'the contingent truths of history can never serve as the demonstration of eternal truths of reason'. He leaves no doubt as to his judgement that the eternal truths of reason are the important thing and that history necessarily belongs to a provisional and inferior order. We may question whether there are any eternal truths of reason of the kind that Lessing, that true man of the Enlightenment, so devoutly believed in. We must agree with him that history cannot be used, in the strict sense of the term, to demonstrate anything; whether we conclude that history is for this reason to be judged as inferior will depend on certain basic views as to the nature and significance of our human experience of our world.

German theology has perhaps never quite freed itself from the influence of this judgement of Lessing. Another profound philosophic influence is that of Hegel, who saw in history the gradual self-revelation and realization of the Idea, and desired to bring history also into the broad and all-encompassing limits of his system. We may perhaps add as a third David Friedrich Strauss, and his remark that 'the infinite grudges the pouring out of the fulness of its being in one particular instance', a remark pontifically thrown out without any attempt to produce evidence in favour of its truth.

Against the prejudices of the metaphysician, the historian must stick to his last, and must maintain the integrity of his own calling. It is almost inevitable that the historian should have some philosophic ideas, perhaps not more than semi-consciously held; but any intrusion of these ideas is bound to be gravely prejudicial to his work as an historian. He is bound, of course, to accept the basic axioms of thought, and that logical law of contradiction which makes it rational and correct to speak of certain things as impossibilities. Beyond this he has no knowledge of the meaning of the words 'possible' and 'impossible'.

Renan started out to write the life of Jesus on the assumption that the supernatural does not occur; thereby he confessed in a sentence that he was not writing as an historian. Forty years later, Kirsopp Lake in his book *The Historical Evidences for the Resurrection of Jesus Christ* (1907) took the view that the Resurrection could not possibly have occurred in the way in which it is recorded in the New Testament; therefore it must have occurred in some other way. The historian, if he is wise, does not commit himself to any view of the definition of the 'natural' and the 'supernatural'—philosophical terms with which he has no concern. What he does know is that history is to a large extent made up of the improbable, and of what by any sober calculation of reason would be regarded as the impossible. One of the most brilliant of twentieth-century historians, Mr. F. A. Simpson, has remarked that it would do historians no harm to believe six impossible things before breakfast every day. This, it will at once be seen, is not an argument in favour of credulity, still less in favour of an uncritical handling of historical evidence. It is a picturesque and emphatic demand that history should be content to be history and should not allow itself to be influenced by ideas or principles which belong to other disciplines but not to history itself.

It is at this point that we begin to feel difficulties about Bornkamm's work on the life of Jesus. We have seen at an earlier stage of our investigations that Professor Bultmann had accepted the 'Philosophy of Being' of Martin Heidegger as the framework within which he would expound the Gospel. The influence of this particular philosophy in Germany is widespread, and almost all the scholars of the school of Bultmann have at least in a measure fallen under its spell. Bornkamm is no exception. Now this is a perfectly legitimate procedure for the systematic or philosophical theologian; if the historical theologian happens to hold such views, he must keep them rigidly out of sight throughout the whole course of his historical investigations; otherwise it is most unlikely that he will arrive at a genuinely historical conclusion. But this is just what Bornkamm has not done. Having rightly affirmed that 'faith cannot and should not be dependent on the change and uncertainty of historical research' (p. 9), he goes on to ask on what it can then be dependent, and finds the answer in certain formal ideas which are constitutive of all true religion. This may be true, but it is not historical. The historian turned philosopher has laid down certain axioms, he 'has already arrived at the knowledge of the religious truth before he opened his New Testament, and consequently everything that is not fit to illustrate this truth is *a priori* doomed to be rejected'.[1]

It is a mistake to isolate the story of Jesus from all that had gone before it; one of the strands that together make up the Gospel story is distorted by this error. It is essential to the ministry of Jesus that it takes place within the framework of Jewish history, that it is the continuation and culmination of all those mighty acts of God in the past through which Israel had been constituted a people, and in face of grave historical improbability had been preserved by God in existence as a people. Amid all their diversities, all the traditions are united in this— that the salvation promised of old has now become an accomplished fact, and it has become fact through the ministry, the death and resurrection of Jesus Christ. This is accepted by the writers of the New Testament as objective fact and not as a reality created by their own faith. Is it likely that the believers came to this understanding of the centrality of Jesus for faith, but that Jesus himself was unaware of his own significance in the purpose of God? The historian is entitled to his own views on all these matters. But, if he persists in maintaining no more than a very tenuous connexion between the actual ministry of Jesus and the faith that was evoked by it in the disciples, it must be clear that his rejection of so much that is plainly present in the Gospel traditions is due to philosophical rather than to historical considerations.[2]

In his desire to minimize any claim that Jesus may have made for himself, Bornkamm is led to the paradoxical view that in all probability 'the historical Jesus never used the title "Son of man" for himself'.[3] The argument is developed with great ingenuity; yet I cannot imagine any historian reading it without the uncomfortable feeling that this is a notable example of that special pleading for which German theologians are famous. A view which runs so directly contrary to all the historical evidence which we possess surely needs to be supported by overwhelming historical arguments. For it is the remarkable fact that this title, in all our Gospels as we have them, is used by Jesus of himself a

[1] Otto A. Piper, loc. cit., p. 474.

[2] This has been grasped by some who are prepared to go rather further than Professor Bornkamm in recognizing the historical character of the Gospels. It does not really matter much whether Jesus ever made *in words* the claim to be the Messiah, the final word of God to men. The claim was present *in him*, in the whole of what he was and did and in every part of it. This is what I take Conzelmann to mean when he speaks of 'Christology *in nuce*' —as we might say, in embryo, in undeveloped form.

[3] G. Bornkamm, *Jesus of Nazareth* (1960).

great many times, but is never used by anyone else either as a form of address to him, or in referring to him. It is a mysterious title, and whole shelves of literature have been written about its meaning. After the Resurrection the title is no longer used.[1] For this it would seem that there is a perfectly sound historical reason; what follows the Resurrection is testimony *about* Jesus, not the testimony *of* Jesus. No disciple ever ventured to take upon his own lips the title which had such solemn associations as having been heard only on the lips of the Master himself. Professor Bornkamm thinks that the title, never used by Jesus himself, 'is for the oldest Palestinian Church, to which we owe the transmission of the words of the Lord, an expression of the essence of their faith and was to be invested with the authority of Jesus himself'.[2] But this seems to overlook one essential element in the *historical* evidence—that the title 'Son of man' occurs in all the Gospels, no less in those which were expressly written for Gentiles than in those which bear an unmistakably Palestinian stamp. It cannot be said that the view of Professor Bornkamm is absolutely impossible—few things in history are absolutely impossible. But all the arguments that he has assembled are not successful in converting a bare possibility even into a probability.

IX

It is just the fact that the *historical* reconstruction of the life and history of Jesus has as yet hardly begun. The work of the last forty years in analysing and criticizing the sources has been of the greatest value. The materials for further work are all there. What we need now is historians. And real historians, like real literary critics, are rare birds. To knowledge of facts and sources must be added three great gifts. First, the capacity of historical judgement—the delicate process of calculating exactly how much weight is to be attributed to each fragment of evidence. Secondly, historical imagination—the power to project oneself into the minds and thoughts of the men and women of a

[1] The one single exception is Acts 7. 56, in the testimony of Stephen before his accusers. See also Rev. 1. 13, where the reference to Daniel 7. 9 is very plain.

[2] Op. cit., p. 230. P. Vielhauer ('Gottesreich und Menschensohn in der Verkündigung Jesu', in *Festschrift für Günther Dehn*, ed. W. Schneemelcher (1957), pp. 51–79), makes the important point that the Son of man sayings never speak of the Kingdom of God, and the Kingdom of God sayings never speak of the Son of man. The fullest study of the problem of the Son of man in recent years is H. E. Tödt, *Der Menschensohn in der Synoptischen Überlieferung* (1959).

generation very different from our own. Thirdly, historical synthesis—
the capacity to put together bits and pieces of historical evidence in
such a way as to make a consistent and convincing whole.

An interesting illustration of the difference between analysis
of documents and true historical reconstruction may be provided from
a sphere remote, but not too remote, from the New Testament.
Every schoolboy knows that St. Patrick was the apostle of Ireland,
that he converted the country, reduced the Druids to subjection, and
expelled the snakes. The whole romantic, heroic tale had become part
of the common memories of Christendom, and very few were aware
of the imperfections and problems attaching to the documents on
which this great superstructure of legend had been erected.

In 1901, a brilliant Celtic philologist produced the article on the
Celtic Churches for the famous German encyclopaedia, the *Realen-
zyklopädie für protestantische Theologie und Kirche.* Mercilessly he
exposed the inconsistencies and improbabilities in the lives of St.
Patrick, written at least two centuries after his death; the preponderance
of purely legendary elements in what is reported of him; the difficulty
of knowing anything about him. By the time that Zimmer has completed his 'Form-critical' investigations, all that is left of poor Patrick
resembles a heap of small fragments on the floor. His activity, such as
it was, was limited to a small area in the south-eastern part of Ireland
(Laigin). He accomplished little, and died a poor, unsuccessful, and
forgotten saint. Then, about A.D. 625, a party in Ireland decided to
resuscitate him. For this two reasons are suggested. This was an
attempt of the Southern Irish Christians to enter the Roman world by
surrendering to the Pope on the vexed question of the date on which
Easter should be celebrated. Alternatively, the motive was the pious
desire of Irish Christians to have an apostle of their own who could rank
with Columba of Scotland and Augustine of England. In either case,
their pious inventions can hardly be accepted as having any historical
value.

Luckily for Patrick, just about the time of the appearance of
Zimmer's article, an eminent historian, J. B. Bury, who was not a
Christian, was led to the study of Patrick and Ireland as further
developments of that expansion of the Christian faith which he had
been studying in countries further east. He found everything in confusion. The art of *Quellenkritik*, the scientific analysis of sources, had
hardly been practised on the documents at all. The theories of Zimmer,
highly plausible as they can be made to sound, were seen, when

critically handled, to be as full of inconsistencies as the documents they so ruthlessly tore to pieces. Bury's competence and impartiality were both above suspicion or reproach; as an historian of the eastern Roman empire he had proved his mastery of the art of documentary study, as an unbeliever he had no interest whatever in supporting the claims of any particular ecclesiastical view.[1] Then, having dealt faithfully with the sources, Bury set to work on the much more difficult task of historical reconstruction. He was a good enough historian to recognize that even legend can be most important, if rightly handled, as historical evidence; but at the same time he is cautious never to allow a mere probability to acquire a certainty which does not intrinsically belong to it. Yet, when all this minute critical work has been done and the results gathered together, a notable rehabilitation of St. Patrick is seen to have taken place. It is frankly admitted that much is still doubtful and uncertain; but gone is the extreme scepticism of Zimmer, and the picture which finally emerges is much more like the Patrick of Christian recollection than we might have expected.[2]

In the whole history of modern scholarship, only two great historians have concerned themselves with the events of the first Christian century—J. B. Lightfoot and Eduard Meyer. Of the permanent value of Lightfoot's contribution we have already said enough. Eduard Meyer's *Ursprung und Anfänge des Christentums* ('Origin and Beginnings of Christianity', 1921–3) was unfortunate in the moment of its appearance. Meyer, inevitably, based his work on the accepted critical canons of the day—the two-document theory of the Gospels and so forth—and was not always fortunate in the authorities on whom he relied. But this was just the moment at which German scholarship was turning over to 'Form-criticism'; Meyer's book appeared to be antiquated almost from the moment of its publication, and Germany has

[1] His own claim to impartiality runs as follows: 'The business of a historian is to ascertain facts. There is something essentially absurd in his wishing that any alleged fact should turn out to be true or should turn out to be false. So far as he entertains a wish of this kind, his attitude is not critical. The justification of the present biography is that it rests upon a methodical examination of the sources, and that the conclusions, whether right or wrong, were reached without any prepossession. For one whose interest in the subject is purely intellectual, it was a matter of unmixed indifference what answer might be found to any one of the vexed questions' (J. B. Bury, *The Life of St. Patrick* (1905), p. vii).

[2] A careful study of St. Patrick and all the problems connected with him would be no bad preparation for the student about to launch out on the critical study of the Gospels. This is not to say that all Bury's conclusions have been substantiated by subsequent research. But his methods, both analytic and constructive, seem to me almost flawless; and it is the acquisition of the right methods which is so enormously important for the conscientious student.

hardly done justice to its very solid merits.[1] For Meyer, who was an historian and not a theologian, drawing on his immense knowledge of the ancient world saw Christianity, as it ought to be seen, historically, as part of the immense ferment of the human spirit, which ranges from the first writing prophets among the Hebrews and the beginnings of Greek philosophy to the preaching of Muhammad in Arabia and the extinction of Greek philosophy in the reign of Justinian.[2] We await the successors, who will carry on what Lightfoot inaugurated and Meyer carried out with only partial success. We may confidently expect that the reconstruction will go much further in a positive direction than anything that has yet been produced by the school of which Professor Bornkamm is so distinguished a representative.

As it happens, this expectation is something more than a mere supposition. A few years ago one of the most distinguished of living Church historians, Hans Freiherr von Campenhausen, Professor of Church History in the University of Heidelberg, produced a long study of the Resurrection narratives;[3] his method and conclusions are rather different from those of the 'Form-critical' school. It has become almost traditional to say that 'the Resurrection does not belong to history; it dwells entirely in the realm of faith', and that therefore historical criticism can neither reconstruct nor interpret the event of the Resurrection. That there is a measure of truth in this affirmation no scholar is likely to deny; but stated in this bald form it will not do for von Campenhausen:

For all its contemporary, vivifying reality, the resurrection is still an actual event of the historical past, and as such it was handed down, proclaimed and believed. And so the proclamation of it cannot evade the historical question, and cannot in any circumstances be withdrawn from the testing of historical investigation. Exactly this was the attitude of the Evangelists in their account of Easter. With all their naiveté and clumsiness, they took serious account of the 'critical' suspicions which had come to

---

[1] Since German theologians on the whole take a low view of Luke as an historian, Meyer would not endear himself to them by taking Luke as his starting-point, and by paying him this tremendous tribute: 'All this assures for the author a conspicuous place among the most important historical writers in the history of the world. He has found in Eusebius a successor who in many ways is of equal value' (op. cit., vol. i, p. 3).

[2] Meyer's great work was a history of the Ancient World (*Geschichte des Altertums*), in five volumes, of which the second edition appeared between 1907 and 1928. Meyer criticizes other secular historians for their failure to treat the origins of Christianity *historically*, as a part of the general history of the world.

[3] This has been republished among his collected essays, *Tradition und Leben: Kräfte der Kirchegeschichte* (1960).

their notice, and, as far as they were able, offered a 'historical' refutation of them. So also did Paul, though it is quite clear that for him faith could not rest on purely historical considerations.[1]

To the historical evidence of 1 Corinthians 15 von Campenhausen attaches very much weight. The Epistle was written probably in A.D. 56, less than thirty years after the events referred to. Paul had been in touch with the leaders of the Church in Jerusalem; it is most unlikely that his conversations with them were limited to the purely practical questions of the admission of the Gentiles to the Church. Probably not more than ten years had elapsed between the Resurrection itself and the day on which Paul received first-hand information as to the Christian tradition from those who had been leaders in its formation; and this tradition he claims to have passed on to the Corinthians when he led them to Christ.[2] It is only rarely that we have such good historical evidence for anything in the ancient world.

Von Campenhausen goes further; he is prepared to take seriously the statement of the New Testament that the grave of Jesus was found empty on the third day after his death. For many years it has been almost an agreed point among New Testament interpreters that the belief of the disciples in the Resurrection depended only on their encounters with the risen Jesus, and that the 'legend' of the empty tomb grew up at a later date to reinforce a belief that was already held. Much is made of the fact that there is no reference to the empty tomb in our earliest account of the Resurrection manifestations, that in 1 Corinthians 15. But here the weight of evidence tells in exactly the opposite direction; Paul's statements that the Lord was buried, and that he was raised *on the third day*, are almost unintelligible if he was not familiar with that part of the tradition which dealt with the empty tomb. And it is further the fact that, though there are many and perplexing divergences between the Gospel narratives of the Resurrection, this is the one point on which they are all emphatically agreed. What we are left with,

---

[1] Op. cit., p. 110.

[2] Paul recognizes that his own encounter with the risen Christ was different from that of the other Apostles, though he stoutly maintains its reality. He uses of himself the very strange expression τῷ ἐκτρώματι, 'the abortion', which may well have been a contemptuous expression used of him by his enemies. But ἔκτρωμα means 'something born *before the right time*'; if we take this seriously, Paul can only mean that he has seen by anticipation the glory of Christ as that will be manifest in the *Parousia*. This fits in with the fact that there is no suggestion that, in this meeting with Paul, the risen Christ was seen standing firmly on the earth, as he is in all the other records of his post-Resurrection appearances.

as historians, is the very strongly attested fact that the grave of Jesus was empty. What we may make of that fact as philosophers, or as believers, or as sceptics, or as anything else, is an entirely different story. Here we are talking only of the work of the historian in the handling of historical evidence.

Now, of course, it is absurd to suggest that the emptiness of the tomb proves the resurrection of Jesus. The fact that the tomb was empty, if it is a fact, proves that the tomb was empty and nothing more. But this is only half the argument. The distinction between a physical and a spiritual resurrection would have been unintelligible to the people of that time—to fail to recognize this shows a serious lack of that historical imagination of which we have been speaking. The empty tomb could not prove the resurrection of Jesus or create faith in it. *But the contrary is not true.* If the Jewish authorities had been able to produce the body of Jesus, they would have been able finally and decisively to *disprove* the resurrection of Jesus, as the disciples believed it and were proclaiming it.

It cannot be too often affirmed that the disciples were *not* stating that Jesus continued somehow to survive in the unseen world. They affirmed that death had been conquered; that by a tremendous manifestation of his power God had raised Jesus out of Sheôl, the home of the departed spirits. They did not imagine that Jesus, like a ghost, had returned to spend some further period upon earth; they affirmed that death hath no more dominion over him. They did not say simply that God had in some way mysteriously vindicated his servant Jesus; they affirmed that the whole universe had become a new place, that the new world-order was already here, because Jesus had risen from the dead.

This is a matter of faith, not of demonstrative proof; but it is one on which history is not qualified to pronounce a negative judgement. For history deals all the time with the unique and unparalleled, and it always keeps in mind the possibility of the wholly new and unforeseen. It is just the plain fact that we have no precedent to guide us in our estimate of what may happen, when a wholly sinless person yields himself up to death in total obedience to the will of God. The whole process of nature as we know it[1] is of a continually advancing subjection of matter to spirit. In the universe as we know it, this advancing freedom has reached its highest point in the creativity of man. We may, if we like, *dogmatically* deny that any further advance is possible; as

---

[1] And as it has been impressively delineated for us by Fr. Pierre Teilhard de Chardin in his now famous book, *The Phenomenon of Man* (1956. English trans., 1959).

historians we must keep open the possibility that a further advance is possible and may in particular circumstances have taken place.

It is interesting to read the comments of the historian von Campenhausen on this particular historical problem:

The only thing which remains perplexing in this whole course of events is that which set the whole thing in motion—the question of what happened to the body of Jesus. We have no reliable testimony of eyewitnesses as to the manner in which the grave of Jesus was opened, and the body disappeared from it. From the side of the Christians we have only the confession of faith in the resurrection which relies on those appearances of the risen Jesus that followed upon it; from the side of the Jews we have only a number of tendentious tales, which counter the Christian explanation with alternative explanations, but do not give the impression of resting upon positive observation, or going back to old and reliable sources of information. From the historical point of view, then, the whole situation remains dark. This does not, of course, mean that we simply call in 'miracle' as an explanation of it. As we have already said, we have to reckon with the possibility of a later reburial, or alteration of the site of the grave; of theft of the body (not necessarily only by the disciples); of malicious activity on the part of the enemies of Jesus; of one or other of the many accidents that could have happened . . . But all this will not alarm one who believes in the physical resurrection of Jesus. Since what this involves is a literally unique event, in the sense that with it the new Aeon came into being and the old world with its laws really comes to an end, the 'natural impossibility' of conceiving anything of the kind to be 'probable' seems rather to be 'necessary' and from the theological point of view, so to speak, 'natural'. The situation is really difficult for those who want to take seriously belief in the resurrection, but regard belief in the physical resurrection as superfluous or as completely unacceptable. For them the only possible, and rather distressing, solution is to follow the early Christians in their confession of faith in the Risen One, but in the main to follow the Jews in their explanation of what it was that originally called belief in the resurrection into being.[1]

Naturally, von Campenhausen's views have not everywhere won approval; the controversy about the resurrection of Jesus will continue. The aim of this discussion has been simply to make plain the nature of the *historical* approach to historical problems, and to indicate that the possibilities of historical research into the life and history of Jesus are very far from having been exhausted. We have quoted one instance from Germany. This may be supported by the somewhat confident

[1] Op. cit., pp. 108–9.

statement of an English scholar, who, though not a professional historian, was very far from being ignorant of the categories of historical research:

I am increasingly convinced that in the Gospels we have the materials—reliable materials—for an outline account of the ministry as a whole. I believe it is possible to produce such an outline and that, when produced, it will dovetail into the rest of the picture, that it will fit into what we otherwise know about contemporary Jewish faith and life in Palestine ... And it will give an adequate explanation of the existence of the Church. We shall not be able to fit in all the details ... the gaps are enormous. But we have *some* details; and I think it is true to say that these short stories, parables, sayings, poems and so on, which go to make up the Gospels themselves, epitomize the whole story. Each of them is, as it were, a little window through which we can view the ministry as a whole; a vantage-point from which we can take a Pisgah-view of the authentic kingdom of God ... There is a vast deal to be done and it is infinitely worth doing. The quest of the historical Jesus is still a great and most hopeful enterprise.[1]

But does it really matter? Many faithful Christians find themselves disturbed and irritated by this emphasis on the historical, and on the vagaries and uncertainties of historical research. Is this what faith is all about? Does not faith move in an entirely different realm?

Certainly it is not the case that we can be saved by the acceptance as true of certain historical phenomena in the past. Certainly it is true that Christian faith will not collapse, if this or that historical detail is shown *not* to be true.[2] Certainly it is not the case that, if every single detail of the Gospel narratives was faithfully and exactly authentic as history, faith in Jesus Christ would automatically result. But having allowed all this, I still think that it is possible gravely to underestimate the significance of the historical in Christian faith. Theologically, history is important. If we believe that in Jesus Christ God did finally and definitively intervene in the world of men, we are committed to the view that history is the chosen sphere of his working, and that therefore history, all history, including the history of you and me today, is related to the process of revelation. But there is something even more important than this. Professor Bultmann and his colleagues insist again and again, and rightly, on our *encounter* with God in Jesus Christ. But

[1] T. W. Manson, *Studies in the Gospels and Epistles* (1962), pp. 11–12.
[2] Some think that it would not collapse, even though it could be shown that Jesus of Nazareth had never existed. I am not in agreement with this view.

whom do we encounter? Is he, as Schweitzer thought, one who comes to us without a name? Is he, as Giovanni Miegge has paraphrased the thought of Bultmann, one who is no more than the geometrical point, which has position but no magnitude? Is he a strange conflation of the Gnostic myth with certain Palestinian legends? When the believer comes to the Holy Communion, what does he imagine himself to be doing?

These are questions that cannot be answered in a sentence; but they must be answered. It is the view of many competent scholars today that all the fragments of Christian tradition which we possess in the New Testament bear witness with singular unanimity to one single historical figure, unlike any other that has ever walked among the sons of men; and that, though much about him must remain unknown and even more must remain mysterious, though an immense amount of work has still to be done on that historical reconstruction of his story which has as yet hardly been begun, he is even now not so much the unknown, the problem, as the one who to the believer is the well known. In the words of Alice Meynell, he is the one 'whom we have by heart'.

Chapter VIII

SALVATION IS OF THE JEWS

TOWARDS the end of the year 1922 that excellent scholar Dr. A.
Lukyn Williams[1] put into my hands a book with the remark: 'I
think this would interest you.' It was the first volume of Strack-
Billerbeck's Rabbinic commentary on the New Testament: *Kommentar
zum Neuen Testament aus Talmud und Midrasch*. Few of us learn
Rabbinic Hebrew. In the dark days before Strack-Billerbeck we
referred to Rabbinic matters cautiously, if at all; in this bright post-
Strack-Billerbeck epoch, we are all Rabbinic experts, though at
second hand.

The idea that much of value to the Christian scholar can be acquired
through the study of the Rabbinic writings was not, of course, new. It
had a famous exponent and practitioner in the seventeenth century,
John Lightfoot (1602–75), Master of Catharine Hall in the University of
Cambridge and member of the Westminster Assembly of Divines. The
brief account of the first Lightfoot in the *Dictionary of National Biography* tells us a great many interesting things about him,[2] among others
that in 1628 he moved to Hornsey, Middlesex, 'chiefly with a view to easy
access to the rabbinical treasures of Sion College', in the library of which
I am writing these lines.[3] He later studied Hebrew and the writings of
the Rabbis with such effect as to receive from Gibbon the tribute that
'by constant reading of the rabbis, he became almost a rabbi himself'.[4]
In the Preface to his *Horae Hebraicae et Talmudicae: or Hebrew and
Talmudical Exercitations upon the Gospels of St. Matthew and St.*

[1] Dr. Lukyn Williams was born in 1853 and was thus already eight years old at the
beginning of the period which we have been studying in this book. He had been a missionary to the Jews in London and had made himself an excellent Rabbinic scholar. His
notable book *Adversus Judaeos*, a study of Christian apologetic against the Jews, was
published in 1937, when he was 84 years old.

[2] Such as that at the Westminster Assembly he vigorously resisted the 'vehemence,
heat and tugs' of the Independents!

[3] But not, of course, in the same building. The contemporary Sion College, with its
entrancing view over the Thames, is Victorian.

[4] I have been unable to trace this quotation.

Mark[1] Lightfoot sets out the purpose of his studies and the benefits which he believed could be obtained from them:

> For, first, when all the books of the New Testament were written by Jews, and among Jews, and unto them;—and when all the discoveries made here, were made in like manner by Jews, and to Jews, and among them;—I was always fully persuaded, as of a thing past all doubting, that that Testament could not but everywhere taste of, and retain, the Jews' style, idiom, form, and rule of speaking. . . .
> For it is no matter, what we can beat out concerning those manners of speech on the anvil of our own conceit, but what they signified among them in their ordinary sense and speech. And since this could be found out in no other way than by consulting Talmudic authors, who both speak in the vulgar dialect of the Jews, and also handle and reveal all Jewish matters; being induced by these reasons I applied myself chiefly to the reading these books. . . . The ill report of those authors, whom all do so very much speak against, may at first discourage him that sets upon the reading of their books. The Jews themselves stink in Marcellinus; and their writings stink as much almost among all; and they labour under this, I know not what, singular misfortune, that, being not read, they displease; and that they are sufficiently reproached by those that have read them—but undergo much more infamy by those, that have not.
> The almost unconquerable difficulty of the style, the frightful roughness of the language, and the amazing emptiness and sophistry of the matters handled, do torture, vex, and tire them, that read them . . . so that the reader hath need of patience all along, to enable him to bear both trifling in sense, and roughness in expression.[2]

The Preface written by this most pleasing sage ends with an affectionate address to the students over whom he presided in Catharine Hall in that year of the death of Oliver, the Lord Protector:

> But this work, whatever it be, and whatever fortune it is like to meet with, we would dedicate to you, my very dear Catharine-Hall men, both as a debt and as a desire. . . . Let this pledge, therefore, of our love and endearment be laid-up by you; and while we endeavour to give others an account of our hours, let this give you an assurance of our affections. And may it last in Catharine-Hall, even to future ages, as a testimony of service, a monument of love, and a memorial both of me and you.[3]

[1] Contrary to the custom of the learned of that time, Lightfoot wrote not in Latin but in English, in spite of the formidable Latin title by which the work is usually known—and good, vigorous seventeenth-century English at that.

[2] I have used the collected edition of the works of Lightfoot, published in London in 1823. *Horae Hebraicae* forms vol. xi in this edition, and my quotation is from pp. iii, iv, and v.

[3] Op. cit., p. vii.

Lightfoot was not, strictly speaking, a pioneer in the study of the Rabbinical writings. Much had already been printed in the sixteenth century, and Christians were naturally indebted for their knowledge of Hebrew in the main to Jewish scholars. But he was the first systematically and methodically to apply his Talmudic knowledge to the elucidation of the New Testament text. The task which he had set himself was indeed a formidable one; the Talmudic literature is vast and chaotic, and he had few clues to guide him. It is amazing that he brought up so much that was of value, and that in the main he was so successful in laying the foundations for one aspect of the historical and critical study of the Scriptures. Inevitably, after three centuries, much of his work is out of date; but for more than two hundred years Lightfoot was the authority to whom men turned, if they lacked his close acquaintance with the original languages.

One single quotation may serve to illustrate the method followed by Lightfoot:

[On Matthew 5. 22] The Jewish schools do thus distinguish between a brother and a neighbour; that a 'brother' signifies an Israelite by nation and blood; a 'neighbour' an Israelite in religion and worship. . . . Maimonides writes thus: 'It is all one to kill an Israelite, and a Canaanite servant; for both the punishment is death; —but an Israelite who shall kill . . . a stranger inhabitant, shall not be punished with death . . . it is needless to say, he shall not be punished with death for killing a heathen'. . . . But under the gospel, where there is no distinction of nations or tribes, 'brother' is taken in the same latitude, as among the Jews, both 'brother' and 'neighbour' were; that is for all professing the gospel,—and is contradistinguished to the heathen. . . . But 'neighbour' is extended to all, even such as are strangers to our religion. Luke x. 29, 30 etc.[1]

Lightfoot's heavy tomes continued, as we have seen, to be reprinted; but they were for scholars and experts.[2] The book from which, at the turn of the last century, many Christians obtained their first acquaintance with the Jewish background of the Gospels was Alfred Edersheim's *Life and Times of Jesus the Messiah*, which first appeared in

[1] Op. cit., p. 105.

[2] A link between Lightfoot and later times was the great New Testament commentary of J. J. Wettstein already referred to. This had been described by its compiler, in its full Latin title, as enriched by a *commentario pleniore ex scriptoribus veteribus Hebraeis, Graecis et Latinis historiam et vim verborum illustrante*. *Hebraeis* here means 'Rabbinic', and the commentary is in fact remarkably rich in Rabbinic illustrations and parallels to the text of the New Testament.

1883. Edersheim was himself a converted Jew, and wrote from within that living experience of the Jewish faith which cannot be shared directly by any Gentile, however sympathetic. He was a real scholar, who had taken the degree of Doctor of Philosophy at the University of Kiel in 1855 and was appointed Grinfield Lecturer on the Septuagint in the University of Oxford in 1886. His pages breathe a profound evangelical piety and devotion to the person of our Lord; but his book is far more than an edifying tract—he has brought together an immense amount of authentic material from the treasure-house of Rabbinic Judaism. His work has, however, one fatal defect; he pays little or no attention to the chronology of the Rabbinic literature, and evidences from many different centuries are quoted as though they had equal relevance to the period of the life of Christ.[1]

This question of the chronology is crucial and exceedingly difficult to answer; for Judaism has not stood still, and what was true of the later periods may be wholly misleading if applied to the time in which Jesus lived. It is the odd, but I believe incontrovertible, fact that the oldest account of a synagogue service to be found anywhere is that in Luke 4. 16–30—our one Christian source apparently antedates all the Jewish sources on the subject! The significance of the chronology is rightly stressed by Professor W. D. Davies, in one of the best recent studies in English of the Rabbinic background in relation to New Testament thought. Commenting on the position taken up by the great Jewish scholar C. G. Montefiore in his book *Judaism and St. Paul* (1914), he writes:

Montefiore drew a very pleasing picture, which we shall describe later, of the Palestinian Judaism of the first century. He could do so only on the bold assumption that that Judaism was like that of the fourth century, 'that there are no signs of improvement in the teachings of the famous Rabbis of the fourth century over those of the first'. It is clear, however, that our sources for Rabbinic Judaism do not warrant such a definite conclusion. Thus the *Mishnah* was not compiled till the end of the second century, and most of the other Rabbinic sources are later than the third century. While it is clear that the Rabbinic sources do preserve traditions of an earlier date than the second century, and that it is legitimate to define the *Mishnah* as a 'deposit of four centuries of Jewish religious and cultural activity in Palestine beginning at some uncertain date possibly during the earlier half of the second century B.C. and ending with the close of the second century A.D.', it must never be overlooked that Judaism had made much history during that period. It

---

[1] It is interesting that Edersheim's book is one of the very few English books referred to with respect by A. Schweitzer in his *Quest*, p. 234.

follows that we cannot, without extreme caution, use the Rabbinic sources as
evidence for first-century Judaism. Especially is it important to realize that
our Rabbinic sources represent the triumph of the Pharisee party, and moreover of a 'party' within the Pharisee party as it were, that of Johanan ben
Zakkai. . . . It is almost certain therefore, . . . that Judaism was much more
variegated than such sources would lead us to expect.[1]

It is one of the great merits of the work of Strack-Billerbeck that it
has, at least in some measure, tried to sort out the date and provenance
of the innumerable quotations which have been brought together in the
collection. This was a work of many years' duration. In the Preface it
is explained that Dr. H. L. Strack had planned to bring together everything in the Jewish traditions that could be of service for the illustration of the New Testament; finding that the work was beyond the
strength of one man, in 1906 he associated with himself Paul Billerbeck;
and it was in fact by the second of the two collaborators that by far the
greater part of the work was done—as the spare-time occupation of a
busy pastor!—and done with resounding success. Whatever we want to
know, we are likely to find something about it here. How often is the
ancestry of Jesus referred to by name in the Jewish writings? Here are
six pages of information from every kind of source (vol. i, pp. 36–
41). What actually happened in the Temple at the time of the feast of
tabernacles, which seems to be referred to in John 7? Here it all is in a
long excursus in vol. ii, pp. 774–812.[2]

II

'Judaism was much more variegated than such sources would lead
us to expect.' These words were written probably in 1946. Never was
the prophetic utterance of a scholar to be more startlingly fulfilled. It
had generally been taken for granted that Palestine, unlike Egypt, was
not well suited to the preservation of ancient documents. In the dry

[1] W. D. Davies, *Paul and Rabbinic Judaism* (1948), pp. 3–4.
[2] It is unlikely that the whole of Strack-Billerbeck will ever be translated into English;
the production of a careful selection of the material would be an excellent undertaking for
some enterprising publisher. Dr. Strack died within a few months of the publication of the
first volume. There is a pathetic note in some words of the Preface to vol. i. In acknow-
ledging indebtedness to various friends who had helped financially in the publication of the
book, the editors add 'and even two in England—evidence that men are beginning to
come to an awareness that Christendom, so terribly torn in twain, must begin to draw
together again to the honour of the Church and of science' (pp. v–vi). We did better
after the Second World War than after the First!

climate of Egypt, as we have seen, papyrus will last almost for ever, though it has a tendency to crumble, and the wealth of papyri from Egypt in half a dozen languages is almost embarrassing. Though the level of rainfall in Palestine is not very high, the rain is heavy while it lasts, and the humidity is sufficient to make sure that such material as papyrus will perish, unless very special steps have been taken to secure its preservation. And, in fact, archaeological exploration in Palestine had been singularly unproductive of documents. There had been certain discoveries of ostraka—broken fragments of pottery, on which something had been inscribed: these are practically indestructible. Most notable of all are the Lachish letters, eighteen ostraka contemporary with the siege of Jerusalem in the time of Nebuchadnezzar, which therefore can be dated almost with certainty in the year 587 B.C. It was known, for instance from the Book of Jeremiah, that important documents were sealed up in jars, and there was always the possibility that such jars might somewhere be discovered—in archaeology it is nearly always the improbable that happens, as with the discovery of a Roman settlement of the first century A.D. on the southeast coast of India near Pondicherry.[1] It is by no means impossible that the sands of Egypt might yet disgorge a manuscript of parts of the New Testament written in the first century A.D. But, whatever the hopeful imagination of archaeologists may have been, nothing had prepared them for the dazzling discovery of what have come to be generally known as the Dead Sea Scrolls, though scholars tend to refer to them more precisely as the Qumran Texts.

The story of the discovery has so often been told that we need give no more than the minimum of space to it.[2]

[1] Unfortunately this site contained hardly any written material. It gives us fresh evidence of the liveliness of trade between the Roman Empire and India in the early years of our century; but we are no nearer than we were before to knowing whether St. Thomas really came to India and founded the Church of the 'Thomas-Christians', as all the members of that Church most devoutly believe.

[2] The literature on the Qumran Texts is enormous. One recent survey refers to upwards of 4,000 books and articles. Many matters of controversy are still unsettled and no doubt the controversy will go on for a very long time. In my opinion the best general account of the documents and their contents is still Millar Burrows, *The Dead Sea Scrolls* (1956), supplemented by the same writer's *More Light on the Dead Sea Scrolls* (1958). An excellent study of the results to date, written by a layman for laymen, has appeared just in time to be included in this note—A. N. Gilkes, *The Impact of the Dead Sea Scrolls* (1962). One translation, by T. H. Gaster, appeared as a paper-back in 1956; this rather free translation has been subject to a certain amount of criticism. Now a new translation, *The Dead Sea Scrolls in English* by G. Vermes (Penguin Books, 1962), has just come to hand. For our immediate subject the most important book is *The Scrolls and the New Testament*, a collection of essays by twelve scholars under the editorship of K. Stendahl (1958).

It seems that the first discovery was made, entirely by accident, in February or March 1947. Although the event is so recent, it has proved impossible to determine exactly what happened—the kind of uncertainty that, as we have seen so often, tends to weigh on historical research.[1] According to one story, the fifteen-year-old Bedouin boy who made the discovery was looking for a lost sheep when he stumbled on the cave in which the priceless manuscripts were hidden; another account is that he, with one or two companions, was taking refuge from a thunderstorm; yet a third that he threw a stone after a runaway goat, was intrigued by the sound of breaking pottery, and so forced his way into the cave.

As soon as word of the discovery reached the learned world, most scholars were convinced that the Scrolls were really ancient—though some doubted the claims to extreme antiquity made for them—and that one of the most exciting discoveries of all time had been made. Since the first discoveries, made in the caves of Qumran in the neighbourhood of the Dead Sea, many other caves have been penetrated and fresh documents brought to light; there is no reason to suppose that all has yet been discovered, and it is possible that new discoveries, as astounding as those already made, lie before us in the future. There is now almost universal agreement that many of the documents, written in Hebrew and Aramaic, belong to the first century B.C. and the first century A.D., and that they give us information concerning a quasimonastic community which at that period lived in isolation in this secluded area, and of which previously we had no direct knowledge.

There is great variety in the manuscripts which have come to light. In the first place, there is a large collection of manuscripts of the Old Testament in Hebrew, some of them almost complete, and beautifully and legibly written. These are of the utmost importance for the study of the Hebrew text of the Old Testament. It was the custom of the Jews, whenever a manuscript became old or worn, to withdraw it from use and to store it in a special room of the synagogue called the *Genizah*. So far from liking and valuing old books, the Jews had no use for them, and it was the cleanest and latest copy that was accepted for use in synagogue worship. The *Genizah* of an ancient synagogue in Cairo was discovered in 1896-7 and, as we shall see later, delivered up some remarkable treasures. But, as a result of this Jewish policy, until

[1] But in this case the Scrolls are there. Doubts regarding the details cannot invalidate the central fact—that the Scrolls really were discovered!

recently we had no really ancient Hebrew manuscripts of the Old
Testament—the earliest manuscripts which can be dated with fair
accuracy are not earlier than the ninth or tenth century A.D. We have
much older manuscripts of the Greek translation, the Septuagint. Now
suddenly from the Dead Sea caves have emerged manuscripts, most
notably one of the prophet Isaiah, which at one stroke carry our
knowledge of the Hebrew text back another thousand years. This new
evidence on the whole confirms the reliability of the so-called Masso-
retic text, that is the text which is found in almost all our printed
Hebrew Bibles; it is clear that the Jews took extraordinary pains with
the correct copying of the text, and that, though there are many
passages in which the original text has been lost through errors in
copying, on the whole the Hebrew words have been reliably transmitted through more than two thousand years.[1]

Popular attention was naturally concentrated on this mysterious
community, with its buildings, its library, its very strict conditions of
membership, its rules of life, and discipline. Who were these people?
What was the nature of their life and witness?

Before the discovery of the Scrolls, we had information from the
Jewish writers Philo and Josephus, who wrote in Greek, and from a
Roman writer, the elder Pliny, about a sect of the Jews called Essenes.[2]
These people lived a community life which was highly organized.
They had a three-year novitiate for those who intended to join the
community, and oaths of obedience and secrecy to be taken on joining.
It is now the almost universally accepted opinion that the Dead Sea or
Qumran community belonged to the sect of the Essenes, and that we
now have first-hand evidence for this group, of whom previously we
knew only at second-hand.

It seems that the buildings, which have now been excavated on a site
not far from the caves where the Scrolls were discovered, known as
Khirbet Qumran, were first occupied about 135 B.C., and, with an
interval of perhaps thirty years in the time of Herod the Great, continued in occupation until about A.D. 66, when with the defeat of the
Jews by the Romans in the great war of that period the community
appears to have been dissolved. From the literature of the community
itself we have commentaries on Old Testament books, notably one on

---

[1] It was a rule that any copy in which as many as three mistakes in copying were detected in a single column must be committed to the *Genizah*.

[2] It is remarkable that there is no reference to the sect in the Old Testament, the
Apocrypha, or the Talmud. All that is known about them has been collected by J. B.
Lightfoot in his commentary on the Epistle to the Colossians, pp. 83–95 and 114–79.

the Book of Habakkuk; a 'Manual of Discipline', giving the law of the life of the community, and the rules to which obedience was required on the part of its members; a number of Psalms of Thanksgiving, which bear witness to the deep religious sense of the community, but which only in very rare cases rise to the level of inspiration of the Old Testament Psalms; and a strange apocalyptic work which has come to be called 'The War of the Sons of Light against the Sons of Darkness'.

All the evidence makes it clear that this was from the start a sectarian community. It felt itself to be in the strongest opposition to the official Judaism of Jerusalem. These sectaries had withdrawn into the wilderness in order to keep pure their faith and devotion to the God of Israel. Among their duties none ranked higher than the study of Scripture, and especially of the law.

How did the community come into existence? Much still remains mysterious, and perhaps will always remain so. But one figure emerges with a certain measure of clarity from the darkness. And here we must turn aside for a moment to one of those remarkable documents which emerged from the *Genizah* of the synagogue at Cairo in 1896–7. In 1910 the great Rabbinic scholar Dr. Samuel Schechter published, under the title *Documents of Jewish Sectaries: i, Fragments of a Zadokite Work*, one of the Cairo fragments, which he believed to belong to the seventh century and to represent the views of the obscure sect of the Zadokites. It is now generally believed that the fragment is much older and is probably of pre-Christian origin. In this fragment, we find the following passage:

But all they that hold fast to these rules . . . and who give ear to the voice of the Teacher of Righteousness and do not reject the righteous ordinances when they hear them—they shall rejoice and be glad and their heart shall be strong and they shall overcome all inhabitants of the universe, and God shall make conciliation for them, and they shall witness his salvation, for they have taken refuge in his holy name.[1]

The mention of the Teacher of Righteousness makes it almost certain that in this so-called Zadokite fragment we have another document emanating from the sect that had its central dwelling in the wilderness of the Dead Sea. For in the documents peculiar to that sect we meet again and again this mysterious Teacher of Righteousness.

[1] The fragments have been re-edited by Chaim Rabin, with translation, *The Zadokite Documents* (2nd ed., 1958); the above quotation is taken from this edition, pp. 42–43.

For instance, in the *Commentary on Habakkuk* (2. 1–2) we are told that

God told Habakkuk to write the things that were to come upon the last generation, but the fulfilment of the appointed time he did not make known to him. And as for the words 'so that he may run who reads it', their interpretation concerns the Teacher of Righteousness, to whom God made known all the mysteries of the words of his servants the prophets.

Again, in a fragment of a commentary on the Book of Micah, the Teacher of Righteousness is described as 'the one who teaches the law to his people and to all who offer themselves to be gathered into the elect people of God, practising the law in the Council of the community, who will be saved from the day of judgment'.

It appears that the Teacher of Righteousness had to face bitter opposition, and especially from one who is called in the documents the Wicked Priest. On one particular occasion the hostility of the Wicked Priest manifested itself with special venom: 'he pursued after the Teacher of Righteousness to his place of exile, to swallow him up in his hot fury, and on the occasion of the appointed season of rest, the day of atonement, he burst upon them to swallow them up and to make them stumble on the fast-day, their sabbath of rest'. But vengeance fell on the Wicked Priest; once again the commentary on the Book of Habakkuk is our authority (2. 7): 'Because of the evil done to the Teacher of Righteousness and the men of his council, God gave him into the hands of his enemies, to afflict him with a stroke, to make him waste away in bitterness of soul, because he acted wickedly against his elect.'

It is a reasonably safe inference that the Teacher of Righteousness was the founder of the Qumran community, and as such was held in deep respect by all who followed him in this austere and narrow way. But his anonymity is strictly preserved in the documents; nowhere is there any hint of his name. Who was this Teacher of Righteousness, and who was his adversary the Wicked Priest? Scholars have exhausted their ingenuity in a great variety of solutions drawn from the tortuous and unhappy history of the people of the Jews in the first century B.C. But none of these solutions has proved convincing; we can only say that the secret has been well preserved, and to this, as to so many questions that we may legitimately ask, the historian can give only one answer: We do not know. It is possible that the Teacher of Righteousness met a violent end; but there is no clear evidence, and once again prudence demands that we should accept the limitations of our knowledge.

This brings us to the major question raised by the discovery of the Scrolls, and by all the new knowledge that they have brought to us. How far does this knowledge affect our understanding of the New Testament, and how far is a radical reconsideration of earlier views and theories demanded? The answer of the scholars will be found to be very cautious; but there seems to be a rather widespread idea that the Scrolls have somehow 'disproved Christianity', and that, if their evidence is accep ted, the whole of the early history of Christianity will have to be rewritten, and many of the claims made by and for Jesus Christ abandoned.

There appear to be two sources for this impression.

The first is an article by the American literary critic Mr. Edmund Wilson, published first in the *New Yorker* (1955) and later reproduced in book form as *The Scrolls from the Dead Sea*. Mr. Wilson is a brilliant and perceptive writer. He correctly discerned the importance of the Scrolls and wrote an admirable introduction to them. But he went further and drew from his studies the conclusion that 'the rise of Christianity should, at last, be generally understood as simply an episode of human history rather than propagated as dogma and divine revelation'. Wilson made the suggestion that Christian scholars were alarmed by the possible effect of these discoveries on their faith, and further suggested that for this reason they had been slow to make the fruits of their researches available to the world in general.[1] It is easy to see the way in which Mr. Wilson's mind worked. Christians have claimed that the revelation in Jesus Christ is absolutely unique. But now we find close parallels to that revelation in other and almost contemporaneous documents, for which the same claim to uniqueness as divine revelation is not made. The Christians must, therefore, give up their claims and recognize that the Christian gospel is only part of a wide movement of the human spirit, with just as much claim as these others to be regarded as truth, but no higher claim. Mr. Wilson was thinking in terms of ideas, and not in the categories of historical investigation. It is easy enough to point out *similarities* between certain Christian ideas and ideas of the Rabbis and the Greek philosophers. History is concerned more deeply with the *dissimilarities*—with that which makes each event unique and unrepeatable. The gospel is not,

[1] A glance at any bibliography of the Dead Sea Scrolls will show the baselessness of this reproach. Publication was as rapid as is consistent with the canons of good scholarship; and the discussion was carried on in an enormous number of periodicals—technical, professional, and semi-popular.

essentially, a set of ideas which can be compared with other ideas; it is the recitation of a number of events which are believed to have happened (as we recall them in the historic creeds of the Church), and which *as a whole* are interpreted in the light of a particular understanding of the purpose of God in and for the world.

Mr. Wilson is not alone in the attempt to produce in readers without special knowledge the sense of a remarkable similarity between the Qumran documents and the New Testament. On 23 January 1956, in a talk broadcast by the British Broadcasting Corporation, Dr. J. M. Allegro reconstructed the fate of the Teacher of Righteousness, and the attitude of his followers towards him. Alexander Jannaeus (High Priest, King, and conqueror, who ruled over the Jews 103–76 B.C., here identified with the Wicked Priest) probably handed over the Teacher of Righteousness to the Gentiles to be crucified. The disciples took down the broken body of their Master, reverently buried him, and settled down 'to await his glorious return as the Messiah of God'. The suggestion is implied that what we read in the New Testament of the attitude of the disciples of Jesus has already been anticipated in the Qumran sect; the Christians were merely taking over and applying to their own Master ideas which were current in the Judaism of their time, and have no particular claim to be regarded as 'true'.[1]

It would be impossible to imagine a better example of the difference between documentary analysis and historical research and reconstruction. What are the facts? It is certain that the Teacher of Righteousness was scorned, persecuted, and exiled; but nowhere in the text is there any clear statement that he was violently put to death. The prudent summary of Dr. Vermes is as follows:

Several scholars assert that he was killed during the course of a persecution commanded by the Wicked Priest, but none of the texts justify anything so categorical. Indeed from the expressions used in the Damascus Rule and the Commentaries on Habakkuk and Psalm 37, it might be inferred that the Teacher escaped a violent end. For the moment the question of both the manner and the date of his death must be left open.[2]

[1] The broadcast had an astonishing sequel. Dr. Allegro's colleagues in research on the Scrolls immediately published a statement to the effect that they had found nothing in the texts corresponding to any of the affirmations made by Dr. Allegro. In his well-known Penguin Book, *The Dead Sea Scrolls* (1956), Dr. Allegro suppressed the more speculative elements in his reconstruction, but repeated the conjecture that the Teacher of Righteousness had been crucified by Alexander Jannaeus.

[2] *The Dead Sea Scrolls in English* (1962), p. 67.

It is known that Alexander Jannaeus on occasion crucified his enemies. After a revolt which he had been able with difficulty to suppress, says Josephus, 'as he feasted with his concubines in the sight of all the city, he ordered about eight hundred of them to be crucified, and while they were still living ordered the throats of their wives and children to be cut before their eyes'.[1]

In the commentary on Nahum, found in Cave 4, there is a reference to the practice of 'hanging men up alive', which could reasonably be understood as meaning crucifixion. The identification of the Wicked Priest with Alexander Jannaeus is far from certain, though perhaps he more nearly meets the requirements of the evidence than any other figure known to us in the first century B.C. But there is not a shred of evidence that the Teacher of Righteousness was one of those whom he 'hanged up alive'; as we have already seen, what evidence there is almost certainly excludes this possibility.

Furthermore, there is no evidence whatever that the Qumran sect identified their founder with the Messiah. Their minds were filled with apocalyptic expectations. It seemed that they believed that the Messianic age would dawn forty years after the death of the Teacher of Righteousness. There is no evidence that they attributed atoning significance to his death, as the Christians from the start did to the death of Jesus. There is no evidence whatever that they expected him to rise from the dead; 'there is no evidence that he did rise from the dead, or that anyone ever thought that he had done so'.[2]

In one further point the Qumran Scriptures are unlike the Scriptures of the New Testament. The Qumran commentaries are concerned with the fulfilment of prophecy. Again and again the old words of Habakkuk are interpreted as referring 'to persons and peoples contemporary with the interpreter—the wicked priest, the teacher of righteousness, the Kittim'.[3] There is a sense of fulfilment yet to come: 'in the day of judgment God will destroy all the worshippers of idols and the wicked from the earth'.[4] But fulfilment, in the New Testament sense

[1] See F. F. Bruce, *Second Thoughts on the Dead Sea Scrolls* (1956), p. 97.
[2] Op. cit., p. 98. Professor Bruce goes a good deal further than I would go myself, when he writes, just before the sentence that I have quoted in the text: 'It may well be that his followers for this reason conceived the belief that he would rise again in the latter days to continue the work which his death had interrupted, until the messianic age had fully come.' In view of Jewish ideas about the return of Elijah as one of the signs of the coming of the end, this is not wholly impossible, but I regard it as extremely unlikely.
[3] C. F. D. Moule, *The Birth of the New Testament* (1962), p. 62.
[4] The last words of the Habakkuk commentary, as translated in Millar Burrows, *The Dead Sea Scrolls* (1956), p. 370.

of that term, is conspicuously absent. The time of Messiah is yet to come. When Jesus, according to Luke's account, said in the synagogue at Nazareth: 'Today this scripture has been fulfilled in your hearing',[1] he introduced something that was entirely new; the fathers had looked forward to the *eschaton*, the decisive word and act of God; now in Jesus of Nazareth the *eschaton* is already here.

Various writers in earlier times have held that there was a close connexion between the teachings of John the Baptist and those of the Essenes, and even that Jesus himself had derived much that was characteristic in his doctrine from them. It must be recognized that the discovery of an Essene community so near to the area in which John the Baptist carried out his mission lends new probability to an idea which had been almost entirely abandoned by scholars. In the Qumran community we find the same intense eschatological expectations as in John; in the Qumran rites of purification there may be certain parallels to John's baptism; in earlier times baptism had been required of proselytes, John required it of all who came to him, with the clear implication that the whole nature was sinful and in need of cleansing, an idea which is not very far from the puritanism of the Qumran group. Amid certain similarities, however, it is important not to overlook the essential difference. John came before the people as a prophet; it was as a prophet that he was recognized and acclaimed. It is impossible to exaggerate the significance of this fact. Some time in the fourth century B.C. the authentic voice of prophecy had died away. The hope that it might be born again had never been lost, as we learn clearly from the decision taken in the days of the Maccabees that Simon 'should be their leader and high priest for ever, until there should arise a faithful prophet'.[2] Now with John the voice of prophecy was heard again, and the stir and emotion among the people was immense. The founder of the Qumran sect had been the *Teacher* of Righteousness; he was of a different lineage, and no one had ever claimed for him that he was a prophet. John may have learned much from Qumran; at certain points his message may have been related to their tradition. But what was essential in John's message was precisely that which was new—not what he derived from Qumran or from the atmosphere in which the Qumran community lived, but that in which he diverged from it—a

---

[1] Luke 4. 21. The New Testament sense of fulfilment does not, of course, depend on this verse alone.

[2] 1 Maccabees 14. 41; and see also 4. 46, 'until there should come a prophet to give an answer concerning them'.

new relatedness to the prophetic message of the Old Testament Scriptures, and a different emphasis in the expectation of the Messianic age.[1]

If this is true of John the Baptist, still more is it true of Jesus of Nazareth. It is possible to point out a number of parallels in phraseology between his teaching and that of the Qumran Scrolls—just as attention has often been drawn in the past to parallels between his words and those of the Rabbis. But similarities in detail may all too easily blind us to the radical difference in essentials. John spoke with the authority of a prophet; Jesus claimed an even more than prophetic authority. His 'it was said unto them of old time, . . . but I say unto you', as recorded in Matthew, strikes a new note and puts him on a level with Moses the great lawgiver and recipient of the divine revelation. It is paralleled by the sense of his authority, power, and independence which is reflected on every page of the Gospel according to St. Mark. Messianic expectation played a great part in the thought of the Qumran sect; but the Messiah, as they saw him, was to be the victorious captain of the sons of light in the last great battle with the sons of darkness; and following upon his victory he would be established as prince in the kingdom that was to be established.[2] Jesus, from the beginning of his ministry onwards, deliberately and emphatically repudiated any identification of himself with the kind of Messiah that the Qumran sect, and probably a great many others among the Jews, were expecting; this was not the kind of kingdom that he had come to inaugurate, and this was not the way in which the true kingdom could be established.

III

Any great discovery, in archaeology as in science, sets the bells ringing down all the corridors of the world. Inevitably many rash statements are made and a great many temerarious theories advanced. Time gives perspective, and, although only fifteen years have passed since the first discoveries, the dust is beginning to subside and we can

---

[1] F. F. Bruce gives a cautious estimate of the facts in *Second Thoughts on the Dead Sea Scrolls* (1956), pp. 127–31. His conclusion, with which I agree, is that 'even if John did owe some debt to the Qumran community, or to any other Essene group, the ministry by which John made his mark cannot be brought within an Essene framework'. Dr. W. H. Brownlee has more elaborately studied the relationship between John and Qumran in *The Scrolls and the New Testament* (1958), pp. 32–53.

[2] Qumran seems to have believed in a priestly as well as in a royal Messiah; the dignity of the former would be even higher than that of the latter.

see a little more clearly the real bearing of this immense new fund of information with regard to the Judaism of the time of Christ. Sober criticism suggests that no radical reconstruction of our ideas about Christian origins will be required. We can even go a little further. We shall not expect to find in the Scrolls direct light on the New Testament, on the ideas of John the Baptist or Jesus, or on the views and practices of the early Church. Nevertheless, these documents are of immense value in helping us to fill in gaps in our knowledge of the Jewish world in the days of Jesus, and in providing illustrative material, the value of which we must now attempt to assess.

The Qumran documents represent not the classical traditions of Judaism, but the views of a sect—a sect that by strict Jewish canons must be classed as heretical. But not infrequently true religious life is to be found in the sects when it has died down among the orthodox; the nonconformists have been from time to time the salvation of the Church. The Church in the end rightly condemned the Gnosticism of the second century. Our more sympathetic eyes may see in Gnosticism a genuine though bewildered Christian faith seeking a philosophy by means of which it could make itself intelligible in the Mediterranean world; and may recognize the immense service that Gnosticism rendered to the orthodox Church by compelling it to think out and formulate its own doctrine of Christ, of revelation, of Scripture, and of authority. Qumran has compelled us to recognize that Judaism in the first century was much more flexible and varied than we had supposed.

It has been customary to draw a sharp contrast between the Judaism of Palestine and the Judaism of the Diaspora, that is of the Jews scattered abroad in the Gentile world. Palestine spoke Aramaic, the Diaspora spoke Greek. The Judaism of Palestine lived in the authentic tradition of the Old Testament and of its authorized interpreters, the Scribes; the Diaspora had been corrupted by the infiltration of Greek and pagan ideas. We now see that this sharp contrast cannot be maintained; the barriers were much less rigid, the walls much less impervious, than we had supposed. Even the Judaism of Palestine had been unable completely to insulate itself; it, too, was affected by ideas, phrases, fragmentary concepts which were part of the climate of men's thinking in that cosmopolitan age.

Even apart from the evidence of Qumran, looking at the history we can see quite clearly that it could not have been otherwise. Palestine was never in any manner an insulated country; shut ourselves up as we will, it is almost impossible to escape the pervasive effects of contemporary opinion. Scholars detect in the later books of the Old Testament the influence of ideas derived from Iranian dualism. From the time of Antiochus Epiphanes the Jews had been subject to Greek influences; the elders had violently repudiated them, but the efforts of the Hellenizers had not been entirely in vain, and the angry young men of the day scandalized the older generation by taking part in gymnastic exercises and wearing Greek hats. The party of the Herods, unorthodox and disliked as they were, stood for the reconciliation of the Jewish world with the dominant civilization of Greece and Rome. Superficial and unstable, the members of this intelligent and sometimes brilliant family, with their surprisingly close contacts with the emperor himself, could not but exercise widespread influence. Qumran has shown us in a new way just how deep this influence went. The Essenes were devoted to the study of the Old Testament; they had no unorthodox or syncretistic purposes; the whole background of their thinking is Semitic. Yet their writings are studded with phrases which, if found in any other context, would have been unhesitatingly classed as 'Hellenistic' a generation ago. It is clear that the antithesis of 'Hebrew' and 'Greek' cannot be so rigidly maintained as was at one time supposed.

The most interesting point about these 'Hellenistic' phrases which occur in the Qumran texts is that in so many cases they are closely parallel to the vocabulary of the Fourth Gospel. Here we meet such expressions as 'the sons of light', 'the light of life', 'walking in darkness', 'doing the truth', 'the works of God', which in the New Testament are found exclusively, or almost exclusively, in the Fourth Gospel.[1] Does this mean that we must consider afresh the whole question of the origin and the interpretation of the Fourth Gospel, and must take seriously the possibility that many things in that Gospel which have been confidently written off as 'Hellenistic' may really be Palestinian in origin?

It will be convenient to make clear the bearing of this question by a consideration of one limited aspect of the problem, the so-called dualism of the Fourth Gospel, and here the clue is provided by an admirably clear comparison of the Fourth Gospel and the Qumran

[1] A special study of these words has been made by W. F. Albright, 'Recent Discoveries in Palestine and the Gospel of St. John', in *The Background of the New Testament and its Eschatology* (essays published in honour of C. H. Dodd, 1956), pp. 153–71. The expression 'to do the truth' is not unknown in the Old Testament, especially in its Septuagint version; e.g. Genesis 32. 11, 47. 29; Isaiah 26. 10; but the resemblances to the Johannine usage do not seem to me to be as close as in the contexts where the same phrase is to be found in the Qumran documents.

texts by the Heidelberg scholar K. G. Kuhn.[1] It is plain even to the casual reader of the Gospel that its message is couched largely in pairs of opposites—light and darkness, belief and unbelief (or disobedience), life and death, and so forth. What is the origin of this dualism? Such a dualism is not clearly marked in the Old Testament, and there are few, if any, traces of it in the Rabbinic literature as it has come down to us. It has become almost an unquestioned principle in several schools of New Testament interpretation that the origin of this dualism is to be found in Gnosticism; this forms the basis of the notable commentary of Rudolf Bultmann on the Fourth Gospel.[2]

Here it is necessary to repeat briefly what has already been said on this subject in an earlier chapter. The Gnostic myth, as it has been put together by these scholars, runs roughly as follows: Long before this universe came into being, the conflict between the divine world of light and the daemonic world of darkness was a great reality. The coming into being of this world was not due to a creative act of God— this material universe of its very nature belongs to the world of darkness and is hostile to God. Some fragments of the world of light have become imprisoned in this lower world. We, as far as we are physical, belong to the world of darkness; but there may be in us some fragment of the world of light. It is, then, all important that we should become *aware* of our true origin and nature, and should strive towards it. This *awareness*, to which the name *Gnosis*, knowledge, is given, is in itself deliverance and salvation. The communication of this knowledge does not necessarily demand the presence of a *Redeemer*; but in many forms of the Gnostic myth, it is held that the 'sons of light' in the midst of this dark world are so deeply sunk in sleep or in intoxication that they can be awakened only if a Redeemer descends from the world of light into these lower realms to overcome the adversaries who would imprison the sons of light for ever in the realms of darkness, and to open the way on which all who have been enlightened can follow him back to the realms of light. In Christian forms of Gnosticism, naturally, Jesus is identified with the Redeemer.

[1] K. G. Kuhn, 'Johannesevangelium und Qumran texte' in *Neotestamentica et Patristica*, a set of essays presented to Oscar Cullmann in honour of his sixtieth birthday (1962), pp. 111–22. This was originally given as a broadcast talk. German theology can be very heavy and turgid; Dr. Kuhn's paper, though truly scientific, is delightful in its lucidity. This is the clearest short statement I have ever read of the basic position of Professor Bultmann in relation to the interpretation of the Fourth Gospel.

[2] The first edition of this appeared during the war in 1941; it has been more than once revised and reprinted.

It is against this background of Gnostic dualism that Rudolf Bultmann tries to interpret the Fourth Gospel. But, as a careful and honest expositor, he strikes again and again against the difficulty that this Gnostic dualism is wholly different from the dualism of the Fourth Gospel. The Gnostic dualism is one of *substance*; matter in itself is evil, and the material world is necessarily identical with the realm of darkness. Light and darkness are in eternal antithesis. The sons of light are so by nature; this nature is unchangeable; what happens to them is *imprisonment* in the realm of darkness, but in no sense an identification with it. They may *forget* their origin, but as soon as their true nature is revealed to them, they are saved by knowledge. But the darkness-light dualism in the Fourth Gospel is of an entirely different character; it is exactly parallel to the dualism of truth and falsehood, of righteousness and lawlessness. Man's situation is determined not by nature but by moral choice: 'This is the judgment, that the light has come into the world, and men loved darkness rather than light *because their deeds were evil*' (3. 19). What determines a man's standing is not an immutable nature but his relationship to God in Christ—whether of obedience unto life, or of disobedience unto death.

Moreover, the Fourth Gospel knows nothing of an eternal, self-existent world of darkness, separate from the world of light. It takes its stand firmly on the side of the Old Testament, with its doctrine of God as the Creator of all things, of the sons of darkness no less than of the sons of light—it was as a defence against Gnosticism that the Church inserted into the Nicene Creed the words 'by whom all things were made'.

Bultmann, therefore, is in the very curious position that, having laboriously built up the supposed 'Gnostic myth' as the background of the Gospel, he has then continually to knock it down again by showing that at every crucial point the Gospel is in tension with the Gnostic point of view, indeed repudiates it. Bultmann's own theology is one of *Entscheidung* ('decision', his great word); he sees very clearly that the Fourth Gospel, although there is in it an element of predestination, is not a Gospel of immutable destiny, but of choice and decision; faith and unbelief develop in men according to their response to the light that is manifest in Jesus Christ.

The Gnostic myth does not give us the clue that we need to the interpretation of the Fourth Gospel. Can we look for it elsewhere?

It is here that the Qumran texts offer certain passages which are at least impressive in their approximation to the teaching of the Fourth

Gospel. In the Book of the Rule of the Community (I QS 3, 15 ff.), there is a long passage which deals with the spirits of *truth* and *falsehood*, which are also the spirits of *light* and *darkness*:

From the God of knowledge comes all that is and shall be. Before ever they existed, he established their whole design, and when, as ordained for them, they come into being, it is in accord with his glorious design that they fulfil their work. The laws of all things are unchanging in his hand and he provides them with all their needs.

He has created man to govern the world, and has appointed for him two spirits in which to walk until the time of his visitation: the spirits of truth and falsehood. Those born of truth spring from a fountain of light, but those born of falsehood spring from a source of darkness. All the children of righteousness are ruled by the Prince of Light and walk in the ways of light; but all the children of falsehood are ruled by the Angel of Darkness and walk in the ways of darkness.

The Angel of Darkness leads all the children of righteousness astray, and until his end, all their sin, iniquities, wickednesses and all their unlawful deeds are caused by his dominion in accordance with the mysteries of God. Every one of their chastisements, and every one of the seasons of their distress, shall be brought about by the rule of his persecution; for all his allotted spirits seek the overthrow of the sons of light.

But the God of Israel and his Angel of Truth will succour all the sons of light. For it is he who created the spirits of Light and Darkness and founded every action upon them and established every deed upon their ways. And he loves the one everlastingly and delights in its works for ever; but the counsel of the other he loathes and for ever hates its ways.[1]

Here, certainly, is a very remarkable dualism—of light and darkness, of truth and falsehood, terms so familiar to us from the Fourth Gospel. What is the source of this dualism? We may be inclined at once to speak of 'Gnosticism'. But 'in this Qumran dualism there is no trace of that thinking in terms of substance and matter—none of that physical dualism which is so characteristic of Gnosticism. This dualism is rather ethical in character. The dualistic conflict between the two powers is accomplished by means of the righteous or sinful actions of men'.[2] Clearly we must look for its origins elsewhere than in Gnosticism. Professor Kuhn mentions briefly the view, which he has worked out in detail in a number of learned articles, that the source of this dualism is to be looked for in Iranian religion, in that tradition which goes back to the mysterious

[1] Here quoted from G. Vermes, *The Dead Sea Scrolls in English* (1962), pp. 75–76.
[2] K. G. Kuhn, loc. cit., p. 119.

teaching of Zarathustra.[1] If we recall that Palestine was for two centuries a province of the Persian empire, we shall see that there is
nothing unlikely in such Persian influence on Jewish thought. Here,
too, we find a dualism which is ethical rather than physical; light and
darkness are to be identified with 'good' and 'evil' rather than with
'spirit' and 'matter'. On which side man stands is determined by a
choice made by the man himself in his existence before birth into this
world.

This may, indeed, be the source of the Qumran idea. But once
again the differences between the Iranian and the Jewish viewpoint are
to be noted. For all its acceptance of an ethical dualism, the Qumran
sect is profoundly convinced of the unity of all things, since it holds
fast to the tradition of an uncompromising monotheism—it is God who
has *created* both spirits, the spirit of truth and the spirit of error. Man's
situation in the world is determined not by an ante-natal choice, but by
the will of God, who holds all souls in life and rules them all according
to his purpose. Furthermore, it is to be observed that in the Qumran
Texts the victory of the good is not attained by the deliverance of the
fragments of the light-world out of the world of darkness, but by
God's intervention at the appointed time, when 'at the time of the
visitation he will destroy falsehood for ever . . . God will then purify
every deed of man with his truth; he will refine for himself the human
frame by rooting out all spirit of falsehood from the bonds of his
flesh. He will cleanse him of all wicked deeds with the spirit of holiness;
like purifying waters he will shed upon him the spirit of truth. . . .
There shall be no more lies and all the works of falsehood shall be
put to shame.'[2]

The parallels, then, between Qumran and the Fourth Gospel are
remarkably close. This does not, of course, prove that the Fourth
Gospel borrowed directly from Qumran, or that the author of the
Gospel or the authorities on whom he depended were members of the
Qumran sect or stood in any close relationship to it. It does show that
many of the ideas and phrases which we meet again in the Fourth
Gospel were current in Palestine and in purely Jewish circles before,
during, and after the time of Jesus Christ. For two generations it has
been taken as axiomatic that the origins of the thought and language of
the Fourth Gospel are to be sought almost exclusively in the Greek-

---

[1] This difficult subject has received its latest treatment in English at the hands of
Professor R. C. Zaehner, *The Dawn and Twilight of Zoroastrianism* (1961).

[2] *The Dead Sea Scrolls in English*, pp. 77–78.

speaking world. The new evidence suggests that this conviction needs
to be carefully reconsidered; it is as yet too soon to assess the extent to
which it may come to be finally abandoned or modified.

IV

The history of the interpretation of the Fourth Gospel is an extremely
interesting study. As we have seen, traditionally it was regarded as the
most faithful and reliable of all the Gospels—how could it be otherwise, if it was indeed the work of the beloved disciple John, who stood
nearer to the Lord in understanding and affection than any of the other
disciples? Westcott still took the conservative view that the Gospel is
substantially the work of the Apostle John, and that the great differences between it and the other Gospels are due to a different theological
purpose more than to anything else. Even those who could not go so
far as this in the conservative direction were inclined to admit a measure
of apostolic authority, though not perhaps of apostolic authorship, in
the Gospel. When did the critical turning-point in the approach to it
take place?

In 1904 Dr. William Sanday of Oxford delivered a course of lectures
at Union Theological Seminary, New York, which he later published
under the title *The Criticism of the Fourth Gospel*. In the first lecture
he expounded, with his accustomed sobriety and judgement, the
recent literature on the subject. The radical criticism of the middle of
the nineteenth century had denied all historical value to the Fourth
Gospel—it was dismissed as a late theological construction with no
claim to historical veracity. In the last quarter of the century there was
a rather remarkable return to a more conservative position; better
methods and a more judicious weighing of the evidence led a considerable number of scholars, especially in Germany, to a reconsideration of earlier verdicts on this Gospel. Sanday quotes a summary of the
position as seen by Professor von Dobschütz:

That the Gospel not only shows a good knowledge of Palestinian localities
but also a thoroughly Jewish stamp in thought and expression, is one of the
truths rightly emphasised by conservative theology, which critical theology
is already, though reluctantly, making up its mind to admit: the Hellenism of
the Fourth Gospel, together with its unity, belongs to those only too
frequent preconceived opinions, on the critical side too, which are all the
more obstinately maintained the more unfounded they are.[1]

[1] W. Sanday, op. cit., pp. 15–16, quoting E. von Dobschütz, *Probleme des apostolischen
Zeitalters* (1904), pp. 92 ff.

The conservative view was expressed in a great variety of forms. Much attention was drawn to the existence of another John, called by the early Christian writer Papias (*c.* 130) John the Presbyter, and referred to by him as a disciple of the Lord. If it is found impossible to regard John the Apostle as the actual author of the Gospel, may not the gap be filled by this other John, of whom we know so little, but who seems to have lived in Ephesus, the place at which it is more than likely that the Fourth Gospel was actually written?

Just at the end of the century another and rather sudden reaction takes place. Sanday[1] lists six scholars who in the few years before 1904 had written on the Fourth Gospel—Jülicher, Schmiedel, Wrede, Wernle, Jean Réville, and A. Loisy. There are, of course, differences between these writers; but in the main they take up the same position— and this Dr. Sanday, as the heading of this section of his studies, qualifies as *Uncompromising Rejection*. The Fourth Gospel is not to be taken as history; any connexion with an Apostle is a mere myth; in one form or another the Gospel is to be understood as an attempt to translate the message of the Gospel into the terms of Greek philosophy, in that attenuated form in which it survived in the decaying world of Greece and Rome.

Sanday has some rather hard things to say about the methods pursued by the scholars of that generation:

When I read an argument by Professor Schürer, and try to reply to it, I am conscious that we are arguing (so to speak) in the same plane. . . . But when I pass over to the younger theologians, I no longer feel that this is so; we seem to be arguing not in the same, but in different planes. There is a far-reaching proposition not merely far back but near the front of their minds. . . . I take it that on this point their minds are made up before they put pen to paper. They all start with the 'reduced' conception of Christianity current in so many quarters, that is akin to the ancient Ebionism or Arianism. But so far as they do this their verdict as to the Fourth Gospel is determined for them beforehand. . . . If a writer starts with a conception of Christianity that is 'semi-Ebionite' or 'semi-Arian', he is bound at all costs to rule out the Fourth Gospel, not only as a dogmatic authority, but as a record of historical fact.[2]

We cannot but ask what set in motion this violent reaction against a reaction. No doubt Dr. Sanday is right in recognizing an element of dogmatic prejudice in the work of these six writers. Another factor must, I think, be taken into account. The last decade of the nineteenth century saw the rise of that religio-historical method of interpretation of which as we saw Professor Pfleiderer was the first great apostle,[1] and which saw the origins of Christianity and the rise of the New Testament as phenomena in the religious history of an age, to be interpreted exactly like any other phenomenon. It was taken as proved that Paul had been deeply influenced by the syncretistic Hellenistic religion of his times; the writer of the Fourth Gospel carried further the theological thought of Paul, and liberated it yet more completely from any connexion with the historical events of the life and death of Jesus of Nazareth. In him, consequently, the Hellenistic tinge is deeper even than in Paul. We have here one stage in that acute Hellenization of the Gospel, of which the Gnosticism of the second century is another manifestation,[2] and the dogmatic definitions of the early Councils a third.

Forty years ago the religio-historical school had great influence. Its findings were very widely accepted. It was taken for granted that its solution of the problem of the Fourth Gospel was the right one, and that only a purblind conservatism could hold on to any idea of apostolic influence on its composition, or look in its pages for anything like historical evidence.

One reaction leads to another. In the year 1923 or 1924, Dr. Israel Abrahams, Reader in Rabbinics in the University of Cambridge and an orthodox Jew, startled the learned world by remarking in a paper read to the Theological Society that 'to us Jews the Fourth Gospel is the most Jewish of the four'.[3] If a learned Jew makes a remark of this kind, it is impossible for a Christian to say that he does not know what he is talking about. It is probable that not every Jew would agree with Israel Abrahams; but he was a man of great Rabbinic learning, who had at the same time a close acquaintance with the Christian Scriptures. To say that there were certain Jewish elements in the Fourth Gospel which

[1] Pfleiderer in *Das Urchristentum* (2nd ed., 1902) described the Fourth Gospel as 'a transparent allegory of religious and dogmatic ideas'; he placed the original Gospel about the year 135, the appendix (c. 21) and the First Epistle about 150. The discovery of the precious papyrus fragment referred to above and dated by the experts not later than A.D. 130, shows that the dates suggested by Pfleiderer are much too late. Dr. Sanday says rather unkindly of Pfleiderer: 'I have long thought that this attractive writer, though interesting and instructive as a historian of thought, is a "negligible quantity" in the field of criticism proper' (op. cit., p. 26).

[2] This estimate of Gnosticism would not be generally accepted today; it had wide currency at the beginning of the century.

[3] I cannot find the quotation in the published works of Dr. Abrahams; I am not certain whether the paper in which it occurred was ever published.

had been overlooked would not have been particularly startling; to maintain that this, even more than the Gospel of Matthew, was the Jewish Gospel seemed to run counter to everything that the scholars had been saying for a generation. Clearly it was necessary to re-consider a great deal that had been for a long time taken for granted.

Naturally, the Jewish element in the Fourth Gospel had never been entirely forgotten;[1] and all the time scholars were at work who were vigorously opposed to the idea that this Gospel represents the Helleniza-tion of the Gospel message. In our studies we have had to devote the greater part of our attention to the more radical schools of New Testament interpretation, and this may have given a false impression. There has always been a conservative tradition in Germany; but the word 'conservative' has come to have a slightly contemptuous flavour, for reasons that were earlier indicated; and the value of the contribution made by these men has not always been fully recognized.

One great scholar who stood in this conservative tradition was Adolf Schlatter (1852–1938), who, unlike many New Testament schol-ars, had a deep knowledge of the Semitic background of the New Testament and of both classical and Rabbinic Hebrew. Just at the time at which the Hellenizing interpretation of the Fourth Gospel was gain-ing in strength, Schlatter produced, in 1904, a book called *Die Sprache und Heimat des vierten Evangelisten*, 'The Language and Home of the Fourth Evangelist', in which he showed, point by point, that a great many phrases and expressions in the Gospel which were commonly regarded as 'Hellenistic' could be paralleled from the Rabbinic writings, and argued strongly that the Palestinian strain in the Gospel could not be accounted for, unless the writer was a Jew who had lived in Palestine and was familiar in detail with its life.[2]

Twenty years after the appearance of Schlatter's work, but in ignorance of it until he had almost completed his own writing, Professor C. F. Burney of Oxford, an Old Testament scholar, took up the same theme and carried it further in a work entitled *The Aramaic Origin of the Fourth Gospel* (1922).[3] Dr. Burney 'had been impressed

---

[1] It is one of the weaknesses of Professor Bultmann's outstanding commentary on the Fourth Gospel that so little attention is paid to the Old Testament and Semitic background.

[2] Schlatter wrote two further works on the Gospel—*Das Evangelium nach Johannes* (4th ed., 1928) and *Der Evangelist Johannes* (1930). Hoskyns always mentioned Schlatter as one of the scholars from whom he himself had learned most about the Gospel; in the Index to his great commentary, after the list of Schlatter's works appears the word *passim*.

[3] See a valuable note by Burney (op. cit., pp. 2–3) on the previous history of this view, and a warm appreciation of the work of Schlatter.

(as every Hebrew scholar must be impressed) with the Semitic character of its diction, and . . . had realized that this was a subject of research fundamental to the problem of authorship which called for closer and more expert attention than it had hitherto received; and he had been amazed at the lightness with which it was dismissed or altogether ignored by New Testament scholars who confidently asserted the Hellenistic character of the Gospel'.[1]

Where Burney went further than even Schlatter was in his belief, not merely that there was a Semitic element in the thought and style of the Fourth Gospel, but that the book itself was originally written in Aramaic:

> Thus it was that the writer turned seriously to tackle the question of the original language of the Fourth Gospel; and quickly convincing himself that the theory of an original Aramaic document was no chimera, but a fact which was capable of the fullest verification, set himself to collect and classify the evidence in a form which he trusts may justify the reasonableness of his opinion not merely to other Aramaic scholars but to all New Testament scholars who will take the pains to follow out his arguments.[2]

Burney's thesis is worked out in great detail, and with such a wealth of illustration from Rabbinic, Aramaic, and Syriac sources that it is impossible for one who is not an accomplished Semitic scholar fully to appreciate or criticize it. It can be stated with confidence that very few scholars competent to form a judgement have accepted Dr. Burney's view in its entirety; nevertheless, his book did good service in that it made it difficult for any subsequent commentator to evade a problem which is a real problem and must be faced.

With the careful study of the language of the Gospel has come also a renewed interest in the question of the acquaintance of the writer with Palestine and with Palestinian custom. Here archaeological discovery has added some points of interest to what was already known. In chapter 5, the healing of a paralysed man is described as having taken place at the pool of Bethesda, 'which has five porticoes'. Excavation in Jerusalem has brought to light a pool which has five porticoes, and an accumulation of detailed and interesting evidence has led highly competent archaeologists to conclude that this probably was the Bethesda to which the Fourth Gospel alludes.[3] In earlier years we were

---

[1] Op. cit., pp. 1–2.   [2] Op. cit., p. 3.

[3] Professor J. Jeremias has been kind enough to give me a copy of his valuable and detailed survey of the evidence for the identification of this pool with the Bethesda of the Gospel, *Die Wiederentdeckung von Bethesda* (1949).

told with confidence by one group of expositors that the five porticoes stood for the five books of the law, and that the thirty-eight years of the illness of the paralysed man represented the thirty-eight years of the wandering of the children of Israel in the wilderness, although the Old Testament almost invariably speaks of the *forty* years of wandering. The writer of the Fourth Gospel is so subtle in his use of language, and numbers play so large a part in the structure of his Gospel,[1] that we cannot regard it as impossible that he saw in these numbers exactly the significance that has been found in them by the commentators. It is, however, at least interesting that at the basis of his story there appears to lie the actual physical fact that there were five porticoes, no more and no less, at this particular pool.

It is only a short step from such geographical and archaeological details to the question whether the Fourth Gospel represents a separate and independent *historical* tradition, of which account has to be taken, as we try to understand the life and times of Jesus. For those who take the view that the writer of the Fourth Gospel is simply a theological allegorizer this question can hardly arise; and, in fact, for a considerable period the question was hardly raised. It had come to be generally taken for granted that the writer of the Fourth Gospel was acquainted with the Synoptic Gospels, more or less as we have them today; and that, where they differ, the Synoptic tradition is always to be preferred. As we have seen, up till the time of Strauss and Baur, John had been regarded as the authoritative Gospel, into the framework of which the others must somehow be fitted; now the wheel had come full circle, and it was generally taken for granted that, though the Fourth Gospel is of supreme importance as showing us what a number of Christians believed about Jesus in the second century, it has no value at all, if judged by the standards of strictly historical evidence.

A little breach was made in this almost solid wall of opinion by a small and unobtrusive work, the importance of which is in inverse proportion to its size. In 1938 Mr. P. Gardner-Smith published a book, under the title *Saint John and the Synoptic Gospels*, in which he carefully reviewed the evidence and came to the conclusion that the use of the Synoptic Gospels by St. John must in every case be regarded as doubtful. Naturally there are certain traditions which are common

---

[1] Almost everyone is familiar with the sevenfold 'I am' of the Gospel, but there are in fact a great many other sevens lying not far below the surface, and these can be detected by any careful student.

to all the Gospels, and certain episodes, such as the feeding of the five thousand, which occur in them all. But it is much more probable that in each case John is working on an independent and unwritten tradition than that he is modifying for his own purpose a narrative which is already before him in written form. It cannot be said that the question is closed. In a book which has just appeared, the revised edition of Peake's *Commentary on the Bible* (1962), the learned commentator on the Fourth Gospel, Professor C. K. Barrett, can write: 'A strong case can be made for his having known Mk., a fairly strong case for his knowledge of Lk.'[1] This is a good deal further than I would be prepared to go myself; I am not convinced that the arguments adduced by Mr. Gardner-Smith have ever been effectively answered.

One of the first scholars, as far as I am aware, to raise in modern times the question of the independent historical value of the Fourth Gospel was Dr. Barrett's predecessor as commentator on St. John in the first edition of Peake's *Commentary on the Bible*, the quiet Cambridge scholar Alan England Brooke, who gave much of his life to work on the great Cambridge edition of the Septuagint, and whose published works are far less than a due memorial to a singularly acute, patient, and devout mind. At two points the chronology of the Fourth Gospel differs markedly from that of the other three. First, the cleansing of the Temple is placed at the beginning of the ministry and not at the end. Harmonizers are driven to the unlikely expedient of supposing that there were two occasions on which Jesus cleansed the Temple. But unless we are firmly convinced on other grounds that Jesus visited Jerusalem only once—in the last week of his life—is it not possible to think that at this point the Johannine chronology is right? If this was so, we find a ready explanation for the early development of hostility to Jesus, which comes in rather perplexingly in the Marcan scheme. In the second place, according to the Fourth Gospel the death of Jesus took place on the day of the Preparation, the day before the Passover, and not on the Feast Day itself. One view is that the writer of this Gospel has changed the chronology deliberately, so that we are presented with the Lamb of God dying on the Cross just at the moment at which the lambs for the Passover were being killed in the Temple. But Brooke raised the question, and in this he is in the company of many other scholars, whether it is not possible to think that here the Fourth Gospel is following an independent, and actually better,

[1] Op. cit., p. 844.

tradition than that which is represented by the Synoptic chronology.[1]

It may be taken as certain that this question of the historical value of the Fourth Gospel will be the subject of extensive research in the future.[2] Already there is visible a tendency to think that, in view of its Palestinian connexions, the Fourth Gospel may be a good deal earlier than we had been led to suppose. But, after all, this Gospel is a theological Gospel; the really important questions regarding it relate to the nature of that theology and to its sources. Why does the author of this mysterious book think in the way that he does think? And where did he learn to think in this way?

As part of the reaction against the purely Hellenistic explanation of his sources, there has been a tendency in recent years to look again at the use of the Old Testament by the writer of this Gospel.[3] I have myself long been convinced that the central clue to the understanding of the Fourth Gospel is to be found in the Old Testament and nowhere else, and that much careful work on the use of the Old Testament in the Fourth Gospel still remains to be done.

In the very first verse and in his opening words, 'In the beginning', which are the same as the opening words of the Book of Genesis, the author seems to tell us that his prologue is going to be an inspired commentary on the first verses of the Bible. He introduces the Logos, 'the Word'. The term has already had a long history in the Greek-speaking world; it speaks not merely of utterance, but of reason and the proportion by which all things are held together. But at once the writer jumps to something that was entirely unknown in the world of Greek thought, the idea of creation: 'All things were made through him, and without him was not anything made that was made' (1. 3). The reader familiar with the Old Testament can hardly fail to recall the words of Psalm 33. 6: 'By the word of the LORD were the heavens made, and all their host by the breath of his mouth.' A little later the writer introduces us to one of the main themes of his Gospel—the contrast between the light and the darkness: 'The light shines in the darkness, and the darkness has not overcome it' (1. 5). It is true that

---

[1] It seems possible, indeed likely, that more light may be thrown on this problem by a study of the calendar in use by the Qumran sect; but this is a matter on which as yet nothing can be said with certainty.

[2] An interesting contribution has been made by the Norwegian scholar N. A. Dahl in an article 'The Johannine Church and History' in W. Klassen and G. F. Snyder, *Current Issues in New Testament Interpretation* (1962), pp. 124–42.

[3] See, for instance, a highly significant article by Dr. C. K. Barrett in the *Journal of Theological Studies* (1947–8), pp. 155–69, entitled 'The Old Testament in the Fourth Gospel'.

this contrast was emphasized in many forms of Hellenistic religion; but once again we are moving in the world of Genesis: 'And darkness was upon the face of the deep . . . and God said, "Let there be light"; and there was light' (Gen. 1. 2, 3). 'The deep' is the old Tiamat of the Babylonians, the principle of chaos and opposition to the world of the gods, here demythologized, but shown as the sphere of darkness, exactly as that word is used in the Fourth Gospel.[1]

As we have seen, one of the main activities of the early Church was hunting down prophecies, types, and analogies in the Old Testament for the illumination of the mystery of the Christ. In the Fourth Gospel we find some of the familiar references. But the remarkable thing is that so few of the quotations or allusions in the Fourth Gospel belong to what appears to have been the common stock of early Christian *Testimonia*. An excellent starting-point for study of the use of the Old Testament in the Fourth Gospel is the extraordinary *midrash* in chapter 10. 34 on the phrase of Psalm 82. 6: 'I said, You are gods.' The meaning of the phrase in Psalm 82 is far from certain; the application made of it in this passage of the Gospel is what we should be inclined to call at least far-fetched. Most of the commentators pay little attention to it.[2] Hoskyns discusses it at some length and ends with a comment perhaps not very much more lucid than the original *midrash*:

The Evangelist has so phrased the contrast that the readers of the gospel recognise the distinction between those *unto whom the word of God came* and the Son of God, sanctified and sent into the world, a delicate reference to the Prologue, according to which Jesus is Himself the Word become Flesh (1. 1, 14). The author is satisfied with this delicate suggestion, because, whereas Jesus as the Son of God is completely justified in the earlier tradition, Jesus as the incarnate Word, though rightly included in the preface to a narrative of His Ministry, cannot, without hopeless anachronism, be included in the record itself.[3]

We are left asking the question, what kind of a mind it was that so

---

[1] Naturally the writer, using Greek, is aware of the subtle changes that will take place in the meaning of the words he employs, as they move out from the Semitic world into the Hellenistic world with its very different use of terms. The point is that it is from a Semitic world that these words move out to start their new life.

[2] There is a useful article by J. A. Emerton in *J.T.S.*, New Series, vol. xi (1960), pp. 329 ff.

[3] *The Fourth Gospel* (2nd ed., 1947), p. 392.

reflected on an apparently insignificant phrase in the ancient Scriptures, and found it full of theological significance.[1] Is it not clear that the nearest parallel to this is in the Epistle to the Hebrews, where we find the same sensitive and imaginative attitude to the earlier writings?

Again, it has long been recognized that one of the many elements which have come together in the Prologue to the Gospel is late Jewish speculation on the Wisdom of God, which has its origin ultimately in certain passages of the Book of Proverbs. But we have to ask ourselves what kind of a mind it was in which this transition from Wisdom to Word has taken place, in which this quiet substitution of Word for Wisdom has been made. Hoskyns has stated the problem for us, this time with perfect lucidity: 'How is it that the wealth of imagery descriptive of the glory of Wisdom has been transferred to honour the Word? And, what has brought about the reference to the Word as a clearly defined person, rather than as a circumlocution for God, or as a poetic personification of an abstract idea?'[2]

In one case we have had direct quotation; in the other, indirect but fairly obvious allusion. But I believe that at a great many other points —and this is characteristic of the extraordinary subtlety of thought that the writer veils under the simplicity of his language—there are allusions and hints of allusions to the Old Testament, and that until these are fully worked out and classified, much will be lacking to our understanding of the Gospel. The writer is writing in Greek, and for readers whose natural language is Greek; but presumably his readers are familiar with the Old Testament in Greek—otherwise his more obvious allusions would have been quite unintelligible to them. I am convinced that, the more carefully the Gospel is studied, the clearer it becomes that the Hellenistic elements belong to a secondary phase of interpretation, and that the deepest elements in the thought, the bony structure on which the whole Gospel is constructed, are derived from the Old Testament, reinterpreted under the influence of an over-whelming sense of the presence of God in Jesus Christ.

This is a matter on which there is as yet no agreement among scholars.

[1] It is, of course, possible that the mind in question was that of Jesus himself: it is more likely, however, that this passage belongs to the interpretative elements introduced by the writer of the Gospel.

[2] Op. cit., p. 156. There is a useful study of 'The Wisdom Background of the Fourth Gospel' in one of the most recent books on the Fourth Gospel, E. M. Sidebottom, *The Christ of the Fourth Gospel* (1961), pp. 203–9.

The veteran American scholar Dr. F. C. Grant, in two recent books,[1] rejecting the Qumran hypothesis to which we have devoted some pages, declares himself as firmly convinced as ever that this is the Gospel of the Hellenists, that the writer himself is a Hellenist who has rethought and reinterpreted the Gospel in order to make it intelligible to the Greek-speaking world.[2]

Dr. C. H. Dodd, in his great book *The Interpretation of the Fourth Gospel*, does recognize frankly both the influence of the Old Testament and the apparent acquaintance of the author with the Judaism of Palestine in the first century A.D. But he does also attribute great weight to the Hellenistic environment, and particularly to that peculiar collection of documents known as the Hermetic writings.

Richard Reitzenstein had drawn attention to the importance of these writings, and especially among them to that section which bears the name *Poimandres*.[3] Dodd himself carried the study a great deal further in the second section of his book *The Bible and the Greeks* (1935), in which he made a most careful examination of this work, and of its relations to the New Testament and to the Hellenistic world by which it was surrounded. He reached the conclusion that *Poimandres* probably dates from the first quarter of the second century A.D., and thinks that a date in the first century is not impossible. He summarizes the parallels between the thought of *Poimandres* and that of the Fourth Gospel in the following terms:

In particular, it has several points of contact with the Fourth Gospel, the date of which may be taken to be not very far from A.D. 100. Such points of contact are the conception of the divine as life and light, of the creative Logos, of the heavenly Man who descends and ascends again, of immortal life as a return to the Father, and of knowledge of God as the condition of attaining immortality. These points of contact, however, are not such as to suggest a literary dependence of *John* upon *Poimandres*, or *vice versa*.

This is extremely interesting. It indicates the existence, in the non-Christian world of the first century, of groups of thoughtful people who were familiar with some of the ideas which meet us in the Fourth Gospel and also in second-century Gnosticism. Our difficulty is that we have no means of identifying these circles, or of estimating how

---

[1] *The Gospels: their Origin and their Growth* (1959); *Roman Hellenism and the New Testament* (1962).

[2] Dr. Grant assigns the Gospel to a surprisingly late date, perhaps A.D. 120. I regard any date after the end of the first century as quite untenable.

[3] In a book bearing the name *Poimandres*, published in 1904.

extensive and influential they may have been. It is largely chance that has determined which of the writings of the ancient world have come down to us, and which have irrevocably perished in the destructions of the Dark Ages. The group for which 'Hermes' or 'Poimandres' wrote may have been very small; in any case these writings can do no more than serve as an illustration of the kind of thing that was current in that largely unknown world; no one, I think, would suggest that they were in any sense directly or indirectly a *source* of the thought or teaching of the Fourth Gospel.

At one point, however, the judgement of Dr. Dodd on these writings is of the most immediate relevance to the direction in which our chapter is moving. *Poimandres* is a writing of the Hellenistic world. Yet it is quite clear that the influence of the Old Testament upon it has been considerable:

It has been customary of late to emphasize the influence of Gentile thought upon Judaism, and that influence was unquestionably enormous. But it would not be safe to assume that where Hellenistic Judaism shows parallels with non-Jewish thought, the debt lies always and wholly upon one side. The *Poimandres* shows that it was possible for a thinker who remained quite outside Judaism to become steeped in ideas which go back by direct lineage to the Pentateuch and the Hebrew prophets. It was not wholly by its own native impulse that paganism moved towards ethical monotheism, and the spiritual worship of God.[1]

v

We speak of Jews and Greeks as though they stood at the very antipodes of human thought and experience; of Judaism and Hellenism as though they were mutually exclusive entities. Prejudice inclines us to think that what is Judaic is genuinely Christian, and that what is Hellenistic is in some way a perversion or distortion of it. But can this distinction be so rigidly maintained, if we look realistically at the state of thought and religion in the period of the rise of the New Testament?

That there is a radical difference between classical Greek thought and the world of Old Testament religion no one is likely to wish to deny. One of the best delineations of the difference comes to us from one of the greatest intellects of this century, William Ralph Inge (1860–1954):

The difference is indeed striking between the narrow and fierce absorption

[1] *The Bible and the Greeks*, p. 247.

of the Jew in the fortunes of his nation, his indifference to all but concrete, tangible marks of divine favour, his intense will-power and defective aesthetic sensibility, and (on the other side) the genial open-minded mentality of the Greek, full of curiosity and enjoyment of nature, an artist to his finger-tips . . . whose religion was a practical and symbolical mythology; who lived in a present which he loved to enjoy, and ardently desired to understand; who, like a child, craved only to *see* all that is to be seen of this wonderful world and the spiritual mysteries which may lie behind it; whose intellect was so much more developed than his will, that he sincerely believed that to see the truth was to possess it, vice being only ignorance, and virtue knowledge; and whose sense of the finer values of life was so keen that he frankly despised unnecessary apparatus, and lived a hardier and healthier life than any civilised race has lived before or since. . . .

So, 'Thy sons, O Zion' stood confronted with 'thy sons, O Greece'. Two racial types utterly unlike each other; two histories equally dissimilar; two philosophies of life, and two religions, were now to unite in begetting that strangest product of time, Catholic Christianity. How was it possible that fire and water could thus coalesce?[1]

To this sharp and clear differentiation between the two races Dr. Inge admits two important qualifications.

In the first place 'there were (speaking broadly) no Greeks left in the time of Christ. The race was all but extinct, or swamped in the mongrel hordes with which the Roman Empire was filling its Eastern provinces'. Hellenistic thought is a wonderful and exciting thing; but from the beginning it was cosmopolitan, subject to all kinds of Oriental influences. The hard, clear lines of Athenian thought no longer anywhere existed. As we have seen, much the same can be said of Judaism; barriers were down, and influences of many kinds had flowed into it.

Dr. Inge's second qualification is even more important. We err if we try to explain the Gospel in terms either of Judaism or Hellenism:

The deepest and truest explanation is surely this, that the Divine Founder of Christianity was above the antithesis. His character and view of life were unlike those of the typical Jew; but we can hardly call them Hellenic. . . . It is idle to pretend that this Teacher, and this teaching, can be explained within the lines of Jewish pietism. Christ burst these cramping fetters at every movement. It was a new faith which he brought, a new view of time and

[1] F. J. Foakes-Jackson (ed.), *The Parting of the Roads* (1912). Introductory Essay by W. R. Inge, pp. 8, 10. Did the reader immediately recognize the allusion to Zechariah, 9. 13?

eternity. Judaism could no more imprison the soul of this revelation than the tomb at Jerusalem could retain the body of its Founder. The universality of Christianity is based upon, and explained by, the universality of Christ.[1]

This warning of Dr. Inge is one to which we do well to pay attention. New Testament research in recent years has developed in so many directions that it has become increasingly difficult to see the wood for the trees. The material of the New Testament has been analysed into so many streams, tendencies, influences that it has become almost impossible to see the unity which holds it all together. Yet the principle of unity is there, in the towering originality and spiritual force of Jesus of Nazareth, in whom all these things had their origin. Perhaps in our detailed study we come too near his feet and are not able to look up and see his face; when we do look up, we find that we have to do with one who refuses to be imprisoned in any of our categories—of language, of race, or of time; and, when we have done our best with all our scientific approaches, we fall far short of the reality which it has been our aim to understand.

Dr. Inge's first reservation, though his essay was written fifty years ago, is also of peculiar relevance to the present time, since the contrast between Greek and Hebrew thought is one of the favourite fields in which the contemporary theologian roves. One of the foundations of what is today commonly called 'Biblical theology' is a return, as it is supposed, from the analytic method of Greek thought, which takes things to pieces, to the synthetic Hebrew method, in which things are seen as wholes. Greek tends to be abstract, Hebrew to be concrete. Greek is interested in eternal relationships; the Hebrew mind sees the expression of reality in history, and so on. It is widely believed that these differences are reflected in the linguistic structures; and that by a careful study of this structure we can reach certain theological conclusions. Grammar and etymology are called in as aids to the understanding of theological structure.

One of the most influential writings in this field is the work of the Norwegian scholar Thorleif Boman, *Hebrew Thought compared with Greek*.[2] This is a careful and, at certain points, enlightening piece of work. The title, however, does not indicate exactly the nature of the contents of the book. Dr. Boman is convinced that essential

[1] Op. cit., pp. 10–11.
[2] English trans., 1960, from the German *Das hebräische Denken im Vergleich mit dem griechischen* (1954).

qualities of thought reflect themselves in the structures of language, and his book is really a study of the Semitic[1] and the Greek languages, as a clue to the basic structures of thought that lie behind words and constructions. It is well known that in Indo-European languages, especially in their ancient forms, the verb is very highly developed, and that an extraordinary intricacy of tense and mood (and aspect, if we include Russian) makes possible a minute precision of expression. This is seen in its most extensive development in Sanskrit; Attic Greek has retained much of it, Latin much less; in English hardly anything of the old structure is left, though we have arrived at a new flexibility by developments of a very different order. The Semitic verb by contrast, is comparatively undeveloped, especially in the matter of tenses; the Indo-European method by which the exact relationship of events to one another in time can be shown is almost unknown. In consequence, the period, with its accumulation of subordinate clauses, so characteristic of Greek, is hardly known in Hebrew, in which the almost monotonous sequence of principal clauses 'and . . . and . . . and' makes up the narrative. From undeniable facts like these Dr. Boman draws rather extensive conclusions as to the differing Greek and Hebrew concepts of space and time; and then, further, to the dynamic character of the Hebrew tongue as contrasted with the static character of the Greek.

Up to a certain point, these arguments are well worked out, and the conclusions follow from the evidence presented. Obviously the structure of a language corresponds to, and is in some way the expression of, a certain structure of thought; this in its turn represents a certain psychology, or outlook upon the world. Anyone who has had anything to do with African languages knows well that these languages are 'non-generalizing'; the Zulu language has, I believe, forty-seven different words for 'to break', but no general word, since each particular word calls up a clear picture, and the picture of breaking off a twig from a tree is quite different from that of letting a pitcher drop and breaking it. In consequence of this linguistic structure, the African finds it difficult to think in general terms, and the African Christian tends to be more at home with the particularized law of Moses than with the generalized law of Christ. Or is it the other

---

[1] Or rather 'Hebrew'. One of the criticisms made of Dr. Boman's book by the Semitic experts is that he bases his conclusions on too narrow a linguistic survey, and that many of his conclusions would be modified by closer attention to the wide variety of Semitic forms of speech which are now available for comparison.

way about—that the African's vividly pictorial and dramatic sense has imposed itself on his language, and kept it vivid, concrete, and dramatic, but poor in general or abstract terms? The student of languages who has had to deal with several families of languages, and not only with the two that we study in our schools and colleges—the Indo-European and the Semitic—becomes very cautious indeed in the affirmations he makes about general problems of linguistics.

At once such a student wishes to raise certain questions relating to the thesis supported by Dr. Boman and widely accepted in certain theological circles.

In what sense is it true that there is such a thing as Greek thought? One who is accustomed to range through the whole of Greek literature, from Homer to the Greek anthology, nearly two thousand years of it, is perpetually amazed at the extraordinary creative vitality of the Greek mind. To give a single example, although Aristotle was the pupil of Plato, the differences in manner of thought and expression as between the two men are more immediately evident than the similarities. This creative vitality reflects itself in the language. At school we are driven to write the Attic dialect, and perhaps rightly, since Athens produced so great a number and variety of incomparable writers. But no sooner have we done so than we are set to read Homer and Herodotus and Theocritus, and find ourselves wrestling in each case with a markedly different form of the language, to which corresponds in each case a notably different point of view. When we come down to the *koinē*, we encounter again another type of language, simplified for international purposes, and, in the New Testament *koinē*, already deeply influenced by Semitic traditions and linguistic forms. What do we mean when we say 'Greek thought'?

Secondly, it cannot be assumed that accurate and exact translation from one language-structure to another is impossible. Very often the exact representation of a single word is difficult. Who will find for us the exact English equivalent of the French *esprit* or the German *Weltanschauung*? A large philosophical treatise could be written on the fact that the German word for 'fair', in the sense of 'fair-play', is 'fair'! But differences of grammatical construction are not in themselves hindrances to communication. In Tamil there is no objective genitive. 'The love of God' can mean only the love which God has or manifests (though alas! under the influence of English the purity of the Tamil language is being gravely endangered). If we wish to speak of the love which we have for God, we have to spell it out—'the love which loves God'. But when the Tamil Christian speaks in the General Thanksgiving of 'the hope which says "we shall attain to glory" ', I believe him to mean exactly and precisely what the English Christian means when he speaks of 'the hope of glory'. Over wide areas, perfect communication is possible, and difference of linguistic structure does not *necessarily* imply any difference of outlook or understanding of the world.

Some scholars, who are also philologists, had been for a considerable time anxious as to the tendencies of the so-called Biblical theology, and unconvinced by many of its verbal pyrotechnics. In the year 1961 a large stone was thrown with great violence into the calm pool of Biblical studies; Professor James Barr, then of Edinburgh and now of Princeton, published a book entitled *The Semantics of Biblical Language*. The book shows signs of hasty composition, and it is certain that not all its contentions will find general acceptance in the world of scholarship. But it is an important book, since it challenges a great many commonly accepted assumptions and raises the whole issue of the relation of language to thought in the field of theological interpretation.[1]

Out of Professor Barr's many contentions we may cite four as having relevance to our immediate theme:

1. The philosophy of speech put forth by W. von Humboldt in the middle of the nineteenth century can serve only as a delusive guide. Von Humboldt wrote:

Their differences (i.e. of languages) can be regarded as that process of striving through which the power of speech which is the common possession of all men, favoured or hindered by the intellectual power that resides in the peoples, comes to expression with greater or less success. . . . In languages . . . nations as such are peculiarly and immediately creative.[2]

[1] In the *Scottish Journal of Theology* for September 1962 Dr. T. Boman has published a long and important and somewhat ill-tempered review of Professor Barr's book—not unnaturally, since Dr. Boman is one of the chief objects of Professor Barr's wrath! To indicate the radical difference between Greeks and Jews, Boman cites in his review 1 Corinthians 1. 22: 'For Jews demand signs and Greeks seek wisdom.' No one would deny a difference. But the papyri show us the intense passion with which 'the Greeks' sought after signs, and a large part of the Old Testament, including the Apocrypha, is made up of the Wisdom literature! The trained philologist is always very hesitant about making generalizations of this kind.

[2] W. von Humboldt, *Sprachphilosophische Werke* (ed. Steinthal, Berlin, 1884), pp. 193, 245, quoted by J. Barr, op. cit., p. 48.

Nations, languages as the striving of Spirit on the way to self-expression, and so forth—these are imaginative and idealistic expressions, and have no connexion with the hard facts of linguistic science. Only a small part of linguistic change can, in fact, be traced to the peculiar point of view of any people.

2. Though the creative effect of the Christian experience on the language of the New Testament was immense, it is vitally important not to mix up grammar, lexicography, and theology. We must not first arrive at a general concept of Biblical theology and then use this as a criterion to determine the meaning of Biblical words and structures of language.

Barr quotes with great effect some sentences from a generally excellent article by Professor B. M. Metzger on 'The Language of the New Testament':

With the advent of Christianity there was let loose in the world a transforming energy which made itself felt in all domains, including that of language. Old, worn-out expressions were rejuvenated and given new lustre. In a few cases, when nothing adequate seemed to be available, new words and phrases were coined. Words expressing servility, ignominy and sin were washed clean, elevated, and baptized with new meaning. Others, standing in the bright light of the gospel, were revealed to be even more sombre and wicked in their significance than had been previously realized.[1]

On this Professor Barr comments, not in my opinion unfairly:

I cannot regard this paragraph as other than a romanticization which comes from a simple transfer to the sphere of linguistic change of the soteriological effects which Christianity claims to have made in life in general. . . . Its character as a linguistic allegory is clear from the impossibility of clarity within linguistic method of such terms as the 'cleansing' or 'rejuvenation' of words. Especially striking is the picture of words the full wickedness of whose meaning had not been known to anyone before the Gospel came to reveal it.[2]

3. The etymology of a word, its origin, is not a safe guide to its meaning, unless it is constantly checked by reference to its actual usage. Etymology is a starting-point; it is not a controlling power. As an example of the false use of etymology, Barr quotes a passage from T. F. Torrance on the significance of the Hebrew word *dabar*, 'word', one of the commonest words in the Hebrew Bible:

This appears to derive from a Semitic root *dbr* meaning 'backside' or 'hinterground', which is apparent in the expression for the Holy of Holies just mentioned, the *debir*, which was lodged at the very back of the Tabernacle or Temple. This term *dabar* has a dual significance. On the one hand it refers to the hinterground of meaning, the inner reality of the word, but on the other hand, it refers to the dynamic event in which that inner reality becomes manifest. Thus every event has its *dabar* or word, so that he who understands the *dabar* of an event understands its real meaning. . . . All through Israel's history the Word enshrined in the form of *debarim* was hidden in the *debir*, but was again and again made manifest when God made bare his mighty arm and showed his glory.[1]

As imaginative interpretation this will do; as accurate philology it is less acceptable; not one single passage can be quoted from the Old Testament to show that the Hebrews ever thought of the Holy of Holies in the way suggested by Torrance. Barr comments again quite frankly:

It should be said that the 'hinterground of meaning' is a semantic indication which is quite unreconcilable with any use of the Hebrew *dabar*. No lexicon recognizes a sense even remotely approaching this. . . . Not only however is the 'hinterground' suggestion impossible, but that of 'the dynamic event in which that inner reality becomes manifest' is also exaggerated and far-fetched.[2]

4. Theological thinking is done primarily in the phrase and the sentence, not in the word. The gravest dangers will result, if we insist on attaching theological significance to words taken in isolation. Words, as the linguistic analysts so potently remind us, are not solid unchanging realities like marbles; woe betide us, if we imagine that they are!

Once again, Professor Barr illustrates his point by a quotation from Professor T. F. Torrance. Israel, we are told, 'became *laos*, God's people', but had a will or aspiration 'to be *ethnos*, a nation like other nations'; this aspiration meant 'a refusal of Israel to be *laos*'.[3] Now in point of fact the Greek words *ethnos*, nation or people, and *laos*, people in general, in their origins differ very little in meaning. A striking illustration from the first century A.D. is the fact that Josephus in his

---

[1] T. F. Torrance, *Royal Priesthood* (1955), pp. 1 ff.
[2] Op. cit., p. 131.
[3] *Conflict and Agreement in the Church* (1959–60), vol. i, pp. 290 ff.

History of the Jewish War regularly uses *ethnos* of the people of the Jews, whereas in his *Antiquities* he uses *laos* with almost equal regularity. Had Josephus undergone some mysterious conversion between A.D. 77, when he completed the *Jewish War*, and A.D. 93, when he completed the *Antiquities?* There is, unquestionably, a tendency in the New Testament to distinguish between *laos* and *ethnē* (the plural but not the singular). But this is due not to some intrinsic mystery in the words themselves, but to the fact that *laos* is often found in the phrase *laos theou*, the people of God, used both of Israel and of the Church; whereas *ethnē* has come to be used as the Greek equivalent of the Hebrew word *goïm*, which is often used in the Old Testament of the nations that know not God. But, just to make it quite clear that this meaning does not reside in the word itself, in Psalm 106. 5 Israel is the *goi* of the Lord; in Isaiah 26. 2. it is the righteous *goi*; and in Zephaniah 2. 9 God speaks of Israel as 'my *goi*'. Torrance's theology is quite correct; but the philological basis which he believes himself to have found for it is non-existent.

It follows from what has been said that Barr is highly critical of certain aspects of the work that has been put into Kittel's immense *Theological Dictionary of the New Testament*,[1] and devotes a long section of his work to the criticism of it (pp. 206–72). Here is his conclusion:

> Far from it being the case, therefore, that *TWNT* is 'in many ways the most valuable achievement in biblical studies of this century', it is rather true that progress can only begin to be made, even with the material assembled by *TWNT*, through an awareness of the great and sweeping linguistic misconceptions which have become more widespread through its influence.[2]

These are hard words. I can only register my opinion that they are in very large measure justified. Of the value of a great deal of the material here for the first time assembled there can be no doubt at all. Under each heading we are given a history of the word from the earliest beginnings of the Greek language, comparison with Jewish usage, notes on the evidence of the Old Testament, studies in such nearly contemporary writers as Philo of Alexandria and Josephus. Most of this is accurately and conveniently set forth. Some of the

---

[1] *Theologisches Wörterbuch zum Neuen Testament*, 7 vols., 1932 onwards, and not yet complete.
[2] Op. cit., p. 262.

articles are masterly in their grasp of what a theological article ought to be. But, when all is said and done, the anxiety remains. How far is the work really reliable, and how far is it tendentious, written to support a general theological position that has already been arrived at on other grounds?

Barr formulates the difficulty as follows:

Thus the articles in *TWNT*, while apparently organized under a Greek word (like *agapaō*, or *hamartia*) have a tendency to be an essay on the biblical conception of Love or Sin; and in difficult cases to leave it somewhat uncertain whether that whole conception can be taken to be indicated in a particular passage by the word which is the subject of the article.[1]

Barr quotes as an example the article on *agathos*, good, by Professor Walter Grundmann. It is first laid down that Matthew 19. 17, 'one there is who is good', and Hebrews 9. 11; 10. 1, 'the future good things', determine the meaning. The word 'good' applies only to God himself or to eschatological realities lying in the future. 'There is nothing in this world that strictly speaking deserves the predicate *agathon* and no one who has the predicate *agathos*. . . . The natural existence of man is excluded from the good, and cannot realize it for all its longing.'

No one reading this article would guess that, in point of fact, two individuals are referred to in the New Testament as 'good'—Joseph of Arimathaea, 'a good and righteous man' (Luke 23. 50), and Barnabas, who was 'a good man, full of the Holy Spirit and of faith' (Acts 11. 24). Unless I have read the article carelessly, these vitally important passages are not even alluded to. It is true that they both occur in the writings of Luke, who is regarded by some as dangerously 'Hellenizing'; but even so it does not do to treat them simply as though they did not exist. And in the article on *agathōsunē*, goodness, which according to Paul is one aspect of the fruit of the Spirit (Galatians 5. 22), no attempt whatever is made to show exactly what the word means, and what its relation is to the other excellent qualities of which Paul speaks.

So in the article on *eirēnē*, peace, the general standpoint is that 'peace is that eschatological salvation (or well-being) of the whole man which has been introduced by Christ'. This being so, the most important utterance of Jesus on the subject of peace, 'Do not think that I have come to bring peace on earth; I have not come to bring peace but a sword' (Matthew 10. 34), is misinterpreted in the following terms:

[1] Op. cit., p. 217.

'Yet this salvation is not identical with the outward situation of man—
it can in fact lead him into the experience of bitter hostility.' This takes
seriously neither what Jesus says nor the tremendous significance of
what he means.[1]

As we have said, Professor Barr's work shows signs of having been
hastily written;[2] it is unlikely that all his contentions will be accepted
by all New Testament scholars. What is already clear is that he has
set up a ferment which no serious New Testament scholar can disregard. A considerable number of what had come to be regarded as
established principles have been challenged. Recent linguistic work has
been shown to have been at many points unscientific, and too much
influenced by other than purely linguistic considerations. It is
likely that much that has been done in recent years will be found to be
in need of revision; and scholars may in the future find it prudent to
test more carefully the foundations for any statements they may make
as to the relations between language and theological thought.

It may seem that this chapter has come down with a sudden bump
from the hills to the plains. We were considering the highest flights of
New Testament understanding and now we have come back to words
—to the details of linguistic theory, of grammar, and of syntax—
subjects that many readers will feel glad to have left behind in their
schooldays. But is this really a come-down? Is it not simply a frank
recognition of the nature of the revelation which is there in the Bible?
'We have this treasure in earthen vessels', says St. Paul of his own
ministry; by analogy the same phrase can be used of the Scriptures.
If revelation comes to us as the Word of God, it can come only through
words; every word has its history, it is related to other words, it stands
somewhere in a complex linguistic structure. Words, as we said, are not

[1] In another context Barr quotes a saying of Professor G. Kittel on the 'New' that has
come in with the Gospel: 'This "new", however, is real, incarnate, personal. And at this
point we reach the ultimate stage of all lexicography and of all history of religions. The
history of the word εἰρήνη comes to an end in Ephesians 2. 14: "HE is our peace"....
He does not bring a new conception of the term "peace"; he *is* it.' On this Barr comments
very properly: 'The ultimate Kittel is talking of here is purely theological, and not lexico-
graphical or historical' (op cit., p. 214, n. 1).

[2] A later work on *Biblical Words for Time* (1962) is more carefully written and more
guarded in expression. Yet even here he writes (p. 161): 'In so far as certain theological
positions . . . claim to stand upon, and to do best justice to, modern biblical and linguistic scholarship, the discovery that these positions depend upon, or tend to produce,
repeatedly and systematically faulty assessments of linguistic evidence is finally and in-
controvertibly fatal to these positions. . . . Good scholarship and good theology alike
require that when an interpretative method is found to be systematically faulty, no pains
should be spared to make the necessary adjustment.'

solid objects like marbles; they are flexible, always changing their meanings and their connotations, difficult to seize in their integrity, always a little recalcitrant in the hands of the one who uses them. Try as we will we cannot get away from the words, in themselves, and in those subtle grammatical structures that build up sentences and paragraphs and books. In theology no one renders us more valuable service than the scholar who helps us to understand the words better, who guides us through the subtleties of idiom, who heads us off from the blind alleys of false etymology or false interpretation of usage. For him the work may be tedious—for those who profit by his labours the results may be illuminating in the extreme.

Up to the middle of the eighteenth century, an arid theory of verbal inspiration made any scientific progress in Biblical studies almost impossible. The text was treated as though it was divinely inspired, and equally inspired in every particular; ordinary canons of interpretation were forbidden, and it was held that Biblical speech was a special kind of speech, which followed its own laws, and could be interpreted only in accordance with those laws. Today we move in a freer atmosphere; Biblical language is recognized to be simply a part of that great movement of the development of speech in which thought finds expression. We draw in to our help all that can be derived from sources Greek, Hebrew, and oriental, from the general study of language everywhere, from the clearer understanding of the processes of human thought which contemporary psychology has made available to us. But all these things will not avail unless there is present with them a certain quality of reverence—not the reverence which tends towards idolatry of the text, towards a pedantry which becomes lost in a jungle of grammatical formulae; but that constructive reverence of Browning's *Grammarian*, or of Bishop Westcott, convinced that no labour is superfluous or in vain that is directed to the elucidation of so precious a thing as the New Testament; and that out of the patient gathering together of little fragments of the truth the glorious mosaic will at length emerge in the centre of which, as in the great Byzantine mosaics, Christ will sit as the Pantocrator, the Lord into whose hands all things have been committed by the Father.

CONCLUSION

WHERE do we come out as the result of all this long survey of the labours of nearly two centuries?

To one who is not a trained theologian it may well seem that the task of the New Testament scholar is no more productive than that of the devils in Milton's Pandaemonium, who spent their time in endless debates on 'fate, freewill, foreknowledge absolute', and never reached a conclusion. So many theories have been put forward, found wanting, and rejected—only perhaps to be rehabilitated after a century has passed.

Is there any real progress? Is there any solid ground underfoot at all, or is all nothing more than the fruit of misplaced human ingenuity? Physical science goes on from strength to strength, through its endlessly cautious checking of data, its constant use of the principle of verifiability, its building on established results as the starting-point for progress in the future. Is there anything comparable in theology? Has it any claim at all to be regarded as scientific in method and achievement?

The irritation of the non-theologian is natural, and perhaps no complete answer can be given to his questions. But certain considerations ought at this point to be raised.

Up to a point the parallel with the operations of physical science is close. There progress becomes impossible unless the utmost liberty is given for the formulation of hypotheses, and for the constant criticism and reappraisal of results that have long been taken as firmly established. Exactly the same is true in theology. No question must be forbidden; no conclusion must be regarded as sacrosanct; every hypothesis must be given serious consideration, and rejected only if it is clear that it fails, in Plato's phrase, to 'save the phenomena', to do justice to all the facts that have been brought to light in the course of research. The sifting out of truth is a long and slow business; but has it not been so also in the physical sciences?

So far the parallel is sound. But we must never forget that the material with which we are dealing in the New Testament is not the same as that which comes before us in the physical or natural sciences. Gabriel Marcel, the French existentialist philosopher who in mature years became a believing Roman Catholic, has reminded us that in philosophy, in a very real sense, there are no definitive results.

Each generation must take up the quest afresh, and can rely only to a very limited extent on the achievements of the past. The available material is always the same—the sum-total of reality. But each generation comes with its own questions; and, more than we perhaps care to realize, the answer is already determined by the nature of the questions that we put. We read Plato and Aquinas and Kant for inspiration and the disciplining of our minds; but their questions are not our questions, and their methods will help us only a short way towards the answering of the questions that we are asking today. So it is with the scientific study of the New Testament. There are certain writers of the past— Augustine, Calvin, Bengel, Westcott, Schlatter—to whom we shall always turn with gratitude for the timeless insights that are to be found in their writings. But at point after point we find them antiquated. What they had to give they have given, and we are grateful; but gratitude does not deliver us from the hard and exacting task of being honest with ourselves and with the men of our times. New questions demand new answers; and often the answer eludes us until we have, as it were, invented the new mathematics by which this particular equation can be solved.

There is a yet further difficulty; the personal equation can never be completely eliminated. The austere picture of the physicist, completely objective, whose work is entirely unaffected by any personal element, is now seen to be an imagination. Even the work of the physicist is affected at every point by his attitude, his sensitivities or lack of them, his interests, his manner of handling his material. In the physical realm, however, the maximum of objective independence can be attained. As we come nearer and nearer to the realm of life, the difficulty increases. This is notoriously so with the historian. As the ratio of personal engagement advances, so does the difficulty of any real objectivity. And when we approach the field of religion, quite evidently the problem is at its acutest; here no man can possibly be neutral, and, however great the care that the scholar may take to allow for his own convictions, prejudices, and predilections, he remains himself—he cannot jump out of his own skin. Every writer who handles matters of this kind is something of an apologist; the more convinced he is of his own neutrality, the less likely is it that he will be genuinely neutral.

This brings us to the point at which we can attempt to assess what has really happened in New Testament studies in the century to which our attention has been particularly directed in this book. We shall not look for the kind of established results from the past on which the physicist builds, but this does not mean that we must completely abandon the idea of progress. In the study of New Testament externals—what used to be called the 'lower criticism'—we may at least hope for certain results which in their scientific validity will be comparable to the achievements of the physical scientists. In more central matters we may hope to find that certain theories have so successfully resisted criticism that they may at least for the time being be accepted as useful working tools. We should be able to indicate certain probabilities, which though at present far from having been established, must at least command respect. Furthermore, we may hope to be able to indicate some of the problems that remain unsolved, and the direction in which solutions may be sought with some reasonable hope of success.

We may start by listing what appear to be the positive achievements of New Testament studies in the century that has elapsed since 1861:

1. First and foremost, the liberty of the scientific and critical approach has established itself almost beyond the possibility of cavil. There are still in existence groups of devout students of the New Testament whose doctrine of inspiration would almost preclude any application of scientific methods; but their influence steadily declines. The so-called 'liberal' and the so-called 'conservative' of today differ in their results; in the definition of the methods to be employed there is hardly the shadow of a difference between them.

2. We now have the materials for the construction of a text of the Greek New Testament which will be almost wholly reliable. Scholars will differ as to the weight to be attached to different forms of evidence; as to the scientific method to be followed in the construction of a text there is only a narrow margin of disagreement. New discoveries may produce many changes in detail. It is unfortunately the case that adequate use has not yet been made of all the material which is in our hands. But a student who today acquires any contemporary edition of the New Testament in Greek, and has some idea of how to use the critical notes at the foot of the page, may feel confident that what he reads is not far from what the apostolic writers actually wrote.[1]

3. Now that the new material from the inscriptions and the papyri has been sorted out, we can say that we have a good knowledge of what

[1] The same is, of course, true *mutatis mutandis* of most modern translations of the New Testament, with the exception of that by Mgr. R. A. Knox, which was made from the Vulgate Latin, and not from the original Greek.

New Testament Greek really is. It cannot be exactly squeezed into the categories of any other form of the Greek language—it is a flexible language, on which both the Greek Old Testament and the experience of Christian living have left their traces. We may hope for more illustrative material as new discoveries are brought to light; but, in the main, we may venture to say that our grammatical, linguistic, and lexical tools for the study of the New Testament are in good shape.

4. The settlement of the date of the Ignatian letters and of the first Epistle of Clement has given us a fixed starting-point for the determination of the dates of the New Testament books. Many good scholars hold that all the books of the New Testament belong to the first century; every serious scholar agrees that the majority of the books were written not later than A.D. 100, that is, within seventy years of the death of Jesus Christ, and in the lifetime of at least some believers who had seen him in the flesh.[1]

5. It is universally agreed that New Testament study must begin with the Epistles of Paul, and in particular with those of his earlier period—1 Thessalonians, Galatians, Romans, 1 and 2 Corinthians. Here we have our earliest pictures of the Christian Church and of Christian faith, since all these Epistles almost certainly antedate the earliest written Gospel.

6. Mark is almost certainly the earliest written Gospel. There is no valid reason for thinking that it was written later than A.D. 70. It may have been written considerably earlier, and in any case was written not more than forty years after the death of Christ.

7. It is almost certain that Matthew and Luke both used Mark's Gospel. In addition they had available, probably in written form, a collection of the 'Sayings of Jesus'. This collection probably existed first in Aramaic, and may in one form or another have been written down within a very few years of the death of Jesus.

8. By careful study of the existing Gospels, it is possible to go behind them to the period of oral tradition, in which the Christian understanding of the life and death of Jesus Christ was being hammered out. Even at this early date interpretation was at work; and out of the vast mass of material available the churches preserved those parts which were felt to convey the challenge of the Gospel to decision and belief, and to

---

[1] Doubts are still felt by some about John, Acts, the Pastoral Epistles, James, 1 and 2 Peter, the Johannine Epistles, and perhaps one or two other books—both by number and length less than half the New Testament.

serve as guides to the members of Christian community in the difficult business of living as Christians in a non-Christian world.

9. Central in the message of Jesus Christ is the proclamation of the kingdom of God. This kingdom is not an inner experience of men, but the reality of God's sovereignty which can be brought in only by God's own act. This conception must be related to the apocalyptic elements in the Old Testament and in the late Jewish expectations of 'the time of the end', though the original elements in the message of Jesus of Nazareth must always be recognized.

10. The new discoveries of Qumran have shown us that the Judaism of the first century was more varied than we had thought, and that much which was previously regarded as 'Hellenistic' is in fact to be found in the Jewish tradition. These discoveries help to light up for us the Jewish background of the time of Christ; but there is no reason to suppose that either John the Baptist or Jesus was deeply influenced by the Essenes, or that any major changes will have to be made, in the light of these discoveries, in our understanding of Christian origins.

11. In interpreting the New Testament, we have to take account of the world in which it was preached, when once it had left the confines of Judaea. It is clear that, through this ceaseless dialogue with the non-Christian world, the vocabulary and to some extent the thought of the New Testament were affected. But all the elements which came in from the Hellenistic world were profoundly influenced, in their new Christian setting, by the creative power of the Gospel.

12. The Fourth Gospel cannot be treated in the same way as the first three, and no artificial attempt should be made to harmonize its account of the life of Jesus with theirs. This Gospel holds firmly to the historic manifestation of God in Jesus Christ; but it is primarily a theological restatement of the meaning of that manifestation, in which the details of the presentation are all controlled by the significance for the faith of the believer which the writer has found in the events which he selects for record.

Now if I am right in thinking that this deliberately brief and rather arid summary fairly represents the agreements to which the majority of New Testament scholars would be prepared to commit themselves today, this must be regarded, in view of the difficulty and complexity of the subject, as no inconsiderable deposit of achievement from the work of a century. But a statement of the agreement immediately leads us on to the many matters in which so far no general agreement has been reached, and where progress towards agreement can come only as the result of much patient and detailed research by many scholars.

What, then, are the fields which present a challenge to the worker in the field of New Testament studies today? Here is a short list of the matters to which, in my opinion, immediate attention needs to be directed:

1. We have, as was said, a vast amount of lexical and grammatical material at our disposal. Are we sure that the best use is being made of this material, and that the linguistic principles which underlie much current work of interpretation are reliable and genuinely scientific? Have New Testament studies taken adequate advantage of the general progress in the sphere of 'linguistics' and 'semantics', the theory of speech and of the nature of communication between human beings?

2. What do we mean by Gnosis? A tremendous task awaits the experts in the interpretation of all the new material from Nag-Hammadi. When all this lies before us, we shall have far more knowledge than before of the world of Christian deviations in the second century A.D. To what extent is it possible to infer back from this material to the first century, and to the period of the writing of the New Testament books? Shall we at last be able to sort out the various elements—Oriental, Hellenistic, Jewish—which went to the making of Gnosticism? Will it then be possible to say what Gnosticism really was, where and when it arose, and what its relation to the New Testament and its composition must be held to have been?

3. As we have seen, no evidence of any kind has yet been produced that a 'pre-Christian Gnostic myth' was in existence in the days when the New Testament books were being written. Has the time come at which scholars should abandon the Gnostic myth and accept the conclusion that the myth was not the cause but the consequence of the development within the Church of the doctrine of Jesus Christ as Redeemer? If this is accepted, it will involve an extensive reconsideration of much New Testament interpretation that has been accepted as authoritative in many areas of the Church. Has the time come at which this reconsideration should be undertaken, and, if so, how far should it go?

4. Old Testament theology has entered on a period of extraordinary creative vigour. Scholars such as Professor G. von Rad in Heidelberg maintain today that the traditional division between Old Testament and New Testament studies is artificial and can no longer be upheld; a

scholar who has found in the New Testament the fulfilment of the Old can undertake his work on the Old Testament only in the light of this fundamental conviction. Is not a similar retroactive process overdue also in New Testament studies? Some good work has been done in recent years on the relation between the New Testament and the Old; is this not a field in which much more work is needed, in the light of recent progress in Old Testament studies, and of the many new evaluations which have to be made as a result of the Qumran discoveries?

5. We know today far more of the Jewish background of the New Testament than was known even fifty years ago. Jewish scholars have made a number of notable contributions in this field. But the gaps are still many. The mutual interpenetration of the Jewish and the Hellenistic worlds, before and during the New Testament period, would seem to be a field in which significant results may yet be attained.

6. Christianity is a historical religion in every sense in which this expression can be interpreted. But there is no subject on which the theologians are less agreed than 'the meaning of history'. A good deal has been written in recent years by philosophers such as Collingwood, and their work has had a deep influence on a number of New Testament scholars, as is evident, for instance, in Professor Bultmann's Gifford Lectures, *Eschatology and History* (1958). But can there really be such a thing as a philosophy of history? Ought we not now to be asking the question as to the *theology* of history?[1] An understanding of history which is incompatible with a Christian doctrine of revelation is bound to land the New Testament scholar in grave perplexities; a true theological understanding of history would not of itself solve any New Testament problems, but it would, so to speak, hold the ring within which a solution can be found.

7. This point leads on directly to the next—history and the Gospels. As we have seen, one of the most recent movements in New Testament studies has been the attempt to get behind the 'traditions of the believers' to the actual figure of Jesus of Nazareth himself. Many of the objections to this quest which have been raised in the past are now seen to rest on philosophical and not on historical grounds. If the problem has been correctly redefined in terms of a true understanding of the nature of history, the stage should be set for notable progress in

[1] Hendrik Berkhof's *Der Sinn der Geschichte: Christus* (1962) seems to be a pointer in the right direction.

that historical reconstruction of the story of Jesus which, as we said, has as yet hardly been begun.[1]

8. An entirely new approach to the Fourth Gospel seems to be possible today. Date, authorship, relationship to the Old Testament, Palestinian connexions—on all these points a number of questions have been reopened. Everyone today recognizes that the Fourth Gospel is theological in character. But of late there has been a fresh recognition of the strange fact that the writer is determined to cast his theology in historical form. Why? What is his understanding of history? To what extent is he making use of a genuine historical tradition, independent of that represented by the other three Gospels and in its own way no less reliable? In a sense these problems are old; but in another sense they present themselves as quite new, in view of all that has happened in a century of study.

9. Another field in which reconsideration will be urgently needed is the later Pauline or 'deutero-Pauline' Epistles. Here there has been marked division between the German and the British tradition, the Germans tending to regard all the later Epistles, especially Ephesians, as non-Pauline or 'deutero-Pauline', the British almost unanimously accepting Colossians, though with greater reservations on the subject of Ephesians.[2] A new understanding of the nature of 'Gnosticism', and so of the possible course of the development of early Christian thought, will involve at least a fresh weighing of the nature of these Epistles and of their relation to the development of the thought of Paul.

10. In a very real sense, the little Epistle called 1 Peter is the storm-centre of New Testament studies. Ten years ago two scholars, as to whose competence and intellectual integrity no question could be raised, published commentaries on the Epistle almost simultaneously. Dr. E. G. Selwyn, Dean of Winchester, took the view that the Epistle is mainly Petrine in context, that its place of origin was Rome, and that it need not be dated later than A.D. 65. Dr. F. W. Beare of Toronto argued that the Epistle in its present form cannot be earlier than about A.D. 112, when Christians in Asia Minor were first threatened by

[1] Professor H. E. W. Turner, *Historicity and the Gospels* (1963), appeared from the press just too late to be used in the preparation of the chapters in this book which are concerned with this subject.

[2] Professor Henry Chadwick in an important article published in the *Zeitschrift für die neutestamentlich Wissenschaft* (1960), pp. 145 ff., points out that the first question to be settled is not so much 'Who wrote the Epistle to the Ephesians?' as 'For what purpose was it written?'

persecution on a large scale, that its authorship must remain completely unknown, and that its connexion with the historic Peter must be regarded as tenuous in the extreme. Now if two scholars can arrive at such widely divergent results, both on the basis of theoretically scientific methods of study, something must have gone seriously wrong somewhere. If it were possible to come nearer to agreement as to the date and origin of this beautiful and perplexing letter, this would provide us with another of those fixed points from which fresh studies could radiate out in every direction, and perhaps new certainties be attained. It may be that definite solutions of this Petrine problem will for ever evade us; we must pursue the matter in hope, and not lie down too easily under the frustration of mutually contradictory solutions.

11. We are as yet far from having reached agreement as to the nature of the Church, the *Ekklesia*, in the New Testament. Some years ago Professor Leuba of Neuchâtel wrote a book with the interesting title *L' Institution et L'événement*.[1] We may not agree with all Professor Leuba's solutions; but he has very neatly fixed for us the difference between what may be called the 'Catholic' and the 'Protestant' approaches to the problem. To the 'Catholic', it is self-evident that every society will have an inner life of its own, which, if it is to persist at all as a society, will naturally find its outward expression in an organization appropriate to that inner life. Inappropriate organization will distort that inner life; excessive organization can suppress it. But there is no necessary or basic contradiction between *Ekklesia* as the life of faith, and *Ekklesia* as the outward, visible, and continuing society. In the Protestant world, for fifty years, to identify anything in the New Testament as *Frühkatholizismus* (early Catholicism) has been tantamount to condemning it as a perversion or distortion of the original Gospel. A new and much more careful definition of this term is needed, as also of the whole concept of 'authority' in the early Church.[2] The results attained by such further studies will affect our judgement on the Pastoral Epistles. Not many scholars today would defend these letters as entirely Pauline.[3] There has, indeed, been a tendency in recent

[1] 1950, English trans., 1953.
[2] Two notable recent studies of this problem are *Church Order in the New Testament* by Eduard Schweizer (English trans., 1961, of the German original *Gemeinde und Gemeindeordnung im Neuen Testament*, 1959) and H. von Campenhausen, *Kirchliches Amt und geistliche Vollmacht* (1953). Neither of these can be regarded as completely satisfactory, the standpoint of the authors being at certain points reflected in the manner in which they handle their evidence.
[3] Though this view has been defended in one very recent commentary, that by D. Guthrie (1957).

studies to ascribe them to a very late date, even as late as A.D. 125.[1] But it is by no means clear that so late a date is necessary; many scholars hold that these letters probably belong to that dark period between A.D. 65 and 90 of which historically we know so little. At this point it is particularly difficult for a scholar to study objectively, without being influenced by his general understanding of the development of life in the early Church.

12. We must come back in the end to the question of eschatology. What is the Church's hope for the future? An extraordinary variety of views on this subject is still held by scholars. Some think that Jesus never spoke at all of his own coming again in glory; the words which suggest this are all editorial additions or explanations supplied by the faith of the early Church. Others hold that this 'coming of the Son of man' was central in the proclamation of Jesus, and that the disciples had rightly so understood it. Some have condemned Luke for bringing the life of the Church into relation to 'history', and so reducing the 'eschatological tension', which is the only true condition of the Church's life. Some seem to bring 'eschatology' entirely into the present; to live 'eschatologically' is to live as though every moment is the moment of decision, in which history is made and the future is determined. It is not perfectly clear how this differs from 'life in the Spirit' as this has been understood in earlier periods of the Church's life. Some maintain that history is moving to a great and final crisis, but that 'the end of history is beyond history'. Others hold that the New Testament clearly speaks of a final triumph of God in time and space, though we can no more conceive what this triumph might be like than the saints of the Old Testament, for all their forward-looking and eager yearning, could really foresee and picture the Incarnation of the Son of God. Clearly, not all of these views can be right. What are the sources and origins of the divisions? We are all trying to interpret the same texts. Why is it that we interpret them so differently? Is it possible to eliminate some of the divisions, and to draw nearer to agreement? Or are we here face to face with a problem that will never be solved?

Evidently, New Testament scholars have enough on their hands to keep them occupied for a great many years. The work must go forward

---

[1] The lowest date suggested by that usually very careful scholar Professor C. K. Barrett in his just published commentary in the New Clarendon Bible Series (1963), the first commentary, I think, to be based on the New English Bible. Professor Barrett tends to the very late dating of New Testament books, a curious aberration in one who is generally cautious and prudent in his views.

in perfect freedom. Progress cannot be made, unless the scholar is free to consider every aspect of the problem, to fashion his hypotheses and to put them forward, in the expectation that only those hypotheses will survive which take all the evidence seriously and 'save the phenomena', that is, provide an explanation of the phenomena which is reasonable and satisfying to the critical intellect.

Yet, when this has been said, the theologian might consider to his advantage the methods employed by scholars who are engaged in other fields of knowledge, and particularly by the physical scientists. He would observe that the physical scientists are strong at two points at which theologians tend to be weak. The first is the ruthless spirit of self-criticism in which the scientist tests his own work; he asks himself again and again whether the hypothesis he is putting forward is really related to the phenomena which it purports to explain, or whether some other explanation is equally possible. In all scientific progress there is an element of inspired intuition, one may almost call it adventurous guess-work; but this is followed up by a long process of experimental verification, before results are put forward with any confidence that they are reliable. The second strength of the scientist is in the rejection of hypotheses that have failed to stand up to the tests to which they have been subjected. The elimination of the impossible and the highly improbable clears the way for the emergence of the highly probable or the certainly established truth. In theology certain proof or disproof is much less often possible than in the physical or biological sciences. But what hinders progress is the persistence in currency of hypotheses in favour of which solid and satisfactory evidence has never been adduced. Because some view has an eminent name attached to it, because it has been often repeated on authority without adequate experimental testing, it comes to be assumed by those who have not the opportunity to test the evidence on which it was originally based that it has a far greater measure of certainty than can legitimately be ascribed to it. In the past there have been notable slayers of hypotheses—for instance, Theodor Zahn in Germany and William Sanday in England. Perhaps one of our great needs today is the clearing away of a vast amount of dead wood, of traditions which survive from the past, views which have never really been tenable, interpretations which have lost such validity as they had, in order that the possible lines of advance may become clear, and that the student may go forward unperplexed by the irrelevancies of the past to such discoveries as will genuinely illuminate the future.

The Temple in Jerusalem in the time of Jesus was approached by a series of courts—that of the Gentiles, that of the women, that of Israel—to which various classes of worshippers had access. Beyond that only the priests could go, and only the high priest once a year into the inmost sanctuary of all. The work of New Testament criticism may be similarly depicted as a gradual approach to the central mystery of faith and unbelief. In the outer court stand those who are concerned with the externals of the New Testament—the manuscripts and their readings, grammar, and lexicography—services by no means to be despised because thay are at some distance from the central issues. Then come the exegetes, whose task it is to say when and how the New Testament books came to be written, what the words and sentences meant to those who wrote them and to those who first read them, in so far as this can be determined today. Clearly, this is an indispensable service; unless it is well done, we shall never be free from fanciful and unreliable interpretations of the New Testament text, determined by imagination and desire and not by knowledge. In the third place come the New Testament theologians, who bring together the scattered lights into a single flame. They are concerned with the issue of revelation. Who is the God who speaks and shows himself in the New Testament? How does he show himself? In the light of this manifestation, how do we understand the world in which we live, how do we understand ourselves, our society, our destiny? What is the nature of this new 'life in Christ', 'life in the Spirit', of which the New Testament so constantly speaks?

All this is approach. But, if all this is no more than approach, what is it that lies beyond?

The New Testament is concerned with *proclamation*. It is a *Kerygma*, the loud cry of a herald authorized by a king to proclaim his will and purpose to his subjects. It is *Euangelion*, good news, sent to those who are in distress with the promise of deliverance. It is the Word of the Lord—and in the East a word is no mere vibration in the atmosphere, it is a living power sent forth to accomplish that for which it is sent. When the New Testament scholar has done his utmost in his sphere, his work remains lifeless, until it is transformed into the living voice of proclamation. The scholar may say, as many have done, that this is none of his business; he will scientifically make known the facts, and it will be the task of others to do with them as they will. But throughout our study we have seen that many of the giants reached out beyond the study to the pulpit, believing that the two are most intimately linked, and that any truth gained by the intense application of labour in the study will find its way out in living proclamation as a Word of God to men. And so, in fact, from generation to generation, the New Testament has taken on new life, as the ancient words have asserted their relevance in every changing scene of human existence, have clothed themselves afresh in human understanding, and have come home to the heart and conscience as challenge, enlightenment, and consolation.

But there is yet one further door through which the human spirit must pass, if it would enter the inmost sanctuary, and through which it can only pass alone. When scholar and prophet and preacher and priest have done their utmost and their best, a question remains on which the individual must make his own decision, since no one can make it for him. The tremendous drama of the Fourth Gospel sets before us the gradual development of faith and unbelief, at first often intermingled in discussion and debate, but gradually crystallizing out in the resolute determination of the enemies of Jesus to destroy him, and the less resolute but still notable determination of his friends to follow him that they might die with him. Beyond question, part of the abiding power of this Gospel to speak directly to the hearts of men lies in those recorded conversations in which the Word of life is seen alone with the individual to whom the challenge to faith is being presented. 'Marvel not that I said unto thee, Ye must be born again.' 'I that speak unto thee am he.' 'Jesus saith unto her, Mary. She saith unto him in Hebrew, Rabboni, which is to say, Master.' 'Lord, thou knowest all things: thou knowest that I love thee ... When he had spoken this, he saith unto him, Follow me ... If I will that he tarry till I come, what is that to thee? Follow thou me.'

INDEX

INDEX OF SCRIPTURAL CITATIONS
AND REFERENCES